... moving . . . full of new informati...

Inaepen...

'*Becoming Steve Jobs* is fantastic. After working with Steve for over 25 years, I feel this book captures with great insight the growth and complexity of a truly extraordinary person. I hope that it will be recognized as the definitive history.'

Ed Catmull, President, Pixar and Disney Animation

'Steve Jobs is the person who most inspires the new generation of Silicon Valley entrepreneurs. In this deeply-researched book, you'll find the most honest portrait of the real Steve Jobs.'

Marc Andreessen

'Square would not exist without the work and persistence of Steve Jobs. I am forever grateful. Amazing read.'

Jack Dorsey, CEO Twitter

'Highly recommended.'

Philip Elmer-DeWitt, Fortune.com

'Offers a new look into the life of the Apple co-founder . . . includes a number of interesting anecdotes and perspectives from those who have rarely spoken of their relationships with Jobs over the decades, all tied together by one of the few reporters to have had access to Jobs on a regular basis throughout that time.'

MacRumors

'What makes their book important is that they contend – persuasively, I believe – that . . . [Jobs] was not the same man in his prime that he had been at the beginning of his career. The callow, impetuous, arrogant youth who co-founded Apple was very different from the matu... ...ling creation

and turned it into a company that made breathtaking products while becoming the dominant technology company of our time.'

Joe Nocera, *New York Times*

'The book about Steve Jobs that the world deserves. Smart, accurate, informative, insightful and at times, utterly heartbreaking . . . *Becoming Steve Jobs* is going to be an essential reference for decades to come.'

John Gruber, *Daring Fireball*

'Brent Schlender and Rick Tetzeli render a spectacular service with this book, giving fresh perspective on Steve Jobs' journey . . . Becoming Steve Jobs gets the focus precisely right: not as a success story, but as a growth story. Riveting, insightful, uplifting-read it and learn!'

Jim Collins, author of *Good to Great*

'One of the best things Brent Schlender and Rick Tetzeli do in writing about Jobs is undoing the 'lone genius' myth, and complicating his persona.'

Anil Dash, CEO of ThinkUp

About the authors

Brent Schlender covered Steve Jobs intimately for over 25 years, and knew him better than any other journalist. 58 years old, he is one of the 'graybeards' of Silicon Valley journalism, having covered the digital revolution almost since its inception, including 10 years at *The Wall Street Journal*, and two decades as *Fortune's* lead technology writer. He has won numerous writing awards, and in 2010 was named a 'Silicon Valley Visionary' by SD Forum, the software industry's international trade association.
@BrentSchlender

Rick Tetzeli is executive editor of *Fast Company*. He was Managing Editor of *Entertainment Weekly*, and Deputy Editor of *Fortune*. He lives in Brooklyn with his wife, Mari, and their three children.
@tetzeli

Becoming
Steve Jobs

HOW A RECKLESS UPSTART
BECAME A VISIONARY LEADER

BRENT SCHLENDER AND **RICK TETZELI**

SCEPTRE

First published in Great Britain in 2015 by Sceptre

An imprint of Hodder & Stoughton
An Hachette UK company

First published in paperback in 2016

1

A CIP catalogue record for this title is available from
the British Library

Paperback ISBN 978 1 444 76201 3
eBook ISBN 978 1 444 76200 6

Typeset in Adobe Garamond

Printed and bound by Clays Ltd, St Ives plc

Hodder & Stoughton policy is to use papers that are natural,
renewable and recyclable products and made from wood grown in
sustainable forests. The logging and manufacturing processes are
expected to conform to the environmental regulations of the
country of origin.

Hodder & Stoughton Ltd
Carmelite House
50 Victoria Embankment
London EC4Y 0DZ

www.sceptrebooks.co.uk

For Lorna, my lifesaver, many times over
—*BS*

For Mari, forever
"It is not often that someone comes along
who is a true friend and a good writer."
—*RT*

Contents

Introduction to the Paperback Edition
Marc Andreessen

When entrepreneurs come to our venture capital firm to pitch themselves and their companies, they walk up the stairs and into a conference room named for Steve Jobs.

If you polled the thousands of founders that come through that room during the course of a year, you'd find that 99.9% of them never met Steve. You'd also find that a fairly large number of them entered the tech industry after Steve passed away.

But overwhelmingly if you ask them who their hero is, who they have tried to learn the most from about how to build a company and how to have an impact on the world – Steve is #1 on that list by a very wide margin.

I see Steve's influence in everything they do. It's in their behavior. In the polish and flair of their pitches. In the design of their slides. In the use of the word "beautiful." Before Steve, no startup ever used the word "beautiful." Now everything has to be beautiful. Every product needs to be fantastic out of the gate. Every product has to live up to its promise and bring delight to the lives of its users.

At its most basic, that's the impact Steve had. His existence, his accomplishments at Apple – ultimately the mere presence of Apple – raised the bar for everybody, within and beyond technology. That effect seems likely to last for decades.

Before Steve staged his comeback at Apple, however, that wasn't the way of things.

Pre-Steve

If you rewind the tech industry to before Steve's return in 1997 and Apple's eventual dominance, Microsoft played the role that Apple does today. The well-understood script from Microsoft was that the first version of any product was going to be a clunker. But you also knew they would keep coming. The second product wasn't going to be all that great either. It was the third version of a Microsoft product that mattered, that's the one that would be successful, and if not necessarily great, then at least OK.

The corollary was that business strategy is more important than product strategy. If you had enough sales and marketing hype, or used enough FUD – Microsoft like IBM before them, was famous for pre-announcing products that weren't even on the drawing board to freeze the market – you could bluff your way through to market success while your product wheezed along.

One of the things that went wrong in Silicon Valley in the '90s – and one of the things that caused the crash in 2000 – was too many Valley companies bought into that approach. So you had too many Valley companies that launched into market too fast and shipped sub-par products. A lot of the products people used in the dotcom era, especially business products, were used out of fear – the fear of being left behind. Then 2000 and 2001 came around and everybody collectively said, "Holy Lord, these products are all crap." And they all got dropped overnight, in many cases killing their companies.

Steve never believed that business strategy trumped product. He always believed that the product has to be great, and if it isn't great, well, we're not going to ship it.

The iPhone Arrives

For anybody coming of age in tech in the mid-2000s, the iPhone was the definitive product of the time. The iPhone set the benchmark for what a great technology product should be, and with a shove from Steve, it was arguably a higher benchmark than any set before.

The iPhone launched in 2007, but there were years of hard work prior to its debut. In 1999 Apple registered the domain iphone.org. In 2003 Apple began working on the hardware and software for touch screens. In 2004 the Apple skunkworks team on the project shifted focus from a tablet to what would become the iPhone.

The work on touch began years before the iPhone came out. Apple could have shipped a phone or a tablet at any number of points along that development timeline, and Steve chose not to because the product had to be great.

Pre-Steve and the iPhone I would try to keep up with all of the emerging mobile gear. I'd always have the latest Treo, or the latest Samsung, or the latest LG. You name it, I had a drawer-full. They'd have Java BREW, 18,000 buttons, and a 400-page manual translated into 7 languages. They'd come in all these odd colors, and the graphics would be weird. Either the touch wouldn't work right, or the keyboard would flake out. At their best they were laggy and slow. Dozens of models came out in the course of a year without any significant steps forward.

And then the Apple phone came out. It was just a slab of glass, and it was gorgeous. The software was butter-smooth. There was no giant manual to wade through. Every time you pulled your iPhone out of your pocket, you had this proud feeling, "Wow. I'm really special. I have an iPhone. This is amazing. I'm part of the future."

The immediate and desperate need people had to write applications for the iPhone was another sign of how good it was. People were so motivated to build their software on top of the iPhone that they would "jailbreak" their iPhone to do it – voiding their warranty at a minimum, and risking turning it into a useless (but pretty) glass and metal brick if things really went south. Meanwhile, every other phone vendor had to beg people to develop for their phones.

That's the quality bar that Steve set, what it meant to ship products. But also the bar for what it meant to have a customer, and whether that customer was happy – ideally, *giddily* happy. Steve made real the notion of customer delight. He did it with the products that Apple shipped. The fetishistic unboxing video trend took off only when Apple made stunning, simple packaging deserving of the device inside. And, of course, there was the breakthrough experience people had when they entered an Apple Store.

We experience so much of life today through our phone, our tablet, or our computer. We're on these devices literally hundreds of times a day. It's how we stay close to people we care about, and it's how we work. It's how we express ourselves. It's how we participate in democracy. So how these things work, how they look and feel, really matters in determining how we live. Steve understood that better than anyone.

Apple-like

There's a story told by Comcast CEO Brian Roberts of getting a call from Steve when he was on medical leave from Apple. Comcast had launched a new high-definition TV interface, and Roberts thought he was getting a congratulatory call. He wasn't. Steve told him everything that was wrong with it. It didn't meet the bar.

Roberts took that to heart, you can see it in Comcast today. Its X-line of cable set-top boxes are much more Apple-like. Would Steve have some choice comments? Undoubtedly, but the point is, even the cable company is trying to get better now.

The new Microsoft is also trying to be more like Apple. The products coming out of Microsoft over the last five years are clearly better. It's no longer "third time's a charm, and it's OK if the first two suck." Satya Nadella is running Microsoft more like Steve ran Apple.

That same Apple-like influence has rippled across other industries.

Take online banking. We see startups all the time that make this point. Go to an incumbent big bank website and you'll see it's still pre-Apple. There will be too many words, too many menu choices, odd fonts, off-putting colors, and bad layout. It's all very confusing.

Then you go to a modern financial services website or mobile app, and the recognition comes unbidden: it's just clean and smooth and fresh. Simple and easy. It's Apple-like.

Ask any of the Apple devout and they will offer a list of products, services, and experiences that they would love to see get an Apple-like redo. Better yet, they would like to see Apple just get into the business.

In the automotive world Tesla is bringing that Apple-like experience to cars, but they are the exception for now. Climb inside most vehicles, and it's still buttons and knobs and levers all over the place. On top of that, most cars are still perfectly happy to collide head-on with another car and never even give you advance warning. Whereas, you just know when Apple comes out with a car, it's never going to let you do that. And it won't require a 900-page manual in 14 languages with a massive index to operate.

An example: Since I have a degree in computer science, I pride myself on never opening the manual on anything electronic. But I could not change the clock on the center console screen of my father-in-law's German sport-utility truck. There's a "Systems" button, and there's a "Settings" option in the "Systems" menu. But there's no setting for changing the clock. I finally broke down and went into the manual for the console display, and I looked up in the index under "time." Under "time" it said, "Refer to the other manual." It turns out you can't change the truck's clock from the center console. You have to change the clock from the steering wheel because the clock is controlled by the car's firmware, not the dash display software. It took 25 minutes to change the clock. Pre-Apple in the extreme.

The way Steve would react to that is simple: Everybody involved in allowing this product to leave the factory without that being fixed would get fired.

"Nice" CEOs

Would Steve, in that case, be "mean" to fire, or at a minimum, yell at people for shipping a lousy product? Or is it the people who made the lousy product that are being "mean" to the rest of the world?

Steve yelled. There is no debating that. He wasn't the easiest guy to work for, BUT he was the best guy to work for. Apple couldn't have accomplished all it has if Apple wasn't a place where people loved to work.

Talk to the very large number of people who not only worked at Apple, but worked at Apple for a very long time, and they all say the same things: "I did the best work of my life at Apple. My work had the biggest impact. I built products there that are so much better than anything else I've ever done. I learned the most. And it wasn't just me, I was surrounded by the best people."

What they describe is a real sense of having something very, very special. And it is probably the most special thing that they – employee or executive – are ever going to have. Steve's ability to create and foster and maintain a company of that size and scale, with that feeling among the employees and executives, was an extremely rare and special thing. There are a lot of "nicer" CEOs who never even get close to that.

Steve may have chewed people apart in a meeting, but afterward they almost always had two things to say: One is, he was right. What they'll tell you next is that they learned "good enough" isn't good enough. And the next time they came back to meet with Steve, they came in with something great.

It's like anything in life. There are standards. The standards have to be enforced. If the standards aren't enforced, then the standards slip. This is the role of the CEO in any company. Some care and some don't. Great CEOs care a lot. Steve cared a lot.

"Nice" CEOs who don't hold the line on standards do not build great places to work. They may build a nice place to work, but they will not build a great place to work. Then the great people will leave, and then the company will degenerate into mediocrity. Steve built Apple into the best place to work.

People watching Steve's personal behavior too closely often miss the broader point of what he was doing, and why he was putting so much energy and so much passion into what he was doing. The experience most people had at Apple was not just, "I had a meeting with Steve and he yelled at me." The experience most people had at Apple was, "I worked at Apple for 10 years, and, oh my God, did we do amazing things."

Good Enough, Goodbye

There's a concept in some countries called the *tall poppy syndrome,* where everybody has to be average. It's culturally very important for everybody to be the same. If everybody ever sticks their head up and says, "No, no, I can do something special, or I can be special," they get it chopped off.

There's a major urge in American society today to implement the tall poppy syndrome. It's this movement right now in politics and economics, this purported ideal that everybody ought to be equal, which is to say, for nobody to be special. Steve embodied the other side of that. The whole point of Steve, and the whole point of Apple, was to be special, was to be the tall poppy.

It's not just Apple that can do this. It's everybody. It's a question of expectations. It's the difference between good enough and great. Good enough was good enough for a long time, but thanks to Steve, it isn't any more.

Authors' Preface

Even before the March 2015 publication of *Becoming Steve Jobs*, the press anticipated that last year would be "the battle for the identity of Steve Jobs." Our book, the opening salvo of this supposed battle, became a national bestseller. A documentary on Jobs was released in 68 theaters in September, and later broadcast on CNN in January of 2016. The most expensive effort was Paramount's theatrical movie, *Steve Jobs*, which stars Michael Fassbender and Kate Winslet, and premiered in October to generally positive critical reviews.

The movie, to the surprise of many, bombed. How could a movie about the world's most famous business leader and visionary, featuring an all-star cast, an estimated $35 million publicity campaign, a 2,047-theater launch and a script by Academy Award winner Aaron Sorkin, tank? (The film grossed less than $30 million worldwide before it was yanked from theaters three weeks after its release. By contrast, *The Martian*, which was released at the same time, had a global box office topping $300 million during that same period.) What went wrong?

For one thing, even Apple fans are tired of hearing so much noise about whether Steve Jobs was a "good" or a "bad" person. The Sorkin movie reinforced the classic stereotype of Steve Jobs as a tortured genius incapable of empathy, who berated people mercilessly into delivering the best work of their lives. Its three acts hammered this home in fictionalized backstage accounts of the launch of three products: the Mac, the NeXT computer, and the iMac. The acting is brilliant, and the dialogue snappy. But (perhaps because of its claustrophobic setting) the movie provides no answer to the fundamental question about Jobs: if he remained the quasi-sociopath portrayed in the movie throughout his life, how did he manage to succeed so brilliantly at Apple, creating breakthrough after breakthrough, and permanently changing the way we interact with one another, after failing to do so in his early years at Apple? Human stories are about change, and the Steve Jobs of Aaron Sorkin does not change. The man we follow in *Steve Jobs* could never have created what became the most valuable and, for many Apple fans, the most beloved company on the planet.

We wrote this book with the goal of showing how Jobs changed, and how that change affected his performance as a leader, innovator and businessman. The fact is Jobs, due to a host of influences, matured and even, arguably, mellowed a little over time. He didn't care if the world at large recognized this change. He himself never spoke of it. But colleagues and friends who knew him over the decades witnessed it, and we have tried to chronicle that slow but profound evolution and education.

Over the course of his life, Jobs became more patient, more considerate, and more loving, particularly to those in his small inner circle. This gradual transformation is one aspect of why he was so successful in reviving Apple when he returned to the company in 1997. He was wiser, a better strategist, and more capable of focusing on what mattered. Always whip smart, he remained an autodidact, a perpetual learner. He also developed remarkable peripheral vision, which helped him lead Apple into new industries like music and telecommunications.

His maturation was slow and complicated, with many hiccups along the way, moments where he remained as belligerent and stubborn and awkward and slighting as ever. Jobs, famously, didn't look back. He moved as fast as he could into the future, with the kind of speed that guarantees some rough passages.

Jobs launched the personal computing era, *and* the mobile computing world that still defines our technological experience today. He is a figure of lasting historical importance. As the years go by, the idiosyncrasies of his personality will become less interesting. What will matter is what we can learn from the way he saved Apple and transformed computing not once, but twice. That story, a tale of insight, collaboration, risk, and the way personal change can alter business success, is the account we try to chronicle here.

Batley Library

Tel: (01484) 414 868
Email: Batley.lic@kirklees.gov.uk

Customer ID: *****1888

Items that you have renewed

Title: Can't we just print more money? :
economics in ten simple questions
ID: 800869357
Due: 13 November 2023

Title: Very bad people : the inside story of the
fight against the world's network of
corruption
ID: 800868718
Due: 13 November 2023

Total items: 2
Checked out: 2
Overdue: 0
Hold requests: 1
23/10/2023 15:38

Thank you for using the bibliotheca SelfCheck
System.
We hope to see you soon.

www.kirklees.gov.uk/community/libraries

Authors' Note

The reporting and writing of this book is the work of two authors. The two of us have worked together for years, going back to our time together at *Fortune* magazine. For *Becoming Steve Jobs,* we spent three years researching, interviewing, reporting, writing, and editing together. That said, in the narrative you're about to read, we decided, for convenience's sake, to use the first-person singular throughout to refer to Brent. Brent is the one who had a relationship of almost a quarter century with Steve Jobs, so using the word *I* made it much easier to tell our story.

Becoming
Steve Jobs

Prologue

"Y ou're new here, aren't you?" Those were his first words to me. (His last, twenty-five years later, would be "I'm sorry.") Already he had turned the tables on me. After all, I was the reporter. The one who was supposed to be asking the questions.

I had been warned about the unique challenges of interviewing Steve Jobs. The night before, over beers, my new colleagues at the San Francisco bureau of the *Wall Street Journal* had told me to bring a flak jacket to this first meeting. One of them said, only half jokingly, that interviewing Jobs was often more combat than questioning. It was April 1986, and Jobs was already a *Journal* legend. Bureau lore had it that he had dressed down another *Journal* reporter by posing this straightforward question: "Do you understand anything at all, *anything at all* about what we're discussing?"

I'd had plenty of experience with real flak jackets during my years reporting in Central America in the early 1980s. I'd spent much of that time in El Salvador and Nicaragua, where I'd interviewed everyone from truck drivers motoring through war zones, to American military advisers in the jungle, to Contra *commandantes* in their hideouts, to presidents in their palaces. On other assignments I'd met with obstreperous billionaires like T. Boone Pickens and H. Ross Perot and Li Ka-shing, with Nobel Prize winners like Jack Kilby, with rock stars and movie idols, renegade polygamists, and even the grandmothers of would-be assassins. I wasn't easily intimidated. Yet for the full twenty-minute drive from my home in San Mateo, California, to the headquarters of NeXT Computer in Palo Alto, I brooded and fretted about how best to interview Jobs.

Part of my unease came from the fact that, for the first time in my experience as a journalist, I would be calling on a prominent business leader who was younger than I. I was thirty-two years old; Jobs was thirty-one and already a global celebrity, hailed, along with Bill Gates, for having invented the personal computer industry. Long before Internet mania started churning out wunderkinds of the week, Jobs was technology's original superstar, the real deal with an astounding, substantial record. The circuit boards he and Steve Wozniak had assembled in a garage in Los Altos had spawned a billion-dollar company. The personal computer seemed to have unlimited potential, and as the cofounder of Apple Computer, Steve Jobs had been the face of all those possibilities. But then, in September of 1985, he had resigned under pressure, shortly after telling the company's board of directors that he was courting some key Apple employees to join him in a new venture to build computer "workstations." The fascinated media had thoroughly dissected his departure, with both *Fortune* and *Newsweek* putting the ignominious saga on their covers.

In the six months since, the details of his new startup had been kept hush-hush, in part because Apple had filed lawsuits trying to prevent Jobs from hiring away its employees. But Apple had finally dropped those suits. And now, according to the publicist from Jobs's PR agency who called my boss at the *Journal,* Steve was willing to do a handful of interviews with major business publications. He was ready to start the public fan-dance that would begin to reveal in detail what exactly

NeXT was up to. I was thoroughly fascinated, and equally wary; I didn't want to get taken in by the notoriously charismatic Mr. Jobs.

———

THE DRIVE SOUTH to Palo Alto is a trip through the history of Silicon Valley. From Route 92 in San Mateo over to Interstate 280, a "bucolic" eight-laner skirting San Andreas Lake and Crystal Springs Reservoir, which store drinking water for San Francisco piped in from the Sierras; past the blandly ostentatious venture-capitalist habitat along Sand Hill Road in Menlo Park and traversing the oblique, mile-long Stanford Linear Accelerator, which slashes like a hairline fracture through the landscape and beneath the freeway; past the "Stanford Dish" radio telescope, and the white-faced Herefords and ornate oak trees dotting the expansive greenbelt behind the university campus. The winter and spring rains had resurrected the prairie grass on the hills, turning them briefly as green as a golf course from their usual dull yellow, and peppering them with patches of orange, purple, and yellow wildflowers. I was so new to the Bay Area that I didn't yet realize that this was the most beautiful time of year to make this drive.

My exit—Page Mill Road—was the home street address of Hewlett-Packard, early biotech pioneer ALZA Corporation, Silicon Valley "facilitators" like Andersen Consulting (now called Accenture), and the law firm Wilson Sonsini Goodrich & Rosati. But first you hit the university-owned Stanford Research Park, with its groves of low-slung corporate research-and-development labs situated with lots of grassy elbow room. Xerox's famed Palo Alto Research Center (PARC), where Steve first saw a computer with a mouse and a graphical "bitmapped" screen interface, resides here. This was where he had chosen to head-quarter NeXT.

A young woman from NeXT's PR firm, Allison Thomas Associates, escorted me through the boxy, two-story, concrete-and-glass office building to a small conference room with a view of a half-filled parking lot and not much more. Steve was waiting there. He greeted me with a nod, dismissed the flack, and, before I could get seated, popped that first question.

I wasn't sure if Steve wanted a monosyllabic answer, or if he was genuinely curious about who I was and where I came from. I assumed the latter, so I started ticking off the places and industries I'd written about for the *Journal*. Right after leaving graduate school at the University of Kansas, I'd moved to Dallas for the paper, where I'd written about aviation, airlines, and electronics, since Texas Instruments and Radio Shack were based there. Along the way I had won some notoriety for a profile of John Hinckley, the privileged son of a Texas oilman who shot President Reagan in 1981.

"What year did you graduate from high school?" he interjected. "Nineteen seventy-two," I replied, "and I spent seven years in college but never quite got my master's degree." "That's when I graduated from high school," he interjected. "So we're about the same age." (I found out later that he had skipped a grade.)

I then explained that I'd spent two years each in Central America and Hong Kong writing and reporting on geopolitical issues for the *Journal,* and a year in Los Angeles, before finally wangling my dream job in San Francisco. At this point, it really was beginning to feel like a job interview. Except that Jobs wasn't reacting much to any of my answers.

"So do you know *anything* about computers?" he asked, interrupting again. "Nobody who writes for the major national publications knows shit about computers," he added, shaking his head with a practiced air of condescension. "The last person who wrote about me for the *Wall Street Journal* didn't even know the difference between machine memory and a floppy!"

Now I felt on somewhat firmer footing. "Well, I was an English major, formally, but I programmed some simple games and designed relational databases on a mainframe in college." He rolled his eyes. "For a couple of years, I worked nights as a computer operator processing the daily transactions for four banks on an NCR minicomputer." He was staring out the window now. "And I bought an IBM PC the very first day they were available. At Businessland. In Dallas. Its serial number started out with eight zeroes. And I installed CP/M first. I only installed MS-DOS when I sold it before we moved to Hong Kong, because that's what the buyer wanted."

At the mention of those early operating systems and a competitor's product he perked up. "Why didn't you get an Apple II?" he asked.

Good question, but seriously . . . why was I letting this guy interview me?

"I never had one," I allowed, "but now that I'm here, I got the *Journal* to buy me a Fat Mac." I had convinced the big guys in New York that if I was going to be writing about Apple, I'd better be familiar with their latest machines. "I've been using it for a couple of weeks. So far, I *do* like it better than a PC."

I had picked the lock. "Wait till you see what we're going to build here," he told me. "You'll want to get rid of your Fat Mac." We'd finally reached the point of the interview, the destination Steve had wanted all along—the place where he could tell me how he was going to outdo the company he had founded, and best the people, most notably Apple CEO John Sculley, who had effectively banished him from that kingdom.

Now he would take my questions, although he didn't always respond to them directly. I was curious, for example, about his eerily empty headquarters. Were they really going to assemble computers here? It sure didn't look like manufacturing space. Was he bankrolling the whole thing, or was he lining up some investors? He'd sold all his Apple shares save one, netting him about $70 million, but that wasn't enough to fund a company this ambitious. At times he veered off into completely unexpected terrain. As we talked, he drank steaming hot water from a pint beer glass. He explained that when he ran out of tea one day, it dawned on him that he liked plain old hot water, too. "It's soothing in the very same way," he said. Eventually he would steer the conversation back to his main pitch: higher education needed better computers, and only NeXT could deliver them. The company was working closely with both Stanford and Carnegie Mellon—universities with highly respected computer science departments. "They'll be our first customers."

Despite his evasiveness and his determination to hew to a single message, Jobs was a vivid presence. The intensity of his self-confidence made me hang on his every word. He spoke in carefully constructed sentences, even when trying to answer an unexpected question. Twenty-five years later, at his memorial service, Steve's widow, Laurene, testified to the "fully formed aesthetic" he possessed from a very young age. That confidence in his own judgment and taste came through in his answers. It also came through in the fact, as I realized over the course of our conversation, that he really *was* interviewing me, testing me to see if I "grokked"—understood—what was special about what he had done and what he planned to do at NeXT. Later, I came to realize that this was because Steve wanted whatever was written about him and his work to measure up to his own high standard of quality. At this stage of his life, he thought he could probably do anybody's job better than they could—it was an attitude that gnawed at his employees, of course.

The interview lasted forty-five minutes. The plans he laid out for NeXT were sketchy; as it turned out, this was an early sign of the troubles the company would experience over the years. There was, however, one tangible thing he did want to discuss: the NeXT logo. He gave me a fancy brochure explaining the creative evolution of the snazzy corporate symbol Paul Rand had designed. The booklet itself had been designed by Rand personally, with expensive translucent leaves separating thick, creamy pages embossed with a step-by-step guide to how he had settled upon an image that spoke in "multiple visual languages." The logo was a simple cube with NeXT spelled out in "vermillion against cerise and green, and yellow against black (the most intense color contrast possible)," and "poised at a twenty-eight degree angle," according to the pamphlet. At that time, Rand was noteworthy as one of America's leading graphic designers; he was famous for dreaming up the visual identities of IBM, ABC Television, UPS, and Westinghouse, among others. For this pamphlet, and for a single, take-it-or-leave-it draft of a corporate logo, Jobs had happily parted with $100,000 of his money. That extravagance, albeit in the pursuit of perfection, was a quality that would not serve him well at NeXT.

———

I DID NOT write a story after that first meeting. A fancy logo for an infant company didn't qualify as news, no matter who had commissioned it, no matter who had designed it. (Besides, back then the *Wall Street Journal* never published photographs; in fact, it never printed anything in color. So even if I had wanted to write about Steve's shiny new bauble, its subtle and impractical beauty would have been doubly lost on the *Journal*'s readers, who cared little for design at the time.)

Not writing a feature was the first salvo in the twenty-five-year-long negotiation that marked our relationship. As with most journalist/source relationships, there was one main reason Steve and I wanted to connect: we each had something the other needed. I could deliver the front page of the *Wall Street Journal* and, later, the cover of *Fortune* magazine; he had a story that my readers wanted, and that I wanted to tell better and earlier than any other journalist. He usually wanted me to write about a new product of his; my readers wanted to know about him as much as the product—if not more. He wanted to point out all the glories of the product and the genius and beauty of its creation; I wanted to get behind the scenes, and to cover the competitive ups and downs of his company. This was the subtext of most of our interactions: a transaction in which we each hoped to cajole the other into some sort of advantageous deal. With Steve, this could be like a card game where one day I'd feel we were partners playing bridge and the next I'd feel like a sucker holding eight-high in poker. More often than not, he made me feel like he had the edge—whether or not that was true.

Despite the fact that the *Journal* didn't publish anything at the time, Steve told Cathy Cook, a Silicon Valley vet then working for Allison Thomas, that the interview went fine and that he thought I was "okay." From time to time, he would have Cathy invite me over to NeXT for updates. There wasn't much worth covering, frankly, at least in the eyes of the *Journal*—I didn't write my first big piece about NeXT until 1988, when Steve finally unveiled the company's first computer work-station. But the visits were always intriguing and invigorating.

One time he called me in to crow about persuading Ross Perot to invest $20 million in NeXT. On the face of it, they were the oddest couple: Perot, the crew-cut, buttoned-down, uber-patriotic, navy vet-eran bankrolling a former hippie who still preferred to go barefoot, was a vegetarian, and didn't believe in using deodorant. And yet I now knew Steve well enough to understand that he and Perot, whom I'd interviewed a few times, were actually kindred spirits: both were id-iosyncratic, idealistic autodidacts. I told him that he absolutely had to visit Perot in his office at Electronic Data Systems (EDS) in Dallas, if for no other reason than to see his over-the-top collection of histrionic eagle sculptures and the colonnade of U.S. flags lining the headquar-ters driveway. Steve laughed, and rolled his eyes in amusement: "Been there, done that." He asked if I thought he was crazy for liking Perot. "How could anyone *not* like Perot at least a little after meeting him?" I replied. "He's *funny*." Steve cackled in agreement, and then added, "Seriously, I think there's a lot I can learn from him."

Over time, our similar ages became a bridge more than a barrier. Steve and I had navigated similar adolescent rites of passage. I could say the same thing about Bill Gates, whom I also covered extensively, but he wasn't the product of a working-class upbringing or public schools as Steve and I were. All three of us had dodged the bullet of serving in Vietnam because the military draft was abolished by the time we had turned eighteen. Yet Steve and I, more than Bill, were true products of the antiwar, peace and love, tune in/turn on generation. We were music nuts and gaga for gadgets, and we weren't afraid to experiment with outlandish new ideas or experiences. Steve had been adopted as a child, and we did occasionally talk about what that had been like, but that aspect of his upbringing never seemed nearly as big an influence on his intellectual and cultural development as was the larger social and political milieu—and the high-tech sandbox—in which we came of age.

In those early years, Steve had an important reason to cultivate our relationship. In the ever-shifting computer world of the late 1980s, building breathless anticipation for his Next Big Thing was crucial to attracting potential customers and investors, and Steve would need plenty of the latter, given that NeXT would take nearly five years to produce a working computer. Throughout his life, Steve had a keen sense of the tactical value of press coverage; this was just one part of what Regis McKenna, perhaps his most important early mentor, calls "Steve's natural gift for marketing. Even when he was twenty-two years old he had the intuition," McKenna elaborated. "He understood what was great about Sony, about Intel. He wanted that kind of image for what he was going to create."

Knowing that Apple was also among the companies I covered for the *Journal*, and later for *Fortune*, Steve would call up at seemingly random moments over the coming years to offer me "intelligence" that he'd heard from former colleagues who were still there, or simply to share his opinions on the interminable executive soap opera at his old company in Cupertino. Over time I learned that he was a reliable source about the mess that Apple became in the early 1990s—and I also came to realize that there was nothing random about those calls. Steve always had an ulterior motive: sometimes he was hoping to glean something about a competitor; sometimes he had a product he wanted me to check out; sometimes he wanted to chastise me for something I'd written. In the latter case, he could also play the withholding game; once, in the late 1990s, after his return to the company he had co-founded, I sent him a note to say that I thought it was about time for me to write another Apple story for *Fortune*. I had been out of touch for several months because I'd had open-heart surgery—he had called me at the hospital to wish me well—but now I was ready to jump on another piece. His email reply was simple: "Brent," he wrote, "as I recall, you wrote a rather mean story about me and Apple last summer.

I remember this hurting my feelings. Why did you write such a nasty story?" But a few months later he relented, and cooperated for another cover feature about the company.

Ours was a long, complicated, and mostly rewarding relationship. When I would run into Steve at industry events, he would introduce me as his friend, which was flattering, odd, true, and yet not true all at the same time. During the brief time when he had an office in Palo Alto near *Fortune*'s bureau, I would run into him around town now and then, and we'd stop to chat about all kinds of things. Once, I helped him shop for his wife Laurene's birthday present. I visited his home many times, always for one work reason or another, but with an informality that I've never encountered from another CEO. And yet there was never a minute where the basic terms of our relationship weren't clear: I was the reporter, he was the source and subject. He enjoyed some of my stories—others, like the one that prompted that email, infuriated him. My independence and his hoarding of information created the borders of our relationship.

This necessary distance expanded during the last few years of his life. Both of us got very sick in the mid-2000s; he was first diagnosed with pancreatic cancer in 2003, while in 2005 I contracted endocarditis and meningitis during a trip to Central America, which put me in a near coma for fourteen days and eventually took away almost all my hearing. He knew more about my illness than I knew about his, of course. Still, he did sometimes reveal details—one time we even compared surgical scars, much like Quint (Robert Shaw) and Hooper (Richard Dreyfuss) in the movie *Jaws*. He visited me in the Stanford hospital twice during the weeks when I was recovering—stopping by when coming in for regular checkups with his oncologist. He told me some awful jokes about Bill Gates, and excoriated me for having continued to smoke cigarettes despite his admonitions over the years. Steve always did love to tell people how to conduct their personal lives.

AFTER STEVE DIED, reams of armchair analysis unfurled: articles, books, movies, and television shows. Often they resurrected old myths about Steve, using stereotypes that had been created way back in the 1980s, when the press discovered the wunderkind from Cupertino. In those early years, Steve was susceptible to the flattery of the press, and he opened himself and his company to reporters. He was at his most undisciplined and most intemperate then. As much as he showed a genius for imagining breakthrough products, he also could display a disturbing meanness and indifference toward both employees and friends. So when he started limiting access, and cooperating with the press only when he needed to promote his products, the tales from those early days at Apple became the conventional wisdom about his personality and thinking. Perhaps that's why the posthumous coverage reflected these stereotypes: Steve was a genius with a flair for design, a shaman whose storytelling power could generate something magical and maleficent called a "reality distortion field"; he was a pompous jerk who disregarded everyone else in his single-minded pursuit of perfection; he thought he was smarter than anyone else, never listened to advice, and was an unchanging half-genius, half-asshole from birth.

None of this gibed with my experience of Steve, who always seemed more complex, more human, more sentimental, and even more intelligent than the man I read about elsewhere. A few months after his death, I started combing through the old notes, tapes, and files from my stories about him. There were all kinds of things I'd forgotten: off-the-cuff notes I'd written about him, stories he'd told me during interviews that I couldn't use at the time for one sensitive reason or another, old chains of emails we'd exchanged, even a few tapes I'd never transcribed. There was an audiocassette he'd made for me that was a dubbed copy of one given to him by John Lennon's widow, Yoko Ono, with all the various versions of "Strawberry Fields Forever" recorded during its lengthy composition process. These were all stored away in my garage, and unearthing them triggered many buried memories of Steve over the years. After rustling through these personal relics from

the past for a few weeks, I decided that it wasn't enough to grumble
about the one-dimensional myths about Steve that were ossifying in
the public mind; I wanted to offer a fuller picture and deeper understanding of the man I had covered so intensely, in a way that hadn't
been possible when he was alive. Covering Steve had been fascinating
and dramatic. His was a truly Shakespearean tale, full of arrogance,
intrigue, and pride, of perceived villains and ham-handed fools, of outrageous luck, good intentions, and unimagined consequences. There
were so many ups and so many downs in so short a time that it had
been impossible to draw the broad trajectory of his success while he
was living. Now I wanted to take the long view of the man I'd covered
for so many years, the man who had called himself my friend.

THE MOST BASIC question about Steve's career is this: How could the
man who had been such an inconsistent, inconsiderate, rash, and
wrongheaded businessman that he was exiled from the company he
founded become the venerated CEO who revived Apple and created a
whole new set of culture-defining products that transformed the company into the most valuable and admired enterprise on earth and that
changed the everyday lives of billions of people from all different so-
cioeconomic strata and cultures? The answer wasn't something Steve
had ever been all that interested in discussing. While he was an introspective guy, he was not inclined to retrospection: "What's the point in
looking back," he told me in one email. "I'd rather look forward to all
the good things to come."

A real answer would have to show how he changed, who influenced
those changes, and how he applied what he'd learned to the business of
making great computing devices. As I pored over my old documents,
I kept coming back to the time that many have described as his "wilderness" years, the dozen years between his first tenure at Apple and
his return. That era, from 1985 to 1997, is easy to overlook. The lows
aren't as dramatic as the blowups of his first tenure at Apple, and the

highs, of course, aren't as thrilling as those he engineered in the first decade of the twenty-first century. These were muddled, complicated times, and not the stuff of easy headlines. But those years are in fact the critical ones of his career. That's when he learned most everything that made his later success possible, and that's when he started to temper and channel his behavior. To overlook those years is to fall into the trap of only celebrating success. We can learn as much, if not more, from failure, from promising paths that turn into dead ends. The vision, understanding, patience, and wisdom that informed Steve's last decade were forged in the trials of these intervening years. The failures, stinging reversals, miscommunications, bad judgment calls, emphases on wrong values—the whole Pandora's box of immaturity—were necessary prerequisites to the clarity, moderation, reflection, and steadiness he would display in later years.

By the end of that decade in the woods, despite his many missteps, Steve had, remarkably enough, salvaged both NeXT and Pixar. The legacy of the first secured his professional future, while the triumph of the second ensured his financial well-being. His experience at both companies taught him lessons that, in retrospect, determined the future of Apple and helped define the world we live in. Steve could be intransigent, and nothing was ever learned easily or superficially, but learn he did. Driven and curious even when things were tough, he was a learning machine during these years, and he took to heart all that he gleaned.

No one works in a vacuum. Getting married and beginning a family changed Steve profoundly, in ways that had an enormous positive impact on his work. I had plenty of glimpses into Steve's personal life over the years, and several encounters with Laurene and their children. But I was not a close friend of the family. When I started to report this book, in late 2012, it seemed that I might not learn much more about his personal life. Saddened by his death and feeling burned by some of what had been published about Steve posthumously, many of his closest colleagues and friends originally refused to talk to me. But that changed over time, and those conversations with his most intimate friends and colleagues—including the only four Apple employees to attend his private burial—revealed a side of Steve that I had sensed, but had not fully understood, and that I have certainly never read about elsewhere. Steve was capable of extraordinary compartmentalization. It's a talent that allowed him to master and keep track of the various pieces of an entity as complex as Apple upon his return. It allowed him to maintain his focus despite the cacophony of worries that came with knowing he had cancer. It also allowed him to maintain a deep and meaningful life outside the office, while revealing little of that to people who weren't part of his close inner circle.

Of course, he could be a difficult man, even late in his life. For some people, he was hellish to work for. His belief in the value of his mission allowed him to rationalize behavior that many of us might well deplore. But he could also be a loyal friend, and an encouraging mentor. He was capable of great kindness and genuine compassion, and he was an attentive and loving father. He believed deeply in the value of what he chose to do with his life, and he hoped those close to him believed in the value of their work just as deeply. For a man who so thoroughly "deviated from the mean," as his friend and colleague Ed Catmull, the president of Pixar, puts it, he had deeply human feelings, strengths, and failings.

What I have always loved about business journalism, and what I have learned from the very best colleagues I've worked with, is that there is always a human side to the seemingly calculated world of industry. I knew this was true about Steve when he was alive—no one else I have ever covered was so passionate about the creations of his business. But only in writing this book have I come to understand just how much the personal life and the business life of Steve Jobs overlapped, and just how much the one informed the other. You can't really understand how Steve became our generation's Edison and Ford and Disney and Elvis, all rolled into one, until you understand this. It's what makes his reinvention such a great tale.

AT THE END of our first interview, Steve walked me down the neat and glimmering hallways of NeXT's headquarters to the exit. We didn't exchange small talk. As far as he was concerned, our conversation was over. As I exited he didn't even say goodbye. He just stood there, looking out the glass doors toward the entrance of the parking lot on Deer Creek Road where a crew of workmen was installing a 3-D version of the NeXT logo. As I drove away, he was lingering there still, staring at his hundred-grand logo. He knew *in his bones,* as he would say, that he was about to do something great. In reality, of course, he had no idea what was ahead of him.

Chapter 1
Steve Jobs in the Garden of Allah

On a cold December afternoon in 1979, Steve Jobs pulled into the parking lot of the Garden of Allah, a retreat and conference center on the shoulder of Mount Tamalpais in Marin County, north of San Francisco. He was tired, frustrated, angry, and late. The traffic on 280 and 101 had been at a standstill much of the way up from Cupertino, way down south in Silicon Valley, where the company he'd founded, Apple Computer, had its headquarters, and where he had just suffered through a meeting of Apple's board of directors, which was chaired by the venerable Arthur Rock. He and Rock didn't see eye-to-eye on much of anything. Rock treated him like a child. Rock loved order, he loved processes, he believed that tech companies grew in certain ways according to certain rules, and he subscribed to these beliefs because he'd seen them work before, most notably at Intel, the great Santa Clara chipmaker that he had backed early on. Rock was perhaps the most notable tech investor of his time, but he in fact had been reluctant to back Apple at first, largely because he'd found Steve and his partner

Steve Wozniak unpalatable. He didn't see Apple the way Jobs saw it—as an extraordinary company that would humanize computing and do so with a defiantly unhierarchical organization. Rock simply viewed it as another investment. Steve found board meetings with Rock enervating, not invigorating; he had looked forward to a long, fast drive to Marin with the top down to get rid of the stale stench of seemingly endless discussion.

But the Bay Area was shrouded in mist and rain, so the top stayed up. Slick roads made the traffic stultifying, so much so that it took all the pleasure out of the drive in his brand-new Mercedes-Benz 450SL. Steve loved the car; he loved it the way he loved his Linn Sondek audiophile turntable and his Ansel Adams platinum prints. The car, in fact, was a model for what he thought computers should be: powerful, sleek, intuitive, and efficient, nothing wasted at all. But this afternoon the weather and the traffic had defeated the car. Consequently he was about half an hour late to the initial meeting of the Seva Foundation, a creation of his friend Larry Brilliant, who looked like a little Buddha himself, albeit in track shoes. Seva's goal was pleasingly ambitious: eliminate a certain kind of blindness that affected millions of people in India.

Steve parked and got out of the car. At six feet tall and a trim 165 pounds, with brown hair that touched his shoulders and deep, penetrating eyes, he would have been striking anywhere. But in the three-piece suit he'd worn to the board meeting he looked particularly resplendent. Jobs didn't quite know how he felt about the suit. At Apple, people wore whatever they wanted. He often showed up barefoot.

The Garden of Allah was a quaint sort of mansion, built on a hillock up Mount Tamalpais, the verdant peak overlooking San Francisco Bay. Nestled into a covey of redwoods and cypress trees, it meshed classic California Arts and Crafts style with the feel of a Swiss chalet. Built in 1916 for a wealthy Californian by the name of Ralston Love White, it had been operated by the United Church of Christ since 1957 as a retreat and meeting site. Steve walked across the lawn of the heart-shaped driveway, climbed some stairs to a broad veranda, and entered the building.

Inside, one look at the crew gathered around the conference table would have told any casual bystander this was not your typical church gathering. On one side of the table was Ram Dass, the Jewish-born Hindu yogi who in 1971 had published one of Steve's favorite books, *Be Here Now,* a bestselling guide to meditation, yoga, and spiritual seeking. Nearby sat Bob Weir, the Grateful Dead singer and guitarist—the Dead would be performing a benefit for Seva at the Oakland Coliseum on December 26. Stephen Jones, an epidemiologist from the U.S. Centers for Disease Control, was in attendance, as was Nicole Grasset. Brilliant and Jones had worked for Grasset in India and Bangladesh as part of the World Health Organization's audacious—and successful— program to eradicate smallpox. The counterculture's favorite trickster philosopher, Wavy Gravy, was there, too, sitting with his wife near Dr. Govindappa Venkataswamy, the founder of India's Aravind Eye Hospital, which eventually would help millions of people with an operation that repairs blindness caused by cataracts, a malady that then plagued the region. Brilliant was hoping to pull off something almost as audacious as wiping out smallpox. His goal for Seva was that it would support the work of people like Dr. V (as Brilliant called Venkataswamy) by setting up eye camps throughout Southern Asia to restore sight to the blind in poor rural areas.

Steve recognized a few of the folks. Robert Friedland, the guy who had convinced him to make a pilgrimage to India in 1974, came up and said hello. And he recognized Weir, of course; he admired the Grateful Dead, even though he thought they didn't have the emotional or intellectual depth of Bob Dylan. Steve had been invited to the gathering by Brilliant, whom he'd first met in India, five years earlier. After Friedland sent him a 1978 article detailing the success of the smallpox program and talking a bit about Brilliant's next steps, Steve sent Brilliant five thousand dollars to help get Seva rolling.

It was quite a collection of people: Hindus and Buddhists, rockers and doctors, all accomplished, all gathered in the United Church of Christ's Garden of Allah. Clearly, this was not the place for your traditional corporate chieftain, but Steve should have fit right in. He meditated often. He understood the search for spiritual fulfillment—in fact, he had gone to India specifically to learn from Brilliant's guru, Neem Karoli Baba, also known as Maharaj-ji, who had died just a few days before Steve arrived. Jobs felt a deep restlessness to change the world, not just build a mundane business. The iconoclasm, the intersections of different disciplines, the humanity present in that room, all were representative of what Steve aspired to. And yet for some reason he couldn't settle in.

There were at least twenty people in the room Steve didn't recognize, and the conversation had not quieted or slowed much when he introduced himself. It seemed to him that many of them didn't even know who he was, which was a little surprising, especially in the Bay Area. Apple was already something of a phenomenon: the company was selling more than 3,000 computers a month—up from around 70 a month at the end of 1977. No computer company had ever blossomed this way, and Steve was sure the next year would be even more explosive.

He sat down and started listening. The decision to create a foundation had already been made; the question now on the table was how to tell the world about Seva, its plans, and the men and women who would implement those plans. Steve found most of the ideas embarrassingly naïve. The discussion seemed more appropriate for a PTA meeting; at one point, everyone but Steve heatedly debated the finer points of a pamphlet they wanted to create. A *pamphlet*? That's the best these people could dream up? These so-called experts may have achieved notable progress in their own countries, but here they were clearly out of their league. Having a grand, bold goal was useless if you didn't have the ability to tell a compelling story about how you'd get there. That seemed obvious.

As the discussion meandered, Steve found his own attention wandering. "He had walked into that room with his persona from the Apple board meeting," Brilliant remembers, "but the rules for doing things like conquering blindness or eradicating smallpox are quite different." From time to time he'd pipe up, but mostly to interject a snide remark about why this or that idea could never fly. "He was becoming a nuisance," says Brilliant. Finally, Steve couldn't take it anymore. He stood up.

"Listen," he said, "I'm telling you this as someone who knows a thing or two about marketing. We've sold nearly a hundred thousand machines at Apple Computer, and when we started no one knew a thing about us. Seva is in the same position Apple was in a couple of years ago. The difference is you guys don't know diddly about marketing. So if you want to really do something here, if you really want to make a difference in the world and not just putter along like every other nonprofit that people have never heard of, you need to hire this guy named Regis McKenna—he's the king of marketing. I can get him in here if you'd like. You should have the best. Don't settle for second best."

The room went silent for a moment. "Who *is* this young man?" Venkataswamy whispered to Brilliant. A handful of people started challenging Steve from different sides of the table. He gave as good as he got, turning the group discussion into a donnybrook, ignoring the fact that these were people who had helped eradicate smallpox from the planet, who were saving the blind of India, who negotiated cross-border treaties so they could perform their good works in multiple, even warring, countries. In other words, these were people who knew a thing or two about getting things done. Steve didn't care about their accomplishments. He was always comfortable in a fight. Challenges, confrontations: in his limited experience, this was how you got things *done;* this was how the great stuff broke through. As the conversation heated up, Brilliant finally interjected: "Steve." And then he yelled, "Steve!"

Steve looked over, clearly irritated by the interruption and anxious to get back to his argument.

"Steve," said Brilliant, "we're really glad you're here, but now you've got to stop it!"

"I'm not going to," he said. "You guys asked for my help, and I'm going to give it. You want to know what to do? You need to call Regis McKenna. Let me tell you about Regis McKenna. He—"

"Steve!" Brilliant shouted again. "Stop it!" But Steve wouldn't. He just had to get his point across. So he took up his argument yet again, pacing back and forth as if he'd purchased the stage with his five-thousand-dollar donation, pointing directly at the people he was addressing as if to punctuate his remarks. And as the epidemiologists and the doctors and Bob Weir from the Grateful Dead looked on, Brilliant finally pulled the plug. "Steve," he said, sotto voce, trying to remain calm, but ultimately losing it. "It's time to go." Brilliant walked Steve out of the conference room.

Fifteen minutes later, Friedland slipped outside. He returned quickly, and discreetly crept over to Brilliant. "You should go see Steve," he whispered in his ear. "He's out in the parking lot crying."

"He's still here?" Brilliant asked.

"Yeah, and he's crying in the parking lot."

Brilliant, who was presiding over the meeting, excused himself and hurriedly walked out to find his young friend, who was hunched over the steering wheel of his Mercedes convertible, sobbing, in the middle of the parking lot. The rain had stopped, and the fog had begun to settle in. He had put the top down. "Steve," said Brilliant, leaning over the door and giving the twenty-four-year-old a hug. "Steve. It's okay."

"I'm sorry. I'm too wound up," Steve said. "I live in two worlds."

"It's okay. You should come back in."

"I'm going to leave. I know I was out of order. I just wanted them to listen."

"It's okay. Come back in."

"I'm going to go in and apologize. And then I'm going to leave," he said. And that is what he did.

THIS LITTLE ANECDOTE from the winter of 1979 is as good a place as any to start the story of how Steve Jobs turned around his life and became the greatest visionary leader of our time. The young man making a hash of his visit to the Garden of Allah that December evening was a mess of contradictions. He was a cofounder of one of the most successful startups ever, but he didn't want to be seen as a businessman. He craved the advice of mentors, and yet resented those in power. He dropped acid, walked barefoot, wore scraggly jeans, and liked the idea of living in a commune, yet he also loved nothing more than speeding down the highway in a finely crafted German sports car. He had a vague desire to support good causes, but he hated the inefficiency of most charities. He was impatient as hell and knew that the only problems worth solving were ones that would take years to tackle. He was a practicing Buddhist and an unrepentant capitalist. He was an overbearing know-it-all berating people who were wiser and immensely more experienced, and yet he was absolutely right about their fundamental marketing naïveté. He could be aggressively rude and then truly contrite. He was intransigent, and yet eager to learn. He walked away, and he walked back in to apologize. At the Garden of Allah he displayed all the brash, ugly behavior that became an entrenched part of the Steve Jobs myth. And he showed a softer side that would go less recognized over the years. To truly understand Steve and the incredible journey he was about to undergo, the full transformation that he would experience over his rich life, you have to recognize, accept, and try to reconcile both sides of the man.

He was the leader and public face of the personal computer industry, and yet he was still a kid—just twenty-four years old, still in the early days of his business education. His greatest strengths were inextricably tied to his greatest weaknesses. As of 1979, those failings had not yet gotten in the way of his success.

In the years ahead, however, Steve's tight bundle of contradictions would unravel. His stubborn strengths would give rise to Apple's signature computer, the Macintosh, which would debut in 1984. But his weaknesses would lead to chaos in his company and exile for him personally, just one year later. They would sabotage his efforts to create a second breakthrough computer at NeXT, the company he founded shortly after leaving Apple. They would lead him so far from the heart of the computer industry that he would become, in the damning words of one of his closest friends, "a has-been." They became so ingrained in his business reputation that when he was improbably invited back to run Apple in 1997, commentators, and even industry peers, would call the company's board of directors "crazy."

But then he pulled off one of the greatest business comebacks ever, leading Apple to the creation of a series of amazing products that defined an era and transformed a dying manufacturer of computers into the most valuable and admired company in the world. That turnaround wasn't a random miracle. While away from Apple, Steve Jobs had started to learn how to make the most of his strengths, and how to temper somewhat his perilous weaknesses. This reality runs counter to the common myths about Steve. In the popular imagination, he is a tyrant savant with a golden touch for picking products and equally a stubborn son of a bitch with no friends, no patience, and no morals; he lived and died as he was born—half genius and half asshole.

The unformed youth at the Garden of Allah could never have revived the moribund company he returned to in 1997, nor could he have engineered the slow and deeply complicated corporate evolution that led to the unimaginable success Apple enjoyed during the last decade of his life. His own personal growth was equally complicated. I can't think of a businessman who grew and changed and matured more than Steve. Personal change is, of course, incremental. As all "grown-ups" come to understand, we wrestle with and learn how to manage our gifts and flaws over a lifetime. It's an endless growth process. And yet it's not as if we become wholly different people. Steve is a great object lesson in someone who masterfully improved his ability to make better use of his strengths and to effectively mitigate those aspects of his personality that got in the way of those strengths. His negative qualities didn't go away, nor were they replaced by new good traits. But he learned how to manage *himself,* his own personal miasma of talents and rough edges. Most of them, anyway. To understand how that happened, and how that led to the confounding resurgence of Apple later in his career, you have to consider the full range of personal contradictions Steve brought to the Garden of Allah that December afternoon.

———

STEVEN PAUL JOBS felt deeply entitled almost from the start, thanks to parents who raised him to think that he was every bit as special as they believed he could be. Born on February 24, 1955, in San Francisco, Steve was given up for adoption by his birth mother, Joanna Schieble, who as a graduate student at the University of Wisconsin in Madison had become romantically involved in 1954 with Abdulfattah Jandali, a Syrian PhD candidate studying political science. Schieble moved to San Francisco after becoming pregnant, but Jandali remained in Wisconsin. Paul and Clara Jobs, a childless working-class couple, adopted Steve just a few days after his birth. When Steve was five years old they moved to Mountain View, twenty-five miles south of the city, and soon thereafter adopted a daughter they named Patty. While some have trotted out Steve's adoption as a primal "rejection" that explains the irascible behavior he often displayed, especially early in his career, Steve repeatedly told me that he had been loved and deeply indulged by Paul and Clara. "He felt he had been really blessed by having the two of them as parents," says Laurene Powell Jobs, Steve's widow.

Neither Paul nor Clara had attended college, but they did promise Schieble that they would send their new son. It was a significant pledge for a lower-middle-class family, and it marked the beginning of their pattern of giving their only son whatever he needed. Steve was whip smart; he skipped sixth grade, and his teachers even considered having him skip two grades. After leapfrogging to seventh grade, however, Steve felt snubbed socially and still unchallenged by his schoolwork. He pleaded with his parents to move him into a better school, and they agreed, despite the considerable cost of the switch. Paul and Clara packed up and relocated to Los Altos, a prosperous bedroom community that had sprung up in what were once plum orchards adjoining the low hills rising to the west above San Francisco Bay. The new neighborhood was then a subdivision within the Cupertino-Sunnyvale school district, one of the best in California. Once there, Steve started to flourish.

Paul and Clara may have let his sense of entitlement blossom, but they also nurtured his perfectionism, especially when it came to the rigor that underlies great craftsmanship. Paul Jobs held many jobs over his lifetime, including repo man, machinist, and car mechanic. He was at heart an inveterate tinkerer and craftsman who made furniture or rebuilt cars most weekends and taught his son the paramount value of taking one's time, paying attention to details, and—since Paul was anything but rich—putting in the legwork to hunt for spare parts that were a good value. "He had a workbench out in his garage," Steve once told an interviewer from the Smithsonian Institution. "When I was about five or six, he sectioned off a little piece of it and said 'Steve, this is your workbench now.' And he gave me some of his smaller tools and showed me how to use a hammer and saw and how to build things. It really was very good for me. He spent a lot of time with me . . . teaching me how to build things, how to take things apart, put things back together." In his later years, as Steve would show me a new iPod or a new laptop, he would remember how his father told him that you had to devote as much care to the underside of a cabinet as to the finish, or to the brake pads of a Chevy Impala as to the paint job. Steve had a deeply sentimental streak, and it came out when he told these stories about his father. They were made more poignant by the fact that Steve gave his father so much credit for instilling his own sense of aesthetic excellence in a medium—digital electronics—that Paul Jobs would never fully understand.

That combination, of believing that he was special and of wanting to get things just right, was a potent mix given where and when he was raised. The experience of growing up in what wasn't yet even called Silicon Valley in the late 1960s and early 1970s was unique. The environs between Palo Alto and San Jose were a boomtown of a new kind, attracting highly educated electrical engineers, chemists, optical specialists, computer programmers, and physicists who were drawn to the region's blossoming semiconductor, telecommunications, and electronics companies. It was a time when the market for high-end electronics had shifted from government and military customers to corporate and industrial America, expanding dramatically the number of potential customers for new electronic technologies of all kinds. The fathers of many other kids in Steve's neighborhood were engineers who commuted to work at the nearby headquarters of emerging tech giants like Lockheed, Intel, Hewlett-Packard, and Applied Materials.

Living there, a curious child interested in math and science could easily develop a much deeper sense of the leading edge of technology than those growing up elsewhere in the country. Electronics were just beginning to replace hot rods as the passion of young tinkerers. Geeks lived and breathed the fumes emanating from their soldering irons, and traded dog-eared copies of *Popular Science* and *Popular Electronics* magazines. They built their own transistor radios, hi-fi stereo systems, ham radios, oscilloscopes, rockets, lasers, and Tesla coils from kits offered by mail order companies like Edmund Scientific, Heathkit, Estes Industries, and Radio Shack. In Silicon Valley, electronics wasn't just a hobby. It was a fast-growing new industry and just as exciting as rock and roll.

For precocious kids like Steve, the implicit promise in all this was that anything could be figured out—and since anything could be figured out, anything could be built. "It gave one the sense that one could build the things that one saw around oneself in the universe," he once told me. "These things were not mysteries anymore. You looked at a television set and you would think that, 'I haven't built one of those but I could. There's one of those in the Heathkit catalog and I've built two other Heathkits, so I could build that.' Things became much more clear that they were the results of human creation, not these magical things that just appeared in one's environment and that one had no knowledge of their interiors."

He joined the Explorers Club, a group of fifteen kids who met regularly on Hewlett-Packard's campus in Palo Alto to work on electronics projects and get lessons from HP engineers. This is where Steve was first exposed to computers. It's also what gave him the outlandish notion to reach out and establish a minor, but fascinating, connection with one of the two men who famously created HP, the first Silicon Valley dynamo out of a garage. When he was fourteen years old, he called up Bill Hewlett at his Palo Alto home to ask personally for some hard-to-find electronic components for an Explorers Club project. He got them, in part, because he already could spin a good tale. In many ways, Steve was a prototypical adolescent geek. But he also was a curious student of the humanities, beguiled by the words of Shakespeare, Melville, and Bob Dylan. Glib and persuasive with his parents, he applied the same skills when dealing with friends, teachers, mentors, and eventually the rich and powerful; Steve innately understood from an early age that the right words and stories could help him win the attention he needed to get what he wanted.

———

STEVE WAS NOT really a star in this local crowd of budding technologists. But in 1969 a friend named Bill Fernandez introduced him to someone who was: Stephen Wozniak. Stephen Wozniak from nearby Sunnyvale. The son of a Lockheed engineer, "Woz" was an engineering genius. Steve, it turned out, was a great enabler of genius. This would turn out to be the first great collaboration of his career.

Nerdy and shy, Woz was five years older yet far less assertive than Steve. Like Steve, he had learned about electronics from his father and from other neighborhood dads. But he had immersed himself much more deeply into the subject, in school and out, and had even created a rudimentary calculator, made of transistors, resisters, and diodes, when he was just entering his teens. In 1971, before the single-chip microprocessor had been commercialized, Woz designed a circuit board loaded with chips and electronic components that he called the "Cream Soda Computer," since that was his favorite sugary soft drink at the time. Woz turned himself into an extraordinarily talented hardware designer whose uncanny electronic engineering instincts were coupled with a great software programmer's imagination—he could see shortcuts both in circuits and in software that others simply couldn't envision.

Steve didn't have Woz's innate talent, but he did have a native hunger to put really cool stuff into the hands of as many people as possible. This unique trait fundamentally separated him from other hobbyists messing around with computers. From the start, he had the natural inclination to be an impresario, to convince people to pursue a goal that often only he could see, and then to coordinate and push them toward the creation of that goal. The first sign of that came in 1972, when he and Woz started in on an unlikely commercial collaboration.

With Steve's help, Woz developed the first *digital* "blue box"—a machine that could mimic the tones used by telephone company switches to connect specific phones anywhere in the world. A prankster could hold one of these clever (and illegal) battery-powered gadgets up to the mouthpiece of any telephone and fool Ma Bell's switching systems into making long-distance or even international calls for free.

Woz would have been happy to just build the circuit and share it— as would be his inclination later with the circuit board that formed the heart and soul of the Apple 1 computer. Steve, however, proposed that they try to make some money by selling completely assembled machines. So while Woz polished his circuit design, Steve pulled together the necessary materials and priced the finished boxes. He and Woz netted some $6,000 selling the illegal devices at $150 a pop, mostly to college students. The two boys would wander dormitory hallways, knocking on doors and asking the occupants if this was George's room—a fictional George who supposedly was an expert phone phreak. If the discussion prompted interest, they'd demonstrate what the blue box could do, and sometimes make a sale. But business was spotty, and when they went further afield the venture foundered—the boys closed up shop after one supposed customer pulled a gun on Steve. Still, it wasn't bad for a first effort.

———

IT MAY SEEM strange to include Steve's spiritual life as one of the source materials of his career. But as a young man, Steve, with great sincerity, sought a deeper reality, a plane of consciousness beneath the surface. He pursued it with psychedelic drugs, and he pursued it with religious exploration. This spiritual sensibility contributed greatly to the unusual breadth of his intellectual peripheral vision, which eventually led him to see possibilities—ranging from great new products to radically reinvented business models—that escaped most others.

Just as Silicon Valley was the environment that birthed and nurtured Steve's technological optimism, the 1960s was the decade that fueled an inquisitive teen's natural impulse to search for deeper truths. Like so many other young people of the time, Steve embraced the questioning and yearning of the counterculture movement. He was a baby boomer who experimented with drugs, drank deeply of the insurgent lyrics of musicians like Dylan, the Beatles, the Grateful Dead, the Band, and Janis Joplin—even the radical, more abstract sonic musings of Miles Davis—and delved into the works of people he considered philosopher kings, spiritual thinkers like Suzuki Roshi, Ram Dass, and Paramahansa Yogananda. The messages of the time were clear: question everything, especially authority; experiment; hit the road; be fearless; and work to create a better world.

Steve's own grand quest began immediately after graduating from Cupertino's Homestead High School, when he headed off to Reed College in Portland, Oregon. It didn't take long before the headstrong freshman was only attending the classes that fascinated him, and after just one semester, he abruptly dropped out, without even telling his parents. He spent a second semester auditing classes, including one calligraphy course that he would cite in later years as the inspiration for the Macintosh's ability to produce a diverse panoply of typographical fonts. He also delved more deeply into Asian philosophy and mysticism, and dropped acid with greater frequency, at times almost as a spiritual sacrament.

The next summer, after returning, flat broke, to live with his parents again in Cupertino, he spent considerable time commuting back and forth to work at an Oregon apple orchard that doubled as a sort of commune. Eventually he landed a job back home as a technician at Atari, the video game company started by Nolan Bushnell, the inventor of Pong. He proved adept at repairing game machines that had gone on the fritz, and was able to convince Bushnell to let him fix some coin-operated kiosks in Germany, as part of a deal to pay his way to India, where he would join his pal Robert Friedland, the charismatic owner of that Oregon orchard.

It was all part of a romantic search for a way of life that had real meaning, at a time when the culture smiled on such quests. "You've got to keep Steve in the context of the time," says Larry Brilliant. "What were we all looking for? There was a generational split then, a split that was far deeper than the left-right split we have now, or the fundamentalist-secular split. And even though Steve had wonderfully supportive adoptive parents, he would get letters from Robert Friedland and other people who were in India, who had gone there seeking peace and believed they'd found something. That was what Steve was looking for."

Steve ostensibly went to India hoping to meet Neem Karoli Baba, known as Maharaj-ji, the famous guru who was an inspiration to Brilliant, Friedman, and other seekers. But Maharaj-ji died shortly before Steve's arrival, to his lasting disappointment. Steve's time in India was splintered, as unfocused as the searches of many young people seeking a broader vision than the one they were handed as children. He went to a religious festival attended by ten million other pilgrims. He wore flowing cotton robes, ate strange foods, and had his head shaved by a mysterious guru. He got dysentery. For the first time he read Yogananda's *Autobiography of a Yogi*, a book that he would return to several times throughout his life, and that would be given to everyone who attended the reception following Steve's memorial service at Stanford University's Memorial Church on October 16, 2011.

Early in his stay, according to Brilliant, "Steve had been flirting with the idea of being *sadhu*." Most Indian *sadhus* live a monklike existence of deprivation as a way of focusing solely on the spiritual. But Steve was obviously too hungry, too driven, and too ambitious for that kind of life. "It was a romance," says Brilliant, "with the idea of being a renunciate." But that doesn't mean he came back to the United States disillusioned, or that he dismissed Eastern spiritualism altogether. His interests migrated toward Buddhism, which allows for more engagement with the world than is permitted ascetic Hindus. It would enable him to blend a search for personal enlightenment with his ambition to create a company that delivered world-changing products. This appealed to a young man busy trying to invent himself, and it would continue to appeal to a man of infinite intellectual restlessness. Certain elements of Buddhism suited him so well that they would provide a philosophical underpinning for his career choices—as well as a basis for his aesthetic expectations. Among other things, Buddhism made him feel justified in constantly demanding nothing less than what he deemed to be "perfection" from others, from the products he would create, and from himself.

In Buddhist philosophy, life is often compared to an ever-changing river. There's a sense that everything, and every individual, is ceaselessly in the process of becoming. In this view of the world, achieving perfection is also a continuous process, and a goal that can never be fully attained. That's a vision that would come to suit Steve's exacting nature. Looking ahead to the unmade product, to whatever was around the next corner, and the two or three after that one, came naturally to him. He would never see a limit to possibilities, a perfect endpoint at which his work would be done. And while Steve would eschew almost all self-analysis, the same was true of his own life: despite the fact that he could be almost unfathomably stubborn and opinionated at times, the man himself was constantly adapting, following his nose, learning, trying out new directions. He was constantly in the act of becoming.

None of this was readily apparent to the outside world, and Steve's Buddhism could befuddle even his closest friends and colleagues. "There was always this spiritual side," says Mike Slade, a marketing executive who worked with Steve later in his career, "which really didn't seem to fit with anything else he was doing." He meditated regularly until he and Laurene became parents, when the demands on his time grew in a way he hadn't anticipated. He reread Suzuki's *Zen Mind, Beginner's Mind* several times, and made the intersection of elements of Asian spiritualism and his business and commercial life a regular subject of the conversations he and Brilliant enjoyed throughout his life. For years, he arranged for a Buddhist monk by the name of Kobun Chino Otogawa to meet with him once a week at his office to counsel him on how to balance his spiritual sense with his business goals. While nobody who knew him well during his later years would have called Steve a "devout" Buddhist, the spiritual discipline informed his life in both subtle and profound ways.

———

WHEN STEVE RETURNED to America in the fall of 1974, he landed back at Atari, mainly doing hardware-related troubleshooting tasks for Nolan Bushnell's pioneering—and poorly managed—company. Atari was such a loose, strange organization that Jobs could still comfortably disappear for a couple of weeks to pick apples at Robert Friedland's orchard and not get fired, or even be missed, really. Meanwhile, Woz was working at Hewlett-Packard, in a safe, well-paying, but not particularly challenging gig. Nothing about Jobs's life at this time would have suggested that he would achieve extraordinary success in business, computer technology, or anything else, for that matter. But unbeknownst even to himself, Steve was about to begin the real work of creating his life. In the next three years, he would morph from a scruffy, drifting nineteen-year-old into the cofounder and leader of a revolutionary new American business.

Steve was blessed to live at a moment that was ripe and ready for someone with his talents. It was an era of change on so many fronts, and especially in the world of information technology. In the 1970s, big machines called mainframes defined computing. Mainframes were enormous, room-sized computing systems sold to customers like airlines, banks, insurers, and large universities. The programming required to get a result—say, to calculate a mortgage payment—was beyond cumbersome. At least it seemed that way for anyone studying computer science in college, which is where most of us had our introduction to making a mainframe actually do something. After settling on the problem you wanted the machine to solve, you would painstakingly write down, in a programming language like COBOL or Fortran, a series of line-by-line, step-by-step instructions for the exact, logical process of the calculation or analytical chore. Then, at a noisy mechanical console, you would type each individual line of the handwritten program onto its own rectangular "punch card," which was perforated in such a way that a computer could "read" it. After meticulously making sure the typed cards were arranged in the right order— simple programs might need a few dozen cards that could be held by a rubber band, while elaborate programs could require reams that would have to be stacked carefully in a special cardboard box. You would then hand the bundle to a computer "operator," who would put your deck in the queue behind dozens of others to be fed into the mainframe. Eventually, the machine would spit out your results on broad sheets of green-and-white-striped accordion-folded paper. More often than not, you would have to tweak your program three, four, or even dozens of times, to get the results you were looking for.

In other words, computing in 1975 was anything but personal. Writing software was a laborious and slow process. The big, expensive, high-maintenance computers were manufactured and sold, appropriately enough, by a handful of big, bureaucratic technology companies. As it had been since the 1950s, the computer industry in 1975 was dominated by International Business Machines (IBM), which sold more mainframes than all of its other competitors put together. In the 1960s, those also-rans were called "the Seven Dwarfs," but during the 1970s, both General Electric and RCA gave up, leaving a stubborn group of manufacturers referred to as the "BUNCH"—an acronym for Burroughs, Univac, NCR, Control Data Corporation, and Honeywell. Digital Equipment Corporation (DEC) dominated an upcoming segment of somewhat cheaper and less-powerful "minicomputers" used by smaller businesses, and by departments within larger corporations. There was one outlier at each end of the cost spectrum. At the high end, Cray Research, founded in 1972, sold so-called supercomputers used primarily for scientific research and mathematical modeling. These were the most expensive computers of all, costing well north of $3 million. On the cheap end of the scale was Wang, which was founded in the early 1970s and made a task-specific machine known as a "word processor." It was the closest thing to a "personal" computer that existed, since it was designed for a single person to use in the preparation of written reports and correspondence. The computer industry then was primarily an eastern establishment. IBM was headquartered in the bucolic suburbs north of New York City; DEC and Wang were based in Boston. Burroughs was headquartered in Detroit, Univac in Philadelphia, NCR in Dayton, Ohio, and Cray, Honeywell, and Control Data all hailed from Minneapolis. The only notable early computer maker in Silicon Valley was Hewlett-Packard, but its primary business was making scientific test and measurement instruments and calculators.

This industry bore little resemblance to today's entrepreneurial, innovative, and rapidly iterative tech world. It was a stodgy enterprise most similar to the capital equipment business. Its universe of potential customers could be counted in the hundreds, and these were companies with deep pockets whose demands focused more on performance and reliability than on price. No surprise, then, that the industry had become cloistered and a little complacent.

Out in California a significant number of the people who would have a hand in flipping that industry on its head started meeting regularly as a hobbyist group called the Homebrew Computer Club. Their first get-together occurred shortly after the publication of the January 1975 issue of *Popular Electronics,* which featured a cover story about the Altair 8800 "microcomputer." Gordon French, a Silicon Valley engineer, hosted the gathering in his garage to show off an Altair unit that French and a buddy had assembled from the $495 kit sold by Micro Instrumentation and Telemetry Systems (MITS). It was an inscrutable-looking device, about the size of a stereo component amplifier, its face sporting two horizontal arrays of toggle switches and a lot of blinking red lights. The clunky thing couldn't do too much, but it demonstrated the feasibility of having a computer to yourself, one that you could program twenty-four hours a day if you wanted to, without having to wait in line or punch any cards. Bill Gates read the article, and shortly thereafter famously dropped out of Harvard to start a little outfit called Micro-soft to design software programming languages for the Altair.

Woz knew the MITS machine wasn't all that much more advanced than the Cream Soda Computer he'd created four years earlier, in 1971, when he had to use much less sophisticated components. Spurred by a geek's natural competitive instincts, he roughed out some new designs for what he knew would be a better microcomputer, one that would be easier to program, control, and manipulate. Flipping toggle switches and counting flashing lights was like using flag semaphore and Morse code, he thought. Why not input commands and data values more directly with a typewriter keyboard? And why not have the computer project your typing and results onto an attached television monitor? And for that matter, why not plug in a cassette tape recorder to store programs and data? The Altair had none of these features that would make computing far less intimidating and far more approachable. This was the challenge Woz decided to tackle. In the back of his mind he hoped that his employer, HP, might want to manufacture a version of his concept.

Enter Steve Jobs, the budding opportunist and junior impresario.

He didn't think Woz needed HP. He thought he and Woz could develop a business of their own. Steve knew that Woz was so uniquely talented that any computer he would design would be cheap, usable, and easy to program—so much so that the other hobbyists at Homebrew might want one, too. So during the fall and winter of 1975 and early 1976, as Woz perfected his design, Jobs started to conjure how they might pool their resources to purchase the components they needed to make a working prototype. Every couple of weeks, they would take the latest working version of the computer to the Homebrew meetings, to show off a new feature or two to the toughest audience in town. Steve persuaded Woz that they could make the club members their customers by selling them the schematics, and perhaps even printed circuit boards. Club members could then buy the chips and other components themselves, and assemble them into the guts of their very own working microcomputer. To raise the cash to pay a mutual friend to draw a "reference design" for the circuit boards, Steve sold his treasured Volkswagen minibus, and Woz unloaded his precious HP-65 programmable calculator. After spending $1,000 on designing the board and contracting to have a few dozen made, Jobs and Wozniak made their money back and then some by selling them to fellow Homebrew members for $50 apiece, netting them a nifty $30 for each circuit board.

It wasn't much of a business, but it was enough for two young men who were coming to believe that these microcomputers could change everything. "We felt it was going to affect every home in the country," Woz explained years later. "But we felt it for the wrong reasons. We felt that everybody was technical enough to really use it and write their own programs and solve their problems that way." Steve decided that their new company should be called Apple. There are different tales about the origin of the name, but it was a brilliant decision. Years later, Lee Clow, Steve's longtime collaborator on Apple's distinctive brand of advertising, told me, "I honestly believe that his intuition was that they were going to change people's lives by giving them technology they didn't know they needed, that would be different from anything they knew. So they needed something friendly and approachable and likable. He took a page out of Sony's book, because Sony was originally called Tokyo Telecommunications Engineering Corporation, and [cofounder] Akio Morita said they needed something much more approachable."

Indeed, adopting the name Apple foreshadows the expansiveness and originality Steve would bring to the creation of these new machines. It's suggestive of so much: the Garden of Eden, and the humanity—both good and bad—resulting from Eve's bite of the fruit from the Tree of Knowledge; Johnny Appleseed, the great sower of plentitude from American myth; the Beatles and their own record label, a connection that would lead to litigation years later; Isaac Newton, the plummeting apple, and the spark of an idea; American as apple pie; the legend of William Tell, who saved his own life and that of his son by using his crossbow to pierce an apple perched on the son's head; wholesomeness, fecundity, and, of course, the natural world. Apple is not a word for geeks, unlike Asus, Compaq, Control Data, Data General, DEC, IBM, Sperry Rand, Texas Instruments, or Wipro, to mention some less felicitously named computer companies. It hints at a company that would bring, as it eventually did, humanism and creativity to the science and engineering of computers. As Clow suggests, settling on Apple was a great, intuitive decision. Steve was innately comfortable trusting his gut; it's a characteristic of the best entrepreneurs, a necessity for anyone who wants to make a living developing things no one has ever quite imagined before.

Of course, Steve's gut could also betray him, as it did when he fell in love with Apple's first corporate logo. It was a pen-and-ink drawing, detailed in the way of an etching, of Isaac Newton sitting beneath an apple tree. It was the kind of overworked, precious image that a young calligraphy student might find enchanting, but far too esoteric for a company with big mainstream ambitions. This graphic rendition was drawn by Ronald Wayne, a former Atari engineer whom Steve had recruited to join the team. Wayne would have acted as the wise, elder tiebreaker if Steve and Woz ever came to loggerheads. The three signed a partnership agreement that gave Steve and Woz each 45 percent of the equity, with Wayne taking the remaining 10 percent. But Wayne quickly decided he wasn't prepared to risk his future on this pair of neophytes. In June 1976, he sold back his stake for $800 to Jobs and Wozniak, who a year later would commission a new logo. In the tradition of Pete Best of the Beatles, Wayne would miss out on the ride of his life.

———

SHORTLY AFTER REGISTERING Apple as a California business partnership on April Fools' Day, 1976, Steve and Woz made one more trip to the Homebrew Computer Club to show off the finished, fully assembled version of their new computer. Woz had met every challenge. On a circuit board measuring 9 inches by 15.5 inches, he had assembled a microprocessor, some dynamic random access memory chips, a central processing unit, a power supply, and other parts in such a way that once you connected it to a keyboard and a monitor, you could do a couple of radically new things: write computer programs on your own machine, in your own home, without being tied into a remote mainframe; and for the first time on a microcomputer, you could type your commands on a keyboard and see them immediately displayed on a black-and-white TV monitor, making them easier to edit than ever before. Both steps were radical departures from past practice. Woz had also written a version of BASIC, the simplest and most important hobbyist programming language, to run on the Motorola 6800 microprocessor that functioned as the brains of what he and Steve were starting to call the Apple 1. Woz didn't fully appreciate it, but he had created the first truly *personal* computer. Steve, however, understood the magnitude of the achievement, and the power of the term *personal computer* in the context of an industry that had historically been anything but personal. So that was exactly the term he used whenever people asked him what it was that Woz had dreamed up.

The reaction from most club members, however, was tepid. Most were tinkerers who believed that half the fun of computing was in designing and building their own machines. That's why they called it the Homebrew Computer Club, after all. With an Apple 1, however, all you had to do was set it up, connect it to a keyboard and a monitor, plug it in, and turn it on. Others beefed that Steve was flouting the club's community spirit and its history of sharing ideas freely by asking them to pay for a prebuilt machine.

It was Steve's nature to be out of synch with this kind of groupthink. He was a singular free-thinker whose ideas would often run against the conventional wisdom of any community in which he operated. He and the Homebrewers were cut from different cloth. Their spirited debates often bored him. While a few had broader business ambitions and eventually founded microcomputer companies of their own, most were obsessively focused on electronic intricacies, like determining the most efficient way to link memory chips to microprocessors, or imagining how you might use a cheap computer to play games like the ones they played on mainframes back in school. Steve liked knowing enough to be conversant about electronics and computer design, and later in his life he would boast about his own supposed skill as a programmer. But even in 1975, he didn't fundamentally or passionately care about the intricacies of computers in and of themselves. Instead, he was obsessed by what might happen when this powerful technology got into the hands of many, many people.

Through the years, Steve would be the beneficiary of a fair amount of luck, some of it outrageously good, and of course some of it mortally bad. Pixar's Ed Catmull likes to say that since you can't control the luck itself, which is bound to come your way for better *and* for worse, what matters is your state of preparedness to deal with it. Steve had a kind of hyperawareness of his surroundings that allowed him to leap at opportunities that presented themselves. So when Paul Terrell, the owner of the Byte Shop computer store in nearby Mountain View, introduced himself to Steve and Woz after the presentation and let them know he was impressed enough to want to talk about doing some business together, Steve knew exactly what to do. The very next day he borrowed a car and drove over to the Byte Shop, Terrell's humble little store on El Camino Real, Silicon Valley's main thoroughfare. Terrell surprised him, saying that if the two Steves could deliver fifty fully assembled circuit boards with all the chips soldered into place by a certain date, he would pay them $500 a pop—in other words, ten times what Steve and Woz had been charging club members for the printed circuit boards alone. Without missing a beat, Steve happily promised delivery, even though he and Woz had neither the wherewithal to buy the components nor anything like the "factory space" or "labor force" necessary to build anything.

From this point forward, Steve's opportunism and drive would define the contours of his relationship with Woz. Woz, who was five years older, taught Steve the intrinsic value of great engineering. His accomplishments reinforced Steve's sense that anything was possible when you had technological genius on your side. But it was Steve's ability to manipulate Woz that drove the partnership, and not always for the better. Back in 1974, when Atari had been trying to develop a new version of its big hit, Pong, Nolan Bushnell had asked Jobs to create a prototype, offering a considerable bonus if he could reduce the number of chips required for each circuit board. Steve brought Woz in on the project, promising to split the fee. Woz's design was more economical than Bushnell had thought was even possible, and so Steve was paid a bonus of $5,000 on top of the base $700 fee. According to Woz, Steve only paid him $350, not the $2,850 he should have earned. Walter Isaacson, Steve's official biographer, wrote that Jobs denied shortchanging Woz. But the accusation rings true, because it fits with a few other instances in which Steve took shortcuts with people who were close to him.

Still, like several other close collaborators who later grew disenchanted with Steve, Woz admits that he would never have succeeded so brilliantly without Steve. Terrell's order for $25,000 worth of computer motherboards was about $25,000 higher than anything Woz imagined he might ever sell.

The two young men had created a nice little market for their "blue boxes," but that was trivial compared with this. They had never manufactured multiple units of anything at such a significant scale. They had never formally financed a business. Nor had they ever really sold anything of any real value. None of this dissuaded Jobs. He set about taking care of the details of production. For a makeshift factory, he commandeered a bedroom in his parents' house. He roped his adoptive sister, Patty, into fitting and soldering the semiconductors and other parts into their marked spaces on the circuit board. When Terrell ordered up another fifty, Steve moved the operation into his parents' garage after his father cleared out the cars he was fixing up for resale. He hired Bill Fernandez, the very guy who back in high school had first introduced him to Woz. And he brought in other neighborhood kids to accelerate the process. He signed up an answering service and rented a post office box. He did, in other words, whatever it took.

The garage became home to an assembly line in miniature. In one area, Steve's sister and some friends soldered chips into place. Woz had his own workspace nearby where he could vet the assembled boards as they were finished. On the other side of the garage they took turns testing the "stuffed" boards for hours under heat lamps to verify their durability. Steve's mother answered phone calls. Everyone worked nights and weekends. And Steve was more focused than anyone. He prodded the team ceaselessly. When things went wrong, he moved fast; after an old girlfriend failed to solder a few chips correctly, he made her the team's bookkeeper. His temper was short and he never hesitated to belittle their work when something went wrong. As a child, Steve had rarely been given any reason to hold back his honest feelings. Now he began to learn one of his first management lessons, namely that his temper, properly targeted, could actually be a very effective motivational tool. It was a lesson that would prove hard to undo.

Sure enough, under Steve's gimlet eye, his motley team delivered all the circuit boards Terrell ever ordered. The product didn't exactly fly off the shelf—fewer than two hundred Apple 1's were ever sold. Even so, that summer in the legendary garage represented the first time Steve rallied a group of people to dig down deep and deliver something that was innovative and miraculous, and that they weren't even sure they could create. It wouldn't be the last time he would pull off such a trick. After an aborted stint at college, a picaresque pilgrimage to India, some revelatory travels on LSD, and an internship of sorts at Atari, Steve had discovered his true mission. And now he was totally locked in.

Chapter 2
"I Didn't Want to Be a Businessman"

The story of Steve Jobs's first tenure at Apple Computer is the tale of a young visionary in the adolescence of his career. After playing such a crucial role in making and selling the Apple 1, Steve faced the challenge of moving his vision, intelligence, intuition, and ferocious personality from his father's garage into a much bigger "space"—the corporate and financial and industrial world of Silicon Valley. Steve may have been a quick study, but he didn't have an instinctive sense of how to do this. Some young men and women are bred for corporate life—Bill Gates comes to mind. Steve was not.

If Steve was ever going to do something grander than just cook up something cool with the kids in the garage, he had to learn to play with the grown-ups. But it wasn't going to be easy. As he told me several times: "I didn't want to be a businessman, because all the businessmen I knew I didn't want to be like." Steve's natural inclination was to position himself as the critic, the rebel, the visionary, the lithe and nimble David against the stodgy Goliath of whatever powers might be.

Collaborating with "the Man," to use the colloquial terminology of his day, wasn't just problematic, it was tantamount to collusion. Yes, he wanted to play their game, but by his own rules.

―――――

ALMOST AS SOON as the young men had started selling the first batches of Apple 1's, Woz told Steve that he knew he could design a much better machine. As Woz imagined it, the next model would display its results in full color, pack a lot more power and performance onto the same-size "motherboard," and have multiple "slots" that could be adapted to help the machine perform more tasks. If Steve and Woz were going to have any chance of producing and selling such a snazzy machine, they would have to scrounge up some serious working capital. They needed far more than they could get by continuing to cadge personal loans from friends, parents, and advance payments from proprietors of hobby shops. Not knowing exactly where he could get that kind of money, Steve began to make a real effort to connect with Silicon Valley's cloistered world of successful entrepreneurs, marketers, and financiers.

In 1976, the route to success in Silicon Valley wasn't remotely as well mapped as it is today, when entrepreneurs can find the path to financing by simply Googling "venture capital." Back then the Valley had a much smaller mix of lawyers, financiers, and managers, and most business was conducted face-to-face. But Steve had several qualities that made him a superb networker. "I was really lucky to get into computers when it was a very young industry," he once told me. "At that point in time there weren't many degrees offered in computer science, so people in computers were from mathematics, physics, music, zoology, whatever. Wherever they came from they loved it, and there were some incredibly brilliant people involved." He had no qualms about calling anyone up in search of information or help; heck, he'd been doing that since his phone call to Bill Hewlett when he was fourteen years old. Steve had none of the tentativeness most young men or

women might have as they set out to learn the nuances of a complicated new world like the venture capital business. He had such faith in
the excellence of his work that he assumed someone would eventually
agree to fund. He could be genuinely charming when this confidence
didn't lead him into boorishness.

So he tirelessly navigated the Valley's network of experts, one phone
call and one meeting at time, until he finally found himself connected
with Regis McKenna, the marketing whiz who had helped promote
Intel, and who would eventually be instrumental in establishing Apple's iconoclastic, and remarkably resilient, public image.

Steve and Woz met McKenna at his offices. Steve certainly didn't
dress up for this meeting—as usual, his jeans had holes, his hair was
unbrushed, he wore no shoes, and he smelled. At this point in his life,
he deemed deodorant, footwear, and the like affectations. McKenna
was a unique member of the Silicon Valley elite. Well coiffed, with
magnetic blue eyes, he was frank, unforgiving, and ubiquitously networked, and had a sly sense of humor and brash self-confidence that
matched Steve's. His business card simply read: Regis McKenna, *Himself.* He saw past the boys' nerdy slovenliness to their remarkable intelligence, and found himself liking them. "Steve had breadth," McKenna
remembers, "and a sort of thoughtful way about him that would always
be there." So he and Nolan Bushnell, Jobs's old boss at Atari, steered
Steve to Don Valentine, a founding partner of Sequoia Capital, one of
the first venture capital firms to master the art of early-stage investing
in high-tech companies.

Valentine came from the chip world. He had worked with the
founders of Intel before they abandoned Fairchild Semiconductor to
open their own shop, and he had once held a senior position at National Semiconductor. He met with the boys only because McKenna
was a friend, and quite literally held his nose to hear Steve and Woz
out. After their visit, he called McKenna to ask, "Why'd you send
me these renegades from the human race?" Yet he did point the boys
toward an individual "angel" investor who would be more apt to work
closely with an idiosyncratic startup such as Apple.

That's how Steve was introduced to A. C. "Mike" Markkula, who would become, for better and for worse, one of Steve's two primary early mentors at Apple. One day, Markkula decided to drive his gold Corvette over to the garage and let the boys walk him through the wonders of the Apple 1. A former Intel sales executive who also owned an advanced degree in electrical engineering, he had made a lot of money in a hurry but had "retired" in his early thirties when he was passed over for the company's top sales job. Rather quiet, Markkula was at heart a computer geek, and could do some programming himself. He immediately grasped the potential in the ambitious ideas of Jobs and Wozniak, and he also could see how intelligent, resourceful, and yet malleable they were. After a few meetings he bought in, driving a pretty hard bargain. In one of the greatest angel investments of all time, Markkula ponied up $92,000 out of his own pocket and arranged for a $250,000 line of credit with Bank of America, in return for a one-third stake in Apple.

Markkula insisted that Woz, who was still working at Hewlett-Packard, become a full-time Apple employee. Woz loved working at HP, but he also really did want to create another great microcomputer. So he made one last presentation to HP, to give them a final shot to develop his still rough concept for the Apple II. They weren't interested. "Big experienced companies and investors, analysts—those kinds of people, that are trained in business and much smarter than we were— they didn't think that this was going to be a real big market," Woz remembered. "They thought it was going to be a little hobby thing, like home robots or ham radios, that a few techie people would get into." So he quit his job and signed on.

From the start, Markkula was an unlikely match for Steve and Woz. A short, trim, dapper guy, he seemed to come straight out of central casting for seventies fashion, with his fast car, long sideburns, full head of hair, and flashy leisure suits. His conversational style could be best described as mumbling. While he was smart and technically adept, he wasn't forceful or combative, nor did he express strong opinions with any passion. And while he had made a lot of money already and was very interested in making more, he really didn't want to work all that hard. Later, after Steve left Apple, Markkula would work valiantly to keep Apple afloat. But that was in a crisis. At the point in his life when he met Steve, he was pretty content with his big house and his Intel payout. In a move that clearly reflected his ambivalence, Markkula promised his wife that he would spend no more than four years working with Apple.

So when Markkula decided that the company should convert its limited partnership into a California corporation and employ a professional chief executive, he made it very clear that he was not interested in that job himself. He recruited Michael "Scotty" Scott, a thirty-two-year-old manufacturing manager from National Semiconductor, as Apple's first professional president and CEO. Markkula, thirty-four, became chairman of the Apple board. It was February 1977, and Steve, all of twenty-one years old, had turned Apple over to adult supervision. Unfortunately, neither Markkula nor Scotty could ever become the mentor he needed.

———

THE COMPANY MOVED out of Steve's parents' garage and into real offices on Stevens Creek Boulevard in Cupertino. Scotty and Markkula started hiring people and setting up the basics of a corporation. For the first few months, Steve kept doing what he knew how to do best: rally a small crew to produce something wonderful. This time, it was the Apple II—the machine that would really introduce the world to personal computing.

Once again, Jobs was the impresario and Woz the engineering genius. Steve pushed Woz, cajoling him, berating him, and challenging his thinking. Woz responded by giving his new machine a versatility and instant usefulness never seen before in a microcomputer. It was the most complete computer in a single, manageable box the world had ever seen. All you really needed to add to it was a TV monitor. The Apple II, its innards housed in a sleek, beige plastic case with a built-in keyboard, resembled the consumer-friendly electric typewriters that were popular then. It was designed as a finished product ready for the home, school, or office; the Apple 1, it now seemed clear, could be relegated to the world of soldering irons, oscilloscopes, voltmeters, and other electronic arcana that the average consumer never wanted to worry about.

The new model had a significantly faster microprocessor than its predecessor and more built-in memory, which also improved performance. It had an audio amplifier and speaker, and jacks for plugging in a joystick for game play or a cassette tape drive for cheap data storage. Since Woz wanted it to be useful to the hobbyist programmer the minute it was plugged in, he also built the BASIC programming language right into the system, loading it into a special chip of its own that was hardwired to the motherboard. Perhaps most important, the computer was designed to accommodate unforeseen future hardware modifications that could either soup up its performance or optimize it for a particular kind of computing task, whether crunching numbers, playing games, building searchable lists, or writing programs. Woz built in eight so-called expansion "slots" that would allow the insertion of special circuit cards—essentially smaller circuit boards—that could work in concert with the microprocessor and memory chips on the motherboard for particular purposes, such as adding a floppy disk drive, or more advanced video graphics, or better sound, or the expansion of memory. This gave the Apple II the potential to become a much more capable computer once professionally designed software applications and special expansion circuit cards were available for it, and they weren't long in coming.

As it had in the garage, Steve's perfectionism and his comfort with being out of synch with conventional wisdom led to conflicts. Steve had opposed adding those expansion slots, for example, because he thought a perfect consumer computer should be so easy to use that no one would ever want to add to the hardware's capabilities by opening it up. The instinct—to deliver a computer with the simplicity of an appliance—may have been an admirable long-term goal, but it was a profoundly wrongheaded choice for a personal computer in 1977. Business-minded tinkerers had already expressed interest in designing add-in cards that would let the Apple II interact with or control telephones, musical instruments, laboratory instruments, medical devices, office machines, printers, and on and on. Woz understood this, and won the argument.

But on several other decisions where Steve defied conventional wisdom he was right. You wouldn't want a truly *personal* computer to sound like an industrial machine, he reasoned, so he convinced a talented engineer by the name of Frederick Rodney Holt to design a special power supply that didn't heat up so much that it required a noisy, perpetually whirring fan to keep the machine from melting down. Jobs also pushed for an external shell that looked more like an appliance than a piece of lab equipment, going so far as to visit department stores for inspiration. This insight seems obvious now, but at the time computer hobbyists preferred industrial-looking cases, or even topless machines that showed off the complexity of their insides, and allowed for easy modification. For less hard-core consumers, the Apple II's design was more inviting and self-contained and presentable, and those qualities alone made it very different from anything else out there at the time. Even though its first significant software application— VisiCalc, a spreadsheet program written by Dan Bricklin and Robert Frankston—wouldn't arrive until 1979, the $1,295 Apple II was an immediate hit upon its April 1977 introduction. Within one year the company that was accustomed to selling a dozen Apple 1's every few weeks was selling 500 or so Apple II's every month.

———

TWICE NOW, STEVE had proved himself to be a strong leader of a small group of people. The challenge he faced was to figure out how he himself could be led, by Markkula and Scott, as they set out to do something he knew that he could not possibly manage alone: design, build, and steer a growing company to develop, manufacture, distribute, and sell computers. Ceding control had not been difficult at all for Wozniak, who had absolutely no interest in overseeing the details of a burgeoning business. A world-class electrical engineer, he always seemed happiest at his workbench, where he could tinker, invent, and debate with his fellow engineers about wonky details as Apple's vice president for research and development.

It was far more complicated for Steve, and not just because he had an adolescent problem with authority. He had seen now that his contrarian thinking was essential for the kinds of breakthrough products he wanted to engineer, and he had also seen that his irascible methods could prod a group of people to deliver that vision. Those were qualities that didn't mesh easily with the grown-up leadership that Scotty was trying to bring to Apple.

What Scotty offered were systems. If Apple were a family, Scotty would have handled the nuts and bolts of the household, setting up bank accounts, closing on a mortgage, and so on. Of course, what he did for Apple was far more complicated. An engineer with a strong manufacturing background at National Semiconductor, Scotty was a high-tech dweeb, right down to the plastic pocket protector he really did have in his short-sleeved dress shirts. He came to Apple having already managed hundreds of people and overseen the complex fabrication processes at a chipmaker. At Apple, he provided most of the managerial heavy lifting required to build a sophisticated high-tech company from scratch: leasing office and factory space and equipment, masterminding the design of a reliable manufacturing process, building a sales team, creating quality controls, supervising the engineering, installing management information systems, and putting together an executive staff to handle finance and hiring. He initiated the critical process of developing solid relationships with key components suppliers and software developers. Steve absorbed a lot by watching Scotty handle these tasks.

Adding to the complexity of what Scott was trying to manage was the fact that Apple was pioneering a nascent industry that was different from most others in one crucial way: computers were *systems* that blended three key underlying technologies that all were in a state of perpetual and rapid change—semiconductors, software, and data storage. A company couldn't simply devise a single great, innovative product, tool up, stamp it out, and then sit back and count the money. That had worked for high-tech companies like Polaroid and Xerox during their first decades. But this was different. As soon as a computer company had breathed life into one new system, it had to buckle down and start all over again in order to outdo itself before some other Promethean company reconfigured newer versions of these ever-improving technologies and stole its fire. And it would have to do so over and over again, generation after generation. In fact, it soon became clear that it was smart business for a company to start work on the product that would render obsolete its latest and greatest offering *well before* the first one even made it to market. That's how fast things would change in the tech marketplace that was just beginning to materialize. And each of the system's three underlying technologies was improving independently at its own breathtaking pace, so there was always more leverage to be had by employing the latest, greatest building blocks as they became available.

The great technology CEOs could impose rigor on their companies and yet accept the fact that all this rapid change would eventually disrupt their operations anyway. Mike Scott was not a great CEO. He had the skills and personality of a COO—a chief operating officer. When he didn't get the stability he so avidly tried to engineer, he became frazzled. And, thanks in great part to Steve, Scotty didn't achieve a whole lot of stability at Apple.

Steve certainly knew, intellectually, that he needed the orderly and well-oiled basic operations of a corporation to achieve his vision. But he was enamored with instability. His vision was based on destabilizing the existing computer industry. Stability was a quality that IBM had, and Apple, in Steve's mind, was the anti-IBM.

Needless to say, the arranged marriage between one man who embraced uncertainty and another who craved stability was not destined to last. A harbinger of its eventual demise occurred in the first couple of weeks after Scotty arrived at Apple. He had to assign numbers to the workplace badges everyone wore around the new Stevens Creek Boulevard office. When he decided that Woz would be "Employee #1," Steve went to him and whined; it didn't take long till Scotty relented and gave Steve a new, customized tag: "Employee #0."

IN PART BECAUSE of the way Steve quarreled with Markkula and Scott, in part because he so brazenly asserted his opinions as fact, and in part because, over the length of his career, he neglected to share credit for Apple's successes in the press, Steve developed a reputation as an egomaniac who wasn't willing to learn from others. It's a fundamental misunderstanding of the man, even during his youngest, brashest, and most overbearing years.

While Steve looked to his elders at Apple for guidance, he also sought it out elsewhere. He didn't yet have the skills to build a great company, but he admired those who had pulled it off, and he would go to great lengths to meet them and learn from them. "None of these people were really in it for the money," he told me. "Dave Packard, for example, left all his money to his foundation. He may have died the richest guy in the cemetery, but he wasn't in it for the money. Bob Noyce [cofounder of Intel] is another. I'm old enough to have been able to get to know these guys. I met Andy Grove [CEO of Intel from 1987 to 1998] when I was twenty-one. I called him up and told him I had heard he was really good at operations and asked if I could take him out to lunch. I did that with Jerry Sanders [founder of Advanced Micro Devices] and with Charlie Sporck [founder of National Semiconductor] and others. Basically I got to know these guys who were all company-builders, and the particular scent of Silicon Valley at that time made a very big impression on me."

Most of these older men enjoyed sparring with and advising someone this glib, smart, and anxious to learn. Of course, they didn't work with him, which lowered the stakes on the relationship considerably.

Some were heroes whom he only met once or twice, like Edwin Land, the founder of Polaroid. Steve admired many things about Land, among them his obsessive commitment to creating products of style, practicality, and great consumer appeal, like the groundbreaking SX-70, the folding camera that wowed America in the 1970s; his reliance on gut instinct rather than consumer research; and the restless obsession and invention he brought to the company he founded.

Others became lifelong advisers. Grove served as a behind-the-scenes counselor to Steve at several critical moments in his career, despite the fact that Apple—until 2006—was the one major computer company whose machines didn't run on Intel chips. Jobs deeply respected Grove. A Hungarian Jew who survived a Nazi labor camp, fascism, an aborted revolution, and the prolonged Russian siege of Budapest, who lost most of his hearing at age four from a severe case of scarlet fever, and who made his way to Ellis Island on his own after fleeing the communist regime as a teenager, Grove is as tough and pragmatic as any businessman around. But he is also, just as Steve was, a well-rounded person with wide-ranging interests. At City College of New York he mastered English, including its most scathing expletives, which he could hurl with astonishing venom thanks in part to his Hungarian accent. His combination of pragmatism and expansiveness was something Steve admired, something he aspired to himself.

Grove is the third member—along with Jobs and Bill Gates—of the triumvirate that brought personal computing to the masses. He came into his own after he signed on as the first employee at Intel Corporation, which was founded in 1968 by fellow Fairchild engineers Robert Noyce and Gordon Moore, the originator in 1965 of Moore's law. That "law" was an observation about the price and performance of semiconductors that no one before him had noticed: namely that the number of transistors that could be etched on a single chip of a given size doubled every eighteen months or so, without any corresponding increase in the cost. It was Grove who best understood just how intricate and difficult it was to actually make reliable semiconductor components on a scale that computer makers like IBM, Sperry, and Burroughs could count on. In that sense, he was the one who transformed Moore's law into a business model, allowing the computer industry to expect predictable gains on a fairly regular timetable. Grove was famous for hard-nosed, seemingly counterintuitive strategic decisions, including, famously, abandoning the memory chips that accounted for almost all of Intel's revenues and switching Intel's operations over to making microprocessors for the emerging categories of personal computers, engineering workstations, and bigger systems that would come to be known as "file servers." His flexible, sophisticated approach to management set a high standard for Silicon Valley companies. He even wrote a popular management column for the *San Jose Mercury News*.

Noyce, the Intel cofounder who pioneered the development of integrated circuits, was another early hero. Jobs and Wozniak presented the Apple II to Noyce and the rest of the Intel board in 1977. While Noyce appreciated the technology, he didn't appreciate the two young men, with their long hair and shabby attire. But Steve pursued Noyce, and over the years the two became friends. Noyce's wife, Ann Bowers, was an early investor in the company, and in 1980 she even became Apple's first vice president of human resources.

Steve's relationships with outside mentors could be very personal. "Steve wanted that family thing," remembers Regis McKenna. "He used to come over and just sit at the kitchen table with me and my wife [Dianne McKenna, an urban planner who at one point became mayor of Sunnyvale]. He always wanted to talk to her when he called up. She and I always had the sense that he wanted a family, that he really wanted that. He used to come over from Apple to fix things on my Apple II! I would tell him, Steve, you've got more important things to do than that, but he'd insist on coming over. 'Besides,' he'd tell me, 'then I get to chat with Dianne.' "

Partly because he is so personable, partly because Markkula asked him to work for Apple as an adviser, and partly because his expertise is in something that Steve found instinctually appealing—marketing—

McKenna became Steve's most significant early mentor. McKenna was expert at presenting a company's tale, but he was also a master corporate business strategist. Silicon Valley has long depended on marketers nearly as much as it has depended on engineers. Every technological advance must be framed in a beguiling narrative if it's to get off the workbench and into businesses or homes. These advances often are foreign concepts, after all, with potential that seems opaque if not daunting, so the job of a great marketer is to wrestle the concept back to earth and make it approachable for mere technophobic mortals. McKenna's consultancy would have a hand in the creation of many of the elite companies in Silicon Valley and beyond, including National Semiconductor, Silicon Graphics, Electronic Arts, Compaq, Intel, and Lotus Software.

McKenna quickly saw that Steve was unusually articulate and driven. "He had what I'd call Silicon Valley street smarts," says McKenna. "You know how certain kids who grow up in the inner city know where to go to get what, and how the power structure of the neighborhood works? Here, you're likely to live next door to an electrical engineer or a software programmer, and a smart and curious kid can learn a lot just by wandering around and paying attention. From junior high on, Steve was out there figuring things out."

The two spent many hours in the basement of McKenna's ranch-style Sunnyvale home, talking about Steve's goals for Apple and its wondrous Apple II. Their conversations ranged widely, over design, marketing, product development, and strategy, and how these were intertwined in a healthy business. McKenna was expert at framing a company's development in a narrative Steve could relate to. "We talked about how your financials are your best marketing tools," says McKenna. "To get people to sit up and pay notice, especially in the computer business, you need to be a successful financial company."

McKenna was absorbed and engaged by Steve. "He was very pleasant and enjoyable, and had a lot of depth intellectually. He could talk about a wide range of subjects. We could have real trivial conversations, and then we could talk about Apple and the business. I remember him once asking me if I thought Apple would ever be bigger than Intel. The answer, of course, is that Intel was a component manufacturer, and usually the equipment manufacturers get much bigger in revenue."

McKenna and Jobs connected on so many levels that Regis got to know Steve as well as anyone during those early years. It helped that he didn't tolerate any of Steve's more obnoxious behavior. "He did have that quick, reactive temper, but I never had him shout at me; I never had him upset with me. Did we disagree? Yeah. Did we argue? Yes. But we also got along really, really well," he remembers. "I had an assistant who told me that Steve called up wanting something, and had yelled and yelled at her, using a lot of four-letter words. Next time I saw Steve, I told him, 'Hey, don't ever do that again.' She said the next time he came to the office, he walked in and said he was really embarrassed and apologized. I was trained in the semiconductor industry under Charlie Sporck and Don Valentine and those guys. If you weren't strong, they'd just gobble you up. So it didn't bother me to say, 'Hey, Steve, shut up.' He didn't dominate you to be mean. But when people acted as minions, he let them be minions."

McKenna and his team worked with Steve to craft a marketing pitch designed to make the Apple II stand out as the friendly computer for more than just computer geeks. The headline of the first promotional brochure McKenna created for the machine asserted, "Simplicity is the ultimate sophistication." It was a concept that went against every industry trend, since most of the existing manufacturers, including Commodore and MITS and Vector Graphic, advertised in the hobbyist rags with endless gray type that alerted obsessive geeks to this or that great new feature. Friendly marketing would distinguish Apple from its competitors for decades.

McKenna also helped Steve understand the value of presenting this image across every platform the company touched. Early on, he convinced Steve that since there was nothing remotely quaint about Apple's computers, the company would need an unmistakably modern visual identity, rather than Ronald Wayne's archaic etching, which was more appropriate for a Berkeley head shop than a company that hoped to lead a global revolution in computing. The replacement was the now-famous apple with the bite taken out and five exuberant rainbow stripes—each fitting perfectly atop the other, as Steve insisted. It seemed sharp and modern, and seemed to promise that computing from Apple would be something much more fun and easy than those mainframes from IBM, with its sober, stratified, white initials against a deep blue palette—almost like a pin-striped suit laid sideways. As Steve explained at the time: "Our whole company is founded on the principle that there is something very different that happens with one person, one computer. It's very different than having ten people to one computer. What we're trying to do is remove the barrier of having to learn how to use a computer."

Like McKenna, Steve had the gift of being able to explain profoundly complicated technology in simple, clear, and even rhapsodic terms. McKenna and Jobs knew this was a profound asset for Apple, especially given the company's other nondescript leaders. There's a long and wonderful extemporaneous quote from a *New Yorker* piece in late 1977 that offers rich proof of Steve's fully formed verbal mastery. Written at a time when the average reader knew so little about computers that a writer could delight in titillating terminology like "naked computer" and get away with obvious puns using the words "byte" and "Apple," the magazine's reporter encountered Steve manning the Apple Computer booth at a computer fair. "I wish we'd had these personal machines when I was growing up," Jobs tells him, before continuing on for a total of 224 words:

> *"People have been* hearing all sorts of things about computers during the past ten years through the media. Supposedly computers have been controlling various aspects of their lives. Yet, in spite of that, most adults have no idea what a computer really is, or what it can or can't do. Now, for the first time, people can actually buy a computer for the price of a good stereo, interact with it, and find out all about it. It's analogous to taking apart 1955 Chevys. Or consider the camera. There are thousands of people

across the country taking photography courses. They'll never be professional photographers. They just want to understand what the photographic process is all about. Same with computers. We started a little personal-computer manufacturing company in a garage in Los Altos in 1976. Now we're the largest personal-computer company in the world. We make what we think of as the Rolls-Royce of personal computers. It's a domesticated computer. People expect blinking lights, but what they find is that it looks like a portable typewriter, which, connected to a suitable readout screen, is able to display in color. There's a feedback it gives to people who use it, and the enthusiasm of the users is tremendous. We're always asked what it can do, and it can do a lot of things, but in my opinion the real thing it is doing right now is to teach people how to program the computer."

Before moving on to a booth where a bunch of kids were playing a computer game called Space Voyager, the reporter asks if Steve "would mind telling us his age. 'Twenty-two,' Mr. Jobs said."

Speaking off-the-cuff to a passing journalist from a decidedly non-techie publication, Steve finds so many ways to demystify for the average person the insanely geeky device that he and Woz had created. He understands their fundamental fear that computers may take over too much of modern life (a fear he would capitalize on repeatedly, most notably in the Orwellian imagery of Apple's famous "1984" commercial). He sympathizes with their ignorance. He offers several analogies to comforting examples they *will* understand: Chevys, typewriters, cameras. Indeed, he makes using a computer seem no more complicated than taking a photograph, going so far as to call the Apple II "domesticated." And yet he elevates both his company and its computer into something aspirational. He links this machine made a few months ago by some disheveled California misfits to Rolls-Royce, the seventy-three-year-old paragon of sophisticated industrial manufacturing and elite consumer taste. He even calls Apple a world leader, an absolutely unprovable claim that rockets the little company into the same league as IBM and DEC and Burroughs, which were then the industry's giants. He was an extraordinary extemporaneous speaker, and McKenna helped him wield that tool to great effect.

———

TWO KEY IMPROVEMENTS to the Apple II sent its sales skyward. First, the company incorporated a floppy disk drive that made loading software much easier. Then, in 1979, VisiCalc became the very first massive software hit. VisiCalc was a relatively simple financial modeling spreadsheet, and its existence suddenly gave nongeeks a concrete reason to own a computer, as they realized how much time they could save handling accounting chores, managing inventory lists, and trying out business scenarios. Suddenly Apple enjoyed an unprecedented, meteoric rise. It manufactured computers that cost more than $1,300 a pop, so when unit sales quickly ramped up into the tens of thousands per month, Apple became the electronic equivalent of a gusher. Sales rose from $7.8 million in 1978 to $47 million in 1979 and all the way up to $117.9 million in 1980, the year of its initial public offering (IPO, in Wall Street parlance). No other company had ever grown that fast. The mainstream media began to take note, with publications like *Esquire, Time,* and *BusinessWeek* starting serious coverage. *Inc.* went so far as to put Jobs on its cover, with the hosanna of a headline "This Man Has Changed Business Forever."

But the rosy picture obscured the many problems within Apple, problems that were inherent in the company's motley mix of leaders.

Each of Steve's informal outside mentors had been able to cleverly exploit his own idiosyncratic talents in a corporate setting. Edwin Land was a pioneer whose inventions were dismissed, and yet he'd created a great company by dint of pure stubbornness. Robert Noyce was charismatic and forward-thinking and had only been able to start Intel after leaving the shadow of the most imposing figure in semiconductor history, William Shockley. The systems that Andy Grove put in place were more complex and rigorous than anything Mike Scott had ever seen, and yet Grove had also been able to make his company one of the most creative places in Silicon Valley. And Regis McKenna became so adept at deftly navigating the constant shifts and tremors of Silicon Valley culture that he would wind up writing several books explaining how others could do the same. These were well-rounded, complicated, deep, and fascinating men. They were comfortable with change, and they lived where Steve wanted to live himself—at the intersection of technology and something that was more like the liberal arts. They were people who played the corporate game by rules of their own devising.

It's impossible to say what would have happened next if Steve had had someone like these men as his boss at Apple. Maybe they would have been able to channel his bundle of contradictions to good purpose. But you don't get to replay the experiment. What he had instead was Scotty and Markkula. And they, it would now become clear, could not control him. They could barely even channel his creative energy toward useful purposes. The encounter between young Steve Jobs and the broad, real world around him was about to become something more like a slow-motion collision. It would cost him friends, it would cost him his job, and it would leave him without the company he had created.

Chapter 3
Breakthrough and Breakdown

Every cliché is built on some truth. The cliché that Steve Jobs was half genius, half asshole is based largely on his actions during the nine years that constituted his first tenure at Apple. This is when his highs would shine most famously, and when his lows were reprehensible. It was the period when he most sought the limelight, and when he was most out of control. He developed followers and he created enemies. This is when his bundle of contradictory qualities unraveled, leaving him, and his company, at loose ends. These years provide a baseline for the rest of his career.

Steve's personal life, which had been chaotic in the scattered, sloppy way of most twenty-somethings—especially those throwing themselves at a career without regard for sleep, social life, or family—spun out of control in 1978, when he denied the paternity of his own child. Chrisann Brennan, who had been his girlfriend for some time, gave birth to their daughter, Lisa, in May 1978. She was born in Oregon, at Robert Friedland's orchard, and three days after her birth Steve flew north to be with her and Chrisann. But for months afterward, Steve denied he was Lisa's father and refused to pay child support. He even resisted when a court-ordered paternity test established the likelihood that he was the father at 94.4 percent; it was as if the mere fact of his denial would negate the proof. When he finally starting paying child support of $385 a month, he continued to protest that he might well not be Lisa's father. He saw her rarely, letting Chrisann raise Lisa on her own in a small house in Menlo Park.

It would take years for Steve to bring Lisa into his life in any significant way, and later he would repeatedly express deep regret over his behavior. He knew he had made a terrible mistake. The event obviously crossed the line of what anyone would consider acceptable behavior. Lisa has spoken about the distance she felt from her father, and the confusion and instability she felt as a child. Chrisann has spoken and written about this, too, creating a picture, albeit one-sided, of a careless, indifferent, and cruel lover and father. When people debate whether Steve was a "good" or "bad" man, this is the strongest indictment against him. He was twenty-three years old when Lisa's birth presented him with a clarion call to accept adult responsibility. He rejected the call as fully as he rejected her.

Colleagues he worked with closely knew about Lisa, and heard Steve deny his paternity and complain about being pursued by Chrisann. Arthur Rock would later describe Steve's behavior as "delusional." Especially for someone as unsentimental as Rock, Steve's behavior tied in to a pattern of irresponsibility that was developing at Apple. Whether working with his ostensible superiors, such as Rock, or making decisions that widely affected subordinates, Steve could seem indifferent to the impact of his choices. He conveyed a lack of empathy.

This behavior only worsened in the year after Steve's visit to the Garden of Allah, when Apple made a big splash by going public. Several years later, Jobs told Susan Barnes, a financial manager at Apple and at NeXT, that December 12, 1980—the date of Apple's IPO— was the most important day of his career, because only then was he sure that the folks who had driven Apple's early success would make serious money. But Steve had specifically excluded people like Bill Fernandez and Daniel Kottke, an engineer whom he'd met at Reed, from the options bonanza, even though they had been instrumental in getting Apple started during that summer of 1976 in his parents' garage. Jobs had a bureaucratic rationalization for doing so: they were hourly employees, and therefore not guaranteed the "founder's stock" that helped make three hundred longtime salaried employees millionaires. But Steve's lack of generosity was reflective of something that was starting to seem part of a broader character trait.

"He had this incredible bandwidth," explains Lee Clow, the Chiat\ Day ad director who would become Steve's close friend after working on the famous "1984" television ad, "but he devoted almost all of it to work." Prioritizing things in this way, especially as an immature young man, made most people in his life replaceable. Fernandez and Kottke, for example, had been important to Steve three years earlier, but to Steve's way of thinking they had not kept up. They were not key contributors to Apple, and therefore to Steve's life, anymore. The bigger priority was to reward the people who were improving Apple at present. It was a cold evaluation by a young man whose work life was exploding into something much bigger than he had ever anticipated. But his logic carried an emotional cost the young man didn't even consider. Kottke and Fernandez and others like them felt snubbed and unappreciated. Steve's behavior isolated him within the company. He had little sense at this point of how important it can be to have true allies in a corporate setting. It was a blind spot that would catch up to him eventually.

After the IPO, Steve was worth $256 million. That widely publicized number, along with the fancy cars that started appearing in the Apple parking lot and the talk of country homes and expensive vacations, contributed to a sense within the company that the offering had created a set of winners and losers. Apple, which had grown from a handful of people in 1977 to 2,900 employees by the summer of 1981, was riven in more ways than one. In the fall of 1980, its head count had doubled in just three months. Apple "old-timers" took to calling that short stretch of time "the bozo period," and scorned the newbies.

Steve was rarely showy about his newfound wealth, but he widened the rifts in the company in other solipsistic ways. Broadly speaking, Apple employees were focused either on supporting and milking the revenue from the Apple II or on exploring new products. The Apple II was the breadwinner driving the company's growth. The work going on around it was the classic, incremental work of improving and deepening the usefulness of a product so that it would be successful for years. Apple II staffers built an extensive retail sales channel of hundreds of resellers; worked with the emerging world of software developers to ensure that they had the necessary tools to write more interesting software that would attract even more buyers; and labored on follow-up machines, like the Apple IIe and the Apple II GS. Their work paid off: the Apple II, in its various models, was a remarkably resilient product, selling nearly six million units before it was finally discontinued in 1993. For a decade, the company would depend on Woz's reliable old Apple II to fuel its soaring growth. Indeed, it wasn't until 1988 that Macintosh revenues at long last exceeded those from Apple II sales.

It didn't take long for Steve, whose official job was to head up product development, to simply stop caring about the Apple II. He felt, in his bones, as he liked to say, that Apple would need a great new product, that the industry was moving at such a rapid pace that the company would be fatally wounded if all it had to offer were slightly improved versions of the Apple II. He made his feelings very clear, and suggested that any engineer or marketer worth his salt would be drawn to working on the creation of the next breakthrough product with him. While Steve's narrow attitude slighted scores of the company's hardware and software designers, it was especially insulting to Woz, who eventually chose to nurse along the Apple II rather than join the Mac team. "Some Apple II engineers were being treated like they didn't exist," Woz would later say. As the company grew, he and Steve couldn't help but grow apart.

In a broad way, Steve was correct in thinking that Apple needed a significant new offering, and soon. The best recipe for maintaining steadily rising revenues in the computer hardware business is to have a breakthrough product ready just when your last breakthrough is reaching the peak of its own success. Markkula, Scotty, and the board all agreed that the company urgently needed a new model, ideally one better tailored to the needs of office workers. IBM, which had been the sleeping elephant of the industry, had reportedly started studying the possibility of building its own personal computer. (The device would eventually make it to market in the summer of 1981.) So in 1978 the Apple board gave Steve the budget and the engineering talent to go ahead and start developing a successor to the Apple II.

The personal computer industry was in its infancy, and everyone was flying blind, including Steve. One important thing he didn't yet understand was that most breakthrough products result from a long cycle of hit-and-miss prototypes, the steady accumulation of features, and a timely synthesis of existing technologies. He and Woz, on the contrary, had stuck their heads down, worked hard, and on their very first try created something brilliant that the industry had never before seen. That was Steve's idea of product development. But he was about to discover that that wasn't the way it worked inside a corporation.

The company had concrete and meaningful goals for its new machine, to be called the Apple III. It would be aimed at the office as well as the home, and would support a color monitor that displayed 80 characters of text on each line, twice as many as the original Apple II. Since a typical typewritten document can accommodate 80 characters per line, the Apple III would compete head-on with specialized word-processing computers from Wang Laboratories that over the past two years had cascaded into offices across the United States and Europe in even greater numbers than the Apple II had landed in people's homes. Done right, the new model would have been Apple's entree into the corporate market for personal computers.

The success of the Apple 1 and the Apple II had given Steve a little too much confidence in his own technical judgment. He made a series of bad decisions that would be hard to undo later, the most important being his edict that the Apple III, whose footprint had to be small enough to leave lots of open room on an office desk, would be absolutely silent, which meant no internal cooling fan. This slowed the development process to a crawl, because engineers had to figure out how to create convection currents to draw heat away from the motherboard, which held all the semiconductor chips, as well as from the power supply. Without a fan, those components could make the innards of a small computer hot as a pizza oven. The solution the engineers finally came up with was to make the cabinet itself act as a heat sink to help draw out and dissipate the heat; however, that meant making it out of cast aluminum, a good heat conductor but a material that added considerably to the cost and complexity of manufacture.

It wasn't just Steve's demands that slowed the Apple III. Since Apple would be wooing customers who might have purchased an Apple II, the company had to make sure that that software created for the II would also run on the III. This "backwards-compatibility" was an annoying requirement that was far more complicated than Steve imagined, and the time his engineers spent learning to accomplish it slowed the project almost as much as his fussy hardware demands. Steve pushed the Apple III engineers relentlessly to solve these problems quickly. It didn't matter to him that these were gnarly problems to solve. Accustomed to Woz's magical ability to defy old boundaries and technical obstacles, he expected these new hardware and software engineers to do the same. They couldn't.

––––––––––

STEVE'S IMPATIENCE WITH the nuts and bolts of corporate life was understandable. Steve was a visionary. It's a word that is loosely tossed around these days, especially in Silicon Valley, but it legitimately applied to Steve even from very early in his life. He had the ability to see around corners, to envision how the seeds of existing ideas could be combined to create something unimaginable to others. The challenge he faced was to become an effective visionary—that's what turns a dreamer into someone who changes the world.

A few weeks before he made that drive up to the Garden of Allah in late 1979, Steve had decided, at the urging of Bill Atkinson, Jef Raskin, and several other Apple technical employees, to check out some work being done by a well-known computer scientist named Alan Kay and some other engineers at Xerox Corporation's Palo Alto Research Center, just a ten-minute drive up the peninsula from Cupertino. PARC, as it was known, would become famous for developing the concepts behind any number of important technologies, including Ethernet local area networking, high-resolution video monitors, laser printing, and object-oriented programming. That summer, Xerox had joined a number of venture capital firms in a $7 million secondary investment round in Apple (as part of the deal, Steve sold $1 million worth of his own stock to the investors), and in return had agreed to give Apple a peek at its most advanced technologies, or, as people in Silicon Valley like to say, to "open the kimono." These visits were nothing short of an epiphany for Steve, because the technology at PARC was the visual expression of everything he believed computers could and should be.

It was at PARC that Steve and his group from Apple first saw the nascent technologies that would later become the distinguishing features of the Lisa and the Macintosh, and eventually *all* personal computers. They were shown a computer that featured a screen that was white like a sheet of paper, not black. Moreover, that screen had the exact dimensions of standard typing paper—8½ inches wide by 11 inches tall. On it were projected black characters so sharp and shapely that they looked as if they had been printed on that sheet of paper. The characters had been "bitmapped," meaning that each pixel of the screen followed individual instructions from the computer, a radical new technology that gave developers full graphic control of the monitor screen. (Previously they had only been able to place rudimentary white, green, or orange characters on a black screen. Graphical images, other than meticulously arranged agglomerations of standard characters, were out of the question.) These bitmapped characters were really just the beginning of the changes: that screen also could display and organize the contents of the machine's digital data storage by means of graphical "icons"—little symbolic figures a tad smaller than a postage stamp—representing documents that could be placed "inside" chimerical folder icons by means of a strange pointing device the geeks at PARC called a "mouse." This mouse could also be used to directly move a cursor around a document on the screen when writing or editing. To delete a file or a folder, you would throw it in the trash by using the mouse to "drag" the icon representing a document over to a special icon on the screen that looked like a garbage can, and "drop" it in. Compared to the black screen with eerie green characters that had preceded it, this "graphical user interface"—or GUI (pronounced "gooey"), as it came to be known—represented at least as radical a break as when silent movies shifted to talkies.

The PARC researchers understood full well how significant a development this was, and were dismayed that Xerox had, in effect, paid for the privilege of giving Steve and the other Apple visitors access to technology this radical and new. They believed, correctly, that Xerox senior management back east was not that interested in building a full-blown computer; rather, they wanted to create better photocopiers, and perhaps a dedicated word processor to compete with Wang's. Xerox did not come out with a computer using the PARC technology until 1981. Called the STAR, it was an intriguing device that was sold not to individual consumers but to businesses, as part of a networked system of at least three desktop units that sold for about $16,000 each. While it was a capable microcomputer for its time, customers balked at having to shell out $50,000 or so just to get the minimum setup for an office. It had little impact in the marketplace.

Steve realized that the Xerox GUI could be the foundation of something very ambitious and very personal. Visual iconography on a screen could make computing almost intuitive for just about everyone. Existing computer interfaces put a wall of arcane commands and typographical symbols that looked like expletives between the user and the results spewed back by the computer. If you replaced those commands with visual icons that could be easily manipulated via a mouse, harnessing the data-processing power of a computer might feel more like going to the library and pulling a book off the shelf, or like engaging in a discussion with a really smart friend or teacher. This interaction, this feeling of comfort with the back-and-forth with a computer, could lead to the realization of Steve's overarching goal, the creation of a *truly* personal computer for ordinary people. Steve even had a metaphor for what that computer could be—*a bicycle for the mind*. After visiting PARC he was a changed man; these were technologies he wanted to bring to everyone in the world.

NOW STEVE FACED the challenge of delivering on this promise within the gnawing confines of Apple. It would be a staggeringly ambitious project—one that no one at Apple but Steve could have imagined, and one that no one but he could have made so maddeningly complicated. The long road had many detours and would be pockmarked with collateral damage, but it would eventually lead to the introduction of the Macintosh computer in 1984.

After that visit to Xerox PARC, Steve completed what had been a slow abandonment of the Apple III development. The more he realized that the machine was simply a modest renovation of the Apple II, the more his attention wandered. Now he turned away completely, with the intention of applying what he'd learned at PARC to another computer already under development at Apple. This machine was specifically designed for Fortune 500 companies that required heavy-duty networked computing to accomplish tasks that were significantly more data-intensive than anything that could be handled by the Apple II or even the Apple III.

The Lisa, as this machine was dubbed, had been gestating since mid-1978, without making much progress. So when Steve assumed full control of the project in early 1980, the team felt a brief spurt of optimism. Steve told them that he fully intended to have the Lisa be the first computer to feature a graphical user interface and a mouse. They had, he told them, a chance to make history. He asked Bill Atkinson, the project's lead software architect, how long it would take to translate what they'd seen at PARC into software that could be run on the Lisa. Atkinson predicted that he could do it in a mere half a year—missing the mark by some two and a half years. Clearly, Steve wasn't the only person at Apple who could confuse a clear vision for a short path.

Steve's brief management of the Lisa project revealed all his weaknesses. Once again, he couldn't resolve the disparity between the corporate demands for this computer and his own ambitions. The Lisa was supposed to be for businesses, but Steve focused almost exclusively on what would make the machine accessible and friendly for an individual. Once again, he had the right idea for the long run—years later, easy-to-use computers would make personal computing ubiquitous across businesses both small and large—without the perspective needed to succeed in the short term. He paid lip service to the special needs of corporations and institutions, but what really fascinated him were the rounded edges of the icons on the Lisa's "desktop" interface.

Atkinson and his programmers did create significant improvements on what they'd seen at PARC; the Lisa project is where the modern user-interface concepts of overlapping windows, seamless scrolling, and the mouse came into their own. But Steve was a failure at managing this group, in large part because he didn't offer them a unified vision to rally around, given that his own interests were not those of the target audience—business users. When the project stalled, as was inevitable, Steve lashed out, excoriating the team and threatening to bring in Woz, who could surely get things done better and faster. Scotty tried to help Steve out by recruiting Larry Tesler, one of Xerox PARC's own top researchers, and a group of his associates to try to bring a little more discipline and focus to the project. But two months after Tesler's hire, Scotty looked at where the Lisa was headed and saw that the computer he had been counting on to represent Apple in the all-important business market was going to be too late, too expensive, and most likely a muddled mess of a machine.

In the fall of 1980, Scotty kicked Steve off the team after only nine months of being in charge, and handed its management over to a former Hewlett-Packard senior engineering exec named John Couch. Twice now, in rapid succession, Steve had failed when trying to lead a team to create a computer for the business market. While more and more people in the computer industry were keenly in tune with the needs of enterprise customers, Steve wasn't one of them.

———

STEVE'S INSTINCTIVE PROBLEMS with authority—his inability to successfully manage large teams, his failure to adapt his strengths to the needs of his admittedly weak bosses—were wreaking havoc. The launch of the Apple III was a disaster. The computer didn't ship until May 1980—a year later than planned—and sold for a base price of $4,340, more than double its target price. Within weeks, many buyers were returning their machines and demanding refunds, after an alarming number of Apple III's started suffering catastrophic failures due to overheating. In some cases the motherboard got so hot that the solder softened and chips popped out of their sockets. All told, 14,000 had to be replaced. (The aluminum chassis worked fine for dissipating heat; the problem turned out to be that the parts had been nestled too closely to one another on the circuit board.) Moreover, backwards-compatibility had proved so thorny that very few programs were available out of the gate, so the computers that did happen to work weren't particularly useful. The Apple III was an unmitigated commercial failure, selling only 120,000 units before it was discontinued in 1984. During that same time, the company sold nearly two million Apple II's.

The pressure to get things right, which was amped up considerably now that the company's stock was widely held, fell mainly on Scotty. But Jobs undercut his boss again and again. He humiliated suppliers that Scott had wooed; he complained endlessly and publicly about little things like the color of laboratory benches; and he repeatedly interfered with Scotty's production schedules by insisting on the completion of inconsequential details. Steve's own failures did nothing to chasten him. In fact, they only heightened his antipathy for Scotty, who was trying to balance the competing needs of thousands of employees. Steve didn't accept the idea of compromise when it came to his own ideas, and so he turned every decision that didn't go his way into a confrontation. The battles between the two became known within the company as the Scotty Wars.

Having such a difficult partner was just one of Scotty's many frustrations, and finally it all became too much. Bit by bit, he disintegrated into an unreliable leader of a company that needed a firm hand. He started to develop some physical ailments, which seemed clearly related to stress. When he finally decided to repair some of the damage resulting from the bozo period by laying off some staff, he did so at a company-wide meeting in March 1981, at which he admitted to all present that he didn't find running Apple to be all that much fun anymore.

Soon after that the board agreed that Scotty had to go. He departed after taking one last shot with a letter that attacked what he saw as a culture of hypocrites, yes-men, and "empire builders." Of course, the divided culture was as much his fault as anyone else's. But Steve knew that Scotty had borne the heaviest load as Apple morphed from a startup into a real operation. After his departure, Steve reportedly experienced a sudden bout of guilt; he was quoted as saying, "I was always afraid that I'd get a call to say that Scotty had committed suicide."

———

ON A SEPTEMBER day in 1981, just a couple of months after Scotty's departure, Bill Gates visited the Apple campus in Cupertino. The twenty-six-year-old CEO of Microsoft made the trip fairly often, since his company worked closely with Apple on programming languages for software developers. At the time, Steve was far richer and far more well-known. Gates, however, was the far more precocious and astute businessman.

After dropping out of Harvard, Gates had started Microsoft in 1975 in Albuquerque, New Mexico, with his prep school programming buddy, Paul Allen. Albuquerque was home to MITS, the maker of the Altair computer that had so excited the Homebrew hobbyists. Gates and Allen wrote a piece of software called an "interpreter" that made it possible for hobbyists to write their own programs for the Altair in the simple but popular BASIC programming language. MITS opted to bundle the program with each Altair it sold, and Micro-soft was in business.

The fortunate son of a prominent Seattle attorney and an accomplished, civic-minded mother, Gates came to business naturally. After he and Allen discovered that hobbyists were giving away pirated copies of their Altair BASIC interpreter, Gates wrote a kind of manifesto, asserting that developers of software for microcomputers should be paid for their programs. If that happened, Gates predicted, an entirely new kind of software industry would arise that would benefit software developers, microcomputer makers, and users alike. This would represent a huge change: at that point, software development was mostly in the hands of the makers of computer hardware, who buried the development costs in the final price of the devices they sold. The prospect of making money by building software, Gates believed, would spur innovation and help the new microcomputer manufacturers take better advantage of the breakneck pace of improvement in semiconductor technology promised by Moore's law.

Gates's manifesto was every bit as significant as Moore's law in the explosion of personal computing. Software development requires very little capital investment, since it is basically intellectual capital, pure thoughtstuff, expressed in a set of detailed instructions written in a language that machines can understand. The main cost is in the labor required to design and test it. There is no need for expensive factories or for the invention of fabrication equipment and processes. It can be replicated endlessly for practically nothing. And the prospect of hundreds of thousands of potential customers, or even more, means that developers don't have to charge enormous prices.

Gates was right. Accepting the fact that software was worth paying for led to the emergence of a dynamic new industry. One could argue that Gates's greatest contribution to the world was not Microsoft, or the MS-DOS or Windows operating systems, or the Office productivity applications that hundreds of millions of people use. It was his role as the first champion of the concept that software itself had value. The mind that could envision all that was a mind suited for the organizational matrixes of the corporate world. In those early days, Microsoft never lacked for enlightened leadership, unlike Apple.

On that September morning in 1981, IBM shipped its first personal computer. Steve had always derided Big Blue as a lumbering monstrosity, and truly believed that no discerning buyer would ever prefer a microcomputer from IBM to one made by Apple. Gates, on the other hand, knew this might be the beginning of something big. His MS-DOS operating system software sat on every IBM PC that went out the door, and he had witnessed the speed with which IBM's Don Estridge and Bill Lowe had steered their PC project around IBM's hidebound bureaucracy. In fact, their rush to market had led them to acquiesce to a historic deal with Gates, allowing him the right in the future to license MS-DOS to other computer makers. It was a decision they would forever regret, since it ultimately tilted power from hardware manufacturers to Microsoft—thereby proving the validity of Gates's manifesto and setting the stage for virtually the entire industry to adopt MS-DOS as a standard that would marginalize Apple, which did not license its operating system. But on that fall afternoon, no one Gates spoke to at Apple seemed aware that their world was about to change, much less acted worried. Years later, Gates remembered that "I kept walking around, asking, 'Isn't this a big deal?' But no one seemed concerned."

WITH SCOTTY'S DEPARTURE, Mike Markkula became president and Jobs was elevated to chairman. At a moment when it was about to be blindsided by IBM, and by the series of "clone" computer companies like Compaq that would follow in Big Blue's wake, Apple was led by two men who didn't want and weren't suited for the positions they held. Steve's reckless immaturity and authority issues had left the company rudderless, and Markkula was an ambivalent leader who did little to give staffers a clear sense of direction. Apple muddled along this way for several months before finally getting serious about the search for a new CEO by hiring Gerry Roche, the chairman of the renowned headhunting firm Heidrick & Struggles, to handle the quest for a new boss. Roche was the man who introduced Steve to John Sculley.

Steve's personal courtship of Sculley, then the president of PepsiCo, has been endlessly documented. It's the story of two men who saw exactly what they wanted to see in the other, who salivated at the thought of how pairing up might transform their lives, and who both wound up sorely disappointed.

Sculley was a soda pop and snack food executive, a forty-three-year-old native New Yorker who was the product of the best prep school and Ivy League educations that money could buy, graduating from Brown and getting his MBA at Penn's Wharton School. He made a name for himself at Pepsi designing taste-it-and-rate-it advertising campaigns like the "Pepsi Challenge," and bringing new innovation to supermarket aisle "endcap" promotions and other cosmetic marketing ploys. He was a great champion of consumer research to determine how best to refine product offerings.

Despite his dismissive penchant for ignoring Scotty and Markkula, Steve was fully aware that he still had much to learn about the world of business. In Sculley, he thought he had found an open-minded Fortune 500 exec who would be the in-house mentor he thought he wanted and the enlightened, disciplined leader for a company breaking into the big time. As Steve spun tales of Apple's potential, Sculley seemed full of ideas of how his expertise could fuel Steve's notion of where the company should go. The fact that he played hard to get only heightened

Steve's infatuation. He turned down Apple's initial offer of a salary of $300,000 a year, plus options for 500,000 shares of Apple stock, which at the time were worth about $18 million. On March 20, 1982, the two met at the Carlyle Hotel for the signature moment of their courtship. They wandered around Central Park and the Metropolitan Museum of Art before winding up at the San Remo apartment building on Central Park West. A two-story penthouse apartment in one of the building's distinctive twin towers was vacant and for sale, and Steve had been mulling making an offer to buy it. Standing together on a balcony thirty stories up, Sculley told Steve that before he'd even consider coming to Apple, they'd have to agree to pay him $1 million in salary, plus a $1 million signing bonus, and a guaranteed $1 million severance payment if things didn't work out. It was a stunning demand for the time, but Steve was undeterred. He said he'd pay it out of his own pocket if necessary.

He sealed the deal by challenging Sculley with a line that would become a famous part of the Steve Jobs lore: "Do you want to spend the rest of your life selling sugared water, or do you want a chance to change the world?"

Two days later CBS founder William S. Paley told Sculley that if he were a young man, he would head for Silicon Valley, because that was where the future was being made. Sculley started work in Cupertino on April 8, 1983. His extravagant salary package made him by far the highest-paid executive the computer industry had ever seen.

Falling for Sculley would prove to be another regrettable mistake on Steve's part. In his anxiety to find a big-time manager whose skills would mesh with his, Steve had missed some glaring weaknesses. While Sculley possessed strong, if conventional, marketing skills, he was not well versed in many of the other parts of business, despite his MBA and years at PepsiCo. In his own way, he was every bit as insecure as Steve. He felt he had much to prove to the tech wunderkinds at Apple. He bragged that as a kid he had been a ham radio operator and had invented a color television tube. But he knew little about computers. One of his first hires upon arriving in Cupertino was a technical assistant to help him bone up on digital technology and master the Apple II in his office.

Smart as he was, Steve made his fair share of bad hires, often after deciding all too quickly that a flashy outsider was stronger than the people who were already working for him. Later the cost of such mistakes would diminish, as he learned how to react quickly when he had to clean up a mess he had made. But the Sculley hire was double trouble. First, Steve did not get the strong mentor he needed, the leader who truly could have furthered his business education. Second, Sculley was a much more skilled practitioner of the dark arts of corporate politics than Steve. It would take time for Steve to realize that Sculley didn't bring as much to the table as he had hoped. And when Steve did finally come to that realization, he didn't know how to win the ensuing battle.

———

DESPITE THE MANAGEMENT mess at Apple, veterans of those years remember Apple as a company with a unique soul, and cite Steve as a powerful inspiration. The long and winding development of the Macintosh is the saga that best shows why Steve remained so admired even as he was so instrumental in tearing apart the company he loved.

To understand this, we need to take a step back chronologically, to the fall of 1980, when Scotty dumped Steve from the Lisa team. At the time, he had suggested that Steve take a look at an intriguing side project being run by Jef Raskin, a smart, idiosyncratic, theoretically inclined former college professor whose first job at Apple had been to supervise the preparation of user manuals and product documentation for the Apple II. Steve thought Raskin was a pedantic egghead, but he was intrigued by the goal of his project: to create a consumer-oriented "computer appliance" that would sell for just $1,000. Raskin planned to call his machine the Macintosh.

Once Steve had decided that he wanted the Mac as his own sandbox, he made quick work of Raskin. He repeatedly and publicly contradicted and undermined Raskin, asking his engineers to tackle projects that didn't relate to the project's stated goals. He made clear that he thought Raskin's product plan fell far short of what was actually possible. Ultimately, he forced a meeting with Scotty and Raskin in which he made an impassioned plea for outright ownership of the product. Shortly after Scotty's decision in favor of Steve, Raskin quit in a huff. But before he left he fired off a memo to his bosses that still stands as an angry summary of Steve's weaknesses. "While Mr. Jobs's stated positions on management techniques are all quite noble and worthy, in practice he is a dreadful manager. . . . He is a prime example of a manager who takes the credit for his optimistic schedules and then blames the workers when deadlines are not met," he wrote, adding that Steve "misses appointments . . . does not give credit . . . has favorites . . . and doesn't keep promises."

All true. And yet Steve was right to dump Raskin. He saw that the self-consciously modest Macintosh Raskin had proposed would fall far short of a real breakthrough. To truly expand the consumer market, a transformative step was required, and that meant finally delivering on the promise of those graphical user interface technologies he had first seen at PARC. Steve was convinced he could do this, and equally convinced that Raskin could not. Steve never really cared if people thought he was selfish or that his elbows were a little too sharp. He was willing to do whatever he felt it took to achieve his goals.

To that end, Steve also did everything he could to separate "Mac" from "Apple." He ran the project as a fiefdom that just happened to have access to all the funds of the corporation. He spent a million dollars setting up a new home for the team in a separate building known as Bandley Three, down the road from Apple headquarters. Shortly after they moved in, a programmer named Steve Capps hoisted a skull-and-crossbones flag over the building. It became a rallying point for the team—although the rest of the company, of course, took it as a clear sign that Steve was in it for Mac, not for Apple. Again, this was true insofar as it went. But the Lisa would soon prove to be as big a dud as the Apple III, and the Apple II would come under growing pressure from Big Blue's successful entrant in the market—the IBM PC. Apple needed a breakthrough product. And this time around, Steve would succeed brilliantly in leading the company's talented engineers to heights they never imagined they could reach.

Raskin had opted for a cheap and anemic Motorola 6809e microprocessor chip, which would not have had the processing horsepower to employ a mouse or to create screen resolution high enough to support bitmapped graphics. Playing to the competitive instincts of hardware engineer Burrell Smith, a twenty-four-year-old savant with technical chops that rivaled those of Woz, Steve challenged him to build a prototype of the machine that instead incorporated the Lisa's much more powerful chip—the Motorola 68000—without dramatically raising the overall cost of the machine. It was a daunting goal: you could buy twenty 6809e chips for the price of one 68000.

Smith, like Woz, could never say no to an engineering challenge. His central breakthrough was to find a way to multiply the flow of digital data from the 68000 processor through the rest of the circuit architecture, a trick that ingeniously allowed the computer to take full advantage of the increased processing power without requiring more support chips or circuits. The result: detailed and responsive graphics, exactly what was essential for a machine that employed a mouse and made bitmapped images. Smith literally lived in his lab for a month, while others in the company took off for the Thanksgiving and Christmas holidays. He didn't even stop to celebrate his twenty-fifth birthday on December 19. But he accomplished the impossible.

Egging on Burrell Smith was just the beginning. The Mac project was an expanded version of rallying the gang in the garage, with Steve leading and inspiring a small group of extremely creative people. He stole the best programmers from the Lisa team and other projects around Apple, with a disregard for corporate niceties that was matched only by his boldness. To cite one famous example, when he was unwilling to wait a few days for the extraordinary Andy Hertzfeld to finish up some work on the Apple II, he unplugged Hertzfeld's computer (wiping out his code in the process) and drove him and his computer over to the building where the Mac team was working. Personality traits that failed him elsewhere worked here. As always, he could be more temperamental than his subordinates, but with this group of artiste engineers he was afforded considerable leeway. "If you could take Steve, he made you up your game," says Lee Clow. "People who were too thin-skinned to deal with his abusive approach to demanding what he wanted walked away. But I want to prove to guys like that that I can do it. I'm the kind of person who steps up." So were many of the other stars on the Mac team.

Steve led the group on retreats every once in a while, which gave him occasion to have the team all to himself, separate from the distractions of the rest of Apple. He was an inspirational speaker. "The work fifty people are doing here," he told them, "is going to send a giant ripple through the universe." His language changed over the months as the project, predictably, took longer than he had expected. "The journey is the reward" and "It would be better to miss rather than turn out the wrong thing" gave way to "Real artists ship." But the phrasing always gave his team the sense that he did indeed see them as artists, as creative innovators. "He was so protective of us," one of them told *Fortune,* "that whenever we complained about somebody outside the division, it was like unleashing a Doberman. Steve would get on the telephone and chew the guy out so fast your head would spin."

The best of them felt truly empowered and gained Steve's respect by challenging him directly, using facts, ability, and persistence to change his mind. Sometimes they would simply ignore him outright. One of the Mac hardware engineers, Bob Belleville, worked with Sony to develop a new, much smaller disk drive for the Mac, despite being ordered directly by Steve to not do so. In the end, Sony's disk drive made it into the Mac and prevented a potentially disastrous delay. Jobs applauded Belleville for sticking it out on his own.

"You read the books and you wonder, 'As difficult as he is, why would anyone ever work for him?'" says Susan Barnes, the general manager on the Mac project. A no-nonsense financial whiz with a soothing way of managing both above and below her level, Barnes has a quiet, measured intensity that acted like a gyroscope for Steve. She may have been physically small and unassuming, but she commanded respect. "If you've worked enough, you know the difference between a boss who just gets it and someone you have to drag into understanding what you're trying to do. And when you find that boss that just gets it, you're just like, 'Oh my God, it's wonderful. You're making my life so easy now.' Steve was that kind of person. He was intellectually right up there with you. You didn't really have to go into too many explanations. He cared passionately. And he never dialed it in."

Over two years, the team performed heroic work. Steve drove them as relentlessly as he drove himself. He reminded them that the fate of the company hinged on their work. He harangued them for failing to meet deadlines and for falling short of perfection. The pressure grew steadily over time. It was taxing on both mind and body, and some members burned out so completely that they were never able to work in the high-tech industry again. Others found the experience exhilarating, but not something they'd want to repeat, and left Apple to find a less stressful employment environment. And then there was the small group of folks who loved it so much they stuck around, ready to do whatever it would take all over again, in order to work in the rarefied, exhilarating, and charged atmosphere that Steve created when he was running the show. When the job was over, Steve had the signatures of the forty-six key players on the team engraved on the inside of every Mac. Even people working on the Apple II found Steve's performance inspiring. "We used to say that the Mac people had God on their side," said one only half jokingly.

———

THE DEBUT OF the Macintosh established Steve as a master showman. Between the famous "1984" ad, which played just once, during the Super Bowl broadcast on January 22, 1984, and the Mac's official presentation at the Flint Auditorium on the campus of Cupertino's De Anza College on January 24, 1984, Steve transformed expectations of what a product introduction could be. "Steve was P. T. Barnum incarnate," says Lee Clow, a plain-spoken man who sports a wizardly beard and sprangly white hair. "He loved the ta-da! He was always like, 'I want you to see the Smallest Man in the World!' He loved pulling the black velvet cloth off a new product, everything about the showbiz, the marketing, the communications."

Working with a team of marketers and PR execs, Steve would rehearse endlessly and fastidiously. Bill Gates made appearances at a couple of these events, and remembers being backstage with Steve. "I was never in his league," he remembers, talking about Steve's presentations. "I mean, it was just amazing to see how precisely he would rehearse. And if he's about to go onstage, and his support people don't have the things right, you know, he is really, really tough on them. He's even a bit nervous because it's a big performance. But then he's on, and it's quite an amazing thing.

"I mean, his whole thing of knowing exactly what he's going to say, but up on stage saying it in such a way that he is trying to make you think he's thinking it up right then . . ." Gates just laughs.

Making the "1984" ad with Steve was a pirate enterprise for creative director Clow, art director Brenton Thomas, and Steve Hayden, who wrote the copy. Steve didn't let the board see the ad until a couple of days before the Super Bowl, and they were horrified. Directed by *Blade Runner*'s Ridley Scott, the sixty-second spot features a lone woman, in color, running through a sea of gray men and women listening obediently to a huge talking head nattering threateningly from an enormous screen about the enlightened potential of absolute conformity. As the ad nears its end, the woman hurls the large hammer she's been carrying and smashes the screen. A simple line follows: "On January 24th, Apple Computer will introduce Macintosh. And you'll see why 1984 won't be like '1984.'" Sculley got cold feet and told Chiat\Day to sell off the expensive Super Bowl ad space it had purchased. The agency unloaded a thirty-second spot, but lied to Sculley and told him they couldn't sell the longer one. Marketing chief Bill Campbell decided to air the ad despite the worries of Sculley and the board. Hayden, who was as talented in his own right as Clow, later drew a cartoon that summed up his feelings about Sculley. According to Clow, it showed the CEO and Jobs walking together through a park. Steve is telling Sculley, "Ya know, I think technology can make the human race better." The thought bubble above Sculley's head reads, "I'm gonna win over the board. This kid's gonna be out of here within six months."

As it was supposed to do, the brilliant ad set up Steve's "ta-da!" at the official presentation at De Anza. That day, Jobs was P. T. Barnum at his very best. He strolled the stage confidently. He positioned the Mac on the side of the rebellious, the creative, and the bold by reading lyrics from Bob Dylan's "The Times They Are a-Changin'." He took gleeful aim at IBM. He showed off the computer's beautiful graphics, with its script "Insanely Great" unscrolling across the giant video screen above the stage. The amazing new machine even introduced itself to the crowd, its goofy cyborg voice intoning, "Hello. I'm Macintosh. It sure is great to get out of that bag," referring to the padded canvas tote bag that had concealed it until Steve pulled it out and plugged it in. The crowd went wild, and Jobs, who seemed to choke up, soaked in the admiration. He delivered to the audience the idealized version of what the Mac was supposed to be, and the press ate it up. Primed by a long and brilliant pre-debut press campaign by McKenna, the magazines and trade journals went crazy. The Mac won raves across the board, from *Computerworld* to *Fortune* to *Esquire* to *Money* magazine, which called it "hands down, the best piece of hardware for its price." *Rolling Stone* hailed its subculture bona fides. *Venture* magazine even went so far as to applaud Steve's "maverick" management.

The machine was housed in a cute, seemingly self-sufficient ivory-colored box the shape of a miniature refrigerator, a design so cozy it defanged the word *computer* all on its own. But the user interface was the real triumph of friendliness. For the first time, you could create files that looked like paper documents. You could use your mouse to control a cursor that would drag those documents into folders. If you wanted to delete what you had worked on, you put the document into a trash bin. These things had all been demonstrated at PARC but with none of the wondrous simplicity and playfulness on display at De Anza. The superlative reviews, curiosity, and deals with some of the nation's leading universities fueled strong sales for a few months. But after the initial curiosity wore off, sales declined precipitously.

Truth is, the Mac that Steve had delivered was deeply flawed. It was a brilliant piece of engineering and a gorgeous vision of where computing could go, but it was far too underpowered to be useful. Trying to hold the Mac to a $1,995 retail price, he had refused to include more than 128K of memory—about a tenth of what came with the higher-priced Lisa. The Mac's bitmapping technology soaked up power. The lines and characters that appeared on its screen were pretty, but they sometimes took forever to show up. In fact, the original Mac did just about everything at a glacial pace. It came with a floppy disk drive rather than a hard drive, so copying files from one floppy disk to another was an arduous process in which the user had to pop the two floppies in and out of the computer multiple times. Adding to the machine's woes: the Mac launched with hardly any software, because the operating system was still being tweaked right up to the day of launch. No wonder sales dried up. In his effort to realize a vision, Steve had slighted the machine's utility.

———

STEVE SHOULD HAVE been the guy leading the charge to overcome the Mac's technological faults. There was plenty to be done—develop a hard drive for the machine, increase its memory, work with independent software developers to build more applications that took advantage of its great graphics. In fact, shortly after the Mac shipped, he was officially put in charge of the division overseeing both the Lisa and the Mac. But Steve wasn't interested in supervising incremental improvements for either model. His career to date consisted of a couple of failures—his work on the Apple III and the Lisa—and a couple of breakthrough products. After creating an industry, and then capturing the world's imagination with another revolutionary computer, he couldn't be bothered with the heavy lifting required to make the Mac succeed as an ongoing business.

Moreover, the glittery debut of the Mac sent Steve's life spinning into a new stratosphere of celebrity, one that pumped up his sense of grand accomplishment. He delivered Macs to Mick Jagger, Sean Lennon, and Andy Warhol. For his thirtieth birthday, he hired Ella Fitzgerald to entertain a crowd of a thousand guests at the St. Francis Hotel in San Francisco. He affected a high-handedness that hurt him within his own industry as well. Steve had alienated the critical software developer community throughout the entire development of the Mac by making it seem that it would be a grand privilege if he allowed them to develop applications for his precious machine. "We'd go down to Cupertino," remembers Bill Gates, "and Steve would be like, 'This thing is so fucking cool; in fact, I don't even know why I'm going to let you guys have anything to do with this. You know, I heard what a bunch of idiots you guys are, and, you know, this thing is so golden. It's going to ship for $999, we're about nine months away.'" Other times, Steve would betray his own insecurities. "And then the second day we'd have another meeting," remembers Gates, "and Steve would be like, 'Oh, shit, is this thing any good? Oh, God, can you help us out with this?'" Either way, he wasn't easy to work with.

The arrogance wasn't tempered by the Mac's swooning sales. Mike Slade, who then worked in marketing at Microsoft but later became an Apple employee and one of Steve's close friends, remembers seeing that ego on full display in the fall of 1984, when Slade accompanied Gates to Apple's national sales meeting at the Hilton Hawaiian Village in Honolulu. Getting its application software onto the Mac was critical for Microsoft, which had assigned a slew of developers to create graphical software for the new machine. And eventually Microsoft would become the leading Mac software vendor. But at the time the company had serious competition from Lotus, which had developed a spreadsheet for Mac called Jazz. "Jim Manzi and Eric Bedel [Lotus's

CEO and the Jazz product manager] were like the new girl in the frat," remembers Slade, whose sharp sense of humor masks the kind of analytic chops that made him a favorite of both Gates and Jobs. "Steve and his whole gang were there, and they're ignoring not only me but Bill [Gates]. They're treating Bill like he's the fucking janitor. They even gave us a bad table for dinner." That night, Slade and Gates went for a long walk on the beach. "Bill was so caught up in the thing, so nervous. He had these Bass Weejuns on, and by the time we got back to the hotel they had salt water all over them. He had no idea he had been walking through water. He was oblivious to the whole thing."

Things were no better three months later when Slade and Gates prepared to demonstrate Excel to Steve, Sculley, and the other Apple brass. "We start showing them Excel, but we can't show much, because the demo is barely working. After thirty seconds Steve totally loses interest. If the demo's not working, he's not interested. Sculley gets it, though, and we talk about how to position it as better than what's on a PC. But Jobs is out of there, he's moved to the other side of the table. And he and Bill and Andy Hertzfeld just get into this raging battle about BASIC [the popular programming language]. No one can control Jobs. I mean, I come from a pretty dysfunctional family and I'm thinking, This is the most unbelievable shit fight. But finally, finally, Steve leaves, and the meeting gets better." Years later, after Steve's death, Gates told me, "Steve's a tough character, but he didn't direct his anger at me all too often." (Like many of the people we interviewed, Gates slipped into the present tense when talking about Steve, as if he were still alive.) When I asked him if there was anything Steve was terrible at, he laughed: "Sitting in meetings where he wasn't the person presenting, and the subject was something mundane. Steve was hopeless at that."

MAC SALES FELL off a cliff in the second half of 1984. The Apple II still accounted for 70 percent of the company's revenues. IBM's PC was gaining market share. And the New Year provided no relief. Sales were so far off target that it began to look like the Macintosh might prove to be just as much of a failure as the Apple III and the Lisa. The board of directors, which had been led to believe that the Mac was both the replacement to the Apple II and an IBM-killer, was beginning to see that neither its CEO nor the head of its most important product division had a clear plan forward. As the pressure grew on Steve and Sculley, the two spent less time together, less time finishing each other's sentences and singing each other's praises. And that spelled trouble for Steve.

In March 1985, Sculley decided that Steve would have to step down as head of the Mac product division. Steve tried to dissuade him for several weeks, with both flattery and scorn, the tools he'd used to great, if isolating, effect on those who had worked for him. But Sculley persisted and brought the matter to the board on April 11. The board sided unanimously with Sculley, even though it included Markkula, Rock, and others who had invested so much in Steve over time. For someone who had given his all to the company he had founded, who was known entirely for what he had accomplished at Apple, the prospect of such a demotion was devastating.

After a few weeks, Steve decided that he wouldn't accept the demotion. Instead, he tried to get Sculley fired. He told his closest confidants that he intended to dethrone the CEO over Memorial Day weekend, when Sculley was supposed to be in Beijing signing an accord to allow Apple to sell its computers in China. Steve was so certain of the rightness of his position—and so naïve—that he even laid out his plans to Jean-Louis Gassée, the company's director of European operations, who was in Cupertino only because Sculley planned to bring him in to replace Steve. "I made my choice," Gassée says now. "At that point I'd rather work with Sculley than work with Steve, who was absolutely out of control." Gassée informed Sculley of the plan, telling him, "If you go to China, you're dead." Sculley canceled his trip to China and confronted Steve directly at the next day's executive committee meeting. He asked the company's top management either to support him or to support Steve. One by one, around the conference table, everyone explained why they would support Sculley. Steve watched as the support he'd counted on, which he'd always expected would be there at the end, vanished. Afterward, still in shock, he called his co-conspirators and a couple of friends to tell them he'd lost the battle. "I counted wrong," he told Larry Brilliant that afternoon, recounting, through tears, how the team turned against him, one by one. The board, which Sculley then contacted by phone over the weekend, went against Steve as well. By Tuesday, Steve knew he was finished at Apple. On the following Friday, May 31, he sat in the back of the Apple auditorium and watched as Sculley announced a reorganization that promoted Gassée and left Steve with nothing more than a nonexecutive role as chairman, with no one reporting to him. It was Steve's second demotion, and this time there'd be no recovery. "Steve always had an animal inside him," says Gassée, "and in the early eighties that animal threw him to the ground. Boom!"

———

STEVE'S EXILE WAS complete and designed to humiliate. He was given an office in another building, far from Sculley, Gassée, and the other executives who were now without question running Apple. He was sent to Russia to promote the Apple II, of all things, and to Italy, France, and Sweden, ostensibly on company business. Back in California, he visited the Graphics Group, made up of leading-edge computer graphics technicians who were working for film director George Lucas of *Star Wars* fame, and began to think that the possibilities for computing with high-end, 3-D graphic images were limitless. So he suggested that the Apple board might want to consider buying the group from Lucasfilm. "These guys were way ahead of us on graphics, way ahead," Steve later told me. "They were way, way ahead of anybody. I just knew in my bones that this was going to be very important." But the board wasn't paying much attention to Steve anymore, and they passed on acquiring what would eventually become known as Pixar. Indeed, Steve, the cofounder of Apple, wasn't even consulted on most meaningful decisions anymore.

Sculley made clear that he would take the company in a more "market-driven" direction. Apple would now respond to the demands of its customers, instead of dictating to the market, as Steve had tried to do. Product decisions would be led by the sales and marketing teams, not the engineers. It was a rational decision by a CEO trying to sharpen an organization that had flailed every time it tried to establish some consistency. But it wouldn't re-create the Apple dream that had drawn so many employees to Cupertino, especially the veterans who had experienced the thrilling and terrifying highs and lows of the Mac development. One employee told *Fortune,* "They've cut the heart out of Apple and substituted an artificial one. We'll just have to see how long it pumps." Susan Barnes was one of those who felt the company was becoming mundane, losing its edge. "We were going the wrong way," remembers Barnes. "Apple was reorganizing, and you had to go down seven levels of management to find an engineer. That's a really dangerous place for a technology company to be."

Steve started to think about life without Apple. He spent more time with his daughter Lisa, beginning the process of figuring out how she could fit into his life in a more meaningful way. He gardened, organically, in a plot in the yard of his big house in Woodside. He mused about running for public office. He even applied to fly as a civilian on the space shuttle. For a while he behaved more like a retiree than one of the world's most highly driven thirty-year-olds. "One day he called me," Barnes recalls, "and said, 'We're supposed to have dinner next week, but I'm going to Europe. I may stay there for twelve months.' And I said, 'Thank you, great, but I'm having a bad day at work and don't really need to hear about you in Paris and Italy.'"

He went to Europe on company business, but he made time to visit museums and enjoy the life of a tourist. He spent a lot of time alone, or with his girlfriend. "Apple had been formed when he was twenty-one," says Barnes, "so he never really had any time off to think about what he really wanted to do with his life." It seemed as if this was a time to reflect, to take to heart the hard lessons learned at Apple. It could have been a time to think about what had gone wrong, to understand his own contributions to the quandary that he and the company were in. In some meaningful way, Steve and his followers were right: Steve was the heart of Apple, and without him the company was headed straight for mediocrity. How had he let things get so out of hand?

Self-reflection didn't come easy for the thirty-year-old. In Europe he was still hailed as a revolutionary business figure, and his visits to heads of state, university presidents, artists, and others reinforced his vision of himself as an extraordinary person who had been done in by a conventional bureaucrat. That kind of ego inflation was accompanied by the real pain and insecurity resulting from getting rejected by the company he had founded. Later that summer, Steve phoned Barnes from Italy, so depressed that she started to worry that he might be suicidal.

But when he returned to the United States, he turned his focus right back to where it had always been: discovering the Next Big Thing. In early September, he met with the Nobel Prize–winning scientist Paul Berg, who told him about his frustration that computers were not yet speeding up the scientific research process significantly. Macs and PCs weren't powerful enough to do the kind of computational modeling he needed to do, and mainframes and minicomputers were too expensive and unwieldy for many labs. Steve began to develop an inchoate vision of where computing might go next, and of the kind of powerful computer he now wanted to concoct for demanding users like Berg. With Barnes and others telling him how wrongheaded Sculley was, he knew he could woo a handful of powerful allies from within Apple to start a new company. And at an Apple board meeting on September 13, he told Sculley and the other board members what he planned to do.

He was going to start a new company, he told them. He would like to take a few "low-level" employees with him. The company would try to concoct a radically new, high-end computer "workstation" for a specific and limited market—the upper echelons of higher education. It would not, he assured them, compete with Apple. In fact, he'd be happy to have Apple be a ground-floor investor in the new venture.

In the coming days, all hell would break loose. The employees he wanted were hardly "low-level," Sculley would say. Board members would call Steve a liar in the press. Once again, national magazines like *Newsweek* would put him on the cover. Steve would resign. And Apple would sue him.

But none of that mattered. He was gone. Now his great work could really begin. He was ready to go create the Next Big Thing. Again.

In the balmy autumn days that followed his departure from Apple, Steve and his renegades gathered at his house in bucolic Woodside, a horsey community west of I-280 and nestled in a valley whose western slope swoops up to the coastal range of low mountains that protect Silicon Valley from the Pacific. The house, which he'd bought in 1984, was perhaps the most extravagant, albeit typically peculiar, nod to his rock-star status. It had been built by another controversial innovator, Daniel C. Jackling. In the early 1900s, Jackling had pioneered open-pit mining, the highly efficient yet disastrously polluting method for reaping low-grade copper that is still used throughout the world. Like Steve, Jackling made a bundle developing his idea, and the Woodside house, designed in Spanish Colonial style, was his personal monument. The rambling 17,000-square-foot structure had fourteen bedrooms, custom-made wrought-iron lamps, and a pipe organ that had been expanded to seventy-one ear-shattering pipes. Charles Lindbergh and Lillian Gish had been feted there at parties that flowed forth from the enormous ballroom. The driveway leading to the mansion showed off its ample landscaped grounds, which had fallen into some disrepair. Some of Steve's indulgences—a BMW motorcycle and a gray Porsche 911—were parked out front. On the inside it didn't feel much like a home at all. Steve hadn't gotten around to buying much furniture. Strewn about the house were a mattress, a lamp, some Ansel Adams prints. He'd bought a monstrously big house, but had settled in without bothering to make it a home.

The apostolic high-tech renegades from Apple—Rich Page, a hardware engineer and Apple fellow; Bud Tribble, a leading software programmer; George Crow, another hardware specialist; Dan'l Lewin, who had led Apple's efforts to sell Macs to universities and colleges; and Susan Barnes, the Mac financial manager—converged here with their rock-star leader every few days to plot the next revolution. From the very start, the world was peeking in through the windows. For the *Newsweek* cover story on Steve's departure from Apple, the magazine photographed the six of them outside his house, awkwardly sitting on the lawn in their "business" clothes. (Dan'l Lewin, the chiseled Princeton grad who would lead the sales team, was even wearing a tie.) "It's hard to think that a $2 billion company with 4,300 employees couldn't compete with six people in blue jeans," Steve told the reporter. His humility, of course, was utterly disingenuous.

When he resigned, Steve had told the Apple board that his new company, dubbed NeXT, would not attack any important Apple markets. That was nonsense. His stated target—the higher education market—was in fact very important to Apple, and he had stolen away Lewin, the company's key sales link to the academic world. But Steve had his eyes on even more than that one narrow slice of Apple's potential market. As Steve saw things, he had created the first two signature moments of the personal computing era: the Apple II and the Mac. (There had, of course, been another signature moment: the release of the IBM PC in 1981. But Steve discounted that milestone, since he couldn't imagine a world in which most people would choose to buy machines that were so much harder to use than the ones he created.) Now it was time for a third shift, and he naturally would be the one to drive the change. He would show those bureaucrats who had mismanaged Apple a thing or two about real leadership and innovation.

Steve believed that he now had everything he needed to succeed as a world-class CEO. He had been involved in every aspect of Apple's business over the previous eight years. He was a quick study, a savant who could envision revolutionary products and inspire the close group of folks who designed and made them, and he was an instinctive marketer. In Steve's eyes, no one could say the same for Sculley and his "market-driven" tactics. "I think the question everyone is asking about Apple is this," Steve told me during one of our first interviews. "Does the environment to create the next Macintosh still exist at Apple? Would they know it if they found it?" His new company, called NeXT, would surely grow to be even bigger than Apple, for the sole reason that he had higher expectations for it. "The world doesn't need another $100 million computing company," he announced, scoffing at the thought that he might produce something so trivial.

He was convinced that he really was the only person who could create from scratch the amazing blockbuster products that would give rise to the industry's next great company. So were his renegades. "I had had plenty of experience with the downside of Steve," remembers Lewin, the last of the five Apple exiles to sign up. "I definitely thought about the risk of going to work for him and leaving my job at Apple. But I worried that if I didn't go to NeXT, I would have always said, 'Dammit, I should have gone along for the ride.'" Says another early staffer, who signed on in 1986: "You would have had to be an idiot not to believe that Steve was going to create the next big thing. Everyone believed that."

Little did they know that in due time, NeXT would turn out to be the full, unfortunate blooming of Steve Jobs's worst tendencies at Apple. Yes, Steve had been a product visionary and a great spokesman for the company and the industry he had helped create. But he was hardly poised to be a great chief executive. In many ways, he wasn't even a grown-up yet.

At the very moment when Steve had convinced himself that he had won a richly deserved freedom from an oppressive, dull overseer, he was in fact slave to so much else: to his celebrity, to his unbalanced and obsessive desire for perfection in the most innocuous of details, to his managerial flightiness and imperiousness, to his shortcomings as an analyst of his own industry, to his burning need for revenge, and to his own blindness to these faults. He was immature and adolescent in so many ways—egocentric, unrealistically idealistic, and unable to manage the ups and downs of real relationships.

Steve was too self-centered to see how much of Apple's success had depended upon a combination of perfect timing and the work of others. Nor did he recognize how much he had contributed to its many problems. He didn't realize how little he had truly absorbed from his crash course in business. Steve had been the titular CEO of Apple for only a few brief months at its inception, before Mike Scott was hired, and actually knew quite little of the true demands of corporate leadership. He was smart enough to realize that a successful CEO must prioritize among his employees' many projects and ideas, but it would take years for him to learn how to do so efficiently or without the ego that came with thinking that his own ideas were always best. Nor did he have any real knowledge of how to launch a company into a field crawling with competitors. And he was unaware of each and every one of these weaknesses.

One afternoon that fall, the wind kicked up outside the Woodside house during an early meeting. "The doors were slamming," remembers Barnes, who served as NeXT's CFO, "just opening and shutting, opening and shutting in the wind. It was driving Steve crazy. And I could see, there was a piece of him that wanted to turn on one of us and just take us out. But it was his house. I wasn't in charge of facilities, like I was at Apple! So, hey dude, it's your house, you're the one who's got the door-slamming problem, not me." Jobs, it seemed to Barnes, had no clue about the hundreds of little things other people had been doing over the years to keep Apple afloat while he was dreaming up his big ideas. Now he had to learn. "When you're the CEO and the funder," she says, recalling that afternoon, "*everything's* on your shoulders."

———

UNLIKE IN 1975, when he and Woz had pioneered the personal computing industry, in 1986 Steve was trying to enter a hypercompetitive marketplace with such a wide range of offerings that any newcomer would be hard-pressed to offer anything truly unique. Computer technology, drafting on the amazing multiplicative power of Moore's law, had made tremendous strides in a decade. Nineteen eighty-five was the year that semiconductor makers like Intel and NEC first boasted of cramming a million transistors on a single memory chip. (Of course, that pales next to today's highest-capacity chips, which can hold 128 trillion discrete elements.) But that wasn't the only technology that had improved so swiftly. Hard disk drives were finally cheap enough for consumers to afford: If you shopped around, you could find one that held 10 megabytes of digital storage for about $700. Back then that was enough space to hold all the essential software and applications you used for quick access and then some. (To give a sense of comparison, today, $700 will buy you 10 terabytes of storage, or roughly 100,000 times as much capacity—room enough to stockpile more than a thousand high-definition movies.)

As a result, the performance and capacity of reasonably priced microcomputers were improving by leaps and bounds, and would continue to do so in the foreseeable future. Steve understood this, and thought it was possible to find a perfect niche for his perfect new machine, right between the personal computer and a new category of desktop systems that had come to be called engineering workstations.

The "workstation" segment of microcomputers emerged in the early 1980s, around the time that Apple was working on the Lisa and IBM was gearing up to introduce its machines. Workstations were basically PCs beefed up with more memory, more data storage, faster processors, and, most visibly, gigantic, twenty-four-inch screens. They emerged mainly from computer science departments in academia and were designed to put as much raw processing power as possible in the hands of a single user—most likely an engineer or scientist whose institution could afford the machine, and who could write his or her own applications to perform heavy-duty calculations or mathematical models. Workstations had two other attributes that really made them stand apart. First, they were designed from the ground up to participate in networks with other workstations. Second, they employed the most advanced microcomputer software operating system of the time, which had been originally developed by computer scientists at AT&T's Bell Laboratories, and then nurtured and improved by academic researchers and scientists in national laboratories. Called Unix, it was the operating system that enabled the first data "network of networks," which later came to be called the Internet.

Sun Microsystems, a Silicon Valley workstation maker, got its start in 1982 making such machines for use on the Stanford University Network (hence its name). Sun set a record that still stands in the annals of American business for being the company that from a dead start reached the $1 billion sales mark faster than any other manufacturer—it took all of four years. In fact, Sun was nearing that heady milestone the year that Steve's new venture opened for business. Sun was a no-nonsense company. Its powerful computers had no special flourishes other than their outstanding performance benchmarks. They delivered great bang for the buck, but their lack of aesthetics offended Steve; instead of seeing the utility of such computers, he saw only opportunity—of course, he assumed, the world would be partial to something easier to use and more attractive.

Meanwhile, personal computers sold by IBM, and by the growing number of "clone" manufacturers like Compaq and others, were perfectly serviceable machines for the thousands of businesses starting to make rudimentary computing a standard part of their office workflow. The workplace was a fast-growing market, with ferocious competitors serving business customers who focused on price, productivity, and return on investment. A startup out to make its mark would have to come up with a computer that stood out from the rest, that gave schools, businesses, or consumers something they really couldn't find anywhere else.

Given this fierce competition, it's easy to understand why Sculley and the Apple board sued Steve. With IBM and the makers of other MS-DOS-based clones dominating the market for PCs sold to corporations, Apple needed the school and university market more than ever. Workstations were quickly becoming the lab benches for many disciplines at research universities and in corporate R&D skunkworks. It was only natural that Apple would want to offer its own unique approach to these machines as well. Apple's suit stalled Steve's effort to move quickly, by making it difficult for NeXT to do basic things like arrange deals with suppliers, incorporate, hire employees, and so on.

But Apple withdrew its legal challenge in January 1986, in part because Sculley finally decided he didn't have the stomach for the public relations fallout of a court suit against a popular public figure. In the meantime, Jobs had been able to use the fall of 1985 to study the education market. He, Lewin, and some of the other founders made several trips to universities to hear what professors and researchers really wanted. The founders would remember these treks as fondly as they would the gatherings at the Jackling house. Funded by Steve, who could still be a tightwad, the early employees operated on the cheap, with "that startup hustle," as Steve put it. "We didn't have a lot of money," Bud Tribble told me. "All six of us would squeeze into a single rental car to go make our visits. We even shared hotel rooms. We developed a real pioneer spirit." For a couple of months, NeXT had the feeling of a true startup. And the road crew actually learned something promising: academics truly did want all the power in those $20,000 workstations. But the crew also learned what the company's challenge would be: academics absolutely could not spend more than $3,000 per machine. As he had done at Apple, Lewin created a consortium of schools to serve as consultants—and as pilot customers for the NeXT computer. It wasn't just the allure of signing on with the great Steve Jobs that appealed to the university presidents; it was the fact that the great Steve Jobs had promised that he could indeed deliver the machine they craved for a mere $3,000. It was a promise he wouldn't come close to keeping.

———

LATER IN HIS LIFE, Steve would become more adept at managing the press than any other businessman alive. But as he entered his thirties, his idea of good PR was to get attention of any kind. Launching NeXT, Jobs felt that some initial publicity would help attract the investors he needed to build this new and better version of Apple. So he opened the doors for two prestigious media outlets, *Esquire* magazine and PBS. The results were fascinating: a portrait of a young entrepreneur trying on the clothes of a seasoned businessman, and not quite filling them out.

Steve's segment of a PBS show called *The Entrepreneurs* kicked off with an image of him pulling carrots from garden soil. He did occasionally garden, and he may have intended the image as confirmation of his counterculture roots, but the shot lent an almost laughably gauzy warmth to the introduction, setting the stage for a piece that revealed far more about him than he can have intended. The episode consisted mostly of film clips from the company's first two off-site meetings— intense getaways that were one part group therapy brainstorming, and one part endurance test. Everyone involved in the production wanted to tell the tale of a heroic young entrepreneur, and the voiceover obligingly delivered, describing the show as a chance to see Jobs "at his lucid best, as a company builder and a motivator." But the language didn't match the actual footage from the retreats, which made clear just how hard it would be for Jobs to bring NeXT into focus.

The two off-sites were at Pebble Beach, California, the first in December 1985 and the second in March 1986. They were designed for Jobs and his small staff to define their grand project and to assign clear responsibility for the various strands of its development. Footage from the December meeting shows Jobs at the whiteboard trying to get the group to agree on their top priority: Was it more important to meet the $3,000 price target, create a machine loaded with great technology, or deliver that computer by the spring of 1987? As with any startup, different factions advanced their own agendas; Rich Page claimed that the company was pointless if its computer wasn't a radical technological advance. Dan'l Lewin, the head of sales and marketing, explained that since schools purchased computers during the summer, missing the target date would mean missing a year of revenue. George Crow, another hardware whiz, argued that price was paramount. As always, Jobs was charismatic and confident and clearly aware of when the cameras were rolling. His sentiments were touching, his heart seemed in the right place, and his bold words were inspiring. "More important than building a product, we are in the process of architecting a company that will hopefully be much more incredible, the total will be much more incredible than the sum of its parts," he said. "The cumulative effort of approximately twenty thousand decisions that we're all going to make over the next two years are going to define what our company is. And one of the things that made Apple great was that, in the early days, it was built from the heart." But not surprising for a CEO emphasizing the importance of "twenty thousand decisions," he made little progress in steering the group toward consensus. His one clear conclusion—"The delivery date is a line in the sand"—registered as what it turned out to be: an unattainable fiat. His team seemed smart, passionate, and intelligent; but it also seemed young, naïve, unfocused, and in desperate need of a leader more decisive than Steve.

As they pontificated, deliberated, and pointed fingers, especially during one fraught March discussion on cost cutting, the group made apparent how absurd it was to think that they could actually deliver a great computer in fifteen months. For years, Jobs had been criticized by Scott, Sculley, Markkula, Woz, and others as being a divisive and impulsive manager who sowed chaos unnecessarily, delivered products late, gave unclear and shifting directions, and advanced his own ideas at the expense of the corporation. The squabbling was a clear harbinger that similar troubles awaited the NeXT crew.

For the *Esquire* piece, which was published in December 1986, Steve invited the writer Joe Nocera to spend a week at the company. Nocera (now an op-ed columnist at the *New York Times*) attended planning meetings and strategy sessions at the company's new offices in the Stanford Research Park in Palo Alto (the same building I visited when I met Steve for the first time), where he spoke with a wide range of staffers. He dined with Jobs and visited him at home—activities that would be strictly off-limits to most journalists later in Jobs's career. As always, Steve had a point he wanted to make, in this case that NeXT was "going to take the technology to the next level," as he told Nocera. Getting there would mean re-creating the intensity and passion that he had loved during the development of the Mac. "I remember many late nights coming out of the Mac building, when I would have the most incredibly powerful feelings about my life," Jobs said. "Just exhilarating feelings about my life. I feel some of that now with NeXT. I can't explain it. I don't really understand it. But I'm comfortable with it."

Steve's strong feelings about Apple rippled through the story, so much so that Nocera called Jobs's assertion that he had put Apple behind him "wishful thinking." "Apple," Jobs admitted, "is like an intense love affair with a girl you really, really like, and then she decides to drop you and go out with someone who's not so neat." The story even dipped into Steve's relationship with his girlfriend at the time, Tina Redse, describing how Steve wrote her a long note apologizing for working late one night. Nocera found his single-mindedness lonely. Jobs, who at one point in the article failed to remember if he had curtains in his house, refused to acknowledge feeling any kind of wistfulness or dissatisfaction.

"That impression of eternal youth," Nocera wrote, "is reinforced by some guileless, almost childlike traits: By the way, for instance, he can't resist showing off his brutal, withering intelligence whenever he's around someone he doesn't think measures up. Or by his almost willful lack of tact. Or by his inability to hide his boredom when he is forced to endure something that doesn't interest him, like a sixth grader who can't wait for class to end." Looking back, it's clear that Nocera had landed on something few people, including Jobs, wanted to see—the fact that the Steve Jobs of 1986 was too raw, too self-centered, and too immature to successfully pull off the balancing act required of a big-time CEO.

About the time Nocera had started his reporting, Steve hired a new PR agency, Allison Thomas Associates. He had gotten to know Thomas when she was steering a state commission on industrial in-novation, a project that solidified California's support for high-tech companies and led to corporations getting a tax credit for donating computers to schools, among other initiatives. Steve wanted to reposi-tion his image, to move past all the stories about his erratic behavior. Thomas, who became close to Steve over the years, found a way to dis-cuss the problem without setting him off: What could be done about "the other Steve," the one who came off seeming arrogant and mean? It was an ingenious approach that helped the two work closely for sev-eral years. But in the end "the other Steve" won out: Steve badgered Thomas incessantly, urging her to cut off all communications with any reporters who criticized him. She would quit in 1993, a few weeks after Jobs paged her three times during the inauguration of President Bill Clinton, which she was attending in Washington, D.C.

———

AFTER ONE OF NeXT's early board meetings, Steve pulled aside Susan Barnes, his CFO. "When my life is over," he told her, "people will give me credit for all the creative stuff. But no one will know I actually know how to run a business."

As Steve started NeXT, it was true that he did know certain key things about running a computer business. He was a strong, if some-what confounding motivator, and a restless innovator. He had shown himself to be a good negotiator with parts suppliers, often getting Apple better prices in its early days than its volume had really justified. He could synthesize big ideas, and he could see how different technologies could be combined into something that added up to a whole lot more. "He knew about inventory terms, he understood the mechanics of capital investment, he knew cash flow," says Barnes. "He did understand this, and starting Apple had taught him things you can *try* to teach an MBA. But he actually knew them. [They were] survival skills."

Steve craved recognition for this, and spoke often about how well he was going to manage NeXT, and how much he had learned from the mistakes Apple had made during its years of unfettered growth. "This is really the third time around for me and a number of other people at NeXT," he told me. "When we were at Apple, we spent half the time fixing things that were breaking, whether it be an employee stock ownership plan, or a parts numbering system, or a way of manufacturing a product. At NeXT we have the benefit of having the experience of growing a company from zero to a couple of billion dollars before, and we could anticipate some of the more sophisticated problems that we didn't anticipate the first or second time around. It gives us a certain level of confidence which enables us to take more risks. We're working much smarter. We're thinking things through more, which results in more getting done with less work."

It sounded good. But much of it was chutzpah and self-delusion. When he started Apple, he had not presumed that he knew how to run a business—he was willing to rely, at least for a while, on his mentors and bosses. Now, however, he acted as if he knew everything, from payroll and engineering to marketing and manufacturing. He was out to do absolutely every little thing right this time. You could see it in his body language. Whenever someone nattered on about a subject Steve believed he knew well—knew better than anyone else, in his opinion—he would look away, tap his feet, shift restlessly in his seat, and behave like a teenager undergoing physical torment until he could finally break in and say his piece. And of course all this was done in a way that was obvious to everyone else in the meeting.

Steve's overbearing need to weigh in on everything—to get those "twenty thousand decisions" exactly right—slowed everyone down. This micromanagement was the primary example of the fact that Steve did not know how to prioritize in any kind of holistic way at this stage of his career. Remember how he wanted the group at the first Pebble Beach offsite to decide on NeXT's top priority: a great machine, on-time delivery, or a price tag under $3,000? It was the wrong question. NeXT absolutely needed to do all three things. But Steve couldn't keep his company focused on what mattered when he couldn't focus himself efficiently.

Steve was unable to effectively manage all the cash that he had been able to raise. NeXT was bankrolled by $12 million that Steve put in in two stages, as well as by investments of $660,000 each from Carnegie Mellon and Stanford, and $20 million from H. Ross Perot, the idiosyncratic businessman who offered to back NeXT after seeing the episode of *The Entrepreneurs*. ("I found myself finishing their sentences," Perot raved to *Newsweek*.) The investments gave the young, productless company an exorbitant valuation of $126 million in 1987. (Two years later Canon, the Japanese camera and printer maker, would kick in $100 million more, raising the overall valuation of the company to $600 million.) Steve touted the investments as proof of concept. The Carnegie Mellon and Stanford money showed that the schools were anxiously awaiting his computer. Perot's endorsement just underscored the size of the potential market, and was evidence that the most innovative businesspeople understood Steve's greatness, potential, and maturity. Perot swore that he'd keep a close eye on his investment: "This is going to be hell on the oyster," he said in the *Newsweek* article covering the deal, equating himself in his folksy way to the sand that irritates the oyster to create the pearl inside. But in truth Perot was hands-off with the man he viewed as a young genius. Years before, he had decided against investing early in Microsoft, missing out on billions of dollars as the company's stock soared, and this time he was determined to roll the dice on one of those brilliant techies from the West Coast. Steve promised to be a careful steward of the cash. In the *Entrepreneurs* video, he repeatedly urged his staff to conserve resources, to the point of complaining about the hotel room rates they were getting. Despite having seen him throw money around at Apple, Barnes was initially hopeful that Steve might change his ways. "I thought he'd be better when it was his own money," she remembers. "Boy, was I wrong."

Most great Silicon Valley startups start out lean and simple. The advantage they have over established companies is the focus they can bring to a single product or idea. Unencumbered by bureaucracy or a heritage of products to protect, a small group of talented folks is free to attack a concept with speed and smarts. Eagerly working hundred-hour weeks, the employees want little more from the "company" than that it pay the bills and get out of their way. They know that if they execute their idea so successfully that their enterprise grows big, at some point they'll have to deal with the rigors and strains of a corporation. But generally that's a worry that's tackled later. At the beginning, corporate trappings can just get in the way, and distract from the all-consuming job of creating an object of desire.

As he had explained to Nocera, Steve enjoyed the spirit of a startup. But his definition of lean and mean had been changed by his experience at Apple. "Living on the cheap was difficult for him after he'd lived the high life there," says Barnes. Jobs had enjoyed the benefits of Apple's resources and size, of its manufacturing prowess and rich marketing budget. Despite what he said about wanting to repeat the experience of the Apple II and the Mac, what Steve really wanted at NeXT was the garage spirit of a startup meshed with the safety, status, and perks of the Fortune 500. It wasn't a combination he could pull off.

The first sign of his extravagance came early, when Steve paid Paul Rand $100,000 for his beautifully designed NeXT logo. Choosing Rand to design the logo was an indication of Steve's ambition: Rand's most famous logo is the one still used by IBM. His prestige was such that Steve agreed to Rand's stringent terms that all he'd get for his hundred grand was a single draft—take it or leave it. Fortunately, Jobs loved everything about it. He loved the logo, and he loved the way it was presented in a classy booklet explaining in detail how Rand had arrived at his notable design, including the philosophical rationale for the lowercase *e* and the four vivid colors set on black. The day the members of Team NeXT were given copies of the manifesto, Lewin found himself reflecting on when he had first met Steve in 1977 as a Sony salesman based in an office near Apple's headquarters on Stevens Creek Boulevard. He recalled the way Steve had lovingly fondled the Sony sales materials, making note of the fine paper stock and professional design: "Steve was a freak about Sony, right? Why did people spend fifteen percent more for a Sony product? Steve would walk into our office, and look at the paper and feel the paper that Sony printed their brochures on. It wasn't the products, it was the tactile feel, the surface and the presentation that mattered to him." But NeXT was a startup, not a mature, successful company like Sony with billions in revenues, for whom such a pamphlet would be pocket change.

Extravagant expenditures soon became standard operating procedure at NeXT, especially when it came to the company's headquarters. The Palo Alto offices featured expensive, custom-designed furnishings, Ansel Adams prints, and a kitchen with granite countertops. And when NeXT moved into bigger offices in Redwood City in 1989, no expense was spared. The lobby featured long, lush leather couches imported from Italy. The crowning touch was a floating staircase designed by world-famous architect I. M. Pei, who designed the glass pyramid entrance to the Louvre that opened that year. The staircase was a ravishing predecessor to the showy stairways that now grace some of Apple's retail stores.

Steve's spendthrift ways extended throughout the company. "Our information system," he told me proudly in 1989, "is designed for a company with $1 billion in annual sales." (NeXT's 1989 sales would top out at just a few million dollars, leaving the company at least one hundred times short of that $1 billion mark.) But he justified his spending by explaining that he was creating the infrastructure of a Fortune 500 company from the ground up. Unlike Apple, he told me,

"We were able to make the investment up front to do it right the first time. Let's get the best people we can find, and let's brainstorm and strategize, but let's just do it once. And let's have it be good enough to last for a number of years. It will take a little more startup expense, but it will pay many, many times over in the coming years."

The centerpiece of Steve's spending was a state-of-the-art manufacturing facility to churn out NeXT computers—a factory designed to be the envy of the world. The plant, fifteen miles across the bay from Redwood City, in Fremont, was small, but it was a marvel. Steve took me on a tour of the place, just before it went into production in 1989. The factory was nearly empty; Steve explained that the place had been designed to operate with few people. He took great pride in every detail, pointing out the robots and machines that had been repainted in the tones of gray that he had specified. The production area was on a single floor about the size of a large restaurant. With no one around on that quiet day, it seemed like something of a Potemkin factory—an empty shell for show—but Steve claimed it had the capacity to produce up to 600 machines a day, which was the equivalent of, yes, $1 billion worth of hardware in a year.

The place had been laid out by an army of manufacturing system engineers—for a while, there were more PhDs working for NeXT's manufacturing division than for its software arm. It would be flexible, capable of steadily serving a just-in-time manufacturing scheme. The robots would handle almost everything that required great dexterity, including some of the assembly tasks that Woz and Jobs had performed themselves when making the Apple 1: they placed the chips on the circuit boards, soldered everything into place, and tested and measured to make sure everything was right. A human would step in to do one final check, and would handle the final assembly and pop boards into their appropriate slots inside the magnesium cube.

Steve was right—the place was indeed a paragon. This was at a time when Japanese manufacturers had chased most American companies out of the semiconductor fabrication business and were held up as object lessons for automakers in Detroit. He hoped that his pristine factory would give the world glittery proof that American high-tech manufacturers could still excel. More important, he felt that the seeming perfection of the place and his obsessive focus on its details sent a message to employees: if you aim for perfection in everything you do, you'll achieve greater results than you could ever imagine.

It was a lovely principle. But it didn't come close to justifying spending outrageous sums on a state-of-the-art factory to build computers for which there was not yet any demand. Steve could easily have outsourced manufacturing; by the late 1980s the computer industry had grown to include a host of contract manufacturers right there in Silicon Valley that could build a highly demanding product like the NeXT computer. The cost would have been far less. For all its beauty, from the lush landscaping out front to the meticulously crafted wheeled tables on which the computer components rolled through the assembly process, the NeXT factory turned out to be a sinkhole. Forget producing 600 computers a day: the factory never produced more than 600 machines in a single month.

IN THEORY, THERE'S nothing wrong with a state-of-the-art factory, a beautiful office for your employees, or a fancy logo. It's just that in decision after decision, Steve failed to account for the trade-offs that accompanied his fanciful choices. Steve couldn't distinguish between the extraneous and the critical. As CEO of a fledgling company, that was his key responsibility. At NeXT, he utterly failed to do this.

Steve decided early on, for instance, that the NeXT computer should have an optical disk drive for storing information, rather than a standard hard drive. The optical disk drive had two great advantages: its disks could hold up to two hundred times as much information as the standard hard drive of the time, and they were removable. Steve heavily promoted the idea that regular folks could essentially carry around their life in data, moving from one computer to another armed with their own personal optical disk. It seemed that he wanted to enable the utopian idea of a mobile population carrying its key information with it. (Today, of course, we can access much more data from our smartphones or tablets, but the data resides in the so-called "cloud.") However, the optical option had many problems, primarily that its drives retrieved information from the disks very slowly. Steve had chosen a vision—the potential of abundant storage—over the customers' real need—the convenience of data speedily available. When the NeXT computer did finally hit retail stores in late 1989, competitors like Sun happily cast it as a slowpoke compared with their hard-drive-based machines.

Many of the features of the NeXT computer seemed intended primarily to dazzle. Like a standard-issue PC, the NeXT computer consisted of four devices: a keyboard, a mouse, a cube containing the computer, and the monitor. Its designer was Hartmut Esslinger, the German industrial aesthete who had worked with Steve on the first Mac. Esslinger was another expensive choice, a world-class designer who was just as uncompromising as Steve. He ordered up a true cube, with sharp right angles as opposed to the infinitesimal curves found on the edges of the machines from other manufacturers, including Apple. Those curves on the conventional machines weren't so much an aesthetic choice; they were a concession to manufacturing realities. Creating a perfect cube with true sharp angles required expensive custom molds, which could only come from a specialty metals shop in Chicago. Esslinger and Jobs also insisted that the case be made from magnesium, which is far more expensive than plastic. Using magnesium was a choice, like Jobs's selection of cast aluminum for the Apple III's case eight years earlier, that had a significant downside. Magnesium had certain advantages over plastic, but it was much harder to machine perfectly, leading to more flaws in the manufacturing process.

Designing a computer laden with details like these made building it for $3,000 absolutely impossible. The flourishes just added up too fast. "The business plan," says Lewin, "called for a cube whose material cost was fifty dollars, without the motherboard. Steve went off on this fantasy of wanting the paint job to be of the same quality as some titanium tone arm he'd seen on a four-thousand-dollar turntable. So he sends three people off to General Motors to learn how to do paint that way—Perot had been on the board there, and GM knew how to paint metal better than anyone in the world. And so we figured out how to do that. But that cube that was supposed to cost fifty dollars all-in? The paint job alone cost fifty dollars. It was really fantasyland."

Even more damaging were some of Steve's aesthetic fiats about the inside of the machine. One in particular stands out. In a typical production sequence, engineers are told the specifications a computer must achieve; they design circuitry to meet those demands; and only then do they wrestle with the question of exactly what size and shape the computer's circuit board must be. Steve reversed the process at NeXT. He told George Crow and his hardware engineers that the circuit board for the NeXT computer would have to be a square that fit exactly into the magnesium cube. A square was an odd configuration for the engineers. Insisting on the exact shape of the board, Steve severely limited the engineers' ability to create something inexpensive that met the computer's specifications. He added an unnecessary level of complexity, meaning yet more money spent for more engineers working more hours to accommodate a design that contributed nothing meaningful to the final product.

Again and again, Steve made choices that seemed justifiable in isolation but that damaged the company's critical mission. Steve did a poor job of evaluating these ideas against one another. He couldn't accept that it was impossible for him to have everything exactly the way he wanted it.

In part, this was because he believed his own press. He was a genius, according to the media and his investors. Ross Perot frothingly described Jobs as "a 33-year-old with 50 years' worth of business experience." Little did he know how wrong he was. President Ronald Reagan's secretary of commerce, Malcolm Baldrige, called Jobs for advice. Editors of the most important publications in the land kept sending their reporters to the West Coast to find out what Steve was thinking about all kinds of subjects, not just computing and technology. (I once tracked Steve down for such an assignment, and listened to him confidently opine on industrial policy, competition with Russia, the drug war, and General Manuel Noriega of Panama.) The fascination with his new company, so out of proportion for a startup with no product entering a highly competitive industry, confirmed his own sense that he was destined to do great things. That sense of genius and destiny made it harder for Steve to sideline any of his own ideas. He acted as if each detail he advanced could make the difference between creating a breakthrough product and putting out the kind of dreck he thought was offered by other manufacturers. Years later, Perot admitted that he had been snowed. "One of the biggest mistakes I ever made was to give those young people all that money," he said.

Also, Steve could not resist pursuing anything that would show up Apple. Since Apple had a logo that had become iconic, Steve needed one with the same potential and a great pedigree. Apple had a state-of-the-art factory, so Steve's tiny company built an outrageously expensive factory that could handle as much volume as Apple needed. His obsession with Apple seemed to ooze out of his pores, despite the silence he'd imposed on his handlers. The first time that John Huey, then the editor of *Fortune* magazine, went to visit NeXT, Huey was waiting in the lobby when Steve returned from a lunch date with other visitors. Not recognizing Huey, Jobs sat down on another of those expensive lobby couches and spent fifteen minutes flipping through a set of magazines, excoriating Apple's "stupid" advertising created by whatever "bozos" they had running the show over there now.

Some writers have tried to cast Steve's obsessiveness, and his hunger for the spotlight and success, as a Freudian attempt to bring down the birth parents who "rejected" him by letting him be adopted. It always struck me, however, that at his childish worst Steve was really nothing more than a spoiled brat. Brilliant, precocious, and meticulous, he had always gotten his way with his parents, and had brayed like an injured donkey when things didn't turn out as he planned. As a grown-up he could behave exactly the same way, sometimes exploding in a temper tantrum. At NeXT there was no one to keep that side of him in check. While more grounded and cooler-headed folks like Lewin and Barnes would disagree with him and weigh in with advice, he ignored them with impunity and, often, scorn. Talking about the days after the historic introduction of the Mac, Steve had told Joe Nocera, "I think I know what it must be like to watch the birth of your child." Unfortunately for the team at NeXT, in many ways Steve himself was still the child, rather than the more mature and supportive parent.

———

STEVE'S ARBITRARY DECISIONS dumbfounded those under him at NeXT, and his micromanagement gave them no peace. He assumed they would work nights and weekends. He wouldn't hesitate to call them at home on Sundays or holidays if he'd discovered some "urgent" problem. And yet hardware and software engineers still could not resist working for Steve Jobs.

Steve understood their sensibility. Engineers, at heart, are problem solvers. They thrive on digging their way out of sinkholes, especially the gnarly kind with no clear path forward. Steve challenged them in ways they had never imagined. No one else in the computer business had such radical goals and expectations; no one else seemed to care so much about their work. The idea of creating a computer that could transform the very process of education was cool; but to his incredibly talented programmers and gearheads, the idea of creating this particular computer for this particular boss was irresistible.

As the years went on, it became apparent that Steve's goals for the NeXT computer went way beyond serving the university market. Lewin and his salespeople were courting customers in all kinds of businesses, thinking that the NeXT computer could transform the corporate workplace, blending the computing power to do 3-D modeling and to interpret copious data with the ability to connect with others easily on corporate networks. A machine like that, made available not just to the denizens of the ivory tower but also to the quants of Wall Street and the merchants of Main Street, truly would be revolutionary. So even as the company drifted from month to month, year to year without delivering a final product to the market, many of the engineers continued to do great work and viewed their jobs as both a noble mission and a labor of love. Engineers ruled the roost at NeXT. They had their own special wing at headquarters, equipped with a grand piano and locks that kept out all other employees. And indeed, Steve's amazing collection of geeks at NeXT produced some genuinely great work.

Richard Crandall, a physics professor from Reed College, became the company's chief scientist and was given enormous latitude to see just how far computing could expand the scope of high-level teaching in fields such as computational science. His work at NeXT carried over into decades of advanced research on cryptography; he later became the head of Apple's Advanced Computation Group. Michael Hawley, fresh out of the Massachusetts Institute of Technology, worked with a group of folks to create the world's first digitized library, which included the complete works of Shakespeare and the *Oxford Dictionary of Quotations*. And when it finally did appear, the NeXT computer would have easy multitasking, easy ways to attach documents to email, and an intuitive user interface to facilitate the networking it made possible.

Most important, Jobs convinced Avie Tevanian, a young software whiz from Carnegie Mellon University, to come to NeXT rather than join Microsoft. At CMU, Tevanian had worked on Mach, a supercharged version of Unix, the powerful operating system for workstations. At NeXT he became Bud Tribble's key developer on the computer's operating system, called NeXTSTEP. For years, Tevanian kept a calculator window open on his computer that tallied daily the total value of the stock options he gave up when he turned down Microsoft. But he loved the work, in part because Jobs recognized his genius and handed him enormous responsibility as soon as he walked in the door.

Steve said many times that the difference between NeXT and the manufacturers of traditional workstations was that he cared more about software than they did. The NeXTSTEP operating system that Tribble and Tevanian developed truly was elegant; in typical Jobs fashion, it put a gorgeous, approachable face on an operating system that previously only engineers had been able to decipher. And Steve recognized that a technique called object-oriented programming (OOP for short) had great potential to help developers slash the amount of time required to create applications. One OOP toolkit that Tevanian's team created, called WebObjects, eventually became a profitable product for NeXT; after the rise of the Internet, it proved to be a great help to companies looking to quickly build Web-based services.

As much as he depended on Tribble's and Tevanian's skills, Steve could not resist managing them ferociously. "Early on," remembers Tribble's wife, Susan Barnes, "Bud would complain to me about the fact that Steve kept pushing to see what he was working on in action, on a screen. 'Steve can yell that the sun shouldn't rise in the east,' Bud would tell me, 'but it's going to rise in the east, and it's going to take time to get this software to the point where you can see something visually on the screen. I know he's a visual learner, I know he can see that way, and I know it's frustrating for him to look at lines of code. But that's life!'"

"The company was so small," says Tevanian, who looks like a professional soccer player, with his dark curly hair, deep-set eyes, and athletic frame, "that everybody knew everyone else. I'd be working late at night and Steve would come by and I'd show him what I'm working on, and then he'd yell and scream at me, tell me how terrible it was and all that kind of stuff. But in the end, there was a bunch of stuff that I knew that he didn't know. He knew that he didn't know it, so we developed this mutual respect where I could tolerate some of his criticisms because he would also actually listen to me when I had something to say. We made it work."

EARLY ON AT NeXT, Steve said the most important thing he could do was "architect a great company." This potentially noble sentiment became a half-baked and confused endeavor, and yet another distraction. Sometimes Steve's good intentions could lead to a deep intellectual self-deception, in which trivial issues loomed larger than life and fundamental realities were swept under the rug.

He did try to be a good boss. For example, Steve hosted annual "family picnics" for his employees in Menlo Park. They were kid-oriented Saturday affairs, featuring clowns, volleyball, burgers and hot dogs, and even hokey events like sack races. At his invitation, I attended one in 1989 with my daughter, Greta, who was five years old at the time. Steve, who was barefoot, sat with me on a hay bale and chatted for an hour or so while Greta wandered off to watch the Pickle Family Circus, a Bay Area comedic troupe of acrobats and jugglers that Steve had hired. NeXT staffers would come up from time to time, thanking him for throwing the bash. We talked about his business a bit, but mostly Steve rattled on about how important families were to NeXT, and about how many families there were over at Pixar, the small graphics computing outfit he'd acquired from George Lucas. Some of it was hot air, but some of it was a reflection of the fact that Steve really was wrestling with the issue of paternal responsibility. Down deep, he ached for a family of his own. He was spending more and more time with his daughter Lisa, a reconciliation process that was never entirely successful, but that would eventually lead to her living with him during her high school years. I had the feeling that he looked at those picnics as evidence that he could in fact be a good father, if not to his daughter, then at least to his employees. "I think he looked around those gatherings and thought, 'Oh God, I'm not just carrying all these employees, I'm carrying their families, too,'" says Barnes. "It added to the pressure he felt."

Steve's budding paternalism carried over into his efforts to develop friendships with some of his closest executives. When Tribble and Barnes had their first child, Steve snuck into the hospital after hours to visit. "Steve so much wanted to be a father figure," remembers Jon Rubinstein, who joined NeXT in 1991 and eventually replaced Rich Page as the lead hardware engineer. "He's just a year older than I am. But he had this father-figure thing going that was very funny because, you know, he thought he knew more about life than anyone else around him. He always wanted to know about my personal life."

But when he tried to intellectualize or institutionalize his paternalistic feelings, he often did so in shallow, poorly designed ways. As part of "architecting a great company" Steve tried to implement an idealistic social experiment he called the "Open Corporation." Salaries were set by category, so that everyone with a certain job title would be paid the same amount. And every employee's salary information would be available to everyone else. It was, Steve once claimed to me, an example of his commitment to treating everyone at the company fairly. Then he launched into the "heartfelt" soliloquy he'd prepared for that particular moment:

> *"It's people who* make our factory work. It's people who write the software, who design the machines. We're not going to have to out-scale our competitors, we have to out-think them. Every time we hire somebody, we put a brick into building our future.
>
> *"Hiring the right* people is only the beginning—you also have to build an open corporation. Think of it this way: If you look at your own body, your cells are specialized, but every single one of them has the master plan for the whole body. We think NeXT will be the best possible company if every single person working here understands the whole basic master plan and can use that as a yardstick to make decisions. Sure, there is some risk with giving everybody access to all the corporate information, and potentially some loss. But what you gain vastly surpasses what you lose.
>
> *"The most visible* sign of the open corporation at NeXT is our policy of allowing everybody to know what salary everybody else is making. There's a list in the finance department, and anyone can go look at it. Why? In a typical company, a typical manager

might spend three hours a week on compensation issues. Most of those three hours a week is spent defusing false rumors and talking in caged terms about relative compensation. In our company, the manager still spends those three hours, but we spend them defending in a very open way the decisions we made and explaining why we made them, and coaching the people that work for us about what it will take for them to achieve those levels of compensation. So we tend to look at those three hours as an educational opportunity."

Talking about the Open Corporation gave Steve a way to cast a sheen of moral exceptionalism on NeXT. But his actions soon contradicted his words. By the time he was telling me this, the practice had already been exposed inside the company for the twaddle it was. That's because Steve was always hell-bent on hiring the very best people in the world, especially engineers. "In most businesses, the difference between average and good is at best 2 to 1," Steve once told me. "Like, if you go to New York and you get the best cabdriver in the city, you might get there thirty percent faster than with an average taxicab driver. A 2 to 1 gain would be pretty big. In software, it's at least 25 to 1. The difference between the average programmer and a great one is at least that. We have gone to exceptional lengths to hire the best people in the world. And when you're in a field where the dynamic range is 25 to 1, boy, does it pay off."

The hiring process at NeXT was rigorous, with multiple interviews. In many cases, even one interviewer's "No" could blackball a candidate. And there were candidates aplenty, vying for the chance to work with Steve. But of course, even at NeXT it wasn't possible to hire the best of the best without strong financial incentives. So Steve started making exceptions for certain hires. Some folks got extraordinary signing bonuses. Others were simply granted higher salaries than their category would mandate. And when these backdoor deals started to make their way onto that list in the finance department, well, all of a sudden that list became a lot harder to find.

Not only was the Open Corporation logistically and managerially unrealistic; it was emotionally out of synch with the reality of a Steve Jobs workplace. He would repeatedly undermine the vision of harmony, peace, and equality he had promised to foster with his irascible temper and anger and his penchant for using passive-aggressive methods to drive his people harder and harder. Steve was as erratic and verbally abusive at NeXT as he was anywhere else during his career. Moreover, he was an equal-opportunity abuser, yelling not only at his engineers but also at his executive team and his own personal administrative assistants on a regular basis.

His inner circle came to understand the pattern of his anger, but that didn't make it any easier. Tevanian did his best to protect his software engineers from the wrath of Jobs, by making sure they were away from the office when he informed Steve of a slip on schedule, or when a user interface feature he had ordered up turned out to be unworkable. Barnes, who had become familiar with Steve's unpredictable anger while at Apple, had clear strategies for herself and her employees. "If he'd get mad and start screaming, I'd hang up the phone. He is the only person I knew that you could hang up the phone on, and then pick it up and call him back and he'd be calmer. I mean, if you hung up the phone on me, I would kill you. But with him, if yelling isn't getting him what he wants, disengage. Leave the room and he will come back nicer, in a different way. I understood that this was something he could turn on and off, and that he would use if it worked." As for her staffers, she routinely told them to mentally plug their ears and try to "listen through the yelling." Explains Barnes: "You had to get through the yelling to the reason for the yelling—that was the important part, something you could try to fix."

———

THE SENSE OF urgency around the company ratcheted up as Jobs pressed everyone to prepare for the October 22, 1988, debut of the NeXT computer. Steve always relished putting on a show to unveil his digital creations, but he hadn't performed onstage since pulling the Macintosh out of the bag, like a rabbit out of a hat, back in 1984. Steve believed that these magic-act announcements not only were good salesmanship but also helped galvanize employees and energize a company that was weary after its Sisyphean struggle to ready the product for launch. His performances would grow more and more elaborate over the years, his stagecraft would show increasing sophistication, and the amount of groundwork involved would increase correspondingly, as well as the stress for anyone involved with staging the event. It was exhausting work, and afterward anyone who could do so would immediately head off on vacation.

Introducing the NeXT computer called for more sleight of hand than ever. The operating system, which was at least a year away from being released, was buggy. The optical storage drive ran too sluggishly for a demo. There were no apps written by outside software developers. With the possible exception of the iPhone nearly twenty years later, Steve would never unveil a product that was less ready for prime time. But he couldn't wait any longer. Steve needed the event to be a success. The halo of being "Steve Jobs's next great company" was wearing off; even potential like Steve's comes with an expiration date.

More than three thousand guests packed Davies Symphony Hall, the sleek modern home of the San Francisco Symphony Orchestra. Security was tight, and dozens of self-proclaimed VIPs were bluntly turned away. Inside, an exhibit of photography by folk rocker Graham Nash graced the curvilinear vestibules, hinting at the possibility of the presence of some real celebrities on the program.

Once audience members stepped into the concert hall they could see a giant video screen serving as a backdrop for the darkened stage. A tall table on the left held a large vase bursting with white French tulips and an array of remote controls. On the right side of the stage, shrouded in black velvet, was what appeared to be a phalanx of computer monitors on an elliptical table. Behind the desk chair facing them stood a pillar about four feet tall with another black velvet mantle draped over it.

The Evolution of a CEO

Steve Jobs and Steve Wozniak in 1979. The two had founded Apple four years earlier, and the company was growing like crazy. But the best years of their collaboration were already over. *Ted Thai/Polaris*

A 1979 gathering of the Seva Foundation, which Steve backed with a $5,000 donation. His close friend Larry Brilliant is at the center with his baby boy, Joseph; Brilliant's wife, Girija, is to the right, arms crossed and leaning back. Dr. Venkataswamy, the Indian opthamologist whose anti-blindness operations were funded by the group, stands to the left of Wavy Gravy, sitting and wearing the propeller hat. Ram Dass, author of the bestseller *Be Here Now*, is squatting at the far left. *Courtesy of the Seva Foundation*

Lee Clow, here with Steve at an advertising industry awards show that honored their triumphant "1984" Super Bowl ad introducing the Mac, was one of Steve's closest colleagues. Steve thought Chiat\Day's creative leader was a true genius. *Courtesy of Lee Clow*

Regis McKenna was Steve's most important early mentor. The marketing wizard helped craft Apple's indelible image. © *Roger Ressmeyer/Corbis*

The renegades who left Apple to start NeXT Computer: (back row) Rich Page, Steve, and George Crow; (front row) Dan'l Lewin, Bud Tribble, and Susan Barnes. "I definitely thought about the risk of going to work for him and leaving my job at Apple," says Lewin. "But I worried that if I didn't go to NeXT, I would have always said, 'Dammit, I should have gone along for the ride.'" © *Ed Kashi/VII/Corbis*

Avie Tevanian joined NeXT out of Carnegie Mellon University and worked for Steve for sixteen years, there and at Apple. At a party honoring him for his promotion to Chief Software Technical Officer in 2003, he was given a set of framed CDs of various pieces of software he had masterminded. Three years later, he left Apple. *Courtesy of Wen-Yu Chang*

Jon Rubinstein, known as "Ruby," also worked for Steve at NeXT and at Apple, overseeing hardware design and manufacture. Ruby was instrumental in helping Apple develop a faster metabolism for coming up with great new devices year after year. He and Steve celebrated at his 2001 wedding, which took place just ten days before the introduction of the iPod. *Courtesy of Jon Rubinstein*

Just a week before Steve's death, Eddy Cue helped introduce the iPhone 4S at an event on the Apple campus. "What I loved about working for Steve," says Cue, "is that you learned that you could accomplish the impossible. Again and again." *Courtesy of Kevork Djansezian/Getty Images*

Katie Cotton, Apple's longtime head of communications, coordinated the strategy of making Steve available to only a few select outlets and writers. *Courtesy of Brent Schlender*

In 2007, Steve visited a class taught by Andy Grove at Stanford University. Grove, the former CEO of Intel, was an important behind-the-scenes advisor. When Steve called in 1997 to ask if he should take the job as interim CEO of Apple, Grove growled, "Steve, I don't give a shit about Apple." *Courtesy of Denise Amantea*

Steve would lunch three or four times a week with his most important collaborator, Jony Ive. The design chief was on the CEO's wavelength, and Steve knew from the moment he met Jony that he was "a keeper." © *Art Streiber/AUGUST*

At the Academy Awards in 2005, the *Incredibles* gang from Pixar paused for a photo on the red carpet. John Lasseter is front and center, flanked by his wife, Nancy, and Steve's wife, Laurene. Director Brad Bird is at the far right, with his wife, Elizabeth Canney. Steve is in the back, with the goofy grin.

Watching Pixar president Ed Catmull, Steve absorbed a series of lessons about managing a creative corporation that became the foundation of his moderated behavior upon his return to Apple. © *Michael Macor/San Francisco Chronicle/Corbis*

In 2004, Steve swore he would never sell Pixar to Disney. But then Disney replaced Michael Eisner with a new CEO, Bob Iger. Iger, at right in 2005 when he and Steve announced that ABC programming would be available on the iTunes store for Apple's video iPods, worked slowly and carefully to wipe away years of mistrust between Disney and Pixar. He and Jobs eventually became close friends. Disney acquired Pixar in 2006. *Courtesy of the Walt Disney Company*

Tim Cook joined Apple in 1998, and eventually succeeded Steve as CEO. A quiet and intense Southerner, Cook became Steve's go-to guy for any particularly gnarly situation, and the two developed a keen friendship. Once, Steve called Cook's mother to encourage her to convince her son to start a family. © *Kimberly White/Corbis*

Steve's presentations were always carefully choreographed, none more so than the 2010 event where he introduced the iPad. The homey set conveyed the sense of how simple and intimate the device was supposed to be, but the leather loveseat was also a concession to Steve's frail health. © *Kimberly White/Corbis*

Befitting the venue, chamber music wafted through the sound system as the crowd settled in. It was a Tuesday morning, yet most of those in attendance were dressed as if they had arrived for a night at the symphony. (I even wore a suit.) That's just the way Steve wanted it.

The show was so extravagant a success that it really could have been considered NeXT's first major product. The crowd went silent as soon as Steve, clean-shaven and with his hair neatly trimmed, stepped into the spotlight. He was wearing a dapper, dark Italian suit, a blindingly white shirt, and a burgundy-and-black crosshatched tie. Pausing to soak it all in, he smiled with pursed lips, trying hard not to break into a toothy grin; the applause went on and on.

"It's great to be back," he said, after the clapping stopped completely. And then, pressing his hands together in a prayerful gesture, he launched into his comeback pitch. It would last two and a half hours. He had spent months polishing his remarks, which were given as more of a business school lecture than a sales spiel. Steve laid out the new taxonomy of the computer industry—a version of that taxonomy that made his new machine seem like the natural next grand step, of course. He did so using presentation slides that had been meticulously put together by hand, because no computer application yet existed to automate the process. Work on the slides had gone on and on; after days of trying to find the exact shade of green for one slide, Steve finally found a tone he liked and kept muttering, "Great green! Great green!" The phrase became a mantra for the beleaguered marketing team.

He explained how what he was now calling a "personal workstation" fit the needs of sophisticated computer users much better than the workstations that Sun and Apollo were selling for tens of thousands of dollars. While at Apple, he admitted, he had overlooked the significance of linking personal computers such as the Macintosh into networks. The NeXT computer was designed from the ground up to be connected to a network.

Computer scientists already knew this history, of course, but the broader public that was so fascinated with Jobs didn't. Steve had always been able to describe the potential of obscure yet real technologies with such aplomb that he created something akin to lust in his audience. He had absolute self-confidence that he could sell people a sense of discovery in the form of technological products they previously didn't even know they wanted, a confidence that was usually justified. When he held up the NeXT computer's innards and described it as "the most beautiful printed circuit board I've ever seen in my life," the audience gasped and then broke out into applause, despite the fact that at any distance over a few feet every circuit board looks pretty much the same. The audience even clapped when he described the Cube's ten-foot power cord. On this day, the crowd would follow wherever Steve would lead. When he called big universities "Fortune 500 companies disguised by another name," they even seemed to believe that this was true.

The tricky part of the show came when he had to explain that this radically new computer would have to make do with black-and-white and grayscale graphics, a cost-cutting decision (it saved NeXT $750 per machine) that had become unavoidable as Steve's persnickety meddling had delayed the machine and driven up its cost. No matter. Steve simply presented the screen as a magnificent design element. He bragged about the subtle shades of gray in a way that almost demeaned a color screen as an unnecessary extravagance. As the demo went on, Steve's claims became more grandiose, as if these NeXT machines might revolutionize the academics of not just science but the arts as well. Given all this potential, he suggested, it was remarkable that the NeXT computer would cost only $6,500; that its printer was priced at a mere $2,000; and that customers who wanted a conventional hard drive to augment the machine's storage capacity would pay just $2,000 more. Still, he couldn't completely conceal the reality that a fully functioning NeXT computer system would cost well over ten grand—some *seven thousand dollars* more than it was supposed to have.

Steve knew he had to end the show with something that would obscure this unfortunate detail, something that would bring the concert hall crowd to its feet. And that something was music. For the previous six weeks, he had pushed Tevanian, who had been with the company just a few months, to build a music synthesizer software application that could show off the Cube as a more multitalented computer than anything else around. Developing that music synthesizer capability was a tricky bit of programming, and one night, after weeks of effort, Tevanian finally figured out how to make it work. "Suddenly, this circuit board was producing sound! I thought, This is amazing!" Tevanian remembers. "It's eleven o'clock at night, though, and there is nobody there to show it to. So I run to the building next door, and lo and behold, Steve is still working. I said, 'Steve, I've got to show you something.' So we run back over to the engineering lab and I show him. And he just starts swearing at me. 'Why did you show this to me? I can't believe you did this!' he yells. And I say, 'Steve, you don't understand, it works!' And he says, 'I don't care, because it sounds horrible. I don't ever want to see anything like this again.'

"I learned a lot from that interaction," Tevanian adds. "Most people who work in a Steve Jobs organization end up quitting or being fired when that happens, but I just put my head down and thought, Okay, so there is a bar that you have to exceed before you can show it to him. I can show it to other people, but not to him."

At the very moment when the audience might have been expected to grow restless, Steve unveiled Tevanian's trick. He had the computer play gamelan music from Indonesia in a percussive demonstration of polyphonic sound generation. The audience sat rapt as amplified, synthesized music swelled to fill the hall. Steve, like a parent trying not to seem overly proud, broke into a taut smile. Nobody had heard anything quite like this come out of a computer. But that was just the warm-up act. Steve next invited Dan Kobialka, the concertmaster for the San Francisco Symphony, to perform a duet alongside the Cube on his violin. The selection was an excerpt from Bach's Violin Concerto in A Minor. Steve backed away and spotlights illuminated the two performers; for more than five minutes, Davies Symphony Hall seemed as intimate as a living room. When Kobialka lifted his bow at the end, the standing ovation was spontaneous. A third spotlight trained on Steve, who was holding a single rose as he bowed to the adoring throng.

Reactions to the premiere were as over-the-top as the event itself. Industry mavens like Stewart Alsop, Dick Shaffer, and Michael Murphy forecast that the machine would make NeXT a $200- to $300-million-a-year company by 1990. Shaffer called himself a "convert." Even leaving the pundits aside—after all, they were in the business of grandiose predictions—the more sober press accepted Steve's claims for his new machine. I called it "dazzling" myself in my front-page article for the *Wall Street Journal,* and even described it as "relatively inexpensive." As Steve had intended, I was comparing the machine to existing workstations, and not to the original price point he'd promised the universities that were supposed to be his key customers.

The truth that all of us missed was that this was a machine that had virtually no chance to succeed in the marketplace. Steve's mismanagement meant that the NeXT computer was only somewhat less expensive than most workstations, with just a few marginal improvements that didn't offset its many shortcomings. The principles on which NeXT had been based were in tatters, the goals of those long-gone off-site meetings trashed. Jobs had been told emphatically from the start that the machine should cost no more than $3,000; more recently, his collegiate advisers had told him that it should probably be priced at half that. Colleges were not about to spend $10,000 on a fully tricked-out NeXT computer system, versus $2,500 for a Mac or $5,000 for a low-end Sun workstation. The game was already over, but few of us knew it.

———

STEVE'S MOST IMPORTANT and direct competitors were not fooled by the glitzy debut. The folks at Sun Microsystems laughed off the introduction. CEO Scott McNealy, a brash Detroiter who played hockey in his spare time, thought that Steve's fancy fonts and magnesium case were wasted on the hard-core buyers of workstations. "We give them what they want," he told me, "and they don't really care how pretty the icons are."

If Steve had started NeXT with a clear mind and even an ounce of humility, Sun is the company he would have acknowledged as his most dangerous competitor—and potentially his best role model. McNealy, one of four cofounders who started the company in 1982, had become CEO in 1984. He was only three months older than Steve but seemed far more seasoned. His father had once been the CEO of American Motors, the now-defunct automaker that is remembered primarily for offbeat car models like the Nash Rambler and the AMC Pacer. At night, as a child, Scott would pore through his father's briefcase when he wasn't looking. As an adolescent, and later as a college student, he became what he called a "factory rat," spending time on the plant floor learning firsthand about the complexities of auto manufacturing, and about the dynamics of corporations that manage large numbers of people. A child of privilege, he went to Detroit's most prestigious private schools, and then on to Harvard for a business degree, finishing up with a Stanford MBA.

McNealy couldn't have been more different from Steve Jobs. Aside from his formal education, he was a rabid jock. He liked country music and heavy metal, not Dylan and the Beatles. McNealy was an irrepressible practical joker who was prone to shoot from the lip, but he managed his company with a maturity that Jobs only pretended to have. Sun had hit $1 billion in sales within four years. McNealy did it by smartly targeting a customer base that had money to spend—corporate R&D departments, the U.S. military, and the National Laboratories, a less glamorous but much more affluent set of customers than the universities Steve went after. Sun next went after Wall Street, which was just beginning to discover the power of using computers to identify quick trading opportunities. These customers didn't much care what the computers looked like, as long as they had big screens and could handle multiple computing threads simultaneously.

Sun succeeded by identifying the market's real need, by delivering just that product, and by keeping its machines reasonably affordable. NeXT failed at all of that. In fact, NeXT didn't actually sell its first computer until almost a year after that splashy debut in Davies Hall—four full years after Steve had started the company. McNealy was focused, budget conscious, and opportunistic. Steve's goals were muddled, and he was a spendthrift who was slow off the mark. McNealy had thrown in with his cofounders at Sun to sell a lot of machines, serve his customers, and make a lot of money. Steve had founded NeXT because he was furious at John Sculley and Apple, because he desperately needed a second act, and because he thought it was his responsibility—and birthright—to keep astounding the world. There had been a market to be attacked when Steve founded NeXT; McNealy's success proved it. But Steve was still young and immature, and didn't think there was anyone else in the computer business who really mattered. He was looking in the mirror while McNealy had been looking out the window to learn what the world really needed.

Another industry leader was equally unimpressed by NeXT. Bill Gates refused to develop software for the NeXT computer, despite Steve's repeated, if confused, efforts to lure him in with promises that Microsoft would profit as much with NeXT as it had with the Mac (for years, Microsoft had been the Mac's leading applications developer). When Bill first visited Steve in Palo Alto to see what Jobs was putting together at NeXT, Steve left him stewing in the lobby for half an hour before coming to get him. It was a spiteful beginning to what would turn out to be a nonexistent relationship between Microsoft and NeXT. Gates rebuffed Steve again and again and again, with venom. "Develop for it?" he told *InfoWorld*. "I'll piss on it." Microsoft software was already on its way to defining the industry standard in nearly all aspects of computing, so Gates's reluctance to support NeXT with custom versions of its application software effectively marginalized the company.

Gates didn't let up after the Davies Hall showcase. "In the grand scope of things," he said, "most of these features are truly trivial." A year later, he said of the NeXT computer, "If you want black, I'll get you a can of paint." To this day Gates remembers the moment he definitively told Jobs that Microsoft absolutely would not develop software for NeXT. "He wasn't livid," Gates told me recently. "He was deflated. He was at a loss for words, which wasn't typical. He knew what I was saying might be right. And it wasn't a particularly pretty picture in terms of what it meant for big black cubes changing the world."

———

TOWARD THE END of the show at Davies Hall, Steve Jobs revealed what should have been the biggest news to come out of the event: computer industry colossus IBM had decided to license the NeXTSTEP operating system for use on a line of its own engineering workstations. The vision of the world's biggest computer company running Steve's revolutionary operating system seemed a great endorsement.

The basic agreement between the companies was that IBM would license the right to use the NeXTSTEP operating system as a graphical interface in return for $60 million—a pittance for IBM, but critical operating capital for NeXT, which was burning through its investors' cash as the years dragged on. Many people believed that the arrangement might have broader implications, an impression that Steve did nothing to dispel. IBM had an existing deal with Microsoft to jointly develop a new operating system for future PCs called OS/2. By announcing the deal with NeXT, IBM seemed to be indicating that it was not comfortable with Microsoft as its sole key partner. (Indeed, within a few months of the NeXT announcement, it became clear that IBM and Microsoft were having serious issues working together.) The tantalizing possibility was that Steve's operating system might eventually power not only workstations but also the personal computers of Apple's most feared competitor. If that ever happened, Steve's comeback would be complete.

But Steve never seemed to quite know how to play his cards with IBM. He displayed an unsettled and juvenile mix of hubris and uncertainty. Jobs could be bold and strong, as when he secured IBM's promised investment before any Big Blue exec had even laid eyes on the NeXTSTEP operating system. But he could also be just plain rude: Walking in late to one meeting with a suite of IBMers who had flown out to NeXT, Steve interrupted the proceedings with the dismissive pronouncement: "Your UI [user interface] sucks." Dan'l Lewin, who would meet with Steve to carefully plot their strategy before every IBM meeting, never knew what to expect from his boss. Sometimes Steve would completely undermine the groundwork the two had carefully laid. "I'd sit there and literally kick him under the table," Lewin recalls. "There was one meeting, for example, where he went in and actually told them, 'I really don't understand why you guys would want to help us.'"

Psychologically and emotionally, signing on with IBM was every bit as complicated for Steve as begging Bill Gates to support his computer. Steve had always envisioned NeXTSTEP as the backbone of his own spectacular computer. He wanted to be the hero, not a secondary partner to a more powerful computer company. If IBM had exploited his operating system, and sold a lot of computers running their version of NeXTSTEP, the glory would have been theirs, not his.

It shouldn't have been surprising, then, that Steve failed to make this important relationship work. He killed the IBM deal by failing to follow through as a good business partner. IBM's Bill Lowe, a veteran who had been instrumental in launching the PC back in 1981, had initiated the deal. But Lowe retired in 1990, and James Cannavino replaced him. Cannavino logically assumed IBM could use NeXT's 2.0 version of NeXTSTEP on its machines. But Steve, who hadn't even met Cannavino, held up IBM for more money, leading to another round of protracted negotiations. He overplayed his hand. Cannavino stopped taking Steve's calls and just abandoned the project, although there was never any real announcement that it was over. It was a minor disappointment for IBM, ending its "Plan B" fantasy of creating a real alternative to Microsoft's new Windows graphical operating system for PCs. But it was a fatal blow to NeXT, ending its last real chance to achieve the kind of scale that would have turned it into, as Steve had said in 1985, "the world's next great computer company."

Lewin quit NeXT in frustration months before the IBM deal dissolved. He was the first of the five original employees to leave NeXT. "We owned the world when we were at NeXT. And it failed because of Steve," Lewin remembers. Steve invited Lewin to lunch two weeks after his resignation. "Well, now that you're leaving, what do you *really* think?" Steve asked him.

"You're going to go through every penny, the way you're headed," said the now former head of sales. At the time NeXT still had some $120 million in cash. "This company is just not going to happen. You may own 51 percent of it, or 58, whatever it is, but more than half the company worked for me. And I've been fighting with you because I believe in what I know we need to do to run this business. If you want to succeed, you need to listen to your people. Otherwise you're doomed."

A few months later, George Crow, another cofounder, left, tired of bearing the brunt of Steve's furor for the delays in hardware development. Susan Barnes left around the same time in 1991. Managing Steve's finances when he had little fiscal discipline and no checks on his spendthrift ways had grown wearying. "It was classic: his visionary optimism versus my reality," says Barnes. "He always felt that we were going to turn the next corner. And I would always tell him that there was nothing in the business model to indicate that that was so."

When Barnes resigned, Steve immediately and without warning cut off her phone and email access. A year later, Rich Page quit the company, and Barnes's husband, Bud Tribble, picked up the phone to ask Scott McNealy at Sun if he could use a highly seasoned software engineer. A few days later Tribble went to work for the company that was everything NeXT should have been. Just six years after those heady brainstorming days at the old Woodside house, the renegades had all departed, leaving their rock star behind.

During that strange and heady autumn of 1985, just after he had bolted from Apple to go start NeXT, Steve found that there was one other intriguing opportunity he couldn't get out of his mind. His thoughts kept returning to the Lucasfilm Graphics Group, the team of engineering whizzes that he'd tried to convince Apple to buy back in the spring. The outfit had the kind of cutting-edge technology in search of a broader purpose that Steve loved. It was cool: its software tools had helped Lucas's Industrial Light & Magic division create special effects for other studios' movies, including *Star Trek II: The Wrath of Khan* and *Young Sherlock Holmes*. It had wide commercial potential, he believed: the outfit's astounding technology for manipulating three-dimensional images might be perfect for the hospitals, corporations, and universities he was targeting at NeXT. It might even be transformative. Looking way down the road, he could imagine the inexorable force of Moore's law driving down the cost of processing power to the point where everyday users could easily manipulate 3-D images. And there was one other thing that seemed really "neat," to use an adjective that Steve quite liked: its people. "He wanted to keep that group together," says Susan Barnes. "To Steve, it was really hard to see this great integrated team under the threat of getting blown up. It was really hard to think about that natural set of huge intellectual energy going away." So Steve decided he'd go back to Marin County and visit the place again. It was a decision that changed his life. But not in any way he had anticipated.

George Lucas, who needed to take care of an expensive divorce settlement, had decided the Graphics Group was a luxury he could sell without hurting his movies. But he wanted tens of millions of dollars for the group, and Jobs wasn't willing to pay more than $5 million. Steve found Lucas to be a tough negotiator. For starters, he didn't handle the discussions himself; he left it to those under him to talk to Steve and his bankers, adding a layer of delay to the process. And Lucas was courting a range of other potential buyers at the same time, including Siemens, Hallmark, General Motors' EDS division, and Philips. But as one deal after another fell through, the balance of power tilted toward Steve, who didn't need the group as much as Lucas needed the money. So he was perfectly willing to play tough himself. "At one point," says Barnes, who helped with the negotiations, "the delays went on forever and he just went and told one of their executives to 'fuck off.' One of the Lucas team said, 'You can't say that to one of our EVPs.' 'Yes I can,' he replied. 'And fuck you, too.'"

As he would show again and again through his life, Steve was a ballsy negotiator. His willingness to walk away paid off. Faced with getting nothing, the Lucas team caved. Steve paid $5 million in cash while promising to capitalize the outfit with another $5 million. Steve told *BusinessWeek* that buying Pixar was an effort to enter an industry (3-D computer graphics) that "has the same flavor as the personal computer industry in 1978." According to Ed Catmull, the Graphics Group leader who became president of Pixar, "He saw Pixar as the core of NeXT."

As it turned out, Steve was right about the importance of Pixar's pioneering technology. Over the next decade the ability to manipulate 3-D images would transform everything from flight planning and oil exploration to medical practice, meteorology, and financial analysis. Unfortunately for Steve, the people doing that work would employ sophisticated workstations manufactured by Sun Microsystems and Silicon Graphics, not by Pixar or NeXT.

And yet Pixar eventually became a revolutionary success. This unlikely side bet turned into the place where Steve would learn more about the consumer technology business than he had at Apple or would at NeXT. At Pixar he would lay the foundation of two of his great strengths: his ability to fight back in times of distress, and his ability to make the most of an innovation that put him ahead of anyone else in that field. In other words, it taught him how to keep his head and fight back when cornered, and how to run like the wind in the open field. And it became the place where he really learned, albeit slowly and reluctantly and against his natural instincts, that sometimes the best management technique is to forgo micromanagement and give good, talented people the room they need to succeed.

What Steve didn't know in 1986 was that Pixar would give him something much more valuable than a technology to squeeze into NeXT. Although it would take almost a decade, Steve's Pixar adventure would help him rediscover his self-respect, make him a billionaire, and align him with people who would teach him more about management than anyone he'd ever worked with. Without the lessons he learned at Pixar, there would have been no great second act at Apple.

————

PIXAR WAS ONE of the most unusual collections of artistically inclined computer scientists ever assembled. The core of the group had first come together at a Long Island institution called the New York Institute of Technology. NYIT's founder, Alexander Schure, was a peculiar millionaire and an iconoclastic educator. His institution offered an array of courses to both returning veterans and students looking to get out of service in Vietnam. But Schure's real dream was to create an animation studio to rival Disney, despite the fact that his qualifications to do anything of the kind were questionable at best. His one effort at moviemaking, a self-financed film called *Tubby the Tuba,* was a fiasco. Still, in the late 1970s Schure was just about the only person who was putting money into the work of computer graphics specialists, so the pioneers in that field started to descend on NYIT. Schure assembled a remarkable team, including Jim Clark, who would later found Silicon Graphics and Netscape Communications; Lance Williams, who went on to become chief scientist at Walt Disney Animation Studios; and Ed Catmull, Ralph Guggenheim, and Alvy Ray Smith, who would all became key figures at Pixar.

Although Schure assembled the team, he didn't really manage it, which of course was ideal for a group of self-confident academic researchers who needed time and equipment to develop their revolutionary ideas. Working from a large converted garage on a great estate on Long Island's North Shore—*Great Gatsby* territory—the team tackled anything involving computers and 3-D graphics, ranging from virtual reality headsets to texture mapping (a critical foundation for getting sophisticated detail into computer-generated graphics) to exploring the possibility of creating anthropomorphized characters out of mundane objects for television commercials. Ralph Guggenheim, who eventually headed up the film division of Pixar, once called it "a great fraternity of geeks." From day one, they all shared the dream of creating a full-length computer-animated motion picture. So when a George Lucas rep called Guggenheim to see if he'd be interested in helping to form a division of Lucasfilm to help the *Star Wars* director introduce computer graphics into his movies, the team jumped—all the way to San Rafael, California, a Marin County city across the bay from San Francisco that is best known as the locale of the San Quentin State Prison. The new unit was called the Graphics Group, and its mandate was to invent software tools that would help Lucas create his bold, visually explosive films.

As he had in Long Island, Ed Catmull headed up the team. Catmull was a Utah-raised computer scientist who had once hoped to be an animator himself. But he had made a calculated decision that he wasn't sufficiently talented at drawing to succeed. Instead, he had become an expert in the new field of computer graphics at the University of Utah in Salt Lake City before joining NYIT.

More important for Steve Jobs, overseeing this motley crew had turned Catmull into an expert, imaginative manager of creative people. For years Catmull found himself occasionally regretting his decision to abandon his dream of being an animator. But as he steered this odd and talented group past one crisis after another, he started treating management itself as a kind of art, and accepted that this was how he could best contribute. Later in his life, he would come to be recognized as one of the most extraordinary managers in the world; in 2014, he published a brilliant business bestseller, *Creativity, Inc.,* about what it takes to lead a company of creative people. In fact, this quiet, bearded man with a measured, professorial demeanor knows more about managing and motivating creative people than anyone I've ever met, including Sony's Akio Morita, Intel's Andy Grove, Bill Gates, Jeffrey Katzenberg, and Southwest Airlines' Herb Kelleher, among others. His success would prove a powerful example for Steve.

Like Schure, Lucas mostly left the group alone. In the early 1980s he was at the peak of his career, building out Skywalker Ranch, the nerve center of his film empire, in the remote wine and dairy country north of San Rafael that is known, coincidentally, as Lucas Valley. He was absorbed with making the second and third *Star Wars* movies and the first couple of *Indiana Jones* features. Catmull's group developed hardware and software tools that sped up and reduced the cost of certain kinds of animated special effects. But they remained committed to the idea of using computers to create an animated feature movie. With an eye to that, Catmull wooed John Lasseter, then a young and frustrated Disney animator, to create a series of animated short films that could show the potential of 3-D computer graphics. Knowing that Lucas wanted the team focused on tools, not on creating movies of its own, Catmull disguised Lasseter's hire so that he appeared on the budget as an "interface designer." "He knew none of the financial guys would want to embarrass themselves by asking, 'What's that?'" says Lasseter.

The short movies, some of which were no longer than thirty seconds, were screened at the annual computer imaging convention, SIG-GRAPH, where they served as superb advertisements for the group. Brilliant pieces like *The Adventures of Andre and Wally B.* and *Luxo Jr.* made clear that Lucas's group had startling technology; they also made clear that Lasseter had a rare gift for storytelling, anthropomorphizing everyday objects such as the Luxo Jr., the pint-sized articulating desk lamp that eventually made its way into the company's onscreen logo.

Amply funded and consistently ignored, the group developed a close bond. Catmull ran the organization in a highly collegial, non-bureaucratic manner. When Lucas decided to sell the division, Catmull made every effort he could to find a buyer who would keep the group together. Lasseter was being heavily recruited by Disney's Jeffrey Katzenberg, who had seen his short movies and come to regret letting such a talent get away. But the culture Catmull had created was so appealing that Lasseter, like most of the other employees, wanted to stay put.

———

AFTER STEVE COMPLETED the deal to buy what was now to be known as Pixar, he walked into a situation that was unlike any he would encounter again. At Apple he had been the brash novice, the founder who, for better and worse, established the corporate culture. At NeXT, too, Jobs was the center of attention, the hub and visionary of the company. But at Pixar, Steve couldn't shape the culture. He wasn't the founder, and even as owner, he could not change the company to reflect his image and sensibilities. It already had a culture. It already had a leader. Its cohesive and collaborative team knew exactly what it wanted to do. And Catmull was not about to let his young new owner mess things up.

Catmull knew about Jobs's reputation as a difficult micromanager. In fact, he at first resisted having Lucas sell the group to Steve, despite having enjoyed a very pleasant visit at Steve's Woodside house in the fall of 1985. After the purchase went through, he started observing Steve calmly, albeit warily. Having dealt with the idiosyncrasies of Schure and Lucas, he knew that managing a third sugar daddy was possible. He also knew it would have its own challenges. Over time, he became perhaps the keenest observer of Steve Jobs, developing an understanding of his boss that allowed him, in turn, to become one of Steve's most valuable mentors.

He quickly homed in on both Steve's potential and his immaturity. "He was smart. God, he was smart!" says Catmull. "You couldn't prep for Steve, because he's too smart. So I'd just go, 'Here's what the problem is,' and I'd never tell him what to think." He could see that Jobs had an innate comfort with the public demands of a big business. "When I would watch him in the room with powerful people, it was clear that there was an immediate match between them. They could talk and work things out in a way that was actually very different. Steve knew how to deal with powerful people."

The flip side was a callowness and open disrespect that ignited suddenly. "Early on, Steve didn't know how to deal with people who didn't have power, almost as if he couldn't 'get' them. When people would come into the room," Catmull remembers, "Steve would quickly make an assessment as to whether or not they were a bozo. And that was not hidden from them. He would say outrageous things, as a way of taking the measure of the room. And the meanness was that if somebody didn't measure up, then he wouldn't hide it. He didn't do it to me, but I witnessed it with other people. Clearly, that wasn't appropriate behavior."

Still, Catmull saw potential for change. "There were times where the reaction against Steve baffled him," he says. "I remember him sometimes saying to me, 'Why are they upset?' What that said to me was that he didn't intend to get that outcome. It was a lack of skill, as opposed to meanness."

Catmull and Alvy Ray Smith, another cofounder, developed a strategy for keeping their new boss satisfied but mostly out of the picture. Perhaps the most important tactic was to keep Jobs at a physical distance. Pixar retained its small offices in San Rafael, a good hour-and-a-half drive away from NeXT headquarters in Silicon Valley. On most Monday mornings, Catmull, joined sometimes by Smith, would make the trek across the Golden Gate Bridge and down the Peninsula to update Jobs. The arrangement suited Steve fine, since he found the trip north annoyingly full of traffic. Catmull would always come primed with an agenda, but Steve would steer the meetings in whatever direction suited his fancy. He kept pushing Catmull to think of Pixar's technology as rarefied hardware and software tools that could be commercialized and sold at a high price. One of the first things he convinced the team to do was to create what would be called the Pixar Image Computer, which wasn't really a computer, but a special graphics processor that plugged into an engineering workstation. He even got involved with its design, insisting that it be a cube. Only this cube would be painted in a faux granite finish.

The Pixarians appreciated his enthusiasm, but Catmull and Smith would often leave the meetings thinking that Steve really didn't understand their company. "Steve actually didn't know anything about our business, and he didn't even know how to run a small business," Catmull reflects. "He knew something about running a consumer products company, but early on he actually had nothing of value to say [about Pixar], and a lot of his advice to us turns out to have been bad advice. Not that we knew any better." They couldn't share his optimism for consumer applications for their remarkable technology. Having worked on 3-D imaging for so long, they understood how hard it was, and accepted the fact that it occupied a highly specialized niche of the market. Furthermore, they didn't share Steve's goal. The one and only reason they sold software and hardware imaging tools was to stay in business until they could finally create a computer-animated film. Steve would claim later in his life that he had always believed that Pixar would eventually create great content, but that just wasn't the case. His goal was to have Pixar become a successful computer company, ideally one that complemented NeXT.

Even the most sophisticated business strategist would have had a tough time turning Pixar into a self-supporting technology business. And in the late 1980s, Steve Jobs was a long way from being a sophisticated businessman. His ideas for Pixar truly were of little or no help at all. One example: Steve decided the company should expand its reach by going after the hospital market, which was awash in high-resolution images like X-rays. The company added a big sales staff to court the medical world, and even entered into a contract with the Dutch manufacturer Philips, which said it would use its own network to place the machines in hospitals. But the Pixar Image Computer cost an exorbitant $135,000—and even at that price required a connection to a high-end Sun workstation, which could cost another $35,000 or so. (NeXT wasn't yet selling its workstations.) Pixar's lead customer was Disney, which bought a slew of the machines as well as a Pixar software application called CAPS, which enabled the animation giant to manage the storage of its animators' hand-drawn cels and track their progress. Disney was happy with the technology, but the high-end Pixar system was too expensive and too difficult to program for more practical, industrial uses.

Alvy Ray Smith, the Pixar cofounder who could be as brash as Steve, did little to hide his disdain for many of Steve's wild ideas. Alvy Ray, a voluble guy from Mineral Wells, Texas, had forgotten more about computer graphics than Steve would ever know, and listening to Steve opine on this or that grand strategy wore on his patience. Inevitably, their relationship came to a crashing end. Like alpha boys on a playground, the two clashed over who had the right to use a whiteboard during a board meeting, leading to a ridiculous bout of name-calling. Though Steve tried to apologize to Smith, Smith had had enough. He quit shortly thereafter to start his own company and eventually wound up as a research fellow for Microsoft.

The company also sold a professional software application called RenderMan, which allowed computer graphics artists to apply textures and colors to the surfaces of computer-generated 3-D objects onscreen with a level of sharpness and resolution that could be blended into conventional film images. As with everything Pixar did, it was top-of-the-line software. Steven Spielberg's techies used RenderMan (on Silicon Graphics workstations) to create the scaly skin and ivory teeth of *Jurassic Park*'s frightening dinosaurs. RenderMan played a key role in the budding field of 3-D computer graphics imaging, helping to enhance movies like *The Abyss, Terminator II,* and *Alien III,* along with Disney's *Aladdin, Beauty and the Beast,* and *The Lion King.* Pixar even released a version that would run on Macintosh computers. But as cool as the software was, it never came close to making Pixar self-sustainable.

———

BY 1990, THERE seemed very little reason for Pixar to continue to exist as a business. Steve Jobs was anything but a tycoon. The stock he sold after leaving Apple had been worth $70 million, and he had made some successful investments. But after several years of funding Pixar and NeXT, only a fraction of that fortune remained. Pixar's revenues were stagnant, and Steve was writing one check after another to keep the thing afloat. The world's most famous computer entrepreneur was in danger of drifting into the middling obscurity that has enveloped so many other one-hit wonders of the technology world. Shutting down this expensive side project would have made enormous sense. And yet Steve persisted.

He had idiosyncratic reasons for doing so. The easiest to understand is that he desperately did not want to admit to having failed. After his ignominious departure from Apple, and in the absence of a tangible success at NeXT, Steve was basically keeping his reputation alive with announcements of milestones that weren't really milestones. The first kind were the "just around the corner" proclamations, alerting the world to the imminent arrival of something sure to be insanely great, like NeXT's first NeXTcube computer. The second were the "seal of approval" kind, announcing the endorsement of a significant backer, the purchase of a computer or some software by a notable company, or, in the case of Pixar, an award for graphics excellence.

But announcements alone couldn't stave off reality forever, and the Steve Jobs story was starting to shift from his past successes to his present failures. Closing Pixar would have only accelerated that story. At a moment when his business life was in worse shape than ever, Steve simply couldn't risk making things worse by shuttering Pixar. "Steve once told us he had nothing to prove when he started NeXT," Catmull recalls. "Now I don't believe that for a second. We knew he had everything to prove with NeXT. We were the only other gamble he took, and he said we turned out to be such a handful to begin with, that he stopped taking any other gambles beyond those."

Steve's main reason for keeping Pixar alive was that he still believed in this little band of geniuses and their leaders. The business seemed to be going nowhere, but Steve still deeply respected Catmull and Lasseter. He had great admiration for Catmull's business and management expertise. And Lasseter? Well, Lasseter was one of those rare geniuses who can always make life seem grander and full of possibilities.

"Steve dealt mostly with Ed," Lasseter remembers, "because they did the business stuff, and I was just the animator in another building. My first real interaction with Steve was SIGGRAPH in 1986. It was in Dallas, at the beginning of August, and hotter than can be. The film show at SIGGRAPH was like a rock concert. People started lining up six hours in advance. And you do not cut those lines because people get really mad. But Steve and his girlfriend come up, and he says, 'Hey, John, do we really have to stand in line?' So I talk my way through to the guard, and basically made up something about why I had to get Steve Jobs and his girlfriend in before anyone else. The guard let us through, just before the flood of people.

"Before this moment, Steve's tangible moments of success were things like showing up at a school and seeing a whole lab filled with his computers. This was different. It had the feel of a big rock concert, an arena rock concert.

"The show goes on, and people are going nuts over, like, crystal balls bouncing on the screen. It was all tech stuff. Nothing with a story. And then all of a sudden, our little *Luxo Jr.* comes up. You know, the little hopping lamp. It's only a minute and a half long, but even before the thing is over, people are cheering. That moment is remembered as significant in computer graphics history because it was the first time a 3-D computer-animated film entertained audiences with its story and characters, not the mere fact of being made with a computer. It got a standing ovation before it was done. The crowd knew they had seen something brand new.

"And Steve turned to me with these big eyes," Lasseter continues, his own eyes bulging, "like, 'This is *great*! Wow! I like *this*!' Getting that immediate response from an audience was something he had never experienced. The bug had bitten him, and he was like, 'I love this.' It bonded us. And then, that I had the balls to cut in front of this line of six thousand people who would skin you alive! It changed our relationship from that moment on."

"*Luxo Jr.* was the breakthrough," Steve told me many years later. If Steve ever was starstruck, it was by Lasseter, whose artistry seemed to be irrefutable evidence of what Steve believed to be the most important attribute of computers: that they were tools that could unleash and enhance human creativity. Despite his boyish ways (his office is stuffed with so many toys it could double as a Pixar museum, and his wardrobe consists exclusively of blue jeans and hundreds of loud, Hawaiian-style print shirts), Lasseter was a confident grown-up, and not persnickety in any way. While he never looked to Steve for creative advice on his short features, he calmly listened to his boss's opinions, before going ahead with his own plans anyway. But he made compromises when needed, too, rather than insisting on perfection: when he couldn't prepare a polished version of a short called *Tin Toy* in time for SIGGRAPH, he simply showed what he could and filled in the rest with line drawings.

Lasseter lived in constant fear that Steve would shutter his little animation group. Even as he kept writing checks to fund Pixar, Steve regularly slashed budgets and froze salaries: "I think I made the same salary from '84 to '89," Lasseter remembers. "And I thought for sure that they'd get rid of Animation. At one point they were contemplating a layoff in Hardware, I think, and there were lots of complaints like, 'What about Animation? They don't do anything to bring in the money.' So I asked the head of Software, a guy named Mickey Mantle, like the baseball player, 'When's the shoe gonna drop, really? When will they just close Animation?' And he said, 'John, they never will.'

"'What do you mean?' I asked him," continues Lasseter. "And Mickey said, 'Computer hardware and software companies, they go through layoffs and it's business. It's the ups and downs of the business. But when people think of Pixar, it's not our computers or our software. They think of those little short films you've made. That's the identity of Pixar to the rest of the world. So if Pixar were to stop making those films and lay everybody off in Animation, that would signal to the entire world that Pixar is done. That,' he said, 'is why they're not gonna close Animation.'"

It didn't hurt, of course, that Lasseter's team was earning greater and greater awards. When Lasseter had gone to Steve to get approval for the budget on the short called *Tin Toy,* Steve's response had been "Just make it great." The one-and-a-half-minute-long piece, featuring a wind-up mechanical tin drummer who lives in fear of a slobbering infant who likes to throw toys around, turned out to be great indeed: at the Academy Awards ceremony in Los Angeles on March 29, 1989, *Tin Toy* won the Oscar for Best Short Animated Film. Shortly afterward, Steve took everyone who had worked on *Tin Toy* to dinner at Greens, a famous vegetarian restaurant in San Francisco.

"He was so proud," Lasseter said. "I remember grabbing the Oscar and putting it right in front of him. 'You asked me to make it great,' I told him. 'There you go.' That was the dinner where Nancy and I met Laurene—she and Steve had started dating a few months earlier. We just loved being with the two of them that night, because Steve was so clearly in love. He had his arm around Laurene all night and . . . he was so happy, so giddily happy, so full of that feeling like everything is champagne bubbles in your life, just effervescent. He was so excited. He had won an Oscar, and here was this marvelous woman."

———

LOOKING BACK, 1989 stands out as the year when the confusion of Steve's mad, youthful rush started to clear, even though his business problems wouldn't evaporate anytime soon. Having Pixar win that Oscar was something legitimate he could brag about in his work life. But the main bounce came from meeting his wife-to-be. Steve first saw Laurene during a lecture he gave at the Stanford Business School, where she was getting her MBA. "She was right there in the front row in the lecture hall, and I couldn't take my eyes off of her," he told me not long afterward. "I kept losing my train of thought, and started feeling a little giddy." He tracked her down in the parking lot, and asked her to dinner. They went out that very night. And with the exception of Steve's rare business trips, they were together pretty much every day of the rest of his life.

They were a good match from the start. Laurene's father had died when she was quite young. Like Steve, she was raised in the middle class, in her case in the town of West Milford, New Jersey, where, like Steve, she learned to fend for herself. Laurene got herself into first-rate schools: the University of Pennsylvania, and later, Stanford's B-school. She was intelligent and well-spoken and very athletic; an avid reader with eclectic interests in literature and the arts, nutrition, politics, and philosophy; and unlike Steve, she followed professional sports. After college she had tried the world of high finance in Manhattan, but it didn't interest her enough; she left Goldman Sachs after a couple of years and entered business school as a way of figuring out what she would do next.

Steve had had serious relationships with several girlfriends by then, including the singer Joan Baez and Chrisann Brennan. But Laurene, who was willowy with a California girl's blond hair and piercing eyes, had a depth of character that touched him in a whole new way. Some of the women he had dated came to seem needy over time; Laurene wasn't that way. She brought as much self-sufficiency to the relationship as he did. And she wasn't interested in his wealth, or in the kind of dazzling social life that was available to him if he wanted it. They both accepted the value of hard work, which made it easier for Laurene to handle Steve's long hours. And their middle-class connection would become increasingly important: when they eventually had a family, Steve and Laurene would do everything in their power to raise their kids with as normal values as they could, despite their growing wealth.

Their relationship burned intensely from the beginning, as you might expect from the pairing of two such strong-willed individuals. But eventually Steve got over his bachelor's anxiety and proposed to Laurene on New Year's Day of 1990, clutching "a fistful of freshly picked wildflowers," as she would say at his memorial service, just twenty-one years later. She took Steve seriously, that morning and in the years to come, when she learned about Buddhism, reading the books that influenced Steve as a young spiritual seeker. Indeed, Kobun Chino Otogawa, the Zen Buddhist monk who served as Steve's guru for many years, would preside at their wedding. They got married at the Ahwahnee lodge, in Yosemite National Park, on March 18, 1991. She was pregnant with their first child, Reed, who was born that September.

———

IT TURNED OUT that Mickey Mantle was right: Lasseter didn't have to worry about his own division. Steve was indeed, to use Lasseter's word, "bit." So when Steve decided to cut his losses at Pixar, he didn't abandon the company completely. Instead, he unloaded the company's hardware division for $2 million, and decided to focus on software and animation instead. By early 1991, Steve had cut the staff from 120 people down to 42—laying off all those sales folks he had insisted on hiring, and retrenching back to almost exactly the number of people who were working there when he first acquired the outfit in 1986.

It was a wrenching, difficult period. Steve's continued funding came at a price, as he bought back employees' restricted stock grants for very little money, robbing the employees who were left of their primary long-term financial incentive. Steve later tried to paint this period as a glorious turning point, a moment where passion won out over the dreary reality of Pixar's dismal computer sales. "I got everybody together," he told me, "and I said, 'At our heart, we really are a content company. Let's transition out of everything else. Let's go for it. This is why I bought into Pixar. This is why most of you are here. Let's go for it. It's a higher-risk strategy, but the rewards are gonna be much higher, and it's where our hearts are.'" The pep talk did occur, but while some employees felt inspired, most saw that his words glossed over the reality of what had happened, and what was required to turn the company around. Catmull, who like Lasseter was stripped of most of his equity stake in the company, told me that this period was anything but exhilarating: "It was one of the hardest things in my life." By this time, Steve had invested close to $50 million in Pixar.

Slashed by two-thirds, the company was now dependent on three sources of revenue: the CAPS image management system it licensed to Disney; RenderMan, which was now offered in a new version that would allow Macs to create 3-D images; and advertising, a new revenue stream that the animation team had introduced. Pixar was able to sign up a few clients on Madison Avenue, like Listerine, Trident, Tropicana, and Volkswagen. As dreamed up by Lasseter and other animators like Andrew Stanton (who would eventually direct *A Bug's Life*), Pixar's ads for these clients were kooky and lively. They showed off the company's unique ability to anthropomorphize objects like a dancing stick of gum or a bouncing orange, and they forced the animators to adhere to budgets and deadlines, "a discipline that we needed to develop," says Catmull. Combined with Lasseter's increasingly sophisticated short films, they showed that the company was getting closer to having the technical and storytelling chops to realize its dream of producing a full-length film. But Pixar still had nowhere near the revenue it needed to sustain itself.

And then, just around this time, Peter Schneider, the president of Walt Disney Features Animation, came calling on John Lasseter. For the third time in three years, he tried to hire Lasseter away from Pixar. Lasseter wouldn't go. "I was living in the San Francisco Bay Area," he remembers. "I was inventing new stuff. I figured I'd just stay on here. I'd had a pretty miserable experience at Disney." He told Schneider that there was only one way that he'd consider working with Disney—the studio would have to make a movie with Pixar.

Chapter 6
Bill Gates Pays a Visit

I n the early afternoon of July 21, 1991, five people converged on Steve Jobs's house in Palo Alto. It was an unusually warm summer Sunday; the temperature had soared well into the nineties, and judging from the stuffy atmosphere inside, it didn't seem that Steve had gotten around to turning on the air-conditioning. He had dashed back from a weekend Yosemite getaway with Laurene at the Ahwahnee lodge, the same rustic inn where the two had been married a few months prior.

Steve had only recently purchased the house. Neither he nor Laurene was interested in raising a family in a rambling, crumbling mansion isolated in the hills of Woodside. They wanted their children to grow up in a more central location, and Old Palo Alto, as the neighborhood was known, was quiet, shady, and within walking distance of schools and downtown. Also, Steve's first child, Lisa—now a teenager—lived nearby with her mother. The house featured enormous wooden beams that had been used as forms for concrete work on the Golden Gate Bridge, yet it was anything but ostentatious, at least by

Bay Area standards. (John Lasseter puckishly calls it the "Hansel and Gretel" house.) Steve would call this home for the rest of his life.

Steve and Laurene made a few additions and modifications over the years but nothing really radical, and eventually they acquired an adjoining lot in order to expand the vegetable and flower garden that they both tended. The garden was just getting started that July, but already it was teeming with tomatoes, sunflowers, string beans, cauliflower, basil, and an assortment of lettuces. They had planted wild grasses native to Northern California around the perimeter of the property, which faced intersecting streets on two sides. Some neighbors grumbled at first, but most came to appreciate the way the color and character of the vegetation would change with the seasons. In spring the plantings would explode with wildflowers, and in summer the untrimmed clumps of grass would shimmer in the wind. There was no security wall, just a short split-rail fence bordering the sidewalk. There wasn't even a garage. Steve and Laurene rarely used the big wooden front door of the house. Most visitors would park on the street behind Steve's Porsche or Mercedes, enter the gate by the garden, and knock on the kitchen door, if it wasn't already standing wide open to catch the breeze.

This was the first of many visits I would make over the next ten years, and Steve made a point of having me, the photographer George Lange, and his assistant come to this kitchen door, which was indeed standing wide open on this warm day. The guest of honor apparently didn't get the word to use this entrance, or else he simply forgot. He arrived about fifteen minutes after the appointed time, and used the big knocker on the front door to let us know he had arrived. Steve and I went to greet him, and Bill Gates waved to the driver of his black limo to leave. We all shook hands and went inside.

The house was a fraction of the size of the Jackling Mansion in Woodside, and just as sparsely furnished, at least at that point. The living room had a half dozen or so framed prints by Ansel Adams leaning against the walls, yet to be hung. An audiophile-quality stereo system in a vertical rack had been set up with a couple of speaker towers carefully placed along one wall, and about a hundred LPs sat on the floor, some in a box and others loosely propped near the stereo.

The only seats were two classic Eames lounge chairs with footstools. Bill and Steve sat in the chairs, and I sat on an ottoman. Bill occasionally would move to the other ottoman or get up and pace a little, while Steve, who was barefoot, remained seated with his legs curled up underneath him for most of the session. George roamed the room freely, snapping pictures as the two men talked.

The occasion: the first of only two formal joint interviews that the pair would ever grant. (The latter would take place sixteen years later, onstage at a high-tech business conference.) I had arranged the meeting as the key element of a package of cover stories in *Fortune* to commemorate the tenth anniversary of IBM's shipment of its first PC, and to contemplate the future of the young industry. It had been relatively easy to get Bill to buy in to the idea of the interview. Indeed, he was willing to interrupt a beach vacation with his friend Ann Winblad, a fellow coder from Minnesota, who was now a venture capitalist. Like Bill, she too enjoyed taking a stack of thick books along so they could read and discuss them. Bill had begun dating Melinda French, his future wife, several years before, but even after their romance blossomed, he let her know that he planned to continue to take his "think week" vacations with Winblad.

Steve, on the other hand, had played hard to get. Unlike Gates, he insisted on setting certain parameters for the get-together, primarily that it occur on his turf. Bill would have to come to his house in Palo Alto, and only on this particular Sunday. The interview violated what had become Steve's basic criteria for publicity—he would only put himself out for stories that promoted his company's products. If I was going to get this kind of exclusive, unfettered access on an occasion where he had nothing to sell, it was damn well going to be on his terms.

THE CAREERS OF Bill Gates and Steve Jobs intertwine in ways that il-
luminate the entire history of the personal computer industry—and
that help explain why Steve was so unsuccessful at NeXT, and, more
important, why he was able to succeed so brilliantly upon his return
to Apple. While *Fortune* would cast the interview as a retrospective, it
turned mostly into a discussion that forecast the directions in which
the two men would eventually take the world of computing. Bill
and Steve were two very different people with two very different approaches to computing, approaches that perfectly suited and reflected
their personalities. *Fortune* was right to recognize them as cofounders
of the PC revolution, but in 1991 it would have been a stretch to predict that these same two men would shape the industry for yet another
two decades. But that's how it turned out: for thirty-five years, from
the creation of the Apple II until Steve's death in 2011, their differing
philosophies helped determine the design and purpose and marketing
of everything from smartphones and iPods, to the cheapest laptops and
desktop machines, to the massive mainframe computers that drove the
productivity of Fortune 500 companies.

By 1991, their differences had placed the two thirty-somethings
(Steve, then thirty-six, was eight months older than Bill) on opposite
trajectories. Quite simply, Steve's career had been spiraling downward,
while Bill's was soaring to unseen levels. One simple proof of Bill's rising power: For this interview reviewing the decade since the shipment
of the first IBM PC, *Fortune* hadn't even considered inviting someone
from IBM. That's because Gates had neutered Big Blue even before the
company manufactured its first personal computer, when he convinced
them to license his operating system, MS-DOS, without an exclusiv-
ity clause. That brilliant gambit meant that by 1991 it was Gates, not
IBM, who held the keys to the industry's future.

Bill's end run around IBM hinged on the fact that he had understood something IBM had not: that the software IBM was looking
for—that is, an operating system—held the potential to be a corner-
stone of the entire computer industry. An operating system manages

the flow of data within a computer, and gives programmers access to its hardwired information-processing capabilities. It is the crucial intermediary between the programmer who has a task he wants to accomplish and the semiconductor chips and circuitry that can make that happen. What Bill realized, and no one else saw, was that a standardized operating system could ultimately have enormous benefit for the industry, and therefore enormous strategic potential for its steward.

That was back in 1981. In the decade since, while Steve had been on a quest to make a series of breakthrough computers, Gates had been executing a far grander plan. IBM had given instant credibility to the concept of the personal computer, in a way that Apple had never managed to do, especially in the business world. Sales of its computers had quickly outpaced those of other manufacturers, including Apple. The proliferation of those IBM PCs had spread Microsoft's MS-DOS widely, rivaled only by the proprietary operating system that Apple used on its machines. But Apple didn't license its operating system to other computer makers. Gates, on the other hand, readily licensed his operating system to other manufacturers, who promptly started beating IBM at its own game. The new entrants, like Compaq and Dell and Gateway, were lean and aggressive companies that could take the two standard pieces of the IBM PC—Microsoft's MS-DOS and Intel's microprocessor chips—and produce clones that were faster, more innovative machines than those coming out of hidebound Big Blue. It was Compaq, for example, not IBM, that introduced the whole concept of a portable PC, opening up an important new slice of the market. Gates encouraged the clone manufacturers, licensing MS-DOS to them under the same terms he gave IBM. And his developers worked steadily to improve the operating system. MS-DOS eventually became the foundation of Windows, the operating system that supported the kind of graphical interface that Steve had pioneered with the Lisa and the Mac, and Windows became the standard of just about every personal computer other than those made by Apple. By 1991, Bill Gates's operating systems were on 90 percent of all the PCs in the world. And the company that owned the other 10 percent? Well, that was Apple, which was becoming less relevant, less innovative, and less important year after year.

The hegemony of its operating systems paid off in multiple ways for Microsoft. Early incarnations of its applications, like Word and Excel, had been designed from the bottom up to work with MS-DOS and then Windows, giving Microsoft an edge over other software companies like WordPerfect and Lotus, which also made productivity-oriented applications. In 1990, Gates had bundled all his productivity applications into a package called Microsoft Office. Sales of Office were so robust that other software developers were pushed even further to the side. By 1991, Microsoft was far and away the world's dominant software company. And Bill was nowhere near done. He was about to steer Microsoft into a position so powerful that only the government could restrain the company.

All the success had transformed the public's perception of Gates himself, of course. He had started the 1980s as something of a supplicant to IBM and Apple. Back then, Jobs was the rich face of the computer industry, his stake in the company he founded worth $256 million immediately after its IPO. When Microsoft went public in March 1986, Gates's 45 percent in equity was worth $350 million. By the time of our interview, he had become the world's youngest billionaire. Steve's bank account, meanwhile, had plummeted while he scoured around unsuccessfully for another great new product. Now Bill ruled the roost, while it was becoming increasingly difficult to forecast a future in which Steve Jobs would have any important role to play in the computer industry.

IN THEORY, the interview had the potential to be a fistfight. Both men had developed—and, in many ways, earned—serious reputations as prickly, cut-throat competitors.

Many people have forgotten what a difficult guy Bill Gates could be. In the years since his 2000 resignation as Microsoft's CEO, as Gates has transformed himself into a global philanthropist, the public has seen a thoughtful, caring, and sharply focused elder statesman try to tackle enormously difficult public health and education problems. All those qualities (minus the "elder" part) were in place in 1991, but back then Bill was competing in the computer industry, not investing in a cure for malaria and prodding countries to attack AIDS, provide cleaner drinking water, and find ways to help farmers weather global warming. Gates was trying to execute a plan to make Windows ubiquitous, running on anything that could compute, and he lived in constant paranoia of leaving weak spots that would allow a competitor to pierce the shell he'd built around the industry. "That is the stupidest thing I've ever heard," he would snap at coworkers whose business analysis failed to live up to his standards, and then drive his point home by shaking his head in exasperation and muttering, "That is so *totally* random." Bill, with some justification, always thought he was the smartest guy in the room. He was willing to explain his rationale for a decision once, but pity those who needed a second recitation; that too could provoke a sarcastic outburst or, worse yet, a simmering passive-aggressive anger that would later reveal itself unexpectedly, in withering fashion.

In public, the two men had attacked each other regularly, even gleefully, and they would continue to do so for years. Steve cast Bill as a philistine with zero aesthetic sense and little originality. It was a view he'd hold throughout his life. Bill, he told me repeatedly, knew no other solution than throwing money and people at a problem, which was why Microsoft's software was so convoluted and mediocre. (Steve conveniently ignored his own spendthrift ways at NeXT.) Bill bluntly painted Steve as a loser who had fallen from importance because of his own stupid decisions. He was relentless about NeXT's insignificance. Later in the 1990s, when Jobs supported the Department of Justice's effort to rein in the Microsoft monopoly, Gates repeatedly threw Steve in with the vast set of "losers" who "whined" about what he saw as his company's deserved success.

But that Sunday in July they behaved themselves, with little friction and no open acknowledgment of the obvious disparity in their wealth and power. Steve was too proud to concede Bill's preeminence. Bill was too well-behaved to gloat over Steve's current woes. They accorded one another a certain level of respect. They understood each other's strengths. With nothing at stake and the country's leading business magazine there to pat them on the back, none of the negative sentiments flared.

Face-to-face on this Sunday afternoon, the slights—and there were a few—were couched. After Bill attacked John Sculley for wanting to license Apple's operating system so other manufacturers could create Apple clones, Steve got a shot in at both Sculley and Gates. "I'm not interested in building a PC," Steve said, criticizing the standardization that Bill had promulgated. "Tens of millions of people needlessly use a computer that is far less good than it should be." That eventually led to the only outright insult, which they both found funny. Making the case that Microsoft's dominance hindered innovation in the industry, Steve said, "In the MS-DOS world, there are hundreds of people making PCs."

"Right," said Bill.

"And there are hundreds of people making applications for those PCs."

"Right."

"But they all have to pass through this very small orifice called Microsoft to get to one another."

"It's a very large orifice," Bill replied, leaning way back in his chair as he laughed. "I keep telling you it's being extended. . . . It's not even an orifice. We shouldn't have used that term."

"It's been used before," said Steve, grinning like a little kid.

"Which orifice?" Bill asked, grinning right back at Steve, before catching himself and leaning forward again. "Anyway . . ."

Bill was the steadier and more consistent of the two. His vision of the history of the industry was as assured as his sense of where it would go. "I wrote down in 1975, when I started the company," he explained,

casting his extraordinary foresight as nothing more than a simple vo-
calization of what should have been obvious to everyone, "that there
were two focuses of technology in terms of building computers. One
was chips, the other was software." He went on to add, "My approach
to the PC market has been the same from the beginning. The goals
of Microsoft to create the standards for that machine have been the
same from day one." He didn't apologize for any aspect of Microsoft's
success. He wouldn't outright acknowledge its near monopoly, but he
argued forcefully that standardization around his operating system
and Intel's chips benefited everyone. "Now the latest chip technology passes through to the consumer so fast and so efficiently," he said.
"When Intel comes up with a new microprocessor chip, a few weeks
later two hundred PC companies have come up with a machine, and
you can drive out to the computer warehouse and buy a machine. It's
the same if you take software. Because the volumes are so immense,
incredible software that's ten times as good as anything that was out
even five years ago is available for essentially the same price. Even in
strange categories you can choose from so much software."

Given his uncertain position at the time, it wasn't surprising that
Steve was the more volatile participant. He was willing to admit a
few mistakes, even allowing that Bill was correct in saying that Apple
should have taken the IBM PC more seriously. Then he took that
thought further. "The singular event that defined Apple's place in the
industry in the 1980s was actually not the Macintosh," he announced.
"That was a positive event. The negative event that defined Apple's
place was the Apple III. It was the first example I'd seen in my career
of a product taking on a life of its own and developing way beyond
what was necessary to satisfy customer demand. The project took eighteen months more than we'd planned and was overdesigned and cost
a little too much. It's interesting to speculate what would've happened
if the Apple III had come out right, as a lean, mean upgrade to the
Apple II that offered incremental features that made it more suitable
for business. [Instead,] Apple left a real hole." Later, he made clear that
much of the blame could be laid at his feet: "One of the reasons that

the Apple III had problems was that I grabbed some of the best people from that project to do research on how to turn what I saw at Xerox [PARC] into reality."

It was a fascinating admission. Steve was never much for looking back at his own mistakes, and yet during this very public conversation with a friend whom everyone but Jobs now acknowledged as the leader of the computer industry, he was downright contrite. Later in the conversation, he even pulled out a story he'd ripped from the pages of *Newsweek* to make sure that Bill wasn't offended by the author's claim that Steve was no longer his friend. "I tore this out and I was going to call you before I knew we were getting together," he said, brandishing the page like a trial attorney. "This is not true at all, and I have no idea where they got that."

Steve became most engaged when we started discussing whether the PC industry would ever again produce a breakthrough machine like the Mac. That was the kind of product that most interested Steve, of course. At every stage of his life, he always wanted to create devices that would completely reset the industry. "Fundamentally," he explained, "the PC industry is taking the existing and repackaging it or making it run faster. I think that's much more valuable than I used to. But I also think that what's the real trick, and the real necessity to keep our industry healthy, is to balance that incremental improvement with some big steps. I worry about the big steps, and where they're going to come from." Later he added, "The standard bearer needs a kick in the ass every once in a while. [Besides,] it's great for the creator of the deviant innovation. If they're right, there's a big pot of gold there, and the ability to make a contribution to the world."

Bill wasn't obsessed with the revolutionary. He knew that there was a place for breakthrough technologies, and that the nature of the tech business—indeed, human nature itself—guaranteed that such milestones would arise. But over the course of the interview he made clear that what was closer to his heart was the pain that such disruptions caused the corporate customers of his software. "All I want is a car that will run on the current streets," he explained. "I'm on this evolutionary path." The huge investments corporate America had started to make in personal computers and in the critical applications it used to run operations "make for some very unusual dynamics," he said. "In an Egghead Software store five years from now you're not going to find business software for six different types of desktop computers. Personally, I would be stunned if you would find software for more than one overwhelmingly successful type of computer, and maybe a couple of others. More than three would be shocking."

When Steve had left Apple in 1985, the primary competition in the computer hardware business had been framed as a battle to design the best machine; whoever did that, it was assumed, would win the most customers. But six years later that wasn't the game at all, a fact that Steve was only slowly coming to understand, in light of his difficulties with the NeXT computer. The game was now all about serving corporate customers with their millions of machines. Those companies were increasingly reliant on their PCs, which ran custom-built applications that helped them execute complicated, data-intensive operations. They needed these applications to work with every new unit. The cost of re-creating their data to fit, say, a NeXT computer that didn't work with the Windows operating system would have been exorbitant, not just in the financial cost of reprogramming but in the opportunity cost lost to all the time required by a retrofit. It wasn't the bells and whistles that excited these customers; in fact, they found bells and whistles kind of scary. Nope, what they needed was more power, more speed, and above all else, reliability.

Very few people writing about this new industry in the mainstream press truly understood how personal computers had already begun to revert to institutional machines. This was mainly because it was easier for most journalists of the early 1990s to envision and get personally excited about the potential of educational software, or of managing their personal finances, or organizing their recipes in the "digital" kitchen, or imagining how amateur architects could design funky homes right on their home computers. Who wouldn't be excited about more power in the hands of people, the computer as an extension of the brain, a "bicycle for the mind," as Steve put it? This was the story of computing that got all the ink, and it was a story no one unfurled as well as Steve.

Bill Gates wasn't swayed by that romance. He saw it as a naïve fantasy that missed the point of the much more sophisticated things PCs could do for people in the enterprise. A consumer market can be an enormously profitable one—put simply, there are so many more people than businesses that if you sell them the right product you can mint money. But the personal computers of that time still didn't have enough power at a low enough price to excite the vast majority of consumers, or to change their lives in any meaningful way. The business market, however, was a different beast. The potential volume of sales represented by all those corporate desktops, in all those thousands of companies big and small, became the target of Bill Gates's strategic brilliance and focus. Those companies paid good prices for the reliability and consistency that Windows PCs could deliver. They welcomed incremental improvement, and Bill knew how to give it to them. Steve paid lip service to it, but his heart wasn't in it. He thrilled only to the concept of how a dramatically better computer could unlock even more potential for its user.

This fundamental difference between the two coparents of the PC was made utterly clear by the interview. What wasn't made clear, and what Bill didn't even come close to revealing, was how his deep understanding of the computing needs of businesses would transform the computer business itself over the next several years, further sidelining anyone who, like Steve, chose to focus on the aesthetics and thrills of personal computers. Even though nobody recognized it at the time, Bill was about to take the personal right out of personal computing. Ironically, in so doing, he would leave an opening for Steve to fill—eventually.

————

THE DECADE OF the 1990s was about to become the Age of Microsoft, a period of time when a single company dictated the direction of the entire computing industry. Microsoft did have a key partner in Intel, whose chips powered almost every machine running the Windows operating system. But the combination of Windows and a growing suite of office productivity applications gave Microsoft an entree to corporations that Intel could never match. While the steadily increasing power and speed of Intel's chips set a rhythm of inexorable advancements for technology, Windows and Microsoft's other software shaped the look and feel of corporate computing. By attending to every need of both the Fortune 500 and small businesses, Bill Gates was becoming technology's king. Intel CEO Andy Grove was, somewhat to his dismay, relegated to the avuncular role of the "elder statesman."

Together, Gates and Grove had exploited something that Steve had ignored. Looking over the horizon, they could see that the architecture of PCs would improve so much in performance as to subsume almost every aspect of computing. In the past, high-end business machines were based on proprietary designs that didn't benefit from the economies of scale of standardized parts. Gates and Grove knew that eventually—and it wasn't going to take very long at all—the expensive, customized guts of engineering workstations would become juiced-up PC circuit boards, and that the same evolution would ultimately subsume business minicomputers, mainframes, and even supercomputers, those rare and superexpensive machines used for everything from modeling weather patterns to controlling nuclear devices. (For example, IBM's Watson, the machine that in 2011 beat *Jeopardy!* phenomenon Ken Jennings, is one such computer based on a PC-like architecture.) As a result, pretty much every computer that companies relied on to manage their most critical operations would adopt the internal electronic architecture of a PC writ large. All were much, much cheaper and easier to program and operate than unwieldy mainframes, because they were built out of the very same semiconductor components as PCs, and usually used a variation of the Windows operating system software. Thus they benefited from the ever-improving economics of scale afforded by the combination of Moore's law and by the breathtaking growth of the PC market itself.

Throughout the 1990s, Microsoft would become the unchallenged steward of corporate computing. And corporations would welcome its standardization. In a headlong rush to improve productivity through technology, they spent trillions of dollars. In 1991, the $124 billion of corporate spending on information technology accounted for just 2 percent of the gross domestic product. By 2000, that percentage had more than doubled to 4.6 percent. The leading beneficiary of all that was Microsoft; over that same period, its revenues rose from $1.8 billion to $23 billion, its profits rose from $463 million to $9.4 billion, and its stock price appreciated 3,000 percent.

Mired at NeXT, Steve enjoyed hardly any of the spoils of this frenzy. He did sell a few computers to businesses, and once the Internet emerged as the world's great network, the company's WebObjects software turned into a useful tool for corporations developing custom websites. But these were table scraps. For the most part, Steve Jobs could only watch from the sidelines as his old friend and nemesis, a man far more suited to the demands of the corporate market, became arguably the most important businessperson on the globe.

———

AFTER ABOUT TWO and a half hours, we wrapped up the interview. I had covered the two men for years, but bringing these dynamic and headstrong competitors together for a conversation had been like seeing them for the first time in three dimensions. A kind of a parallax effect in their interaction helped me better discern and appreciate each. Perhaps it was because they weren't there to sell anything that I could see them with more nuance. Their proximity and innate competitiveness had brought out spontaneous displays of wit, sharp-edged opinions, and even a sense of friendship that they might not have allowed to show in a different setting.

George Lange, who had been circling the two, camera in hand, during much of the encounter, now wanted to set up the shoot for the cover photograph. We didn't have much time—Bill was adamant about getting to the San Francisco airport in time for his scheduled flight back to Seattle. George had considered shooting them outside, but he decided that the main staircase, which curved dramatically up from the living room, would work better for the cover. He explained his reasons to both. Bill was never that particular about press photo shoots—his primary concern was that they happen quickly. But Steve fancied himself a self-taught expert on the art form. The most intense negotiations I ever had with him when proposing a story for *Fortune* were about the photography. Steve had all kinds of advice about the pictures that would accompany an article, especially about the stylistic approach to his cover portrait. He could be more than a little vain about how he was portrayed, and always sought the upper hand in deciding not only who would do the shooting, but *how* the portraits would be set up. This time, however, he didn't put up a fuss. He climbed right up the red clay steps and sat down. As soon as George looked at him he exclaimed, "Steve, you're not wearing shoes! Don't you want to wear some shoes for the cover of *Fortune*?" Steve shrugged and said, "Sure, fine." He ran upstairs, grabbed a pair of sneakers, and came back wearing them—with the laces left untied.

After the shoot, I told Bill I'd run him over to the airport in my Volvo station wagon, but we had to wait a minute so George could take a photo of the three of us in Steve's backyard, for the editor's page of the magazine. Then Bill and I rushed off to the airport. We didn't say much—I could tell that he had moved on and was already thinking about what was next for him. "You guys get along pretty well," I remarked. "Why shouldn't we?" he answered. He was preoccupied, but polite as always. "Thanks. I'm really glad we did that," he said as he jumped out of the car.

George's photo turned out to be my favorite from the many cover stories I worked on with either Bill or Steve. Wrought-iron railings swoop around the two young cybertycoons, who are perched shoulder to shoulder on the staircase, Steve one step higher than Bill. The expressions on their faces seem without pretense to me, and very revealing of their personalities. Bill looks like the cat who ate the canary. And

Steve, who seemingly could sell anyone (except Bill, that is) the Golden Gate Bridge, has the sly smile of a clever young man who would never outgrow his penchant for making mischief.

Despite his business woes, Steve did have reasons to smile. If he was adrift professionally, he was starting to settle personally, in a way that gave him great satisfaction. His daughter Lisa had just come to live with him and Laurene. This was a complicated kind of atonement on his part, given the way he had immaturely and irresponsibly tried to deny his paternity. And the impending arrival of his son, Reed, excited this very untypical man in a deeply normal way. Reed, of course, was the first child he had planned for, and when he arrived in October, Steve reacted as so many fathers do—he became a know-it-all, in that deadly serious way that's deeply amusing to parents who have been through the exercise. "They were classic new parents," remembers Mike Slade. "They did everything wrong. They were both hippies, right? So the kid was in their bed the whole time, the kid was only breastfed. So what did the kid do? Let's see, he screamed all the time and he was hungry all the time 'cause, duh, right? So within a week they looked like prison camp survivors.

"Steve is kind of a baby himself, right?" Slade continued. "And the guy was getting no sleep. So he instantly became a madman. It was right out of the CIA torture training manual. I'm not kidding. Within a week of Reed being born he was like, 'I've gotta hire a president and COO. I've gotta do it. Ooh, it's too much.'" But even this was a reflection of the very standard delight he took in his son, and the seriousness he was going to apply to the endeavor of raising Reed.

There was one other reason for Steve to be happy then, although nobody—including Steve—understood it at the time.

Bill's strategy—to have Microsoft steer the industry toward a standardization that fit the needs of business—would shape everything about computing in the 1990s. Workstations *did* become subsumed by PCs. Mainframes *did* turn into nothing more than vast arrays of circuit boards built upon the PC architecture. The personal computer giants of that decade, companies like Dell and Compaq and HP and

Gateway, churned out one artless machine after another, competing on brute measures like speed, power, and delivery times. The billions of people around the world who came to depend on the PC interacted daily with interchangeable boxes powered by the same chips, and they executed their tasks through applications governed by the same operating system. Apple, which had been the one company producing unique computers for individuals, foundered as Sculley and the hapless CEOs who succeeded him chased the same market as everyone else. By the late 1990s, it was almost as if the Orwellian scenario of the Mac's "1984" commercial had come true. Big Business, with a pair of capital *B*'s, ruled computing. The drones used what they were told. The personal had been stripped out of personal computing. Year after year after year, Microsoft's domination increased with one inevitable and inexorable and dull step after another. It seemed that Windows might rule forever. The rise of Bill Gates was as dull as the computing he enabled. At least that's how Steve felt about the work of his far more successful rival.

All this standardization left an opening, of course. An opening for someone who preferred creating machines that delighted real people, rather than primarily serve the needs of business. An opening for someone just like Steve Jobs. At the time of our interview, Steve was still a confused fellow. His lingering resentment of the way he had been treated by Sculley and the Apple board, his frustration about the misfortunes and secondary importance of NeXT, and his egotistical need to matter in an industry whose direction was being dictated by someone else made it impossible for him then to see a way out of his dilemma. For the next few years, he would press ahead with his goal of making winners of NeXT and Pixar. But eventually he would sense his way to the opening that Gates had left behind—the opening for a company that could once again make insanely great computing machines for you and me. And when he found that opening, and made the most of it, he was rewarded with a kind of adulation that Gates would never come close to receiving.

Chapter 7
Luck

WOODY
Oh, Buzz, you've had a big fall. You must not be thinking clearly.

BUZZ
No, Woody, for the first time I am thinking clearly.
(looking at himself)
You were right all along. I'm not a Space Ranger.
I'm just a toy. A stupid little insignificant toy.

WOODY
Whoa, hey—wait a minute. Being a toy is
a lot better than being a Space Ranger.

BUZZ
Yeah, right.

WOODY
No, it is. Look, over in that house is a kid who
thinks you are the greatest, and it's not because you're
a Space Ranger, pal, it's because you're a *toy*! You are *his* toy.

(from *Toy Story*)

A few months after that 1991 interview with Bill and Steve, I moved to Tokyo with my family to be *Fortune*'s Asia bureau chief. Part of the reason I jumped at the Tokyo assignment was that the computer industry in the early 1990s had grown a bit dull now that Microsoft and Intel, collectively known as Wintel, had basically won the personal computer wars. Innovation seemed at a standstill, and the future seemed to be merely a game of cutting costs and optimizing the various PC clones that were being offered by the likes of Dell, Gateway, Compaq, and HP. Apple had pretty much fallen into irrelevancy.

By the time I returned to Silicon Valley three years later, however, much had changed. Bill Clinton had unseated George H. W. Bush as president, after a single term. Bill Gates's net worth had surpassed $10 billion, and he had edged out Warren Buffett to become the richest man in the world, according to *Forbes* magazine. John Sculley had been fired from Apple (but the company was still irrelevant). And, the computing world was starting to get interesting again. Netscape Communications had released beta versions of the first commercial Internet browser, which it would eventually call Navigator, and the terms *World Wide Web* and *dot-com* and *URL* were creeping into the vernacular. The Internet was clearly something that could change everything in computing, and that was a good thing for a technology and business journalist.

In July 1994, I emailed Steve to tell him that *Fortune* had moved my family and me back from Tokyo, and that I'd call on him sometime to catch up, once I had leased an office and gotten settled in. A few weeks later the phone rang in our new home, on a Saturday morning when I was there alone refinishing the wood floors.

"Hi, Brent, this is Steve," he said, in the singsongy, laid-back, California-cool voice he often used on the phone, so pseudo-cheery that it almost sounded like a recording. Then he fell back into character. "So you're back. What happened? Did *Fortune* get embarrassed when they put John Sculley on the cover as a savior the very same week he got fired?" He cackled. Here we go again, I thought. He's interviewing me.

"You should come over," he said. "We can take a walk or something." I said I had to finish what I was doing, but that I could get over to the house in an hour or so. "Okay," he said, and promptly hung up.

When I arrived at his home, Steve was fussing around in the kitchen, wearing his usual summertime garb: threadbare cutoffs with the white front-pocket linings sticking out of worn-through areas, and a faded, long-sleeved NeXT T-shirt. (He hadn't yet started wearing the black mock turtlenecks custom-made by Issey Miyake.) His feet were bare, of course. A big, luxurious Japanese chow was lounging quietly under an expansive, rustic worktable in the middle of the room. The dog clearly had noticed me, but he wasn't very interested.

"I guess he isn't a watchdog," I said, hoping to get Steve's attention. Steve turned around, and for one of but a handful of times in dozens of meetings and encounters over the years, engaged in a few minutes of small talk. Enough to let me know that the dog was really old, that Laurene was pregnant again, and that she and Reed weren't around.

"I wanted to tell you that I'm feeling really good about Pixar's first animated film," he said as he hooked a stool with his foot and pulled it underneath him. Then he motioned for me to sit down. "It's called *Toy Story* and it will be another year before it's finished. I'm not exaggerating when I say that it'll be unlike anything anybody has ever seen before. Disney is considering making it the big holiday release next year."

———

WHEN PEOPLE LIST the many industries that Steve is said to have revolutionized, they often include the movies, since Pixar brought a whole new art form to the big screen. I'm not of that mind. John Lasseter and Ed Catmull are the men who brought 3-D computer graphics to the movies, and revived the art of animated storytelling.

That said, Steve did play a critical role in Pixar's success. His influence was constrained, because Catmull and Lasseter were the ones shaping Pixar, not he. But that constraint, ironically, freed him up to do what only he could do best, and he did it brilliantly.

Just as significant for the trajectory of his life is what he learned by watching Lasseter, Catmull, and their incredibly talented employees cobble together their magic. At Pixar, especially when the company started down the path of actually making movies, Steve started absorbing an approach to management that helped make him much more effective when he returned to Apple in 1997. These are the years where his negotiating style gained new subtlety—without losing its ballsy brashness. This is when he first started understanding the meaning of teamwork as something that's far more complicated than simply rallying small groups—without losing his capacity to lead and inspire. And this is where he started to develop patience—without losing any of his memorable, and motivating, edge.

Steve was certainly lucky that things went this way for him at Pixar, a sideline outfit that he bought on something of a whim, that succeeded in a business he didn't intend for it to pursue, and that made him far wealthier than the company that was his life's true work. Ed Catmull has thought a lot about the role luck plays at a great company, and how businesspeople manage that luck. It's all in the preparedness, he says, and in creating a culture that can adapt to the unexpected. "These things are always going to happen. What separates you is your response," he says. Steve responded well, and that's in part because of his greatest piece of luck: getting to work with Lasseter and Catmull. In many ways, his response to the principles he gleaned from them would be a catalyst for his later success at Apple.

———

JOHN LASSETER HAD a love-hate relationship with Disney. As a teenager, he worked at Disneyland, and after graduating from the California Institute of the Arts, he landed a job as an animator there. While he loved the privilege of working with some of the great animators from the company's historic past, he chafed under the company's rigid management. "Leadership squished us," he remembers. "They fired me, basically."

Hence Lasseter's ultimatum when Disney's Peter Schneider tried for a third time to lure him back to Burbank: the only way that he would ever work with Disney again was for Disney to make a movie *with* Pixar. To his everlasting credit, Schneider took him seriously, and summoned Catmull to his offices in Burbank. He told Catmull that he thought it was time for Pixar to make its own movie, for Disney. Catmull suggested that all Pixar was really ready for was a half-hour television special. Schneider scoffed: if Pixar could deliver thirty minutes of great entertainment, it could deliver seventy-five minutes. Catmull gulped, and then agreed.

Now it was up to Steve to negotiate a deal with Jeffrey Katzenberg, Disney's powerful head of animation. Dickering with Disney would offer a real acid test of both his negotiating skills and his self-discipline. Both Katzenberg and Jobs knew that Disney was the power player at the bargaining table. The storied studio was in the midst of a glorious run. Starting in 1989, Katzenberg's team would deliver one hit after another for five years running: *The Little Mermaid, Beauty and the Beast, Aladdin, The Nightmare Before Christmas* (based on a story by another animator who had gotten away, Tim Burton), and *The Lion King*. So as much as Katzenberg admired Lasseter's chops and regretted that he would not return to Disney, he knew that his company could survive perfectly well without a Pixar movie.

Lasseter, Catmull, and everyone else at Pixar, on the other hand, fully realized that making a movie for Disney was probably their only chance to survive as a company. The negotiations were their last stand, and their fate was in the hands of Steve. Catmull and Lasseter were very comfortable with this. For years, Steve had been the point man on Pixar's negotiations. "He was tough," remembers Lasseter. "He'd walk into the room and say, 'Which one of you has the authority to buy our computers?' If they said no one, he would just dismiss them. 'I only want to negotiate with someone who can make the deal,' he'd say, and leave. We always said that Steve would take a hand grenade, toss it into the room, and then walk in. He'd get everyone's attention right away.'"

But putting Katzenberg and Jobs in the same room held potential for catastrophe. Both men had powerful egos, and both were accustomed to getting their way. Katzenberg believed he'd be the next president of Disney, and took full responsibility for the successes of his animators. Smart, overbearing, difficult to work for, and yet somehow likable, Katzenberg also shared Steve's certainty and faith in his own opinions. When he walked into the first negotiating session with Pixar, in a conference room near his office, he plopped a basket full of Disney baby toys in front of Steve, who'd recently been at Laurene's side for the birth of Reed. It was a gift, but it was also a clear sign of who held the keys to the vault.

Susan Barnes has observed that Steve entered every negotiation knowing exactly what he had to get, and what his position was versus the other side. In negotiating with Lucas, he had been able to exploit Lucas's need for cash. This time Steve went in knowing that Katzenberg had the power, and that Pixar needed a deal to survive. He kicked off the negotiations with a certain brashness, saying that he wanted Pixar to be a partner on all aspects of the revenue from the film, something no neophyte studio filmmaker would ever get. Katzenberg promptly nixed that.

The two had fundamental disagreements about the true value of Pixar. Jobs was convinced that Pixar's technology could revolutionize the business model for animation, believing that computerizing the process would dramatically lower the cost of animating movies. He was offended by what he perceived as Disney's old-school thinking. "They make the mistake of not appreciating technology," he told me. "They don't have a clue." Katzenberg, who of course knew far more than Steve about the animation business, disagreed. "I was not interested in Pixar's technology," Katzenberg told me a few years later. "I was interested in Lasseter's storytelling. Luxo the lamp had more emotion and humor in a five-minute short than most two-hour movies." He was sanguine at best about the potential cost savings. "The idea that this technology is a new business model for animation is bullshit.

Good luck with that! The artists and storytellers will want to continue to grow the technology, so this year's technology will be obsolete in ten years." Katzenberg was right, of course. No matter how much technology you throw at the art of making an animated movie, a good one will always be expensive. Pixar made *Toy Story* for around $20 million (a number that doesn't include what Disney spent on it for promotion and distribution). Pixar's 2013 movie, *Monsters University*, is rumored to have cost around $200 million, marketing included.

These kinds of personal and philosophical differences with the brass at Disney were something Steve had been unable to manage at NeXT, where his anger and resentment helped sabotage the IBM deal. "The people at the top of IBM knew nothing about computers. Nothing. Nothing," he raged in later years, still furious. In those negotiations he had let the IBMers know his true feelings about them, one of his many blunders as he overplayed his hand. But with Katzenberg he acted more deliberately. He made his points, and held out when necessary: Katzenberg asked for the rights to all Pixar's 3-D computing technology, and Steve refused. But he mostly acquiesced, instead of raging against the more powerful man across the table. Pixar did not get ownership of the films or their characters. And Pixar didn't get a cut of the video revenues, because Steve didn't yet understand the huge market for family-oriented videos. But he did get a deal— Disney would fund the production of *Toy Story* and have the option to fund two more movies as well. Pixar would get 12.5 percent of the box office—and a new life. At long last, the Pixar gang was going to get its chance to make a movie.

———

STEVE LOVED PIXAR, and he especially loved watching the team start to develop the movie that would turn into *Toy Story*. But he didn't love losing money. In fact, he later admitted that he would never have purchased Pixar if he had known how much money he would spend keeping the company afloat. So in the early 1990s, both before and after getting the Disney deal, he shopped the company around, even though the few potential buyers were interested only in Pixar's technology—not its movie-making promise. Catmull looked on as Steve negotiated with companies as varied as Hallmark, Silicon Graphics, and Microsoft, each with different ideas of how Pixar's software could augment their own offerings. But none of the deals crystallized. In each case, Steve would not budge from an outrageous price tag that he'd put on the company. The repeated failures made Catmull wonder if he'd ever really wanted to sell. "I could see why it would happen. Some of the deals made sense. It wasn't the dream we'd wanted, but you're trying to keep things going," he remembers. But nothing worked out. "Afterward, I'm thinking, What was that all about? Was he just looking for confirmation that he'd done something right?" Catmull came to think that Steve might have been subconsciously sinking each deal out of loyalty to Pixar. "He had this sense of what it means to be loyal and to give your word. As I was getting to know Steve more, I could see how this interplayed in complex ways. Not that Steve ever psychoanalyzed himself."

Catmull never discussed the deals with Steve in such a psychological way: "We didn't get philosophical all that often. When we started to edge into personality and so forth, he'd just say, 'I am who I am.'" So Catmull's theory about loyalty must remain just that. But his conjecture reflects the complexity of what Steve was feeling then. He was losing way more money than he'd ever imagined, especially with things at NeXT going in the wrong direction. Yet he was far from poor: he had all the money he needed to raise a family and do the things that mattered to him. And as he watched *Toy Story* develop, he was starting to fall truly in love with Pixar. It was such a welcome respite from NeXT, far less intense and far less demanding.

Steve started coming up to Pixar's offices once a week, even though he often had little to do there. Catmull managed the process of staffing up after the movie deal was done, a process that could have been disruptive, given that Pixar had just downsized dramatically when Steve sold the hardware division. But under Catmull there was no "bozo period" at Pixar.

Steve had no input on the development of the *Toy Story* plot. Lasseter, Andrew Stanton, Pete Docter, and Joe Ranft worked together to create the script, eventually with help from other writers, including Joss Whedon, who would go on to create the *Buffy the Vampire Slayer* TV series and to direct movies such as *The Avengers*. The team on *Toy Story* would turn out to be remarkably productive, and exceedingly close-knit. Stanton would direct Pixar's second movie, *A Bug's Life,* as well as *Finding Nemo* and *Wall-E*. Docter would direct *Monsters, Inc.* and *Up,* while Ranft would serve as cowriter and story chief on several pictures, until his death in a car crash in 2005. The four men became the core of what Catmull calls the Brain Trust—a collection of Pixar writers, directors, and animators who provide constructive criticism to the director of every Pixar movie. It's a unique idea—the Brain Trust has no authority whatsoever, and the directors are only asked to listen and deeply consider the advice of its members. It became a powerful tool, helping to reshape movies like *The Incredibles* and *Wall-E*. But Steve was never a part of it. Catmull kept him out of those discussions, because he felt that Steve's big personality would skew the proceedings.

Watching Lasseter, Stanton, Docter, and Ranft develop *Toy Story,* Steve was witnessing creative thinking at its best—meaning it was chock-full of failures and dead ends. He always remained encouraging. "When we screwed up," says Catmull, "it wasn't, 'Oh, you guys screwed up!' It was always, 'What are we going to do to move forward?' When you're out there on the edge, some things go right and some things go wrong. If nothing's going wrong, you're fooling yourself. Steve believed that." That was a bright contrast to Katzenberg, whose severe critiques kept pushing the movie in a more sarcastic direction than the team was comfortable with. In fact, things with Disney would get so difficult that after a disastrous screening one Friday late in 1993, Schneider shut down production. For three months, Lasseter and his cowriters recused themselves to draft a new version of the script. During that time Steve and Catmull ensured that the production crew stayed together and got paid. And once *Toy Story* swung back into production, Jobs fought for more money to accommodate the changes made necessary by the new script. His battles with Katzenberg over the budget were intense, but eventually he and Catmull were able to wheedle a bit more cash out of Disney.

"Watching our collaboration, seeing us make ourselves better by working together, I think that fueled Steve," says Lasseter. "I think that was one of the key changes when he went back to Apple. He was more open to the talent of others, to be inspired by and challenged by that talent, but also to the idea of inspiring them to do amazing things he knew he couldn't do himself."

———

IN THE YEARS after marrying Laurene and starting a family, Steve developed a few especially close friendships. These weren't relationships he talked about much, at least not in any way that was personally revealing. Steve drew a hard line with reporters about his private life—those of us who had some access to it agreed not to write about it, unless we got Steve's permission to relate a certain anecdote. Ed Catmull and John Lasseter became two of Steve's really close friends, part of a very small group of people he would hold near and dear till the end of his life.

"I liked him from the moment I met him," Steve told me once about Ed. He found him an intellectual match. "Ed is a quiet guy, and you could mistake that quietness for weakness—but it's not, it's strength. Ed's really thoughtful, and really, really smart. He's used to hanging around really smart people, and when you're around really smart people you tend to listen to them."

Steve listened to Catmull. Though he could often come across as a know-it-all, Steve was constantly trying to learn. Trim and professorial, Ed was ten years older than Steve, making him as much of a mentor as a colleague. Ed showed him how a movie came together, explaining all the pieces and processes in a way that eventually fit together. He could dig into the technology of 3-D animation with Steve. And he could explain his managerial decisions with a sincerity, depth of feeling, and rationality that Steve respected. Ed had made it a point for years to try to hire people who he felt were smarter than he was, and the effort showed. "The collection of people at Pixar is the highest concentration of remarkable people I have ever witnessed," Steve told me. For all that he gained from knowing Catmull, however, Steve never quite acknowledged to Ed how much he had learned from him. "The closest he got," says Catmull, "is that he said he valued what I did, and knew it was very different from what he did."

Theirs was a quiet, sincere friendship, enabled in great part by Catmull's maturity. "Steve and I never argued," he says. "We had disagreements; I won several and he won several. But even early on, when he wasn't particularly skilled at dealing with relationships, I always felt that he was talking about a topic, not about who was right or who was wrong. For a lot of people, their egos are tied up in an idea and it gets in the way of learning. You have to separate yourself from the idea. Steve was like that."

The two men would eventually know each other and work together for twenty-six years. Catmull says he saw enormous changes over the years, but allows that this, too, was something Steve would never acknowledge. "I look at Steve as someone who was actually always trying to change, but he didn't express it in the same ways as others, and he didn't communicate with people about that. He really was trying to change the world. It didn't come across as him being personally introspective."

Steve's relationship with Lasseter was different, more buoyant. Their friendship really picked up once *Toy Story* got under way, and Lasseter's animation division went from being an expensive indulgence to the future of the company. He and Steve were contemporaries, with growing families. "We were having babies at the same time," says Lasseter, "so there was that."

Early in their friendship, the fact that Steve was the boss and the wealthier of the two made him something of an older brother. One weekend in the spring of 1995, the Lasseters invited the Jobs family up to their house in Sonoma. Steve was exploring a radical idea: taking Pixar public after *Toy Story*'s premiere, which was scheduled for Thanksgiving. So on the first night, after the kids were asleep and Laurene had headed to bed early, Steve stayed up till four in the morning explaining stock options to John and his wife, Nancy. "I mean, I went to CalArts. I didn't know anything about that stuff. So he gave us Business 101 about stock, how it works, why companies sell it, what's beneficial for people, how you are then beholden to stockholders and have to do earnings reports, all that stuff. He talked about IPOs, getting ready for it, stock options. He just laid it all out."

The next morning, Steve and John were sitting on the porch of the house, taking in the nice view—which was marred only by the sight of John's 1984 Honda Civic, with 210,000 miles on it. "The paint was just sunburned off," says Lasseter. "The seats were shot—I put T-shirts over them. Steve had driven up in their Jeep Cherokee. Now he knew the roads I had to drive on every day."

"Don't tell me that's your car," Steve said.

"Yeah, it is," John told him.

"You drive to and from Pixar on these roads in *that* car?" Steve said. Lasseter sheepishly nodded. "Okay. No, no, no, no. No, that just won't do."

"Steve," said Lasseter, "I've got to be honest, I can't afford a new car right now. We just bought this house and it's far more than we can afford. I just can't do it now."

"I think what he was thinking," Lasseter told me, "was, 'Oh my God, I bet the farm on this guy, and he's driving that crap car . . . if a truck hits him—dink!—he'll be dead.'"

"Okay," Steve said, "we'll figure something out."

When Lasseter got his next paycheck, it contained a small bonus. "You have to use this to buy a new car," Steve told him. "It has to be safe, and I have to approve it." John and Nancy picked out a Volvo, and Steve approved.

Lasseter is one of the world's great storytellers, and Steve loved this side of him. The director approached the construction of movies with the same kind of craftsmanship that Steve applied when building a new piece of hardware. Both men loved the fit and finish. Once, during the production of *A Bug's Life,* John and Andrew Stanton told me about the research involved in creating the "bug's-eye view" of the world. After fitting arthroscopic lenses to video cameras, the team went to all different kinds of landscapes and pushed the snakelike lenses along the ground to see what the world looked like from an ant's perspective. One thing they realized was that most grass is translucent, casting a greenish hue as the light comes through. Since you can emphasize whatever you want with animation, Stanton and his crew gave their bug's world an exaggerated glow.

This kind of attention to detail fascinated Steve. He loved the narrative and visual mosaics that Lasseter was able to assemble for each Pixar movie, and over the years he came to admire the way the animators outdid themselves with each and every film. He and Lasseter paired a child's curiosity with an obsessive attention to detail. At Pixar, Steve was seeing how the two could be combined into the slow, successful, and patient development of a work of art that would live long beyond its creators.

A few weeks before Pixar's IPO, Steve took Lasseter to an early dinner at one of his favorite Japanese restaurants, Kyo-ya, in San Francisco's Palace Hotel. "Afterwards, we were standing outside out on the curb, talking for the longest time," remembers Lasseter. "We had to have been there at least an hour, just talking about stuff. I was telling him I was nervous, that I was kind of scared of the IPO. I wished that we could wait for the second movie. And he did that thing, where he kind of looks off, and he said, 'You know, when we make a computer at Apple, what's its life span? About three years? At five years, it's a doorstop. But if you do your job right, what you create can last forever.'"

BY LATE 1994, Steve stopped shopping the company around. He didn't want to give up control of what was clearly going to become a very interesting enterprise with the release of *Toy Story*. But he didn't really understand just how big things could get until he attended a press conference for Disney's new animated film, *Pocahontas,* in New York City on February 1, 1995. It wasn't just any old press conference; it was held in a huge tent in Central Park, where Mayor Rudy Giuliani and Disney CEO Michael Eisner announced that the June 10 premiere of *Pocahontas* would occur right there—in the park, free, for up to one hundred thousand people. And the premiere was just the appetizer— Disney's marketing campaign for the hand-drawn *Pocahontas* would add up to more than $100 million.

Steve eyes grew really big. He appreciated a masterful product launch, and his own introductions paled against this one. That's when he got serious about cooking up an audacious plan for an initial public offering of Pixar stock. His goal was to raise enough money for the company to fund its own movie productions, thus enabling it to become a full partner to Disney, rather than a mere contractor.

Making the decision about the details for an IPO, of course, was a task for Steve to handle rather than Catmull or Lasseter. He recently had hired a new CFO by the name of Lawrence Levy, a sharp Silicon Valley attorney with a background in patent law. Right away, he and Levy spent weeks studying the ins and outs of film finance and accounting to get a better sense of how studios really make their money. As part of their "homework" they flew down to Hollywood to quiz other executives at other studios about movie budgets and distribution deals. They immediately learned that Pixar was, at least at that point, a long shot for a successful IPO. Its financial performance to date was pretty dismal—it had accumulated losses of $50 million over the years, while generating little revenue. Its potential revenue stream seemed limited and risky. Pixar was largely dependent on one company, Disney, which was the sole licensee of CAPS technology and which would return to Pixar a mere 12.5 percent of box-office revenues of any movies they might make and market together. Moreover, Pixar seemed to move at a snail's pace, having already spent nearly four years on a movie that still wasn't finished. The movie business itself was notoriously unpredictable. And finally, the company relied on the creative ideas of a very few people, like Lasseter and Stanton, who had good reputations but no significant track record.

Steve had his own misgivings about *Toy Story*'s commercial potential, mainly based upon what he was hearing from Disney's marketers. "Disney came to do a big presentation to us about the marketing," remembers Lasseter. "They told us they had a big promotional plan with Sears. Steve looks around the room and goes, 'Has anybody in this room been into a Sears lately? *Anybody*.' No one raises a hand. 'Then why are we making a deal with Sears? Why are we not going for products we like? Can't we be doing a deal with Rolex? Sony high-end audio equipment?' And their answer was basically, 'Um, um, this is what we do!' He poked holes in every one of their ideas. He was just so logical. Why associate ourselves with products we can't stand?" (In the end, the most prominent sponsor would turn out to be Burger King.)

As long as Pixar had not filed with the SEC for an IPO, Steve was free to do what he could to drum up excitement about Pixar in the business press. Still, I was surprised one Saturday morning in May when the phone rang in my home and it was Steve. He asked if I wanted to come over, but this time with Greta and Fernanda, my two daughters, who were then just ten and nine years old. "I'm watching Reed this morning," he told me, "and I've got something cool to show them."

When we arrived, three-year-old Reed Jobs greeted us at the kitchen door, wrapped in blue and red silk scarves and screeching, "I'm a witch!!!" Reed fluttered around while Steve got the kids some juice and made bowls of popcorn. Then he and I followed the three kids into the den, where Steve popped a VHS cassette into the player. After a bunch of crude storyboards, all of a sudden a full-color early version of *Toy Story* burst onto the screen and a sound track kicked in. I had seen storyboards lining the walls at Pixar, but no actual animation at that point. It was truly spectacular and completely unlike anything I'd seen on a screen before. The three kids sat rapt on the floor in front of the TV. They watched the whole thing, even though only about half of it was fully completed, with the rest filled in by line drawings or semi-complete renderings.

When it was over, Steve told me that the Pixar board of directors hadn't even seen this much of the movie. I took *that* with a grain of salt. (Lasseter later told me that Steve showed it to everyone: "He was impossible!" Steve's friend Larry Ellison, the billionaire founder of Oracle, said he saw eleven different versions.) Steve quickly turned from me to the kids. He was busy conducting market research, Steve Jobs–style. "Whaddya think?" he asked the girls. "Is it as good as *Pocahontas*?" Greta and Fernanda nodded vigorously. "Well, then, is it as good as *The Lion King*?" Fernanda pondered for a beat, then replied, "I won't be able to make up my mind until I see *Toy Story* five or six more times."

Steve loved the answer.

ON AUGUST 9, Steve got lucky again, when a little company called Netscape Communications went public. Netscape's product, the first popular Internet browser, was a revolutionary thing, but there was no obvious way for the company to turn it into a big moneymaker. No matter—the public's enthusiasm for technology and this new darling called the Internet was about to soar. Netscape shares were offered at $28, and closed the day at $58.25, giving the new company a valuation of $2.9 billion.

After Netscape's IPO, Pixar didn't seem quite so wispy a bet. Robertson, Stephens, a San Francisco investment bank, agreed to underwrite the IPO and filed a prospectus with the SEC in October. Steve decided to push his luck even further, and set the date for Pixar's IPO on November 29, 1995, merely one week after *Toy Story*'s debut. If the movie had flopped, the IPO would have been a disaster, and all Steve's efforts to get Pixar onto more secure financial footing would have been for naught.

But of course that's not what happened. The movie is a masterpiece, a soulful, funny film of such enduring power that the American Film Institute includes it in its list of the one hundred greatest American movies. And Pixar's IPO the following week was a blockbuster as well, raising $132 million and giving the company a market capitalization of $1.4 billion. Lasseter, Catmull, Steve, and other Pixarians gathered to follow the affair from Robertson, Stephens's offices in downtown San Francisco. Shortly after the opening bell, when the stock was trading above the $22-per-share price that the bank had established, Catmull saw Steve pick up the phone in an office to the side. "Hello, Larry?" Steve said into the handset, once his pal Ellison was on the line. "I made it." Steve, who owned 80 percent of the company, was a billionaire.

———

WHILE STEVE DID enjoy comparing notes and playing games with Ellison, who at the time was one of the very richest men in the world (and still is), money wasn't what thrilled Steve about Pixar. What thrilled him was to once again play a part in the creation of a successful and profoundly beautiful product that employed brilliant new technology that had seemingly unlimited potential. He loved that once again he was an architect of what the world could not help but recognize as a remarkably creative enterprise. Steve hadn't felt that way for what had seemed like eons. Not since the introduction of the Macintosh eleven years earlier.

The incredible success of *Toy Story*, and of Pixar in general, had a huge personal significance for Steve as well. He always wanted to make products that he both loved and found useful. That's part of the reason that things never seemed quite so magical at NeXT; unlike Bill Gates, Steve couldn't throw himself completely into the creation of a product that suited a particular market but that didn't thrill him personally. The NeXT computer and the subsequent software products were admirable, and elegantly beautiful in their own ways, but they were aimed at institutions rather than people. With *Toy Story,* for the first time in his life, he had a hand in the creation of a product that a young family like his own could enjoy as well. Laurene was pregnant with daughter Erin, the second of their three children. Steve reveled in the fact that *Toy Story* was something that his kids could enjoy, and even their kids as well.

In retrospect, the fact that *Toy Story* was the beginning of Steve's professional resurrection seems preposterously appropriate. Its plot established the Pixar formula: a likable character is the cause of his own downfall, often as a result of hubris; but he (or she, once Pixar finally made *Brave*) overcomes weakness through kindness, bravery, quick wits, invention, or some combination thereof, and thereby earns a redemption that makes him—or her—an even better and more complete toy (or bug, car, fish, princess, monster, robot, mouse, or superhero!). The hero's downfall, incidentally, often involves some kind of exile, as in *Toy Story,* where Woody "accidentally" sends Buzz careening into Sid's backyard, and then must join him to engineer a hair-raising escape from that evil child. The parallels to Steve's own exile from Apple are obvious.

Toy Story also gave Steve back his confidence. He and I spoke several times in the months after the IPO, and I could tell he was beyond ecstatic about the way things had gone. He talked about what had happened at Pixar—and about his role in its success—with real pride. He was generous in giving large stock grants to Catmull and Lasseter, and he personally handed out bonus paychecks of an extra month's pay to all Pixar employees in December. Sure, some of them grumbled that they hadn't received higher stock grants. And sure, Steve claimed more credit for Pixar's sudden success than he deserved. But even Alvy Ray Smith, the original partner of Catmull who had left after clashing with Steve, later admitted that Pixar could not have succeeded without him. "We should have failed," Alvy told one interviewer. "But it seemed to me that Steve just would not suffer another defeat. He couldn't sustain it."

As happy as Steve was, however, to bask in the glory of Pixar's success, he quickly moved on. He had another motive for engaging me in all those post-IPO conversations. He was starting to think about his old company down in Cupertino.

Chapter 8
Bozos, Bastards, and Keepers

Thanks to the unlikely, dizzying success of *Toy Story* and the Pixar IPO, Steve was back in the limelight. He got more than his fair share of the attention, but neither Ed Catmull nor John Lasseter cared too much about that. Now that Pixar was on solid financial footing, they were both ecstatic to be developing their next movie, *A Bug's Life*, without having to worry about the fate of their company. To the outside world, it seemed that Jobs had rediscovered his pixie dust. The success of *Toy Story* had given the myth of Steve Jobs a rather nice touch-up.

The question now was whether Steve's Pixar triumph was a one-shot anomaly. For a man whose name eventually would become synonymous with great American second acts, the Steve Jobs of 1996 had had remarkably little success with his own sequels. The Apple II had been followed by the Apple III and the Lisa, both of which had been failures. The Mac became a success only in the more robust versions introduced by John Sculley. His most grandiose sequel of all, NeXT, the company he'd created to be an idealized version of Apple, had proved utterly anticlimactic.

Pixar had provided some redemption. But Steve, of course, had been on top of the world before. The question was whether he'd handle it any better than he had in the past. Would he repeat the same mistakes? Or—to put it in the language of Pixar—would he make like Woody in *Toy Story* and take to heart what he learned in exile? Could he temper his ego, play well with others, defeat his enemies, and emerge a true hero?

———

THE LAST FOUR years of NeXT, following the demise of the IBM deal in 1992, were something of a tragicomedy. Steve tried so many different strategies that the company meandered without direction. He created a cheaper, pizza-box-shaped computer called the NeXTstation, but it never gained any traction. He and his team decided to design another model, based on a new microprocessor called the PowerPC chip—the same one that Apple's newer Macs would be using. But eventually they decided there was no real market for the machine—not a single one was ever manufactured.

Mike Slade, who was head of marketing for a time, would occasionally think fondly of his old employer, Microsoft, "which was like the Yankees," he remembers. "Going to work for NeXT was like being a starting pitcher on the 1998 Florida Marlins, a team that won, like, what—fifty games? In those days, Steve was kind of a forgotten guy. He was like Brian Wilson [after he had walked out on the Beach Boys], someone who had faded, a has-been. He became a pretty irrelevant guy in the high-tech world. Steve was in the wrong business now. He was put on this earth to sell to consumers, not corporate IT managers."

Steve had great marketing instincts, but they were wasted at a company that had not created a competitive product. One day he told Slade that he wanted to "pick a fight" with Sun. So he had Slade ask two programmers to create a fairly basic database application, one using a

NeXT computer armed with the company's software, the other using a Sun workstation and Solaris, Sun's implementation of Unix. Slade had their work videotaped. The NeXT programmer completed his task so much earlier than his counterpart on the Sun workstation that he had time to play a bunch of computer games. The video that they eventually released showed the Sun programmer muttering, as time ran out, "Um, I've just got a couple more things to work on." NeXT followed up with eight spread advertisements in the *Wall Street Journal,* spending the company's entire marketing budget for that year in one swoop. The result? "A shit storm of publicity, just as Steve had predicted," Slade recalls, with a suppressed guffaw. Sun's Scott McNealy went public, whining about NeXT's "immature" marketing. "What people didn't understand," says Slade, "is that Steve could be just as brilliant when he had to think small. I came up with this elaborate marketing strategy, and he said, 'Nope. The only thing that counts is picking a fight.' And he was right."

If he was brilliant at moments, he was still confounded by the ins and outs of running the company. His series of managerial miscues reached its climax when he hired a garrulous Brit named Peter van Cuylenburg to run the company's day-to-day operations. The tale of PVC, as he was called, speaks to how unfocused Steve could be. Having impulsively decided that he really had to hire a president, Steve ran through a series of barely vetted candidates before turning to van Cuylenburg, a veteran of Xerox and Texas Instruments, who had rejected by fax a previous job offer. Steve professed adoration. "If I was about to get run over at a crosswalk," he told the *New York Times,* "I would feel good about leaving [Peter] in charge of NeXT."

Eventually it was van Cuylenburg who got run over, figuratively speaking. He had promised to give NeXT a clear strategy, but that's not what happened. Zeroing in on details, van Cuylenburg found resistance from some employees who felt he was more interested in process than products. Worse yet, he and Steve seemed to often be at odds. Investors like Canon (that had invested $100 million in 1989) would complain that they didn't know who was running the company—Steve or van

Cuylenburg. The staff, too, got mixed signals—at least a couple of top executives believed van Cuylenburg tried to sell the company to Sun Microsystems without telling Steve. Van Cuylenburg denies this, and Sun's CEO at the time, Scott McNealy, denies that the two companies ever came close to a deal. But there's no doubt that the two did not make a successful management team. PVC was not at NeXT for long.

Shortly after he left, Steve, the ultimate "hardware guy," made the painful decision to end production of the NeXT computer. The physical design of computers engaged him more than anything else, and he took great pride in the beauty and functionality of the machines he oversaw. But the sleek NeXT computers weren't selling. Steve reluctantly shut down the hardware division, fired half the staff, and shunted the remaining hardware and factory assets off to Canon in a deal overseen by Jon Rubinstein. The Fremont factory building itself was put on the market to be leased out or sold as what it had been before—basic warehouse space. The original dream—that NeXT would create the world's next great computer—was over. "We got lost in the technology," Steve would later tell me.

There was no hiding NeXT's failure, and there was no hiding the fact that NeXT's failure was primarily Steve's doing. This was the low point of Steve's career. He was distraught over having failed, and, uncharacteristically, he let his disappointment show. One day, Ed Catmull read a NeXT press release about, he says, "how NeXT is *really happy* to be selling software to control government information servers, or data centers, or something mundane like that. I read this and thought, Oh, shoot, this has got to be killing Steve. So I called him up. We met at a Japanese restaurant in Palo Alto, and I said, 'This isn't you, Steve.' And he went, 'Ohhhhh, I know! I hate this so much. I mean, CIOs are nice guys, but God is this awful!' "

In public, Steve tried to portray this shift as a bold bet on the company's software, especially its NeXTSTEP operating system, which had, he said, "no competitors." But this time his sophistry was recognized as such by the media—and by those competitors, like Microsoft, who supposedly did not exist.

Steve did not shut down the entire company. Just as he had never given up on Pixar, he never quite gave up on NeXT. And just as he had at Pixar, he decided to play out two separate end strategies. He halfheartedly pitched the company to Sun (again), Hewlett-Packard, and even Larry Ellison's Oracle, but nothing ever came through. At the same time, he kept pushing Avie Tevanian and his software team hard. Steve genuinely believed he had the sharpest team of operating system software engineers in the business, and he still hoped that the workstation world might embrace the NeXTSTEP operating system. So the software engineers kept beating the bugs out of it, and porting it to other microprocessor architectures, such as Intel's Pentium family, or the PowerPC chip from IBM and Motorola. Steve worried deeply about finding a way to repay his investors, who had provided nearly $350 million in working capital. Not making them whole would have mortally wounded his credibility as an entrepreneur if he ever tried to start another computer company. So Steve waited to see where NeXTSTEP—and Avie's crack team of engineers—would lead him.

By 1996, it began to seem as if their efforts might pay off in at least a modest way. Avie's team had developed another software product that was drawing accolades. WebObjects was a tool for building commercial websites and other online applications out of modules of prebuilt code, called "objects," that sped the development process and allowed the reuse of standardized components. This capability was especially helpful in building online stores, and the World Wide Web was now teeming with independent software developers and corporate coders building interactive websites with a commercial component. Business had grown so quickly that sales of WebObjects licenses now generated more revenue than NeXTSTEP. Finally, NeXT could truly say it was generating a small operating profit. Steve even lined up Merrill Lynch to back a potential IPO. Once again, a company of Steve's had found its footing by transforming into something other than what he had intended.

AROUND THAT TIME—on April Fools' Day 1996, to be precise—a former air force captain named Fred Anderson showed up at Apple Computer headquarters at 1 Infinite Loop in Cupertino for his first day of
work as the chief financial officer. What he found there was a disaster.

"It was a house on fire," he remembers.

Anderson, who was then fifty-two years old, had held a similar
position at a computer services company called ADP, based in Rose-
land, New Jersey. ADP was a well-oiled machine. But its business—
providing data management services to other large corporations—was
about as prosaic as they come in the world of high tech. Anderson had
been there four years and had already fixed whatever needed his special
skills and attention. He was bored. Yet he and his wife, Marilyn, had
spent years renovating and expanding their traditional Tudor home in
Essex Falls, New Jersey, and he was just getting settled into the subur-
ban life of a typical East Coast corporate big shot. He wasn't looking
for a new job. But then an executive search firm for Apple Computer
came calling. The Cupertino company began aggressively wooing him
shortly after CEO Michael Spindler abruptly fired the company's previous CFO in November 1995.

Apple Computer had always meant something special to Anderson
and his wife. Judging from his appearance, you wouldn't suspect that
Fred Anderson was what people now would call an Apple "fanboy." He
looked the part of a wonky, corporate CFO: tall, even-tempered, well
coiffed, and partial to dress slacks and crisply pressed, monogrammed
shirts or, when slumming it, to khakis and a polo shirt. But both he
and his wife were avid Macintosh users and had always felt a special, almost romantic affection for the company since its very founding. Fred
originally hailed from Southern California, and Marilyn had graduated from Stanford University, smack-dab in the middle of Silicon Valley. They had always hankered to move back to the West Coast.

So Anderson listened to what Apple had to say. As with all things
Apple at the time, his recruitment had its own drama. Company of-
ficials didn't bother to tell Anderson that, even as they were pursuing

him, the company was secretly trying to hammer out a merger with Sun Microsystems. Anderson probably should have sensed that something was not right when one of his early phone conversations with Spindler, a gruff German nicknamed "the Diesel," came while the executive was convalescing in the hospital for a health condition brought on by extreme stress. Spindler would be fired in the weeks ahead, after which Anderson found himself being courted as the first big hire of Apple's next CEO, Gil Amelio, a former semiconductor executive who had been a member of the Apple board of directors for less than a year.

Ultimately, it wasn't the sales pitch from Spindler or Amelio that swayed him. It was more as if Anderson sold *himself* on the Apple job, using the same logic Steve Jobs had used on John Sculley when wooing him with that famous taunt, "Do you want to spend the rest of your life selling sugared water, or do you want a chance to change the world?" Anderson liked the idea that he might help save a great American success story from oblivion. "There was a part of me that said, 'You know, I'd hate to see that company die,'" he remembers. "That's reason number one. I knew how passionate my wife and I were about their products, and I believed that there was this loyal, passionate customer base that didn't want Apple to die. What I hoped was that it also translated into a passionate employee base that would fight to save the company, too. But to be honest, I didn't know that for sure. When I told my wife I'd like to take the Apple job, she looked at me and said, 'Are you crazy?! You already have a fantastic job.'"

Apple's troubles were deep indeed and had worsened over many years. John Sculley's "market-driven" strategy failed to produce any significant technological breakthroughs. Apple's efforts to do so were only made worse by the CEO's desire to prove himself to be as much of an innovator as Steve. Most costly of all his misguided efforts was his attempt to carve out a brand-new category of personal computing with a handheld device called the Newton, which was met with widespread ridicule after its highly touted handwriting recognition feature turned out to be prone to absurd malapropisms. It was an expensive failure, made worse by the fact that Sculley decided to open a bunch of Apple retail stores to sell the doomed new device. Sculley's nurturing of the Macintosh did provide some financial cover for the company. But Apple's share of the PC market eroded as Windows steadily improved.

The Apple board grew disenchanted with Sculley's misfires and abruptly dismissed him in 1993. They replaced him with Spindler, the German sales executive whose idea of a strategy was for Apple to ape Bill Gates and license the Macintosh operating system to other manufacturers in a belated attempt to fend off Windows. But this strategy too failed, and the availability of cheap clones tarnished Apple's mystique as a maker of premium hardware. Spindler, who preserved Sculley's old "market-driven" approach to product development, also allowed Apple's product line to swell uncontrollably, as engineers experimented with different bells and whistles in order to target potential markets that they thought warranted entirely new and distinct Macintosh models.

But Apple's biggest problem was Microsoft. Bill Gates's company had become a juggernaut, and with the release of Microsoft's Windows 95 it formally seized the initiative for driving PC innovation from Apple. It even outdid Apple in over-the-top marketing. Gates introduced this landmark version of his industry-standard operating system with a tightly orchestrated, worldwide rollout emceed by Jay Leno from a big white circus tent on the Microsoft campus and beamed by satellite to gatherings in forty-three cities around the world. The fanfare prompted tens of millions of PC users to line up for hours or even days in order to be among the first to be able to buy the software and install it on their machines when it went on sale at midnight on August 24. The Rolling Stones' "Start Me Up" was the official promotional anthem.

Apple's own attempts over the previous eight years to modernize the architecture of its computer operating system had failed again and again. Projects with code names like Pink, Gershwin, and Copland fell by the wayside, and a couple of awkward joint ventures also went nowhere, including one with IBM curiously named Patriot Partners.

The problem was that there were so many things Windows 95 could do that Apple's aging Macintosh System 7 simply couldn't begin to match. The list included nerdy-sounding features like preemptive multitasking, which allowed several applications to operate simultaneously without interfering with one another, automatic document saving, and most important, much greater speed, stability, and reliability. Microsoft went so far as to hire the graphic designer for the original Macintosh onscreen icons to spiff up Windows' look and feel. Windows 95 also introduced the "Start" button, which made it much easier for users to deduce how to launch programs and otherwise manage files in a PC. Overnight, Apple's sales tanked, and inventories of unsold Apple machines and unused components began to pile up. Worse, Apple seemed to have instantly and visibly lost whatever mojo it was that had made it seem cool for nearly two decades. After Windows 95, Apple wouldn't post consecutive years of sales growth again until 2002.

By the time Spindler was bounced in the spring of 1996 and replaced by Amelio, Apple had become an undisciplined and unmitigated mess in just about every way imaginable, with sales shriveling at a truly alarming rate. No longer a growth company, the cash-strapped outfit was beginning to hemorrhage money. It had far more manufacturing capacity, inventory, and, of course, employees than it needed or could afford. There were no promising new products in the pipeline, much less over the horizon. No wonder Spindler had been so stressed out, and no wonder he was fired. No wonder Amelio and longtime Apple director Mike Markkula immediately redoubled their efforts to find a buyer, like Sun Microsystems or the old AT&T or even IBM. No wonder they had to consider filing for bankruptcy. No wonder they needed a great CFO.

Anderson gave his notice to ADP in March, and spent a month consulting for Apple before he and his wife moved west. He knew the situation was getting desperate, but it wasn't until he arrived at corporate headquarters that he began to get a sense of just how bad things were in Cupertino. Nothing in his career had prepared him for anything quite like this. ADP had posted thirty-five consecutive years of double-digit earnings. His employer before that, a minicomputer maker called MAI Basic Four, had been through some rough patches, but nothing comparable to Apple's quagmire. In the previous six months, Apple had swooned from being marginally profitable to posting a loss of nearly three-quarters of a billion dollars in the first calendar quarter of 1996. The company soon would be technically in default on hundreds of millions of dollars of bank loans. On his very first day at Apple, Anderson was shocked to learn that Amelio had already asked bankruptcy counsel to stand by. What Fortune 500 CFO in his right mind would want to step into this mess?

———

STEVE OBSERVED APPLE'S dire straits from a safe distance, fretting and muttering under his breath and off the record, like an embittered and estranged parent, that the famous company he cofounded might collapse of its own ineptitude. After ten years in exile, he still harbored a strong sense of attachment to his firstborn company and many of its employees. "He loved Apple," says John Lasseter. "I mean, he loved Apple the whole time. It was painful for him to watch what was happening to it." Indeed, the reason Steve had held on to one share of Apple stock for the previous decade was to be able to keep getting shareholder information materials and, if the spirit moved him, to be able to attend the annual shareholders meeting. He hadn't cut the cord completely.

In 1995, his billionaire friend Larry Ellison had suggested the idea of making a hostile bid to buy the company outright so they could take it private and run it as they saw fit. Ellison had even offered to raise the bulk of the money, so Steve wouldn't have to risk his own resources (Pixar hadn't yet gone public). "Steve's the only one who can save Apple," he told me. "We've talked about it very seriously many, many times, and I'm ready to help him the minute he says the word. I could raise the money in a week." But Steve had nixed the effort. Despite the allure of Apple, he had made a pragmatic decision. He was in the middle of Pixar's most critical year, when it released *Toy Story* and went public. He was trying to salvage NeXT. And Laurene was pregnant with their second child. It had all seemed like too much.

In retrospect, deflecting Ellison's offer was the first of a series of practical, well-considered, and mature decisions that Steve would make on the road back to Apple. Opportunism, intuition, and manipulation would all come to play a role in his return to the company he loved most. But by also employing a newfound patience and maturity, Steve would return a better businessman.

———

FRED ANDERSON'S FIRST official duty was to announce that Apple had lost $750 million in the quarter that had ended the day before he arrived. He had indeed walked right into a house on fire.

The grisly loss triggered bank agreement covenants that called on Apple to immediately pay back some debt. But if Apple did so, the company would quickly find itself in what is euphemistically called a "liquidity crisis"; in plain English, Apple would not have enough cash on hand or in the bank to make those required payments *and* to pay its other bills and employee salaries. So Anderson knew he would have to move quickly to persuade Apple's banks in the United States, Japan, and Europe to forgo calling their loans for a time. Then he would have to get cracking to accomplish two things that might keep the banks at bay: work out a recapitalization plan to raise more money in the public bond markets, and set in place a restructuring plan that would drastically reduce the company's operating expenses. The word *restructuring* is a euphemism, of course. The very best way to reduce expenses in a hurry is to lay off employees. Lots and lots of employees.

Before April was out, Anderson had personally visited all of Apple's major bank lenders to ask for leniency, and to present his intentions for restructuring and recapitalization. He also went to Apple's lead investment bankers—Goldman Sachs, Morgan Stanley, and Deutsche Bank—to put together plans for a "commercial paper" offering designed to raise $661 million, which the company would use in part to pay its bank lenders and to help fund ongoing operations. It was basically yet another loan, this time from investors and at a somewhat higher rate of interest, but it bought Apple time to put its house in order and to trim its head count. The goal of the restructuring was to eventually eliminate fully half of its eleven thousand full-time employees, so that the company would be able to break even with sales of around $5.5 billion, or half of its annual sales in 1985. In other words, Anderson believed that half of the company would have to disappear before things would bottom out. The layoffs would come in three waves over the next two years.

The restructuring and recapitalization plan bought CEO Gil Amelio more time and flexibility to find a way to address Apple's other big problem—its technological stasis. He needed to go shopping for an existing advanced operating system that Apple could adapt to the Macintosh to help it keep pace with Microsoft's new, improved Windows 95. Doing so would be an open admission of Apple's inability to create competitive technology on its own, but at least it would offer a glimmer of hope that the company had other options than a merger or bankruptcy.

To find a shortcut to developing a more advanced version of the Macintosh OS, Amelio looked for companies that had built a working version of Unix that ran on familiar microprocessors. Sun and several other companies, including IBM, Apollo (by now part of Digital Equipment Corporation), NeXT, and an obscure Silicon Valley startup called Be Inc., all had developed their own implementations of BSD Unix—a version developed by Sun cofounder Bill Joy—and had managed to "port" them to machines employing chips from the very same family of microprocessors that Apple used in its Lisa and Macintosh. The pure software companies were most interesting because they were cheap enough to buy outright, and small enough to absorb. NeXT was one possibility, but because it was run by Steve Jobs, a man many on the Apple board still considered to be persona non grata, that didn't seem a likely match. But Be Inc. seemed like an intriguing possibility.

That's because Be was headed by Jean-Louis Gassée, the former head of advanced product development for Apple, who had left in late 1990 after clashing with Sculley.

———

JEAN-LOUIS GASSÉE WAS the Apple sales and marketing guy who had warned John Sculley that Steve was planning to challenge his authority in the spring of 1985, prompting the CEO to cancel his trip to China and impose a corporate reorganization that all but marginalized the young cofounder. That sealed Gassée's fate in Steve's eye: from then on, he always thought of the Frenchman as a backstabber. Their enmity was hardly surprising. Gassée shared some of Steve's most cagey characteristics: he was glib and charismatic and a master of hyperbole who passed himself off as a technical expert when in fact he had no more background as a software or hardware engineer than Steve did. Like Steve, he prompted strong feelings. "If there's anyone who's a prickly bastard in this world, if there's one guy who actually competes in the prickly bastard game quite effectively," says one industry veteran who worked with both men, "it's the guy who learned at the hand of the master."

They had other similarities. Shortly after quitting Apple, Gassée started his own computer company in a huff, bringing along several key Apple employees. His business strategy was reminiscent of Steve's approach at NeXT. Be Inc. set out to design an entirely new software and hardware architecture for a computer Gassée called the BeBox, which would incorporate an operating system—BeOS—that shared some key attributes of Unix. What made the BeOS and the BeBox computer unique, however, was that they were designed to also be able to use the existing Macintosh OS, and thus operate like a Mac "clone." The intent, essentially, was to build a computer that could be two machines in one.

Much like NeXT, however, Be hadn't been able to build much of a market for its hardware, selling only two thousand machines before shutting down that part of its business in 1996, to focus on selling its software as an alternative operating system for Apple's Macs and clones built by other manufacturers. Gassée felt that becoming a software-only company would position Be to other hardware manufacturers as a potentially attractive acquisition. There seemed to be several potential suitors out there among the seven companies that made Macintosh clones, including Motorola, and a maker of Windows-compatible workstations called PowerHouse Systems, which was founded by Steve's former head of hardware engineering at NeXT, Jon Rubinstein.

When Gassée learned that Amelio had decided to go shopping for an operating system, he was shocked. It was almost as if the stars had aligned for him to sell his company to Apple, even though he would have to deal with some new faces at the company. "I was looking for an exit sign," Gassée recalls, "and here came Amelio." But Gassée made a serious tactical mistake by trying to milk the situation for all it was worth. Amelio offered to buy Be Inc. for about $100 million, which was a reasonable price for a company with its limited track record. But Gassée overreached, rebuffing Amelio's offer, as well as a counteroffer of $120 million.

I ran into Gassée one weeknight in late October 1996 at what was an unlikely haunt for him—the Buffalo Grill, a steakhouse (since closed) in a shopping mall in San Mateo, fifteen miles north of his hometown of Palo Alto. The location was out of the way, and not the kind of place where you would go to ogle Silicon Valley notables. That was precisely why Gassée had chosen the restaurant.

My wife was with me, so I nudged her on toward our table while I hung back to say hello to Jean-Louis, whom I knew socially as well as professionally; our daughters were classmates at a school in Palo Alto. He was clearly embroiled in serious conversation; he hadn't noticed me yet, so I slapped him on the back and asked him something like "What are you doing up this way? Don't you have any good restaurants in Palo Alto?" Gassée recoiled as if I were a ghost. That's when I looked around the table and recognized the others. Seated with him were Ellen Hancock, a former IBMer who was now Apple's executive VP for R&D and chief technology officer; Douglas Solomon, Apple's senior VP of strategic planning and corporate development; and venture capitalist David Marquardt (who also sat on the Microsoft board of directors). Marquardt, I knew, was Be's primary adviser for financial dealings, and his firm was also Be's biggest investor. I realized that the very last thing this group wanted was to be seen by a business journalist. Never before had I seen the voluble Gassée at such a loss for words.

When I rejoined Lorna at our table, I told her how awkward the encounter had seemed. My first reaction was that it was some sort of powwow about bringing Gassée back into Apple's management team. But if that were the case, why would Ellen Hancock, who was so new to Apple, be there instead of Gil Amelio? "Well, what do you think Steve would make of it?" Lorna asked. So, when we got home, I called Steve at his home.

It was a rather short conversation. When I asked Steve what he thought might be going on, he immediately shifted into petulant mode. "Jean-Louis Gassée is evil," he snapped. "I don't say that about many people, but he is evil." Then he made some comment to the effect that whatever Apple had planned, the company should have nothing to do with Gassée or his technology. "We've been at this for ten years at NeXT, and the BeOS is shit. It has to be. Operating systems get better with age and the BeOS isn't old enough or tested enough to be any good." That didn't really answer my question, but it sure showed I had gotten his dander up. I asked him to be sure to let me know if he heard anything interesting. Not surprisingly, he didn't; I didn't talk to him again until December, when I called to see if I could get some comment from him for a story about Apple's surprise purchase of NeXT for cash and stock totaling $429 million.

STEVE HAD SWUNG into action long before my phone call. Earlier that fall, Avie Tevanian had alerted him to the fact that Apple was looking for an operating system, and Steve immediately met with his investment bankers to determine if it made any sense to try to sell NeXT to

Apple. "We felt that we were a generation ahead of everyone else, and now we might have the chance to make that work in a mass-market world," says Tevanian. While it was public knowledge that the NeXT-STEP OS had been ported to Intel's PC microprocessors, it wasn't widely known that Avie and his team had also gotten it running on computers using the PowerPC chip. Avie and his team knew their way around all the major nonproprietary microprocessors, which is more than could be said for Be's programmers. Steve had told Avie to drop the PowerPC effort a few months earlier; now Avie had his team revive it and double down to make sure the OS was ready to present to Apple.

Steve was playing three games at once as he approached Apple. First, he *really* wanted to torpedo Gassée. "Steve was bitter that I chose to side with Sculley," Gassée remembers. "He said I stabbed him in the back, and whatnot." One evening, as Steve was leaving the Palo Alto restaurant Il Fornaio, he passed a table of software execs that included Gassée. "So I hear you're going to save Apple, Jean-Louis," he said, before heading out the door. Gassée had no idea that NeXT was even being considered by Apple. He thought he had the deal sewn up.

Second, Steve wanted to protect and pay back his investors. Third, he wanted to find suitable next acts for the key people who had stuck with him at NeXT. As Susan Barnes once told me, "If you weren't good at your job, he owed it to the rest of the team to get rid of you. But if you were good, he owed you his loyalty." So while the price was important, so was what the acquiring company intended to do with the NeXT technology, and how they would embrace the technologists who built it. Steve knew he had to convince Amelio that the real jewels that Apple would be acquiring were NeXT's people.

Amelio was an easy mark, and Steve knew it. He saw him as a stuffed shirt who enjoyed the fruits of being CEO but knew little about selling personal computers. So Steve was at his flattering best as he wooed Amelio. In a crisp presentation to the CEO and Ellen Hancock on December 2, he explained that he was willing to do whatever it took to make the deal work, and that he was confident that their good judgment would lead them to NeXT. On December 10, he and Avie made what Amelio himself described as a "dazzling" presentation of the NeXT operating system, during a bake-off against Be at the Garden Court Hotel in Palo Alto.

Just ten days later, Steve had a deal, one that was sealed in Steve's kitchen and got him out of NeXT with more than he could ever have imagined. Avie was guaranteed a central role in the development of Apple's system software strategy and a spot on Amelio's senior executive staff. The price was rich, thanks largely to the recent success of WebObjects, and especially compared to what Amelio had offered Gassée: Steve and his investors would get $429 million in cash and Apple stock. "It wasn't about the money," says Gassée, who concedes that he asked too much for Be. "It was about bringing Steve back. He had a choice between bringing Steve back or not bringing Steve back, and he made the right choice. They could do things we couldn't do."

Most of the Apple shares went to Steve, who agreed to sign on as special adviser to Amelio. The annual MacWorld trade show in San Francisco was coming up in a few weeks, so he offered to make one of his trademark stage presentations after Amelio's keynote address to publicly underscore his "return" to the company he helped hatch.

On a Saturday in late December, Steve invited me over to his house. He was already working on his remarks for MacWorld, and he wanted to see what lines would resonate. But he also wanted to talk about Amelio. "You wouldn't believe what a bozo Amelio is," he hissed. What most galled him was that Amelio, he felt, had no clue about selling to walking, breathing people. "All he knows is the chip business, where you can count your customers on one hand," Steve groused. "They aren't people, they're companies, and they buy chips by the tens of thousands."

I reminded Steve that just a few months earlier he had told me about how he and Larry Ellison had briefly mulled the possibility of a hostile takeover of Apple. "If he's such a bozo, why are you sticking around? Couldn't you take your share of the money and just walk?"

"I can't just walk away from Avie and the others, and say 'So long, nice knowing you!' Plus," he continued, "I can tell that there are still a lot of other really good people at Apple. I just don't think Amelio is the right guy to lead them."

"Well then, what about you?" I said, asking the question on everyone's mind. Steve hemmed and hawed. He seemed as unsure of himself as I'd ever seen him.

———

THERE ARE SOME people who have always believed that Steve did everything he could to engineer a triumphant return to the top job at Apple, that he was executing some grand master plan all along. Gil Amelio is one of them; Bill Gates is another.

The truth is more subtle. Over the previous decade, Steve had learned to act less impulsively. In the past, he had overreached time and again. Now he was willing to walk slowly down a path, and if following his nose led him somewhere better than where he thought he was headed, that's where he would go. In the months after the sale of NeXT, as he studied Amelio and understood more about the current state of Apple, Steve displayed the more deliberate approach he would bring to the company when he was in charge.

The two men whom Steve trusted the most at Apple during the period following the sale of NeXT agree that Steve did not intend to become Apple's CEO. Avie Tevanian was now Amelio's chief of software engineering, while Jon "Ruby" Rubinstein had been brought in at Steve's suggestion to run the hardware division. "We didn't think we were coming to Apple to work for Steve," says Tevanian. "He just didn't seem that interested." Steve repeatedly told them he was reluctant to take on the job, much less lobby for it.

Coming to Apple wasn't exactly a dream come true for either Avie or Ruby. A few weeks after the NeXT deal closed and the two were settling into their new roles, Apple revealed that it had lost $120 million during the quarter ending December 31, 1996. "I asked Steve, 'What have we gotten ourselves into here?'" remembers Tevanian. "Because it was clear that Apple was the company that was broken, not NeXT. You could look at the two of us as Steve wanting to get his own people in, but he did it because it was the right thing. He knew these other people. They were the reason Apple was screwed up."

"I don't believe any of the Machiavellian stuff," adds Ruby, a native New Yorker with the svelte looks of a long-distance runner. "When I got there, I took a look around and thought, Oh my God. What did I just get myself into?"

In the weeks after our December chat, Steve and I met a few more times over his kitchen table for a series of off-the-record discussions. Steve described what he was finding at Apple, in the hope that I would push ahead with a story about the sorry state of things in Cupertino. He spoke freely, although he insisted that I disguise any quotes I wanted to use. At one point he rhetorically asked: "Why do I feel like it's my fiduciary responsibility to see a negative story about my own company?".

The main answer was that the more he got to know Amelio, the more he realized that Dr. Gil—and his team—could never lead Apple back to any kind of prominence. He was dismayed by so much at the company, and he blamed the board of directors as much as Amelio. He couldn't believe that any board could ever have envisioned the dour Michael Spindler, "the Diesel," as an inspirational leader, just as he was dumbfounded that the board had then hired someone like Amelio. He believed that Amelio, who ascended to the CEO position after just one year on the board, had maneuvered himself into the gig by positioning himself as a turnaround expert. "But how can he be a turnaround expert," Steve asked me, "when he eats his lunch alone in his office, with food served to him on china that looks like it came from Versailles?"

Amelio did himself no favors. Rather than adapt to Apple, he seemed to try to get the company to take on his personality. He had surrounded himself with top executives drawn mostly from the semiconductor industry he knew so well, and he was never effective in public situations. Once, while talking to a group at a dinner party that included Larry Ellison, Amelio tried to put his company's problems in perspective for the other guests. "Apple is a boat," he said. "There's a hole in the boat, and it's taking on water. But there's also a treasure on board. And the problem is, everyone on board is rowing in different directions, so the boat is just standing still. My job is to get everyone rowing in the same direction." After Amelio walked away, Ellison turned to the person standing next to him and asked, "But what about the hole?" That was one story Steve never got tired of telling.

Steve was unfair to Amelio. Although he did once tell Amelio that arranging the $661 million in new financing was a good move, he gave him little credit for anything else, even though it was Amelio who signed off on the critical restructuring that Anderson was managing. And when Steve did acknowledge that there was some good work going on inside the company, he credited this to employees who had the true "Apple spirit"—the one that he and Woz had instilled years before—and not at all to Amelio.

But Steve was also right about Amelio, as I discovered when I did finally report and write a story about Apple for *Fortune* in early 1997. In dire need of strong leadership, Apple was in the hands of a bumbling CEO. It had almost two dozen separate marketing teams, which didn't communicate with one another. Its product line was metastasizing. The Mac clone licensing program made no sense. And Amelio was letting the problems get out of hand.

His lack of leadership went on public display at the annual MacWorld trade show in San Francisco, on January 7, 1987. Amelio's opening speech was a meandering disaster. Back then, Apple held four annual MacWorlds, with the others coming later in the year at Tokyo, Paris, and Boston. The keynote speeches had become Apple's primary showcases for introducing new products, and for rallying software developers and customers. Amelio, a barrel-chested, stiffly moving introvert, tried his best to appear a little more hip by ditching his usual uniform of wingtips and a pin-striped suit for a brownish shirt with a banded collar, a sport jacket, and loafers. The highlight of his talk was supposed to be the formal announcement of the acquisition of NeXT and of Steve's return as an adviser. Steve, who had dressed up more than usual, sporting tailored, pleated black pants, a matching Eisenhower jacket, and a white shirt buttoned tight at the collar, waited in the wings as Amelio droned on and on. Gripping the podium at an odd angle, the CEO rambled for more than an hour through a scripted pitch that made little mention of the company's continuing financial predicament. Even though he relied on a Teleprompter, he lost his place. At one point, in a display of pseudo-casualness, he removed his jacket, and you could see large dark circles of perspiration emanating from his armpits, like the actor Albert Brooks in the famous scene from *Broadcast News*.

Steve was greeted with rapturous applause when Amelio finally got around to introducing him. It had been six long years since he had made a corporate strategy presentation to an audience of any meaningful size, and he seized the moment. In contrast to Amelio, he kept his remarks short, cool, and crisp. He promised to "help Gil in any way he asks me to," and vowed to help make Apple's products exciting again. Speaking without notes, he calmly worked the front of the stage so people could get a good look at him. He was encouraging and forceful, yet purposefully vague. He didn't want to make any specific promises; after all, he still wasn't sure he really wanted to have anything to do with Apple.

"Initially," Anderson remembers of those early days, "Steve simply didn't engage. Amelio always had these formal staff meetings, and Steve attended one shortly after MacWorld. It was kind of boring, and Steve didn't like how it was going. So in the middle of the meeting he just got up and walked out. I know what he was thinking—this guy is a bozo."

That's exactly what Steve told me again a couple of weeks after MacWorld. "I know I've said it before, but Amelio is a total bozo," he said. "He is the absolute wrong person to be leading Apple. I don't know who the right person is, but it definitely is *not* him."

LIKE RUBINSTEIN AND Tevanian at NeXT, Lasseter and Catmull were "keepers." So, early in 1997, during the very months when he was studying the hapless Amelio, Steve decided he wanted to safeguard their future by renegotiating Pixar's distribution contract with Disney CEO Michael Eisner—the only man other than Jean-Louis Gassée whom Steve ever described to me as "evil." (This was several years later, when relations between Disney and Pixar reached an all-time low.)

Toy Story had become the undisputed blockbuster of the 1995–1996 holiday season, eventually garnering $361 million in worldwide box-office receipts. Some $45 million of that went to Pixar. That was a lot of revenue for a first movie, but meager fare when compared to what Disney pocketed for financing and distributing the film. Furthermore, Pixar had no share of the video rights, which of course would be substantial for a family film this popular.

With work well under way on Pixar's next movie, *A Bug's Life,* Steve decided to right this wrong. With $130 million of IPO cash in hand, Pixar didn't need Disney to finance its films. And if it could pay for its own productions, why should it earn a mere 12.5 percent of box-office receipts? Steve decided he wanted to tear up the very deal that had saved the company just five years earlier.

"Nobody in Hollywood wants to take any risk," he told me a year later. He truly was proud that he and Lawrence Levy had studied Hollywood closely, and had learned enough to understand how Pixar could cut a great deal in an industry that thrived on plundering the "dumb money" of starstruck outsiders. "You can't go to the library and find a book titled *The Business Model for Animation,*" Steve explained. "The reason you can't is because there's only been one company [Disney] that's ever done it well, and they were not interested in telling the world how lucrative it was."

Steve put in a call to Eisner, and headed to Hollywood to renegotiate. "What we wanted to do with our new deal was far beyond what anybody else [other than Disney] had ever done," he crowed. "And far more sophisticated, because in Hollywood, there are very few relationships between companies. There are relationships between companies and individuals, like between a major studio and Steven Spielberg, or a small production company like an Amblin and a studio. But there are very few relationships between peer companies. But that's how we wanted to think about ourselves. In terms of producing animated films, we wanted to think of ourselves as a peer of Disney's own animation business."

On the surface, his entreaty seemed arrogant, quixotic, and ungrateful. It had barely been a year since the debut of *Toy Story*, a film that had been made possible only by the endorsement and support of the world's most successful animation company. But as was true so often when Steve negotiated, the audacity of his demand was matched by his cool and accurate appraisal of the landscape. Six years earlier, when Katzenberg was running animation and Disney had held all the power, Steve had quickly agreed to their terms. But now Eisner was at war with Katzenberg, who was building up DreamWorks Animation with the intent of besting Disney Animation. His new studio had set off a talent war, leading to, among other things, a series of escalating offers to Lasseter from both Disney and DreamWorks.

Steve saw the opportunity and calmly made the most of it. The IPO and *Toy Story* had changed everything about the relationship: Pixar held a lot more of the power now, and there was nothing Eisner could do. Steve's underlying threat to Eisner was simple: give Pixar a new deal now, or the company would walk after its existing three-movie deal expired. Losing Lasseter and Pixar to Katzenberg or another studio would have been disastrous for Disney. In the end, however, the negotiation wasn't as fraught as it might have been. "For us to go in there and say we'd finance half of our films, well, they hadn't heard that very often," Steve told me. "Michael appreciated that, and all of a sudden we were no longer a production company, we were a co-financier." Eisner was offended by Jobs's temerity, but the terms of the new deal were fair, giving each side half of all profits. On February 24, 1997, a new, five-movie deal was signed. Strand by strand, Steve was wrapping up the remaining loose ends of his decade in the wilderness.

————

THE STORY I published in *Fortune* in March 1997 infuriated nearly everyone at Apple. Titled "Something's Rotten in Cupertino," it portrayed a company in utter disarray. It included several unflattering anecdotes about Amelio, and was equally critical of his two predecessors, Sculley and Spindler, and of the Apple board of directors. Amelio would call me a "literary ax-murderer" in his memoir, *On the Firing Line: My 500 Days at Apple.*

The story, along with some other critical press around the same time, added to the public beating Amelio had started taking after MacWorld. Its indictment of the Apple board put more pressure on the directors. By that time, the director with the most credibility and authority was its chairman, Edgar S. Woolard Jr., who was CEO of DuPont, the chemical giant. The more Woolard learned about Apple's woes, the more he knew that Amelio didn't have the right stuff to save the company. "Ed started asking questions, like 'How's morale, Fred?'" Anderson remembers. "And I'd say, 'It sucks, Ed.'" Anderson hid nothing from the chairman; the strategy was ill-conceived, the company was not going to hit its targets, and Anderson was planning to leave if Amelio stayed on.

Meanwhile, Steve had decided to undermine Amelio. He made that crystal clear on June 26, when, after the expiration of the six-month waiting period Amelio had insisted on, he dumped all but one of the shares he'd gotten for selling NeXT, without bothering to tell anyone at Apple. Once again, he held on to a single share so he would be eligible to attend Apple's annual meeting. It was not an exercise in profit-taking. The value of those 1.5 million shares had dropped $13 million during those six months. But the sale *was* a high-decibel vote of no confidence. Amelio felt stabbed in the back, and he had been. On July

Fourth, Ed Woolard called Amelio at his vacation home at Lake Tahoe to tell him he was fired. Then the chairman called Steve to see if he would be willing to come back as CEO.

Steve had cut Amelio's legs right out from under him. He'd had no qualms about that once he'd decided that the Doctor was a bozo. (In private, he would also call him a "doperino.") But that didn't mean he himself was ready to take on the job of running Apple. According to his wife, Laurene, he was still torn about whether to go back. The two of them debated the matter endlessly. She felt that he was the only person who could save the company, and she knew he still loved Apple. She knew, too, that her husband was most fulfilled when he was tackling something gripping and important. But Steve wasn't sure. The long, drawn-out experiences of salvaging NeXT and Pixar had chastened him. Pixar was on the way up. The frustrations of NeXT could now be tossed into the dustbin of history. But did he really want to try to ride to the rescue of Apple when it hardly resembled the company he had tried to build? Was he even convinced it had the people and resources to become competitive? Did he want to work that hard, now that he had a young family? Did he want to risk what was left of his reputation by tilting at windmills? These questions were all on his mind. He had to become convinced that enough of the "true" Apple remained before he would ever consider taking ultimate responsibility for it.

Steve didn't know it at the time, but his indecisiveness was actually a kind of breakthrough. Steve was developing a more nuanced, measured approach to decision making. Steve had grown more comfortable with waiting—not always patiently—to see what developed, rather than jumping impulsively into some new venture where he thought he could once again astound the world. When he needed to—as when the opportunity arose to sell NeXT to Apple—he could strike quickly. But from now on he would act with a piquant combination of quick, committed actions and careful deliberation.

He told Woolard he did not want the job, at least for now, and he offered to help him recruit someone else. Unable to sleep that night, Steve called his friend and confidant Andy Grove at 2 a.m. Steve told

Grove that he was torn about whether or not to return as Apple's CEO, and wound his way through his tortured deliberations. As the conversation dragged on, Grove, who wanted to get back to sleep, broke in and growled, "Steve, look. I don't give a shit about Apple. Just make up your mind."

———

AFTER STEVE REJECTED Woolard's offer, the board announced that Fred Anderson would be in charge of operations, effectively making him the acting CEO. Anderson didn't want the permanent job, but unlike Steve he was certain that there was still much worth saving at Apple. For one thing, he'd been able to move the company out of its financial crisis. More important, in his fifteen months there he had gotten to know all the key players, including a few who felt comfortable complaining to him about Amelio. One of those was Apple's young design chief, a Brit by the name of Jonathan "Jony" Ive, who felt that he was wasting his talent at Apple. He invited Anderson to come by the industrial design lab, which Amelio had not visited. "There was incredible stuff going on there," remembers Anderson. "That was a big part of how I had come to worry about Amelio and his lack of leadership."

Anderson knew that he himself was not the answer. "I was really good at business and, I'd say, finance and operations, but I wasn't a product guy. I'm not an engineer," he says. Like Woolard, Anderson had enjoyed his crash course in Steve Jobs—even though their relationship had gotten off to a rocky start. "I started dealing with him during the period when we were acquiring NeXT," says Anderson. "One night during the negotiation he called me at home at one a.m., irate and cussing and ranting and raving. I was in bed with my wife, and I'm thinking, This is crazy. So when he wouldn't calm down, I said, 'I'm sorry, Steve, it's one o'clock in the morning, so I'm hanging up.' And I hung up." As was so often the case, Steve respected the pushback. He and Anderson developed such a mutual respect that the CFO would become a key member of the team that would revive Apple. "Even though Steve was not an engineer," Anderson recalls, "he had this great aesthetic taste and he was a visionary, and he had the power of personality to rally the troops. I came to the conclusion that the only person who could truly lead Apple back to prominence was Steve. He understood the soul of Apple. We needed a spiritual leader that could bring Apple back as a great product and marketing company. And nobody else great, who had those skills, was going to take on Apple at that time. So we had to have Steve."

When Woolard announced Anderson's appointment, he also noted that Steve was coming on as "an adviser leading the team." The terminology was odd, but it proved to be accurate. "Now he really rolled up his sleeves," says Anderson. The core of the new Apple—Anderson, Tevanian, Rubinstein, Jobs, and Woolard, who led a real search for a new CEO—felt under intense pressure, in large part because Mac-World Expo in Boston was exactly just one month away, on August 6. By then the company would have to be in a position to present some kind of clear strategy to its developers, or else the feeling that Apple was forever in chaos might replace the feelings of goodwill engendered by Steve's return. And given Steve's history, empty promises and airy visions wouldn't be enough. Thanks to all the hot air that had wafted out of NeXT over the years, Steve had lost much of his credibility. This time he needed to show the capacity to make smart, sensible, surgical moves quickly; if not, the market, the press, the developers, and Apple's customers might collectively respond with a sneering sense of déjà vu.

Steve understood this. His first move was to insist that the board reprice all employee stock options to $13.81—the closing price on July 7, the day Amelio's firing was made public. Steve's signature, not Anderson's, was at the bottom of the "all hands" memo from management announcing the change. It was a dramatic gesture, because most employees' options had sunk so deeply underwater that there seemed no hope that they would ever have any value. Overnight, the prospect of someday achieving actual wealth resurfaced for many of the eight thousand Apple employees who had survived the first two rounds of layoffs. (The move did nothing financially for Steve, who had no options.)

Steve's second big move was to convince Woolard to allow him to replace virtually the entire board of directors—the same one that had just ousted Amelio and brought Steve in to play a big role. Steve felt no gratitude. He was convinced that the group was as much to blame as Amelio for Apple's woes. He wanted a board that would give him the backing he needed to start making some real changes at Apple. Originally he sought the resignations of everyone except Woolard, but Woolard persuaded him to also keep Gareth Chang, the CEO of Hughes Electronics. The others would be replaced by Oracle founder Larry Ellison, former IBM and Chrysler CFO Jerry York, Intuit CEO Bill Campbell, and Steve himself. Steve kept these changes under wraps, however. He wanted to announce the move during the MacWorld keynote speech in Boston, where he'd be able to put his own distinctive spin on the news.

While he worked with the team on new product planning and yet another round of restructuring, Steve also took on a unique project he'd been handed by Anderson: to convince Bill Gates to continue to support the Macintosh with new versions of the company's productivity applications, like Excel and Word, which Microsoft would soon begin to bundle into a suite of productivity programs to be called Office.

Earlier in 1997, Gates had said that he couldn't guarantee that Microsoft would build a new version of Office for the Mac. His reluctance made sense. With Macintosh sales in a tailspin following the introduction of Windows 95, it was more difficult for Gates to justify the expense of supporting the Mac. Microsoft made good money from its Macintosh software, but as Mac sales tanked, so too did Gates's enthusiasm for supporting Apple.

"Reaching an agreement with Microsoft was absolutely critical to laying the foundation for Apple to be saved," recalls Anderson. "But Amelio couldn't get it done." If Gates said no to Steve, Apple could have found itself in the same position as NeXT had been back in 1988. Without Microsoft's applications, which had become the de facto standard tools used in most businesses, Apple, like NeXT, might cease to be relevant.

Apple did bring a stick to the negotiations. The company had a long-standing patent suit against Microsoft alleging that Windows, which largely replicated the conventions of the Mac's graphical user interface, infringed on Apple's own intellectual property. Many observers thought Apple had a good case, and Gates really wanted it settled. But Amelio had insisted on a variety of ancillary agreements and never could close the deal.

When Steve called on Gates, he kept things simple. He explained that he would be willing to drop the patent litigation, but for a price. Not only did he want Microsoft to publicly announce a five-year commitment to provide Office for the Mac; he also wanted his powerful rival to publicly, and financially, make clear that this was an endorsement of Apple's new direction by purchasing $150 million in nonvoting shares. In other words, Steve wasn't asking for a loan, he was asking Bill to put his money where his mouth was.

"It was classic," remembers Gates. "I'd been negotiating this deal with Amelio, and Gil wanted six things, most of which were not important. Gil was complicated, and I'd be calling him on the phone, faxing him stuff over the holidays. And then when Steve comes in, he looks at the deal and says, 'Here are the two things I want, and here's what you clearly want from us.' And we had that deal done very quickly."

The deal closed at quite literally the eleventh hour of the night before Steve gave his MacWorld keynote address in a downtown Boston theater called the Castle. By Steve's standards, this speech was on the short side, clocking in at just about thirty minutes. He had no products to introduce or demo. Instead, he presented the corporate equivalent of a State of the Union address. Pacing the stage like a caged tiger, Steve was visibly tense. He wore a white, long-sleeved T-shirt underneath a black sweater vest that was buttoned up in a lopsided way—the lowest button didn't have a free buttonhole, so one side of the vest hung lower than the other. A couple of times he had trouble getting the remote control to advance the slides projected on the enormous screen behind him. But once he got rolling, his presentation was one of his most concise, and a clear signal that things would change—for the better—at Apple.

Much of his talk was more of a lecture than a presentation, in which he outlined his thinking about what it would take to bring Apple back. He dismissed some of the popular criticisms of Apple, namely that its technology wasn't relevant, that it couldn't execute well, and that the company was so disorganized that it couldn't be managed. "Apple is executing wonderfully well, just on the wrong things," he quipped. The reason the company seemed in such disarray was that it hadn't had any real leadership for years. The biggest immediate problem, he added, was that the company's sales were shrinking. To address that, Apple would need to sharpen its market focus, reassert its brand, and shore up partnerships. "And the place to start is at the top." That's when he introduced the new board, describing the strengths of each new director and only then mentioning that he too would join it. He said there would be no chairman named until a new, permanent CEO was hired.

After about twenty minutes he turned to partnerships. What he really wanted to talk about was one business relationship—the one with Microsoft. His first mention of Bill Gates's company drew only tepid applause, and a few hoots. But in short order, he laid out a five-point deal that would prove to the world that "Microsoft will be part of the game with us," and later adding that "we have to let go of . . . this notion that for Apple to win, Microsoft must lose." Once it all sank in, however, the crowd warmed to the idea, booing only at the mention of Internet Explorer becoming the default browser on future Macs. When Steve introduced Bill, who appeared via a live video feed from Seattle, the audience forced the Microsoft CEO to wait while it applauded before he could make his short statement.

The moment turned out to be Steve's worst case of stage management ever. Bill's face, with his familiar smile that can border on a smirk, was about six feet tall on the massive screen above and behind Steve. He looked down on Steve as if to say, "I'm sorry, little people, while I enjoy gracing you with my presence, I can't be bothered to fly down to your little campfire singalong." The comparisons with Apple's old "Big Brother" ad were inevitable.

Overlooked in the ensuing news coverage was the quiet unveiling at the end of the show of a new slogan. One of the themes Steve came back to at several points in the program was how important it can be to try to look at things from another perspective, just to test your assumptions. In other words, he was urging people to "Think Different." Ads sporting that tagline wouldn't appear for another few months. But Steve was already sold on the concept as a rallying cry for the new Apple. In fact, he also was already sold on coming back to Apple full-time.

"I watched Bob Dylan as I was growing up, and I watched him never stand still," Steve would tell me about a year later, in a circuitous attempt to explain why he finally dived back into Apple. "If you look at true artists, if they get really good at something, it occurs to them that they can do this for the rest of their lives, and they can be really successful at it to the outside world, but not really successful to themselves. That's the moment that an artist really decides who he or she is. If they keep on risking failure they're still artists. Dylan and Picasso were always risking failure.

"This Apple thing is that way for me. I don't want to fail, of course. When I was going in I didn't know how bad it really was, but I still had a lot to think about. I had to consider the implications for Pixar, and for my family, and for my reputation, and all sorts of things. And I finally decided, I don't really care, this is what I want to do. And if I try my best and fail, well, I tried my best."

Steve waited till September to announce that he would formally take the reins. Even then, he agreed only to become Apple's "interim" CEO, or iCEO, as he liked to say, because he still was unsure where the gig would take him. "It was amazing," remembers Gates. "NeXT the hardware company disappears. NeXT the software company is going absolutely nowhere. But then the Apple board of directors hands the keys over to Steve, even as they're all thinking, 'It's too bad all the normal ways of saving a company didn't work. Holy smokes, what are we doing here? This is our only chance, but whoa! Here we go!'"

Chapter 9
Maybe They Had to Be Crazy

At a trade conference on October 6, 1997, exactly three weeks after Steve announced that he was taking on the title of iCEO, Michael Dell, the billionaire founder of his eponymous build-to-order PC clone business, was asked what he would do if he were put in charge of Apple Computer. "What would I do?" brayed the CEO, who was a decade younger than Steve. "I'd shut it down and give the money back to shareholders." Steve shot back an email: "CEOs are supposed to have class," he wrote. But just a year and a half earlier he had told me pretty much the same thing: "Apple ain't worth anything like the price of its stock," he'd said.

Dell's flippant suggestion was not just a reflection of conventional wisdom—it also sounded like a much safer idea than putting the company in the hands of Steve Jobs. There was no evidence to suggest that someone with Steve's record had the chops to turn around a mess as daunting as Apple. He had shown himself to be erratic, undisciplined, and petulant. He had only succeeded when leading small groups of people; Apple had thousands of employees scattered from Cupertino to Ireland to Singapore. He had been a prima donna and a spendthrift, but this job seemed to call for a cold-blooded CEO who understood the value of patience, discipline, and cutting costs in a hurry. Perhaps Steve was a genius—the success of Pixar seemed to reinforce that. Perhaps he was an opportunist—selling NeXT to Apple seemed to bear that out. But a great CEO? A proper leader? The world could be forgiven its skepticism.

Yet here in the fall of 1997, facing a corporate mess that would have challenged the world's greatest managers, Steve slowly started to show what he had learned in the eleven years since he was last at Apple. He had developed some discipline as he salvaged NeXT and negotiated a deal and an IPO for Pixar. He had learned the value of patience and had absorbed from Ed Catmull some proven managerial principles for leading a company loaded with creative talent. He had seen the long, slow, and twisting build of a great product, as John Lasseter and his crew followed their instincts for good and for bad, bit by bit, until their little idea of making a movie about playthings turned into the masterpiece of *Toy Story*. He had taken all this to heart, in a way no one could have predicted and he could not have explained. Now, decision by careful decision, he would start to combine this new understanding with his old talents, and shape a slow, careful comeback for Apple.

———

"I CALLED STEVE a couple of times after he sold NeXT to Apple," Lee Clow remembers, "and every time, he said he wasn't sure if he was going back, that the place was a mess, that Amelio was a dummy. Then one day in the summer, I get a call and it's Steve. 'Hey, Lee,' he says, 'Amelio resigned!' as if it was a big surprise even to him. 'Can you get up here? We've got work to do.'"

Talk about an understatement. Apple's litany of woes seemed never-ending.

Just about everything was headed in the wrong direction. In Apple's fiscal year ending September 26, 1997, the company lost a whopping $816 million. Its annual revenues had shrunk to $7.1 billion, down precipitously from a peak of $11 billion in fiscal 1995. The steady erosion of Apple's business had punctured investor confidence, and the stock price since 1995 had lost nearly two-thirds of its value: a block of shares purchased in late 1995 for $3,000 was now worth roughly $1,000.

Those weren't even the scariest numbers. These were the glory years for the PC industry; 80 million personal computers were sold in 1997, up 14 percent from the year before. Sales of Macs, however, had dropped by 27 percent, to a mere 2.9 million machines, giving Apple a minuscule 3.6 percent sliver of the market that year. Much of the pain was self-inflicted: the few buyers who didn't opt for PCs were often making purchases from the growing number of manufacturers turning out Macintosh clones.

But the deepest reason demand had softened was that Apple's products were stale, expensive, and increasingly irrelevant. Lacking the technological advantage of a state-of-the-art operating system, Spindler and Amelio had allowed Apple's marketing teams to order up all kinds of different models of the Macintosh, in hopes that computers with specialized features would appeal to particular customer niches. The effort was a fiasco, littering the market with a confusing and redundant array of slightly different Macs, each requiring unique parts and assembly methods, each promoted with its own inconsistent and frequently conflicting marketing message.

There was also a grab bag of other failures. Apple had spent nearly a half billion dollars developing and promoting Sculley's Newton, but had managed to sell only 200,000 since its 1993 debut. That hadn't stopped Amelio from hatching a Newton sibling, albeit with a keyboard, for elementary school students. Called the eMate, it was an oddly intriguing device that looked like a junior laptop done up in translucent aquamarine, with a bulbous cover and an oblong hole along one edge that functioned as a handle. It too failed to sell well. And then there were the printers. Believing that it had to offer a full-service office solution, Apple still sold its own printers. But its only noticeable contribution to the product was the plastic shell it designed to go around printer engines it purchased from Canon. Apple usually sold the machines at a loss. A hybrid Mac/TV for college students and a cheap consumer multimedia computer/game machine called the Pippin rounded out Apple's desperate array of ill-defined, marketing-driven products. Seen together, this mishmash of offerings represented a company that had lost its soul and become derivative. By the winter of 1997, hundreds of thousands of unsold machines gathered dust in warehouses.

———

THAT PHONE CALL to Clow was the beginning of Steve's first big move as iCEO. Steve decided Apple needed an advertising campaign to reaffirm Apple's old core values: creativity and the power of the individual. It needed to be something radically unlike the meek and confused product advertising that Apple had been offering consumers for years. Instead, this campaign would celebrate the company—not the company as it was that summer of 1997, but the company Steve imagined Apple should be. On the surface, it seemed an outrageous and perhaps spendthrift goal, given the company's losses and layoffs. But Steve was insistent. And that's why Clow made the journey north from TBWA\Chiat\Day's offices in the Venice section of Los Angeles to Apple headquarters in Cupertino.

Technically, Steve made Clow compete for the Apple account with two other agencies. "But he basically told me that it was ours, if I could deliver what he wanted," remembers Clow. He had several advantages over his competitors. First, of course, he had created the most memorable ad in Apple history (and arguably in the history of advertising), the "1984" Super Bowl spot for the original Mac. Second, he and Steve had a good rapport. They were both middle-class kids with limited formal educations, and they both abhorred the conventional patterns of corporate behavior. While Steve had by now given up the open-toed-sandals look for jeans and a standard T-shirt, Clow came to work in Hawaiian shirts and zipped around the offices on a skateboard. Furthermore, Clow admired Steve's brilliance and was unafraid of his temper. "I grew up working for Jay Chiat," he remembers, "and Jay could let loose some tantrums of his own. He was just as ferocious as Steve. But their goals were both the same. Extraordinary work, at any cost. And like Steve, Jay wouldn't get in your way as you tried to achieve that. Both of them understood that you were going to fail a lot."

When the time came for Clow to present his work, he and his team had "Think Different" ready. Steve hesitated briefly when shown the first boards for the campaign, which paired the phrase with photos of noteworthy creative mavericks. His worry? That any campaign celebrating individual genius would suffer from the idea that Steve was simply out to celebrate his own creative genius. But he went with Chiat\Day anyway. "His decisiveness was so different from the crew that had been there," Clow remembers. "No sending things off to some marketing exec somewhere for approval, no vetting by some committee. In the old regime, you never knew who was making the decision. With Steve it was totally different. It was him and me. You don't get that at any companies—no CEO gets involved the way he does." The campaign went through several iterations over the course of a few anxious weeks, with Steve fretting the details right up until the final night. Clow pushed hard for Apple to go with a recording of Steve narrating the stirring free-verse essay that elaborated upon the campaign's motto. He sent the studio that was to broadcast the ad during the network premiere of *Toy Story* both Steve's version and another read by the actor Richard Dreyfuss. In the morning, Steve called Clow to tell him they had to run Dreyfuss's version. "If we go with mine," Steve said, "it'll become about me. And this can't be about me. It's about the company." It was not the decision of an egomaniac, of someone only out for himself. "Which is why," Clow remembers, "he's the real genius and I'm just the ad guy."

So on the day of the broadcast, it was Dreyfuss's voice behind a slide show of portraits of Albert Einstein, John Lennon, Pablo Picasso, Martha Graham, Miles Davis, Frank Lloyd Wright, Amelia Earhart, Charlie Chaplin, and Thomas Edison, among others:

Here's to the crazy ones. The misfits. The rebels. The troublemakers. The round pegs in the square holes.

The ones who see things differently. They're not fond of rules. And they have no respect for the status quo. You can quote them, disagree with them, glorify or vilify them.

About the only thing you can't do is ignore them. Because they change things. They invent. They imagine. They heal. They explore. They create. They inspire. They push the human race forward.

Maybe they have to be crazy.

How else can you stare at an empty canvas and see a work of art? Or sit in silence and hear a song that's never been written? Or gaze at a red planet and see a laboratory on wheels?

We make tools for these kinds of people.

While some see them as the crazy ones, we see genius. Because the people who are crazy enough to think they can change the world, are the ones who do.

The campaign, which played out in posters, billboards, TV spots, and print ads, received unanimous critical praise. The brilliance of "Think Different" is that it celebrated a counterculture philosophy in a way that allowed almost everyone to feel part of the celebration. Its message was the advertising equivalent of an ideal Apple product—bold and aspirational and accessible all at the same time. It was heartfelt.

The language, which Steve worked on along with Clow and others at TBWA\Chiat\Day, focused outward, defining the quality of an Apple buyer, rather than of a particular machine itself. There's no computer mentioned, in fact. Just "tools," created for the creative. The campaign's clarity and simplicity stood out prominently from the morass of other computer advertising and reminded people of the fresh spirit so many had once loved about Apple. The $100 million campaign began the polishing up of Apple's image, a necessary task that would take years.

It paid off in two immediate ways. First, Think Different started a process of bringing pride back to Apple's employees. Billboards and posters went up across the Cupertino campus. Steve's narrated version was featured in a video promoting the whole campaign inside the company, and later, after Apple won the Emmy Award for the best television ad campaign for 1998, the company gave a fifty-page commemorative book to all its employees. "Our audience was the employees as much as anyone else," says Clow. Inspiring them was challenging, especially when Steve was shuttering divisions of the company and laying off thousands of workers. But Think Different gave the surviving employees a sense that they might see better days ahead, for the first time in years.

Think Different also bought Apple some precious time at a moment when the company had little of tangible value to show off. Steve knew, of course, that he would eventually have to deliver products that lived up to the campaign. But he didn't have them in the fall of 1997. The campaign offered cover while Steve and his team began the hard slog ahead.

Even without Steve's own voiceover some in the press did indeed view Think Different as yet another moment of Steve's grandiosity, and as such, cause for more concern than applause. But in retrospect, it seems clear that it was the exact opposite of grandiose: it was the first step of a leader who would now progress *only* in steps, not by leaps and bounds. "He was so focused," remembers Fred Anderson. "He was intense and both patient and impatient at the same time." Steve had begun to move incrementally.

WHILE THE THINK DIFFERENT campaign captured the public's attention, Steve was busy throwing out all kinds of pieces of the old Apple. The restructuring touched every corner of the company. Out went the Newton and eMate product lines, and the stores and engineering and marketing groups that supported them. (In an odd twist of fate, ex-CEO Amelio came back to visit Steve at Apple headquarters late in 1998 with an offer to buy the assets and intellectual property of the mothballed Newton operations. A few days after the meeting, Steve told me he was flabbergasted that Amelio would have any interest in trying to make a go of it with the Newton. But selling it to him would have been "a cruel joke," he told me. "I can be mean, but I could never be that mean. No way would I let him further humiliate himself—or Apple." So the Newton stayed dead. Many of its key engineers were retained, however.)

Out went the contracts that licensed the MacOS to the clone manufacturers. Steve hated the idea of having his operating system in the hands of others, and he had refused to sign on as iCEO without the promise that he could shut down the clones. This was the most expensive of the many decisions Steve made in the course of stabilizing the company. To avoid the litigation that would naturally arise from Apple abrogating the contracts, the company had to pay the clonemakers to disappear quietly. The most successful of these was Power Computing, which had commandeered a 10 percent share of the market for MacOS-compatible computers. Apple paid $110 million in cash and stock to acquire the company and hire some of its engineers.

Out went the inventory. Tim Cook became a new member of the team in March 1998 when he was hired away from Compaq—where he had been called "the Attila the Hun of inventory"—to be Apple's chief of operations. Cook was a wiry bird of a southerner, thin and bookish-looking despite his athleticism—he biked and ran long distances regularly. Cook spoke quietly, with a soft Alabama drawl, but he may have been the toughest executive at Apple. Cook's work drew no public attention, but it was crucial to trimming the company. In the nine months after he arrived, Apple reduced its inventory from $400 million worth of unsold, unwanted Macs down to $78 million. Cook was responsible for perhaps the most dramatic example of Steve's hurry to rid himself of the burdens of Apple's recent past: the bulldozing of tens of thousands of unsold Macs into a landfill in early 1998.

Finally, out went another 1,900 employees. This was the last tranche of Anderson's resizing of the company. All in all, Anderson had taken the company from 10,896 full-time employees down to 6,658. Steve told me that being a father made firing people much harder than it had been. "I still do it," he said, "because that's my job. But when I look at people when this happens, I also think of them as being five years old, kind of like I look at my kids. And I think that that could be *me* coming home to tell my wife and kids that *I* just got laid off. Or that it could be one of my kids in twenty years. I never took it so personally before."

But if he had perhaps grown more sensitive, he had also grown more focused. As Steve pushed through the downsizing, Anderson discerned a profound difference between the iCEO and his predecessors: Steve kept the greater needs of the company first and foremost, whatever the cost. Sometimes his ability to do so could seem almost cruel, as when, in 1998, he decided that 3,600 layoffs wasn't enough and ordered 400 more people to be let go. But he was determined to lead a company staffed by the best people possible—he wanted Apple's staff to brim with the exceptionalism he had witnessed at Pixar. "When I returned to Apple, I was blown away by the fact that a third of the people there really were A to A-plus people—the kind you'd do anything to hire," he told me. "Despite Apple's troubles, they'd stayed, which was the miracle. That was the good karma of Apple. It was carried through by those people deciding to stay through it all. Another third were very good—you know, the really solid kind of people every company needs. And then there was another third who were unfortunate. I don't know whether they'd ever been good or not, but it was time for them to leave. Unfortunately, a lot of those people were in management. Not only were they not doing the right things, but they were instructing everybody else to do the wrong things, too." Steve's narrow determination was critical: the core team could unite around Steve, knowing that he would do absolutely whatever it would take to turn this company around. He was all in, and working as hard as anyone. "It was pretty bleak those first six months," he told me later. "I was running on vapor."

Still, even though Steve had been disciplined about cutting the company down to its proper size, nobody could really be sure that he was the man to lead Apple forward. Despite ostentatiously declining to receive a salary, Steve was an expensive, unproven bet. Some $450 million of Apple's $816 million loss for 1997 could be attributed to the acquisitions of NeXT and to the purchase and liquidation of Power Computing. One way to understand that number is to realize that Apple had paid out more than a half billion dollars for two acquisitions whose asset value, mere months after the deals were concluded, was just one-fifth that number. A more revealing way to think of it is that Apple had shelled out more than a half billion dollars to rehire Steve Jobs.

———

A FEW MONTHS before Steve came back to Apple, I asked him what he thought Apple's top priority should be. Should it be a new operating system, now that Avie Tevanian was there to create it? "Not at all," he replied, with a forcefulness I hadn't been expecting. "What Apple needs more than anything is to ship a great new *product,* not necessarily some new *technology.* The trouble is, I don't think they even know *how* to make a great product anymore." He paused as if he realized how damning that statement sounded, and abruptly added, "That doesn't mean they can't."

This time, Steve didn't immediately set out to solve everything with the introduction of some groundbreaking new machine. This was a big change from what he'd attempted at NeXT and at Apple the first time around. Instead, he laid out a plan in broad strokes for the company's entire product line. Before Steve would ask his engineers to come up with a particular new product, he wanted to be sure they understood how it would fit into Apple's overall plan. He wanted everyone working from the same playbook, and he wanted that game plan to be crystal clear. He couldn't afford any of the strategic confusion that had hampered the development of the NeXT computer.

The key was to simplify Apple's ambitions so that the company could sharply focus its substantial engineering talent and brand equity on a few key products and broad markets. To understand why Steve could pare down Apple's offerings so drastically in 1997, it helps to think of personal computers as protean devices that can be programmed to be any of a number of tools—a word processor, a supercalculator, a digital easel, a searchable library of research materials, an inventory control system, a tutor, you name it. There's no need for the machine to have a different physical form to perform each different service. All it needs is powerful, adaptable software within. And in the mid-1990s, the capability of software was expanding faster than ever, thanks to the advent of local area networks and the burgeoning Internet. When software can link you to other people, and to databases housed on other computers far away from yours, it becomes much more powerful than an application that is limited strictly to whatever is stored on your own personal computer.

Steve set out to show how Apple could transform itself into a profitable company while offering no more than four basic products: two separate models of desktop PCs, one for consumers and one for professionals; and two separate laptop versions aimed at those same constituencies. That's it. Four quadrants, four product lines. No more redundant engineering efforts, extraneous manufacturing processes, or sales pitches aimed at tricking consumers into buying unnecessary features. With only four basic products to design, Apple's engineers and industrial designers could invest the time and effort to make their hardware and their software distinctive.

This critical decision was as controversial as anything Steve did during this period. Employees were outraged that their pet projects, including some truly valuable technologies that Apple had been developing for years, were being cast aside. Some technologies provided consumers with a tangible benefit, but if they didn't fit into Steve's quadrant structure, they had to go—the institution, he decided, could only focus on so much.

The core executive team understood the necessity of the quadrant structure, even though it meant killing projects that were dear to staffers they respected. And eventually the rest of the company came around. They could see that the quadrants put Apple on the exact opposite course of the Windows PC manufacturers, who were busy churning out all manner of unremarkable, albeit faster and more powerful boxes. The quadrants returned Apple to its historic mission—to serve the high end of the consumer and professional markets with leading-edge products.

What the quadrant strategy *wasn't* is equally important. It was not an effort to solve all problems with one insanely great machine. Steve had been twice burned by that strategy. He had developed enough cautious wisdom to see that breakthroughs were not the solution now. Apple's customers—past, present, and potential—would first have to be shown that the company would survive, that it knew how to consistently produce and deliver distinctive products, and that it could reliably turn a profit. Only after that was accomplished—and Steve was the first to admit that it would take several years—could he think about how to exploit emerging technologies to break new ground again.

———

"SAVE APPLE WAS the mission," remembers Jon Rubinstein. "When we came in the company was almost dead. So let's save Apple—it's worth saving. It was that simple."

Steve ran the new Apple through a remarkably strong, remarkably motivated core group, consisting of Anderson, Cook, Rubinstein, and Tevanian, as well as sales head Mitch Mandich from NeXT; marketing chief Phil Schiller, a former Apple guy whom Steve brought back from Adobe; and Sina Tamaddon, a software guy from NeXT who also engineered several key deals. This group—minus Mandich, who would leave in 2000, and with the eventual addition of design chief Jony Ive—would drive operations at the company well through the mid-2000s. Given Steve's volatile reputation and track record as a manager, it's remarkable that they remained together for so many years.

Steve didn't do the kinds of things that leaders often do to cement a strong group. He didn't take the guys out to dinner. "We had good relationships within the senior executive team," remembers Tevanian, "but we built them ourselves. It wasn't through Steve. I can count on one hand the times, in the eight years that I was there, that we went to dinner together, mostly to an Indian restaurant nearby."

Steve didn't give his team much formal feedback. "During the U.S. versus Microsoft antitrust case," says Tevanian, "Microsoft subpoenaed all my personnel records at Apple. So I'm sitting down with our lawyer, George Riley, and he says, 'I've gotten your file from HR.' He pulls it out and there's one piece of paper in it, something meaningless. He's like, 'Avie, where is your file? Where's your annual reviews and all that?' I told him that I'd never had an annual review!"

"Steve didn't believe in reviews," remembers Jon Rubinstein. "He disliked all that formality. His feeling was, 'I give you feedback all the time, so what do you need a review for?' At one point I hired an executive coach so I could do three-sixty reviews with my own team. He was a really good guy, and I tried to get Steve to talk to him, but he wouldn't. In fact, he asked me, 'What do you need that for? That's a waste of time!'"

Steve didn't lavish anyone with praise, or make them available to reporters who wanted to get behind the scenes of what would become a remarkable comeback. This was not because Steve was hungry for personal press coverage. He wasn't, anymore. In his twenties, he had craved the limelight during his first flush of celebrity: "friendships" with Yoko Ono and Mick Jagger, the heady feeling of things like owning a penthouse suite in the San Remo in Manhattan, and attention from *Time* and *Rolling Stone* and *Playboy* confirmed that he had left his prosaic, middle-class upbringing in the suburbia of Northern California far behind. When he started NeXT, he had for a brief time courted the press to help give his startup a boost. But by the mid-nineties, playing up his celebrity held little appeal to Jobs. While he craved recognition for the quality of his work, he didn't desire fame in and of itself. He directed Katie Cotton, his communications chief at Apple, to adopt a policy in which Steve made himself available only to a few print outlets, including *Fortune,* the *Wall Street Journal, Time, Newsweek, BusinessWeek,* and the *New York Times.* Whenever he had a product to hawk, he and Cotton would decide which of this handful of trusted outlets would get the story. And Steve would tell it, alone.

Steve and I talked many times about his reluctance to share the spotlight with the others on his team, since I asked repeatedly to speak with them and was largely unsuccessful. Sometimes he'd aver that he didn't want anyone to know who was doing great work at Apple, since he didn't want them to get recruited by other companies. That was disingenuous, since Silicon Valley was an incestuous place where tech talent was tracked as closely as the stock market. What *was* true was that Steve didn't think anyone else could tell the story of his product, or his company, as well as he could. Steve was a great performer in any setting, and he considered most interviews to be just another performance. He was a terrific extemporaneous thinker and talker, always confident that he could make the most of an opportunity to promote the company. He cared intensely about the look of any article he participated in, because he thought that photography and typography and a stylish layout helped convey the import of whatever message he wanted to get across.

Under Steve's guidance, Apple would develop one of the clearest brand identities in the world. So, while Steve's policy irked some members of his core team, it was hard to argue with his success. Working for Steve meant accepting a whole range of idiosyncratic behaviors. Policies that seemed selfish often turned out to be good for the company. Strategies that at first appeared quixotic might well prove farsighted. The members of Steve's core team learned to anticipate and live with his unpredictability. They knew they were working for someone special.

Steve made sure in his own way that they knew he thought they were outstanding as well. Sometimes he'd ask one of them to join him on a long walk, whether around the Apple campus or near his home in Palo Alto. "Those walks mattered," Ruby remembers. "You'd think to yourself, 'Steve is a rock star,' so getting quality time felt like an honor in some ways." Steve also compensated his key employees richly, arranging lucrative long-term contracts loaded with stock options for everyone in the inner circle. "He was really good at surrounding himself with really good people and motivating them both philosophically and financially. You have to have the right mix. You have to provide just enough financial motivation in there so that people don't just say, 'Fuck you, I'm not taking this anymore.'"

Steve also understood that the personal satisfaction of accomplishing something insanely great was the best motivation of all for a group as talented as his. "You had to believe that it was going to take some time; that you weren't going to wake up tomorrow morning and it was all going to be fixed," Tevanian once told me. "And that two years, three years down the road you were going to look back and say, 'Gee, we got through it.' If you didn't believe that, you were sunk. Because there was a lot of pain along the way, there were a lot of people saying it's going to fail, it's not going to work, this is wrong with it, that's wrong with it, finding a million things wrong. But you just had to know that if you kept your head down, kept working, kept trying to do the right things, it would work out." Saving Apple was an accomplishment everyone on the team would take pride in for the rest of their lives.

"He cared deeply," says Rubinstein. "And that made him a great manager when things weren't going well. At the beginning of this time at Apple, it was such a pleasure because we were all in it together."

"When it was tough," Avie adds, "he'd think carefully about all the decisions. He'd think through the impact of everything very carefully."

While Steve never hesitated to emphatically assert his opinion, some-times his fretting would drive the group crazy, as he delayed impor-tant projects by fussing endlessly over minute considerations, such as whether to change the plug connectors for mice and keyboards. Mike Slade, the head of marketing for a brief period at NeXT, went back to work at Apple in 1998 as a consultant to Steve. "People want to paint him like he's Michelangelo, you know?" says Slade. "But he was a real nervous Nelly, like an old-fashioned, tiny, old, small businessman say-ing, 'Shall I cut another nickel off it?' Like a junk merchant."

His attention to the job at hand was intense, and he set up his sched-ule to ensure that each of his key deputies was equally focused. Every Monday morning at nine o'clock, he convened the executive team (the ET, as it came to be known) in a conference room located in Building 1 of the Apple campus. Attendance was required. Referring to an agenda he himself had written up and distributed, he'd go around the table, asking specific questions about projects under development and getting updates from the team. Each person was expected to be fully prepared for any question he might ask about their area of responsibility. For some, like Fred Anderson or Nancy Heinen, the general counsel, this might be their main encounter with Steve for the week. Others, how-ever, knew to expect rigorous follow-ups. The pressure was intense. Their past successes had earned them a place in the room, but Steve didn't care about the past. With Steve, says Ed Catmull, "The past can be a lesson, but the past is gone. His question was always, 'What are we going to do moving forward?' "

That's why "That's shit!" was as common a response from Steve as a pointed question or a thoughtful discussion. He wanted smart answers, and he didn't want to waste time on niceties when it was sim-pler to be clear, no matter how critical his response. "The reason you sugarcoat things is that you don't want anyone to think you're an ass-hole. So, that's vanity," explains Jony Ive, a crisply articulate Brit with the muscled frame of a boxer and a tendency to hunch forward over a table as he leans in to speak to you. As design chief, Ive was on the receiving end of Steve's blunt criticisms as much as anyone. Whenever he felt abused, he would tell himself that someone who sugarcoats his true opinions "might not really even be all that concerned about the other person's feelings. He just doesn't want to appear to be a jerk. But if he really cared about the work he would be less vain, and would talk directly about the work. That's the way Steve was. That's why he'd say 'That's shit!' But then the next day or the day after, he also would just as likely come back saying, 'Jony, I've been thinking a lot about what you showed me, and I think it's very interesting after all. Let's talk about it some more.'"

Steve put it this way: "You hire people who are better than you are at certain things, and then make sure they know that they need to tell you when you're wrong. The executive teams at Apple and Pixar are constantly arguing with each other. Everybody wears their thoughts on their sleeves at Pixar. Everybody's totally straight with what they think, and the same is beginning to happen at Apple." His inner circle understood that Steve's acerbic criticism wasn't personal. They'd all learned how to, as Susan Barnes said, "get through the yelling to the reason for the yelling." Steve expected them to do that, and he expected them to push back when he was wrong. "I fought with him for sixteen years," remembers Rubinstein. "I mean, it was almost comedic. I remember one Christmas morning, we're on the phone screaming at each other and both of our significant others are in the background, saying, 'Come on, we have to get going, get off the damn phone.' He was always screaming about something or other. Once, we were in this huge fight. And I'm standing, I think, in Target down in Cupertino, pushing my cart around buying toilet paper or whatever the hell it was, right? And Steve and I are on the phone, yelling at each other. It's just how we operate. I grew up in New York City. My family was out of a Woody Allen movie, you know that scene in *Annie Hall* where they're underneath the Thunderbolt roller coaster? That's my family. So fighting all the time didn't bother me. That was probably one of the reasons we were successful together."

From 850 miles up the Pacific Coast, Bill Gates watched with great interest as the limping company he had helped with that $150 million investment and a commitment to make software for the Mac struggled to survive. "It was a much more mature group," he observes. "With the Mac team or even at NeXT, when Steve went on a jag everybody just scattered into their own corner. But this Apple management team would push back and coalesce as a group. When Steve would pull any one individual out of the pack and say, 'Your work is such shit and you're such an idiot,' the pack had to decide, okay, are we going to let this one go or do we really like this guy. And they could go to Steve afterwards and say, 'Hey, come on, there aren't that many people we can hire that are near as good as that guy, go back and apologize.' And he would, even though his intensity was still just incredible.

"That is a really crack team that has gone through hell, and bonded with each other in toughness," Gates continues, falling into the present tense. "I mean, you can point to everybody on that team and say, okay, he earned his pay, he earned his pay, he earned his pay. There's no weakness in that team, nor is there a backup plan or a forward-looking alternative team. It's just this one team."

Steve had assembled a group that was strong enough to deal with who he was, and autonomous enough to compensate for his weaknesses. They developed their own tactics for managing *him*. "It was like we had a common enemy," says Rubinstein. Members of the team would meet regularly with one another to plan how to get Steve to authorize the decisions they felt would be best, to figure out a way through or around Steve's more imperious or ill-considered decisions or prejudices, and to try to anticipate where Steve would steer things next. They had the sense that Steve knew this was going on behind his back. "He knew that he could count on us to make things work," says Tevanian, "even when there was friction or problems. We faced some really hard problems, you know, and he knew he could trust us to do the right thing."

I watched Steve closely, both as he steadily and patiently composed his strategies and as he cajoled this stable, impressive team to execute them. I was skeptical because of his past failures as a manager, but intrigued. One day I asked him if he had come to enjoy the process of building companies, now that he was trying to do so for a third time. "Uh, *no*," he started, as if I were a fool. But if he didn't enjoy building companies, he sure had a thoughtful and convincing way of describing why he kept doing it. "The only purpose, for me, in building a company is so that that company can make products. One is a means to the other. Over a period of time you realize that building a very strong company and a very strong foundation of talent and culture in a company is essential to keep making great products.

"The company is one of the most amazing inventions of humans, this abstract construct that's incredibly powerful. Even so, for me, it's about the products. It's about working together with really fun, smart, creative people and making wonderful things. It's not about the money. What a company is, then, is a group of people who can make more than just the next big thing. It's a talent, it's a capability, it's a culture, it's a point of view, and it's a way of working together to make the next thing; and the next one, and the next one." A talent, a capability, a culture, and a point of view: the Apple he was in the midst of re-creating would have all these things, as would the products it would create.

————

STEVE KNEW HE had to deliver Apple's first new product in 1998. He certainly couldn't expect Apple's millions of investors to wait around for years and years, as Perot and Canon had been forced to do at NeXT. But Apple didn't have any great software applications ready to unveil, and Steve had no desire to offer *any* hardware that had been in the Amelio pipeline. He needed something new, and it had to have enough of his DNA to signal that serious changes were afoot. The personal computer business had been bereft of creativity and excitement for so long that it was now simply known as the "box" business. Steve needed a lot more than just another box.

He found his answer in the skunkworks of a building several blocks away from the corporate offices. That's where Jony Ive, the designer who had so impressed Fred Anderson, was toiling away.

Ive, Apple's head designer, was not yet a member of Steve's inner circle. An unassuming self-starter who turned thirty at about the time that Steve arrived in 1997, Ive had signed on with Apple as a contract designer in 1992 when he still lived in London, working for a design consultancy called Tangerine. The son of a silversmith who taught at the local college in the London suburb of Chingford, Ive gravitated toward industrial design at an early age, and went on to study at what is now called Northumbria University in Newcastle. There he became an admirer of Dieter Rams, the legendary onetime chief of design for Braun, the German small appliance maker, who in the 1970s was one of the pioneers of what is now called sustainable design, and who railed against the industrial practice of planned obsolescence. Rams, who still designs furniture for a Danish company called Vitsœ, had become known for his "Ten Principles of Good Design." According to Rams, Good Design is:

1. innovative
2. what makes a product useful
3. aesthetic
4. what makes a product understandable
5. unobtrusive
6. honest
7. long-lasting
8. thorough down to the last detail
9. environmentally friendly
10. as little design as possible

During Amelio's short tenure I had visited Jony in his workspace, called the Design Lab. After Steve returned, the lab would be moved into the main headquarters complex on Infinite Loop, and would become as off-limits as Los Alamos during the Manhattan Project. But under Amelio it was accessible on the late Friday afternoon when I visited. Ive was the only employee still around that day. The space was piled high with gray plastic or Styrofoam mockups of the multitudes of previous, rather ordinary Macs he and his team had designed. Back then, his objective was to repackage computers in an artfully austere way, more than to create radically new designs. There were just two exceptions, both vivid in their own way.

The first one that he showed me was the eMate, his counterintuitive version of the Newton Message Pad for elementary school students. The clamshell-type device really did look somewhat like a mussel. Its subtle curves gave it a playful look, but what really grabbed your eyes was its translucent aquamarine plastic shell—a throbbing color that seemed to glow as if lit from within.

The other brilliant design Jony showed me was his prototype of a limited-edition machine Apple would release belatedly to commemorate the company's twentieth anniversary. The 20th Anniversary Macintosh was his pride and joy at the time. It was a striking piece of out-of-the-box industrial design thinking. Jony and his team had placed the guts of a top-of-the-line laptop inside a svelte and slightly curved vertical slab, which had on the top half of its surface a color LCD monitor, and on the bottom half a vertical CD-ROM drive, all of which was framed by specially designed Bose stereo speakers. It was packed with state-of-the-art technology, including cable television and FM tuners and the circuitry necessary for the computer to double as TV set or a radio. Finally, Ive and his team had concocted a conch-shaped floor module to house the power supply, a subwoofer, and a powerful hi-fi audio amplifier so that the computer would supply the sonic fullness of a high-powered stereo system without generating too much heat or seeming bulky. The whole package looked as if it belonged on display in the sculpture gallery of New York's Museum of Modern Art. (In fact, one did wind up in the museum's industrial design section.) Technovores lusted after the machines.

The first time Steve made the long trek over to the Design Lab, Ive was nervous and apprehensive. "That very first time we met, he had already started to talk about reengaging Harmut Esslinger [the founder of Frog Design, who had designed the first Mac]," Ive says. "He came over to the studio, I think, essentially to fire me. And he should have done that, based on the products that we were shipping at the time, which weren't very good at all." The products and the prototypes didn't thrill Steve, but Ive himself made a bigger impression. He is quiet and earnest, and can be beguilingly engaging when describing what he is trying to accomplish with his designs, in his proper British accent. Like Steve, Jony has a gift for clearly explaining complex ideas. Steve was impressed. "You know Jony. He's kind of a cherub," Steve told me in late 1997. "I liked him right away. And I could tell after that first meeting that Amelio had wasted his talent."

Just as important, Jony was impressed by Steve. Thousands of Apple employees had scattered their résumés across Silicon Valley as they tried to abandon Amelio's leaky ship, and Jony had resolved to look around himself. But he quickly saw that Steve and Amelio couldn't have been more different. "Amelio described himself as the turnaround king," Ive remembers. "So he was focused on turnaround, which is mainly about not losing money. The way you don't lose money is you don't spend it. But Steve's focus was completely different, and it never changed. It was exactly the same focus from the first time I met him to right to the very end: the product. We trust if we do a good job and the product's good, people will like it. And we trust that if they like it, they'll buy it. If we're competent operationally, we will make money." It was that simple. So Jony decided not to leave Apple, a choice that would lead to the closest and most fruitful creative collaboration of Steve's entire career, even more symbiotic than his original partnership with Steve Wozniak.

Nonetheless, Steve killed both of Jony's pet projects. The eMate disappeared along with all other traces of the Newton (save a few key patents), and the 20th Anniversary bit the dust after selling just 12,000 units. The products didn't fit into his quadrants. Besides, he told me one day, "I just don't like television. Apple will never make a TV again." This was Jony's introduction to Steve's coldhearted decision-making. Like Avie and Ruby and Fred and Tim, he had come to understand that Apple's best chance forward was with Steve, and that if you were in with Steve, you were in all the way, bumps and all.

THERE WAS ONE thing that especially intrigued Steve at the Design Lab: the odd texture and eerie translucence of the eMate's plastic shell. That detail became a seed idea for the iMac, the first product of the new Steve Jobs era at Apple.

Technologically, the iMac was not a radical departure from the past. But working closely with Steve, Ive designed a cosmetic standout that, for the first time in years, gave the personal computer some personality. The iMac was a dramatically rounded shell made of material similar to the eMate's. Through its "Bondi blue" (named for the evocative tropical waters of Bondi Beach, near Sydney, Australia) translucent plastic exterior, a buyer could see the inner workings of the computer, its rigorously arranged wires and circuit boards loaded with chips that looked like 3-D maps of cities. The computer and monitor were housed in a single bulbous module with a circular hatch on the back that doubled as a handle, to allow access for repairs or modifications. Steve loved the handle despite its impracticality, because it was a throwback to the original Mac. The machine weighed thirty-eight pounds, so it wasn't likely that anyone would actually treat it like a laptop to be carried around from one workspace to another. But the handle, the shape, and the translucence combined to make the iMac seem like a bottle of blue fun. It was exactly the kind of hot new product he needed to once again differentiate Apple from the "box" crowd—the Dells and Compaqs and HPs and IBMs.

Two other decisions—one technological, one driven by marketing—also made the iMac stand out from that crowd of putty-colored rectangular slabs. Steve and Jon Rubinstein opted for developing a CD-ROM drive for loading software, rather than the standard floppy disk drive, despite the fact that most people at the time still stored their data on floppy disks. You could buy a separate, external floppy disk drive to plug into the iMac, but Steve reasoned that most software would soon be delivered on CD-ROM optical discs—a technology that was already fast displacing vinyl and tape cassettes as the primary medium for recorded music. He also felt certain that within a year or two, *recordable*

CD-ROM drives would render floppy disk drives redundant. As he had before, he was betting that users would accept a slightly uncomfortable move into the future, one that would force them to convert their data to a new format. This time he got it right.

Steve's other noteworthy decision was to slot the letter *i* in before *Mac*. The iMac was built to be plugged into the Internet, via sockets that could handle either a phone line or, for those lucky enough to have access, a connection to a full-fledged Ethernet network. It sported a built-in telephone modem as standard equipment, while most computer makers sold those only as an optional add-on. Steve had foreseen that buyers would see this "Internet" Mac as a forward-looking computer with an eye toward the future of personal computing, which was clearly going to revolve around the Internet. But the *i* did more than that. The *i* was personal, in that this was "my" computer, and even, perhaps, an expression of who "I" am. And what a bold expression it was, fresh and transparent and different. It seemed like the kind of computer that an individual who could "think different" would use.

Many critics in the burgeoning computer press sneered that the iMac was neither faster nor more powerful than machines from its competitors. After all, for a decade speed and power had been the only way personal computers differentiated themselves. Those same critics disliked the fact that this blue, rotund thing looked more like a toy than a computer. But they had missed the point completely. The iMac's radical design sent exactly the kind of reassuring, friendly, and differentiating message that Steve wanted to send. With one product, Apple had reinforced its position as the "personal" computer company. The iMac was a vivid reminder that personal computers are tools for *people,* and that they should both reflect and amplify an individual's own personality. That's why the iMac was an instant success, selling nearly two million units in the first twelve months of production, and becoming Apple's first bona fide hit in years.

Its success was critical to Steve's plans for a rebound. Steve had returned to Apple believing strongly that design could be a significant part of Apple's resurrection; the iMac supported his theory. "When we did the first iMac," he later told me, "there was such resistance in hardware engineering. A lot of people thought it wasn't a Mac, that it would fail. But the minute that everybody saw it succeed in the marketplace, a lot of the people started to turn around and go, 'Okay, this design stuff is important I guess.' They felt the thrill of success again." Steve and Jony's iMac enabled Apple to make a bold first step toward recovery, buying Apple some precious time at a moment when most observers thought it was headed to its grave.

ONE OF STEVE'S great failures during his first tenure at Apple had been his inability to deliver strong sequels to the Mac or even the Apple II. But that wasn't the case with the iMac. Just one year after its introduction, the company started to sell a new version in five gumdrop colors. They were even cooler than the Bondi blue machines, because they came with a simple slot drive for CDs, replacing the clunkier drawer that came with the first ones. And their optimistic, brilliant colors played well into Apple's marketing, which kept redefining the Apple brand as forward-looking, lively, and creative.

But Steve didn't just focus on the flashy iMacs—that too was a mistake the old Steve would have made. He made sure that his team did an equally excellent job filling the other three quadrants of the grand plan. The so-called towers, as the desktop computers for professionals were known, were the machines that paid the bills. Loaded with faster chips, more memory, better graphics, and slots for adding hard drives and CD burners and other accessories, the towers were engineered for power users—hence their name, the Power Mac. These big machines sat under your desk, linked to a monitor on your desktop, and were so fast that Apple marketed them as the first "personal supercomputers." They were hefty, but Ive's design gave the impression that they were sleek and manageable—they even had dual handles that mimicked the iMac's, and one side that opened up to make tinkering with the innards easier. The base model cost at least a thousand dollars more than the iMac, but it also carried much higher profit margins.

Here, too, Steve avoided a mistake Apple had made the first time around. He didn't claim that the Power Mac was *the* computer for all businesses, and in so doing try to push Wintel-based PCs out of the market. Instead, he targeted the Power Macs at the new, more entrepreneurial class of small businesses emerging with the rise of the Internet economy: engineers, architects, publishers, advertising agencies, website designers, and so on. This was a world that could tolerate and even celebrate "Think Different," while the dominant class of big corporations looked on fearfully at the radical and potentially undermining change the Internet seemed to promise.

The design and engineering genius that was applied to the iMacs and towers was applied to the laptops as well. The personal models, called iBooks, mimicked the fun of the iMac with a beguiling, bright orange clamshell design that echoed the shape of the old eMate. The higher-end PowerBooks for professionals were curvy, too, but they were sheathed in a rubbery-feeling black shell and powered by a PowerPC microprocessor that briefly allowed Apple to claim the somewhat dubious title of "fastest laptop in the world." The cumulative effect of these revitalized iMacs was simple but profound: just three years removed from near death, Apple had reestablished itself as the most, if not the only, truly creative company in the computer business. "When we returned to Apple," Steve told me around this time, "our industry was in a coma. There was not a lot of innovation. At Apple we're working hard to get that innovation kickstarted again. The rest of the PC industry reminds one of Detroit in the seventies. Their cars were boats on wheels. Since then, Chrysler innovated by inventing the mini-van and popularizing the Jeep, and Ford got itself back in the game with its Taurus. Near-death experiences can help one see more clearly sometimes."

The turnaround, however, did not come without expensive failures.

Apple had done a good job embracing the Internet, by making the process of getting access to the Web as simple as any other function of an iMac. But Apple's eWorld, a proprietary online subscription service bundled with new iMacs, was a flop, despite a friendly interface that suggested that going online could be as easy as walking from one neighborhood to the next. All it really offered was email services and a way to download software, and in practice it wasn't any easier to use than bigger services like EarthLink and AOL, which came bundled on Wintel PCs.

A costlier failure was a pet project that Ruby and Steve worked on together and argued about endlessly, the so-called Power Mac "Cube," which was introduced in 2000. Harking back to the design of the NeXTcube, but one-eighth the size, Apple's G4 Cube was such a stunning, clean design that it too wound up in the Museum of Modern Art. Unfortunately, it didn't wind up in many homes or offices.

Steve loved the Cube. It packed a lot of power—although not quite enough to qualify as a true power user's computer—into a translucent cube just seven inches by seven inches all around. Its cables plugged into Apple's first super-wide flat-screen monitor for the desktop. My monitor measured twenty-five inches diagonally, and it rested on my office desk next to the Cube like a minimalist sculpture. But in this case, Steve made similar mistakes to ones he made at NeXT. He overlooked some of the engineering idiosyncrasies necessitated by the stark design he loved. Worse yet, the Cube seemed snakebit by a host of manufacturing problems. Its clear plastic shell cracked on many machines, a flaw that ruined what had seemed a design masterpiece. My Cube never cracked, but the monitor developed its own, strange, aesthetic problem: ants and other insects were somehow attracted to squeeze through seams in the clear plastic frame that surrounded the screen, and once inside they couldn't get out. Over time, the two transparent "feet" of the screen filled up with bug carcasses, but the effect was not as pleasing as when a prehistoric fly is trapped in amber. I teased Steve about the bug-friendly screen he'd developed a couple of times, but he never found it all that amusing. He pulled the plug on the Cube early, and it never sold anything near the numbers he had forecast.

————

STEVE HAD SURROUNDED himself with a mature, experienced, and disciplined team, made up of people who could argue back fiercely. And for once, he allowed them significant authority—Apple was simply too big for him to make all the decisions himself. Gradually, the organization developed in a way that allowed him to get the details he needed without micromanaging those areas of the company where he added a lot less. He primarily managed through his inner circle (although he convened meetings of the top one hundred people from time to time), and the Monday morning executive team meeting became the linchpin of the week. His attempt to delegate worked well, for the most part. In matters of finance, for instance, "I would get him involved when I needed him," remembers Anderson. Steve was trying to keep his fingers on the pulse of a growing company without stifling it.

He also liked having a confidant—someone he could banter with outside the formal lines responsibility of daily corporate life. In the early years of Steve's return, Mike Slade served that function. Slade, by his own admission, isn't any kind of creative "genius," like Lee Clow or Woz. But he had lots of real-world experience, he spoke his mind, and was both easygoing and independent enough to engage in spirited repartee with Steve without any qualms. He also had made it clear he did not want an executive position at Apple, which made it easier for him to have a good personal relationship with Steve. They would sometimes jog together in the early morning, and he even went Rollerblading with Steve and Laurene.

Slade showed up in Cupertino on Mondays and Tuesdays, flying down from Seattle. No one reported to him, and Steve had told the group that he had no particular authority. But when he was at Apple he almost never left Steve's side. Their Mondays would begin with the executive management team meeting. After that the two would usually go eat in the cafeteria, and later venture into the Design Lab. Slade tried to participate in their discussions. "Jony would say stuff like, 'Steve, I'm not sure the design language and the way it's joining with this is quite right. What do you think?'" says Slade, laughing. "And I'm going, 'Yeah, it's cool. Can I have a Coke now?' They'd ask me, 'Do you think we've got the right degree of opacity,' and all I can think is, 'Why am I here?'" Of course, Slade knew more than he'll admit. But his sense of humor and realism appealed to Steve. Steve didn't allow himself to relax with his inner circle the way he would with Slade. "Slade was the court jester," says Ruby, who also became good friends with Slade over the years.

Most Mondays, their visit to Ive would be followed by one to Avie and the team working on Apple's new operating system, which would eventually be called OS X. The radical new operating system would be the flywheel of all the extraordinary developments that would follow over the next decade, from Apple's suite of iLife applications, to iOS—the slimmed-down operating system that would give life to the iPhone and iPad—to the entirely new software industry that emerged to produce the millions of apps written for those devices.

While Steve's gadgets and computers drew the most attention, the software that made them go was every bit as important. Steve always said that Apple's primary competitive advantage was that it created the whole widget: the finely tuned symbiosis between the hardware and the software *together* defined a superior user experience. In the PC world, hardware and software technologies came from different companies that didn't always even get along, including IBM and the PC-clone manufacturers, Microsoft, and Intel.

Without a new operating system that could outshine Windows, the revival of the Macintosh could never be complete. The existing one was based on technology that had been developed fifteen years earlier for the original Mac, and the look and feel on the screen had come to seem passé.

Back at NeXT, Avie had developed a version of Unix that presented a friendlier face to nontechnical users, while also retaining its bona fides as a serious, world-class computing environment. There, too, the goal had been to create the whole widget, so he designed it to dovetail nicely with the NeXTcube. But when the company was forced to refocus solely on software, Avie and his team knew that the only way they could sell the NeXT OS was to make it attractive to users of workstations made by other manufacturers, like Sun, IBM, or Sony, and perhaps even to users of standard PCs. That's why they had created experimental working versions on Sun workstations using SPARC microprocessors, on other personal computers and engineering workstations using Intel's best Pentium PC microprocessors, and even on the PowerPC chip that was now the heart of Apple's latest Macintoshes. This experience of "porting" NeXT OS to other machines would pay off in two ways for Apple. For starters, Tevanian and his crew walked in the door at Cupertino with the code base and the know-how to support the troubled company no matter which microprocessor would be at the core of future Macintoshes. Apple had already switched Macintosh microprocessors once before, and Steve wanted the flexibility to do so again if it made sense. Since his old NeXT programmers had learned the technological idiosyncrasies of several computing platforms, they could help him make a much more objective decision when it came time to switch again. Technologically agnostic, they would push for the architecture that would get the most out of their operating system—in other words, the one that would help them build the best whole widget possible. This was an ace up Steve's sleeve, one he would play to great effect several years down the road.

Second, and more immediately important, the travails at NeXT had turned Tevanian's crew into a first-rate team. The primary task they faced was to turn the NeXT operating system into something that remained robust but had a modernized look and feel that bore enough similarity to the original Apple system for Mac users to migrate over with as little discomfort as possible. Another priority was to preserve compatibility with software applications that ran on the old Mac OS 9, at least in the short run. Finally, they had to build tools for software developers to help them adapt their old applications to OS X or even rewrite them altogether to take full advantage of its capabilities.

The challenges in developing any new operating system are many and varied, and even though OS X was essentially a modified version of a proven, existing operating system, the "Apple-ization" of it was still an enormous job. Steve understood this, and he didn't create unreasonable deadlines for his programmers. Instead, he oversaw them with a mix of patience and impatience that allowed him to be forceful and yet respectful. What eventually resulted was an operating system that mixed the best of Steve's intuitive understanding of the needs of regular people with deep, robust, and flexible code written by some of the greatest programmers in the world. It preserved the winsome onscreen personality that had made Apple customers so loyal through thick and thin.

Steve was particularly obsessed with the operating system's look and feel. In the afternoon OS X meetings that Slade would attend with Steve, each of Avie's direct reports would be admitted into a locked conference room to demonstrate the latest developments on whatever aspect of OS X they were handling. "We went over OS X again and again," remembers Slade, "pixel by pixel, feature by feature, screen by screen. Should the genie effect look like this? How big should the dock icons magnify? What's the type style? Why does this dial look the way it does? Every week, the agenda was to get Steve to approve the look and feel of each item.

"There is nothing in the operating system that he didn't approve," continues Slade. "It was the opposite of how things were done at Microsoft, where they relied on these five-hundred-page specs [documents laying out in detail every feature to be created by the software developers]. We had specs, too, but Steve never looked at them. He just looked at the product."

When Steve saw something he didn't like, he would tell a user interface designer by the name of Bas Ording to mock it up the way he wanted it. "Bas was a wizard," says Slade. "He'd take ninety seconds pecking away, he'd hit a button, and there it was—a picture of whatever Steve had asked for. The guy was a god. Steve just laughed about it. 'Basification in progress!' he'd announce."

What made the OS X development even harder was ensuring that the new operating system wouldn't instantly render users' old applications useless. This backwards-compatibility is one of the most difficult challenges a computer company can face—it was a real problem for Apple back in the early 1980s, when Apple II customers found that their software didn't work particularly well on an Apple III.

Steve believed that Apple's consumers would adapt more easily than conventional wisdom suggested, since they were far more enthusiastic about their Macs than Microsoft's customers were about their PCs. He believed they would be quite willing to make a big leap to a new operating system, even if it also required eventually buying all-new hardware and software. And he was right. Over the next decade, in its quest to keep the OS lean and modern, Apple would slowly stop supporting for a variety of carryover features from previous generations of hardware and software that were dearly beloved by a sometimes-vocal minority. Most Mac customers figured the trade-offs involved in a steadily improving computer platform were worth it, however.

Still, Steve and Avie did everything they could to make the transition to OS X as benign as possible for customers. One thing they exploited was a new way of delivering software updates. With more and more computers constantly connected to the Web, Apple could update users' software frequently by delivering improvements, modifications, and bug fixes directly over the Internet. This applied not just to operating system software but to all manner of applications, and made sense both for the customers and for the software developers, who by nature love to continue tweaking their work once it is "finished." Avie and his team were among the first mainstream operating system developers to take full advantage of this capability, and their approach would change the expectations of hundreds of millions of people, from corporate IT managers all the way down to the individual smartphone user who wants the very latest version of his favorite game.

Indeed, when Apple first released OS X in September 2000, the company called it a "public beta" version, implying that it was a work in progress. The price was $29.95—about a fifth of what was typically charged for a significant operating system upgrade. It was shrewd marketing, because it implied that early adopters would effectively be putting OS X through a shakedown cruise, and thus some bugs and glitches were to be expected. It also gave Apple a test period during which it could work out how to manage those online software upgrades. And during that period Avie's team used the Internet to provide numerous updates that improved the software. This way of maintaining and fixing software would quickly become the industry norm. It also transformed customers' expectations: no longer would they be willing to wait months for their software providers to fix a problem.

Given the breathing room that the success of the iMac had bought them, the UNIX core upon which they built their system, and their own coding expertise, Avie and his programmers had been able to shoot for the moon. So when OS X was finally ready to go, it could make the Mac do things no PC had ever been able to do. Users reveled in the obvious cosmetic improvements, like the ability to have video continue to play even as you used a mouse to move a window around the screen. And OS X was truly beautiful to behold, creating a screen with the illusion of three dimensions, where windows appeared to cast shadows on the layers of objects "behind" them. It still ran most old Mac programs, especially when their makers made a few slight modifications that could be downloaded and installed easily. But underneath it all was Unix, the core operating system that geeks love to tweak.

With OS X, then, Apple finally had a genuinely industrial-strength computing framework. Macs crashed far less than Wintel PCs. A single haywire program wouldn't take down the whole system. The machines seemed almost immune to software viruses. And its basic file system was easy to navigate and gave users the choice of three different ways to view and locate files in a list format. Under the hood, OS X was the state-of-the-art software foundation for everything Steve would want to create in the years ahead.

———

AS RUBY SAID, the mission had been to save Apple. And in early 2000, it seemed by just about every measure available, that Steve and the team had accomplished that goal. They had rebuilt and revived the company's suite of computers. They were starting to provide users with a solid and modern software foundation. Morale was high, and a sense of mission had been restored. Most important, Steve had visibly changed for the better as a leader and as a manager. Over the three and a half years since his return, he had come to recognize that taking this more incremental approach to computer development can result in the kind of equilibrium that allows you to build a business designed to thrive over the long haul.

Or so it seemed. In September 2000, Apple posted a dismal earnings report. Despite all these new products and fresh technology, the company's sales continued to shrink. The stock price tumbled, falling from $63 in early September to $15 by the end of the year. Meager sales of the Cube were just the most obvious disappointment, but sales were stagnant across the board. It was beginning to look as if Steve had pushed the technology of personal computing just about as far as it could go. He had righted the ship, patched up Amelio's holes, and gotten everyone rowing in the right direction. Apple was profitable again. But to complete Apple's turnaround he would have to get back to the business of creating new kinds of products, the kind that puncture the equilibrium of an industry and create new business opportunities. Yet now, at the end of fiscal year 2000, Apple's quarterly sales were less than when he'd arrived. And most of the gains shareholders had enjoyed since he returned had evaporated. As the headline of one of my *Fortune* stories put it, he was the graying prince of a shrinking kingdom. Something would have to change.

Chapter 10
Following Your Nose

It was Bill Gates who first mapped out the future of Apple. He did so on January 5, 2000, at the Consumer Electronics Show in Las Vegas, Nevada. Of course, he'd intended to lay out a game plan for Microsoft, not Apple. But that's not the way things worked out.

CES was an up-and-coming trade show back then. For years it had been the gathering point for people making everything from car speakers to stereo systems to televisions, from electronic football games that beeped as you pushed the buttons to video cameras to home security systems. The arrival of computer companies transformed the event, and within a few years it would become the largest digital technology exposition of them all, drawing audiences upwards of 150,000 and all but paralyzing Sin City for a week each January. Apple didn't attend CES. Steve preferred to announce his products in an environment he controlled.

Microsoft didn't control CES, but it certainly overshadowed everyone else. Chairman Gates, who relinquished his CEO title to Steve

Ballmer in 2000, gave the keynote speech eight years running. Gates was a natural choice as the show's semipermanent celebrity speaker, and he used the dais as a bully pulpit. In 2000, Microsoft really *was* the computer industry. Some 90 percent of the world's personal computers ran its Windows operating system. Its software managed not only desktop and laptop PCs but also the servers that stored and organized the data of the world's biggest corporations, and that undergirded the information technology of most governmental bureaucracies. Inside ATMs and cash registers, at airline check-in counters, and on the decks of aircraft carriers, Microsoft software made the world's most sophisticated technologies hum. If the consumer electronics universe was about to be thrown into turmoil, who better to hear from than the leader of the industry doing the disrupting?

That evening, Gates spoke to a standing-room-only crowd of more than three thousand people at the Las Vegas Hilton Theater, where he revealed how Microsoft would "usher in the 'consumer-electronics-plus' era." PCs running the Windows operating system would become the central component of "home media centers" that would harness the Internet and interact with consumer devices and even household appliances, all loaded with Microsoft software. This would be a bonanza for consumers, he explained, because they would now get "personalized, convenient access to their favorite music, news, entertainment, family photos and email through an array of consumer electronics, including televisions, telephones, home and car stereos, and Pocket PCs."

The speech was a forecast, a warning, and a blueprint. Gates posited a vision of what the home would look like after the realization and interweaving of a set of trends. There would be much more connectivity among devices, access to a new range of digital content and programming via the Internet, newly interactive video games played at home, and gizmos with responsive screens and software smarts to replace mere electronic gadgets with push buttons. This is what we are going to do to your world, Gates was telling the manufacturers of consumer electronics. It is coming whether you like it or not, because this is what digital technology does to an industry. So get on board, you old-timers tinkering with microwave ovens and car stereos and televisions and headphones. Here's how you can fit in to your own future, which actually belongs to us!

Such was Microsoft's power, at that moment, as the unquestioned ruler of the empire of computing. The company had so thoroughly infiltrated and then controlled every aspect of the world's defining digital technology that it seemed obvious to most everyone attending CES that if this was the future Microsoft wanted, this was the future. The obvious implication that Gates left unsaid was that this would be an enormous bonanza for Microsoft, which, by establishing the specifications that all kinds of hardware manufacturers would need to follow, would ensure its own dominance in the next brave new world.

Ruling the market for new consumer electronics devices might have solved Gates's biggest problem: the fact that Microsoft was no longer growing at the galloping 25-plus percent pace investors like to see in a tech company. Remember that when Bill and Steve got into the business, computing still belonged to the IBMs and DECs of the world, with their big, expensive machines sold into a market consisting of a few hundred corporations, governments, and universities. As Moore's law drove prices down, PC manufacturers sold their wares to a galaxy of other businesses, both big and small, that could now afford powerful computing that would make them more efficient. But numerically speaking, the biggest potential audience of all was relatively untapped. Once you can sell computing to consumers directly, and once you get computing into products that become part of their everyday lives, the volumes become transformative. Consider this: According to researchers at the Gartner Group, 355 million personal computers—servers, desktop PCs, and laptops—were sold around the world in 2011. Some 1.8 *billion* cellphones were sold the same year. And that's a number that doesn't include all the other kinds of computing-based or networkable devices that might become part of a consumer's life, including video game consoles, audio players, radios, thermostats, car navigation systems, and anything else that can become smarter through the power of connected computing.

Gates, who is perhaps the world's shrewdest business strategist, saw this future coming. And he expected Microsoft to garner the same slice of this world that it had of the computing world. After all, who else could possibly define the standards for digital interaction between devices? This had been Gates's game: envisioning and delivering the future. The scale of his concerns and ambitions dwarfed Steve's. He wanted Microsoft software on billions of devices; Steve just wanted anything that would help him sell a few thousand more Macs each month. Gates was the only one who could reasonably think about dominating his awkwardly named but clearly inevitable "consumer-electronics-plus" era. He was powerful, and very, very smart: despite his penchant for dense verbiage, he had done a wonderful job describing the future of computing as we now have it, some fifteen years later. All he and Steve Ballmer had to do was execute the strategy. If they could, they would steer the company through its transition to this future, and in so doing return Microsoft to the kind of growth that investors wanted to see.

No one knew it at the time, but Gates's speech that January morning in Las Vegas marked the apex of Microsoft's hegemony. On December 31, 1999, the company had been worth $619.3 billion, with a share price of $58.38. It would never be worth more.

Instead, a company still struggling to survive on the fringes of computing would execute Gates's vision. It would do so by moving incrementally, by following its nose where the technology led, and by being opportunistic. Over the next few years, Steve Jobs would steer Apple toward a whole new rhythm of doing business. No one would have guessed it then, but the future belonged to Apple, not Microsoft.

WHEN WORD GOT back to Cupertino of Bill's ambitious CES presentation, Avie Tevanian and Jon Rubinstein persuaded Steve to convene an emergency off-site executive staff meeting at the Garden Court Hotel in downtown Palo Alto to rethink where Apple was headed. "Bill Gates was already talking about what we would end up calling our 'digital hub' strategy," recalls Mike Slade. "So I just cribbed his talk and pitched it to Steve at the off-site meeting. I said, 'Shouldn't we be doing this? We can't let Microsoft do it. They'll just screw it up!'"

Apple employees had never had much respect for Microsoft's ability to create anything but ungainly, confusing, and half-baked technologies for consumers. The animus went back decades. Even though Microsoft Word, Excel, and PowerPoint were instrumental in the early success of the Mac, Microsoft's unforgivable sin, from the vantage point of Cupertino, was its derivative creation of Windows. Steve was being expedient when he offered to abandon Apple's long-standing lawsuit against Microsoft to seal the deal with Gates upon his return in 1997. But folks at Apple still considered Windows a rip-off of Apple's ideas, pure and simple. Worse yet, they saw it as an inelegant theft, and one that got imposed on the world by a kind of bullying that Apple both despised and envied.

Steve's team sincerely believed that a world defined by Microsoft's "consumer-electronics-plus" vision would be as ugly as that godforsaken name. In 2000, if anyone needed evidence of how ham-handed Microsoft could be when it tried to befriend actual humans, as opposed to the corporate buyers it had always really cared about, all they had to do was open up Word or Excel or PowerPoint on a PC, where they would be greeted by an animated digital "concierge" called "Clippit." An anthropomorphized talking paper clip that was intended to be an informal help center for users of the Office suite of productivity applications, Clippit was, in the minds of many users, a patronizing, useless abomination that was frustratingly difficult to banish from your PC screen. *Time* magazine would eventually call it one of the fifty worst inventions ever, right up there with Agent Orange, subprime mortgages, and the Ford Pinto.

The team at Apple could not abide the idea of letting the creators of Clippit establish the look and feel of whatever new world of consumer computing, communications, and digital media was emerging. They wanted the new consumer digital technologies to be held to the highest standards of elegance, beauty, and simplicity. Apple had always displayed a sense of style and design that was unmatched by anyone in the computing business. All you had to do was compare an iMac to the average PC.

Gates always knew that he could never hope to approximate Steve's aesthetic sensibility. "He had an expectation of superlative things in his own work and in the products they would create," he says. "Steve had a design mind-set. When I get to a hotel room, I don't go, 'Oh, this bedside table is so poorly designed, look at this, this could have been so much better.' When I look at a car, I don't say, 'Oh, if I had designed this car I would have done this and this.' People like Jony Ive and Steve Jobs are always looking at stuff that way. You know, I look at code and say, 'Okay, this is architected well,' but it's just a different way of understanding the world. His most natural, innate sense was a world-class instinct about whether this or that object met certain standards. He had extremely high standards of what was shit, and what was not shit." By those standards, Steve's executive team was right: Microsoft and Apple had dramatically different notions of what constituted acceptable design, much less great design. If these applications and devices were to become as ubiquitous as Gates proclaimed, this was a rare opportunity to establish a benchmark for the functional and stylistic aesthetics of how the average person would deal with digital technology.

Apple had already dipped its toe into this emerging market with a well-designed but ill-chosen application called iMovie. It was introduced at precisely the moment when affordable digital video cameras from Japanese manufacturers like Sony, JVC, and Panasonic were beginning to hit the market. Steve had thought that an elegant and simple movie-editing application was just what the buyers of those cameras would need. iMovie was sophisticated software that radically simplified the tedious process of editing jerky amateur video into slick home movies with almost professional-quality production values. But if iMovie was proof that Apple could create cool consumer software, it was also proof that the consumer market could be diabolically hard to predict. iMovie was an elegant solution to a problem consumers weren't yet dying to have solved.

In October 1999, Steve introduced iMovie as part of the rollout of a new generation of juiced-up iMacs. But sales were sluggish. Steve blamed himself for not explaining it well enough. So at an executive team meeting in December 1999, Steve gave early prototypes of new Sony digital camcorders to six of his top execs, asking each to shoot and edit his own four-minute home movie, with the finished productions to be shown in a week. He would pick the best of the bunch to show during his appearance at the January 2000 MacWorld in an effort to demonstrate how iMovie was something anyone could master over a weekend.

"Fred [Anderson], Ruby [Jon Rubinstein], Avie [Tevanian], Tim [Cook], Sina [Tamaddon], Steve, and me all made four-minute movies. I'll be honest, it was a painfully cumbersome process, even for geeks like us," remembers Slade. "You had to shoot the movie, then spool the video into the iMac, edit it, add music and credits, and then spool it back out onto the camcorder because the hard disk wasn't big enough to hold both the original video clips and the finished movie, and we didn't yet have recordable DVD drives. Many of us thought it was a pretty worthless strategy.

"But the movies were pretty funny," he allows. "I had little kids back then, so I showed them playing in the leaves on a fall day with Van Morrison's 'Tupelo Honey' as the background music. Steve's was about his kids, too. And Fred, well, apparently his life was so boring that all he could do was make a movie about his goddamn cat. Tim Cook made one about trying to buy a house in Palo Alto, and how overpriced they were. I thought Ruby's was the best, though. He had been on a business trip to Dallas on his birthday that week, so he made this totally deadpan movie of the highlights of his day, where he had scenes sitting alone in his hotel room, and in conference rooms, and other boring places showing himself saying 'Happy Birthday, Jon. Woohoo!' everywhere he went. And Sina made a beautiful one about his kids playing with their pets and jumping on the bed to a Green Day song." (That's the one Steve chose for MacWorld.)

The short little movies may have been fun to watch, but most of them had taken many hours to create. Movie editing, even when simplified by iMovie, was a process that required time, dedication, and skill. It was the kind of thing that a parent might do once in a while, but only in rare cases when he or she had a lot of free time over the weekend. It wasn't until after the Garden Court off-site convened by Avie and Ruby that Steve acknowledged that Apple needed to create a much simpler consumer application than iMovie, something that users could engage with easily every day. The consensus at the meeting was that a digital music management application seemed like a good possibility. Rather than dig in his heels and insist on greater effort to make iMovie a hit, Steve chose to follow his team into the world of digital music. The big question now was whether Apple could move fast enough to make up for arriving so late to that party.

IT'S NOT SURPRISING that Steve had been so attracted to iMovie, since it was a piece of software designed primarily for parents. He and Laurene now had three children, after the birth of Eve in 1998, and by the turn of the century had settled into a relatively predictable and normal domestic routine.

Steve's ability to compartmentalize and focus, qualities that were helping him turn around Apple, also shaped the way he balanced his work and family life. Back when he had been leading the Mac team or driving NeXT, Steve had spent many a late night at the office as part of a small team trying to deliver the next great thing. But now his role at Apple was so different: heading up a company with thousands of employees, Steve managed everything through his small team of senior executives. Rather than hover over the shoulders of star engineers and programmers, he could do much of his work via email. So he would make it home for dinner almost every night, spend time with Laurene and the kids, and then work at his computer late into the night. He and I were iChat buddies at the time, and I would regularly see the green light on next to his name on my screen in the wee hours, an indication that he was logged in to his Mac. (iChat was Apple's video chat application, and there were times when we used it to talk about business, although sometimes his son, Reed, then an early teen, would sneak up behind Steve and make faces at me as we talked.)

On a spectrum plotting how much time parents spend with their kids versus time they spend focused on their job, Steve would land far toward the latter end. Both he and Laurene knew Steve would always work very, very hard—it had been a basic assumption when they'd gotten married. "Neither of us had much of a social life," says Laurene. "It was never that important to us." Laurene often worked beside him at night, at first on Terravera, a small health food business she eventually sold, and then on College Track, her first philanthropic venture. They had adjoining studies; she'd run ideas past him, and on many nights he'd spend an hour or two talking over Apple business with her. They'd often catch a TV show before falling asleep, mostly *The Daily Show* with Jon Stewart after it launched in 1999. The bulk of the parenting did fall on Laurene, but they scheduled their lives to ensure that Steve was involved. The Christmas holidays were often spent in Hawaii, mostly at a bungalow at the Kona Village Resort on the Big Island.

Besides creating a schedule that accommodated Steve's heavy workload, the couple did everything they could to try to give their children what Steve himself defined as a "normal" life. He and Laurene created an environment that hewed to what can best be described as upper-middle-class norms. Over the years, their neighborhood was increasingly populated by the rich and famous (Larry Page of Google lived nearby, and Steve Young, the famous San Francisco 49ers quarterback, was a neighbor), but Steve and Laurene did everything they could to make their house feel as homey as possible. It was not a walled compound. The front door opened right to the street. The children roamed the neighborhood. The family biked around the area together.

Very slowly, Steve and Laurene even added furniture. "Those stories are true," Laurene sighs, albeit with a chuckle. "He truly could take forever to decide on stuff like that, but then so could I." While you could see the telltale signs of children around, it usually was far neater than my own house—having a staff can help with that. As lovely as it was inside, I always thought the heart of the place was the rambling vegetable and flower garden outside the kitchen door. It was the property's most distinct feature and completely unlike the landscaping that graced other homes in the area. When I visited I'd sometimes catch Steve having just finished up in the garden, or Laurene walking in with one of the kids and a basket of freshly picked veggies and flowers.

This was his refuge. Although colleagues occasionally would visit him there, he tried to keep his home and family life completely sequestered from the press. As he did with other journalists who knew him well, it was understood that any discussions we ever had about his family were off the record—when I wrote in *Fortune* about my own kids coming over to see *Toy Story* with his son, Reed, I cleared it with him first.

But Steve and Laurene didn't make any effort to hide away from their neighbors. They were regulars in downtown Palo Alto. *Fortune* had its Silicon Valley bureau offices on Emerson Street, just up the street from a building Steve had bought to use as an office closer to home. He didn't use it all that much, but when he did it wasn't unusual to see him out for a walk with a colleague, or running a personal errand by himself. (When *Fortune* eventually closed the bureau as part of a series of cost-cutting moves, I told Laurene about it, and she leased the space as the headquarters of a nonprofit she was starting, which she called the Emerson Collective.) Once when I ran into Steve we wound up shopping for a new bicycle for Laurene's upcoming birthday. Steve had done his research, so it didn't take long. We were in and out of Palo Alto Bicycles on University Avenue in ten minutes. He said, "I'd never have Andrea do something like this," referring to his longtime administrative assistant. "I like buying presents for my family myself."

These normal encounters with someone who, to repeat Catmull's pithy phrase, "veered so far from the mean," were memorable enough that dozens of people, after Steve's death, wrote about such meetings on Quora, an online query site popular with Silicon Valley types. A designer named Tim Smith described the time his old Sunbeam Alpine sports car stalled in front of the Jobs driveway. Laurene came out and brought him a beer while he tried to figure out what to do, and then she offered to call a friend of theirs who knew a lot about Sunbeams. When the friend came by—dressed in a tuxedo for a night out—Steve emerged from the house with Reed. Steve got in the car and tried to crank it while his friend worked under the hood trying to get the thing going, but nothing worked. As Smith writes online: "I have to stop here—it's a Kodak moment—something you want to remember. It's a beautiful Fall evening in Palo Alto. Your car's broken. A formally dressed close friend of Steve Jobs is under the hood working on your engine. You are talking with Steve's absolutely lovely and down-to-earth wife. Steve is in the car, with his kid, trying to crank it. You don't often get close to people like Jobs, much less in a ridiculous situation like this, where you realize that they are just really good people. They're normal, funny, charitable, real people. Not the people the press talks about. Steve is not the maniacal business and design despot the media loves to portray—well he is, but not always."

This was a side of Steve's life that was seldom seen, and he made no attempt to publicize it. The general myth of Steve as a brilliant and driven egotist, who would sacrifice or shove aside anything or anyone for his career, carried the unfortunate corollary that he must have been a bad father and friend, and a man incapable of caring and love. It was a stereotype that never came close to gibing with my own experience of him.

Contrary to that caricature, and unlike most other CEOs I had interviewed at *Fortune* and the *Wall Street Journal,* Steve always seemed human and spontaneous with a penchant for honesty that stung and yet rung. True, some of this could turn negative: he could be scathing when he disagreed with something *Fortune* had published, and more than once I heard him sneer condescendingly at certain colleagues of mine with unreserved arrogance. But he could also be goofy: Once, when he was telling me that a new software interface was "good enough to lick," he actually leaned forward and licked the screen of the 27-inch cinema-display monitor in front of a whole room full of engineers. And he could be deeply funny in the most disarming ways: One time I came to interview him wearing a loud silk shirt with wavy vertical navy blue stripes separating rows of dozens of large, blossomy, bloodred figures, each about three inches across. Those splotches really leaped from that shirt. When I walked into the conference room, Steve looked me up and down and quipped, "Did you have a meeting with a firing squad before you came to see me?" He paused for effect and then cackled. He would cut loose with a good belly laugh when he was truly amused; according to Laurene, she heard it most when he was cracking wise with the kids around the house.

It isn't that I looked at Steve and saw a model father. I knew how hard he worked, and that his relentless drive carried a personal cost. But I had been given a look inside his home life over the years, and it seemed every bit as authentic as that of my own friends and colleagues. These stories on Quora, and the moments I experienced with him around Palo Alto or at his house, are mundane. But as time went on I came to realize that this was exactly the point: he craved a certain normalcy in his life, and he was able to get that most at home. With his family. They provided a therapeutic—and very human—outlet that he needed, especially in contrast to Apple, where he was gearing up to dive head-first into an uncertain future.

———

IF IMOVIE HAD been a sort of exploratory mission into the world of digital applications for consumers, iTunes would prove to be the expedition itself. Armed with a leadership team he trusted more and more, his keen aesthetic sensibility, a belief that the intersection of the arts and technology could lead to amazing things, and the growing understanding that great ideas develop in fits and starts, Steve was ready to see what Apple could bring to the world of music. In hindsight, of course, this seems like such an obvious course of action. But as in all of the most challenging and eventually rewarding journeys, there was little certainty at the outset of where they would end up. Steve would just have to follow his nose.

He had always loved music, but like many people in their forties, the playlist he returned to was pretty well established. Steve and I talked about the Beatles and Dylan, and sometimes one or the other of us would carp about something new we didn't like so much. You can come to seem like an old fogey pretty fast when it comes to music, and in this way Steve was no different from anyone else.

This might help explain why Steve did not react earlier to the explosion, in the late 1990s, of digital sound formats for storing and playing music on a personal computer. During that period, several startup companies started dabbling with "jukebox" applications to manage MP3s—the shorthand term for digital files that contained, in compressed form, recorded music that had been "ripped" (in other words, copied) from an audio CD onto a PC's hard disk. Others developed their own encrypted compression algorithms in hopes of convincing the recording industry to adopt their technology and build a new business model for music to be sold directly to consumers online. Two, in fact, had been started or financed by Microsoft alumni—RealNetworks and Liquid Audio.

Then there was Napster, the brainchild of a Massachusetts teenager named Shawn Fanning. Napster was the software application that really blew the lid off things. In the summer of 1999, Fanning concocted a "peer-to-peer" file-sharing service that allowed individuals around the world—conceivably anyone with a computer and an Internet connection—to upload and download MP3s, creating a way for people to share their own music collections with one another. Since the files were in digital form, the free copies were practically indistinguishable from the originals. It was one of the first truly "viral" Internet applications, a genuine killer app, that attracted tens of millions of users within months. It also was illegal. Napster facilitated the widespread piracy of recorded music, triggering a wholesale behavioral shift among music consumers that would eventually all but wreck the recording industry's traditional business model. The courts would shut down Napster in 2001, but not before it had become a cultural sensation, and Shawn Fanning a celebrity worthy of the cover of *Time* magazine.

All this had gotten rolling while Steve had been busy stabilizing Apple. He had been preoccupied attacking problems that were directly in front of him: rationalizing inventory, stabilizing cash flow, trimming head count, assembling a new management team, and reviving advertising and marketing, not to mention supervising the design of new products. Steve's intense focus had been on Apple's internal needs and issues. Music hovered on the periphery of his narrowed field of vision. But now he realized that Apple had to move into music, and fast.

The story of Apple's move into digital music is the tale of a man, and a team, learning how to adapt over and over again on the fly. Steve had solidified the company by narrowing its product lines so that Apple could once again produce distinctive computers. He had reaffirmed the company's mission, for employees and for customers, with ingenious marketing and respectable financial results. But Apple's product portfolio was still built around computers. Now that Steve was beginning to sense that the merger of consumer electronics and computers was emerging as a critical growth market, Apple's metabolism, and many of Steve's old habits, would have to shift. Starting with the creation of iTunes, Apple had to become a far more nimble company than it had ever been in the past. Steve had displayed a newfound openness by agreeing that the company had to move quickly past iMovie and into digital music. Now he'd have to maintain that same willingness to be flexible, and to follow his nose, wherever it led.

Historically, Steve had always preferred that Apple create its own software from scratch—he didn't trust anyone as much as he trusted his own people. But since Apple was coming so late to digital music, it would not have time to develop a music management program on its own. So Steve decided to go shopping for an existing jukebox app that Apple could adapt to its own style.

Three independent developers had already created jukeboxes for the Macintosh. The best of the bunch was a forty-dollar application called SoundJam, which happened to be developed by two former Apple software engineers. SoundJam was also of interest to Steve because at its heart was a sophisticated database program that would allow music to be cataloged by more than a dozen attributes. It was a favorite of so-called power users who had large libraries of thousands of music tracks to manage. It was simple to navigate and operate, and it could import music files directly from audio CDs and compress them in a variety of formats into smaller chunks of digital data.

In March 2000, Apple bought SoundJam and attached some unusual terms: the authors of SoundJam would come to work for Apple, but their software distributor could continue selling the existing SoundJam product until Apple had reengineered it into iTunes. The other catch was that the whole transaction be kept secret for two years. There would be no public indication that anything had changed at SoundJam, the distributor and the SoundJam programmers would continue to make money, and Apple could keep its designs on building a jukebox application under wraps. Secrecy was key, since so many parties—studios, consumer electronics manufacturers, tech companies, broadcasters—were trying to find a way to lead digital music. Apple had been a leaky ship during its early years and throughout the Sculley/Spindler/Amelio era. But Steve had eradicated that problem by making it more than clear that anyone caught leaking company information or plans would be fired immediately. So the transaction stayed a secret, as he wished.

Tamaddon's applications division, which had learned a lot from the development of iMovie, moved with speed and a minimum of fuss. The SoundJam team was integrated in seamlessly. Its developers worked directly with Avie and Sina to improve some attributes of the old program, including Steve's favorite—a psychedelic "visualizer" feature that generated trippy, colorful, abstract moving full-screen images derived from whatever music was playing. More important, they simplified the software, eliminating options and complexity whenever they could. This, too, it turns out, would become a hallmark of the new Apple that Steve was creating. Saying no—to software features, new projects, new hires, boondoggle conferences, all kinds of press queries, even to Wall Street's desire for better guidance on future earnings, and anything else deemed extraneous or distracting. Above all, saying no became a crucial way of keeping everyone, including himself, focused on what really mattered. The sheer simplicity of the quadrant strategy had laid the foundation for an organization that would say no again and again—until it said yes, at which point it would attack the new project with fierce determination.

The iTunes team moved remarkably fast. A mere nine months after having purchased SoundJam, and just a year after Bill Gates's public christening of the concept of a world of connected computers, consumer electronics devices, and applications, Steve was able to unveil iTunes at the MacWorld trade show in San Francisco on January 9, 2001. He had a strong set of products to show off besides iTunes, including the Titanium PowerBook, the first of what would become Apple's exceedingly popular laptops to be clad in metal rather than plastic, and OS X, which would finally ship as a finished product in March.

But iTunes turned out to be the real star of the show, because it was something that practically everyone in the room knew that they wanted. Steve demonstrated how the software would allow you to rip an entire library of music CDs into a digital archive on your Mac's hard drive, and how the iTunes database would help you easily find and play particular tracks. You could mix tracks into a personal playlist of music that could be stored in the app or burned back onto a recordable, portable CD. And unlike OS X, which wouldn't ship until late March, iTunes was available for download immediately, for free. Steve then showed a television ad with a stage full of recognizable pop music stars that concluded with the slogan that would soon show up on billboards across the country: Rip. Mix. Burn. He may have been in his forties, but the campaign was totally cool.

Also, for the first time in public, Steve took his first steps on the path to publicly co-opting Gates's promised future. In classic Apple style, he began by reworking the language of Gates's vision, trading "consumer-electronics-plus" for the much more felicitous "digital hub." Energetically pacing the stage, he walked the audience through an enormous screen shot showing a Mac in the middle of six spokes extending to a digital still camera, a PDA, a DVD player, a CD Walkman, a video camcorder, and something called a digital music player. It was an image that updated his old principle of a computer as a "bicycle for the mind." The Mac, Jobs explained, would be the ideal tool for managing, editing, and organizing content from *all* these devices, as well as a central repository for software updates, contacts, music and video files, and anything else you needed on your mobile devices. The computer industry's P. T. Barnum made it all seem so much friendlier than the intimidating future Gates had painted. He made it seem accessible and human and *simple*. Apple promised to deliver software and hardware that you could manage and bend to your will. That was the power of the "I" in iTunes. You ruled this future, not Microsoft, or even Apple. Such was the power of Steve's elocution.

Two days earlier, Gates had once again waxed on about what he now was calling the "digital living room" at CES. Microsoft's booth there was tricked out to resemble a series of rooms in a typical home. Nothing about it was very realistic. When it came to the consumer's future, Gates was the one offering the airy visions of a breakthrough future, while Steve was inching ahead with real products. It was almost as if the two men had reversed roles from that interview I'd conducted at Steve's house a decade before.

During the first week after iTunes was introduced and made available online for free, 275,000 copies were downloaded. That was just a slice of the 20 million Macs installed around the world, but it already exceeded the number of actual users of iMovie, which had been available for download for fifteen months. There was just one problem:

other than the iMac sitting in the center of the octopus-like digital hub diagram Steve had shown at MacWorld, none of the connected devices had been made by Apple. That had to change.

———

EARLY IN 2001, toward the end of a meeting with Steve, Eddy Cue, a young software engineer with a good head for business who would come to play a key role in Steve's executive team, bellyached. "We can't make things better than we're making them," he said. "Yet we're at the same place we were at back in 1997." Indeed, while annual sales had reached $7.9 billion in 2000, they were projected to drop well below $6 billion in 2001. "You've just got to hang on," Steve told him. "People will come around." His patience was admirable, but then again, Steve had believed since the 1980s that the world would eventually come to recognize the superiority of Apple products. Here he was in a new millennium, still waiting on humanity. His company was stable, but it wasn't yet strong. It needed something to get it growing. It needed a new *kind* of product.

The desire to create a portable digital music player arose directly from the development of iTunes: as more and more Apple execs and engineers started listening to MP3s on their computers, it was only a matter of time before they wanted to take their digital music with them in some sort of portable digital version of the old Sony Walkman. The few pocket-sized MP3 players on the market were poorly designed and clumsy to use. It wasn't so much that the sound was bad, but instead that the procedures for loading them with music and then finding what you wanted to hear were hopelessly opaque. Steve was proud of iTunes, and especially of how easy it made it for someone to organize and manage large libraries of recorded music. Not one of the existing devices could make the most of his nifty piece of software.

The only solution, the team decided, would be for Apple itself to make something better. It was a gambit that would push the company further out of its comfort zone: the only mass-market consumer electronics product it had ever manufactured was a long-forgotten Apple-branded digital still camera from the Sculley years. Steve himself had been involved in nothing like this since the illegal "blue box" long-distance telephone dialer he and Woz built and sold back in the 1970s. Computers were Apple's focus and raison d'être. But this group was starting to function at such a high level that they welcomed the challenge of making a new kind of device. And none of them thought a portable music player alone would be transformative, so it seemed like a low-risk gamble. The terminology they used suggested the limits of their ambitions: many of them saw a music player primarily as a "computer peripheral," like a printer or a Wi-Fi router.

As the head of hardware engineering, Jon Rubinstein always kept his eyes open for new electronic components—processors, disk drives, memory chips, graphics technologies—that might pique Steve's interest or give Apple a competitive edge. In late 2000, during a trip to Japan, Ruby stopped by Toshiba, the electronic giant that, among other things, made hard drives for personal computers. The Toshiba engineers told Ruby that they wanted to show him the next "big" thing in laptop hard drives—the prototype of a miniature, 5-gigabyte disk drive that wasn't even two inches in diameter. It could fit into a cigarette pack with plenty of room to spare, and yet was capacious enough to hold thousands of digital files, whether these were images, documents, or, say, songs. Ruby couldn't believe his eyes. This was the first thing he'd seen that had enough capacity at a small enough size to form the heart of an Apple music player. Unlike the tapes or CDs that you played in Sony's Walkman or Discman, this hard drive would have enough disk storage to hold copies of perhaps a thousand tracks, rather than just a dozen. And its "random access" capabilities distanced it even more from the likes of a Discman, since it gave you the potential to find a particular song out of that enormous trove almost instantly.

In January 2001, Ruby asked some former Newton engineers to begin work in earnest on some sort of portable audio device around the Toshiba micro-drive. In March he put Tony Fadell, a consulting engineer who had previously worked for Philips NV, in charge of the group. Fadell, an energetic entrepreneur with the build of a college wrestler and the intensity of a high school football coach, had worked at General Magic back in the early 1990s, with Bill Atkinson, Andy Hertzfeld, and Susan Kare, veterans of the original Macintosh team, who had told him horror stories about Steve in his early days. "I expected an overbearing tyrant," he says, "but he wasn't like that at all. He didn't resemble the guy from their stories at all. On the things he cared about he could be very intense, but in general, he was much softer, much more considerate. He wasn't a crazy micromanager. He trusted his guys."

No one had any idea what the end product would look like, or how users would control it, or how much it would have to function like a tiny computer itself, or how exactly it would interact with iTunes song libraries on the iMac, or even when it possibly could be shipped. All they knew were the basic requirements: that it would somehow pack the tiny hard drive, an audio amplifier powerful enough to drive headphones, a small screen to display and navigate through the music it contained, a microprocessor or microcontroller to give it enough smarts, software to make it programmable and to help it interact directly with iTunes, and a high-speed FireWire port to let it mate via a cable with a Macintosh, in the space of something that you could easily slip into a front pocket of your Levi's. Of course it had to look cool and of course Steve wanted it as soon as possible.

In this way, Steve had not changed at all: he still presented his team with outrageous goals that seemed impossibly out of reach. But there were two things that had changed, things that improved the odds that his team could live up to his stretch targets. Steve himself was more willing to reshape his goals as the development process revealed either limitations or new opportunities. And the group he had assembled was the most talented collection of people he had ever worked with, a naturally ambitious crew that knew that Steve encouraged their spirit of constant inquisitiveness and willingness to push boundaries. "What I loved about working for Steve," says Cue, "is that you learned that you could accomplish the impossible. Again and again."

Another reason that Steve felt confident that Apple could create a great consumer device was that a successful music player could only be the result of a holistic mix of great hardware and software. The iPod was truly a "whole widget" challenge, as Steve described it. With a crash schedule in hand, Fadell led the group building the iPod, but contributions came from everyone on the executive team, as well as from engineers who worked elsewhere in the company. Turning Ruby's Toshiba microdrive into the heart of a pocket-sized piece of functioning hardware was not, by any means, the biggest challenge. The hard part was creating a *usable* device, one that would make those thousand tracks accessible with a click or two of a switch, and that would pair simply and directly with a Mac so its owner could import copies of his iTunes digital music files, along with his custom playlists. It also would be nice to be able to display some information about each track and to take full advantage of iTunes' ability to sort them by artist, album title, and even genre. To make all that happen, the music player would need enough smarts to host a rudimentary computer database program. The iPod, in other words, would actually be a tiny, special-purpose computer.

But that was just the beginning. Out of all the various aspects of computing, Steve was always most fascinated with the contact point between a person and a computer. It was the user interface that had made the Macintosh seem the epitome of a *personal* computer in its time. There were good reasons that Steve found this point of interaction so critical. If the point at which a person interacted with a machine was complicated, he or she would likely never unlock its secrets. Most people don't care about the innards of their computer—they care only about what's on the screen, and what they can get to through that screen. Steve understood the profound importance of this from the very beginning of his career. It was part of what distinguished him from so many other computer makers, most of whom were engineers who believed that a rational customer would of course care deeply about the insides of his or her computer. This bias held true nearly two decades after the introduction of Mac. So if Apple could make its portable music device a cinch to interact with, users would revel in portable, programmable music in a way they'd never imagined possible. If Apple couldn't do so, its machine would be a clunker like all the rest.

Getting the interface right meant blending the right software with the right hardware. Some of the software work was already done, of course: the iTunes application on the Mac was the perfect tool to create the database of music tracks and information to be loaded onto the iPod. But the portable device itself needed its own miniature operating system to provide the software underpinnings of the user interface that would be presented on the screen, much like the Mac OS established the graphical user interface that Mac users operated with a mouse and a keyboard. To accomplish this, the software team mashed up repurposed operating system code from the old Newton with the rudimentary file management system that Apple had quietly licensed from a tiny startup company called PortalPlayer and some elements from Mac OS X.

Getting the hardware right was harder. This is where Ruby's hardware guys and Jony Ive and his team of designers really showed their mettle. At the suggestion of marketing chief Phil Schiller, they created something known as a "thumb-wheel," which functioned in some ways like the "scroll-wheel" on many computer mice. The iPod's thumb-wheel was basically a flat disk that you could rotate clockwise or counterclockwise with your thumb to rapidly navigate up and down the long lists displayed on the screen. The iPod software team gave the thumb-wheel a series of imaginative touches that made it truly intuitive to use. The faster you spun the wheel, the quicker the list would move up or down the list. In the middle of the wheel was a button you clicked to make a choice, just as you clicked the button of a Mac's mouse. Situated around the perimeter of the thumb-wheel like a rim were other buttons that let you jump forward to the next track, restart a track from the beginning, or jump back to the previous track without having to locate it on the screen.

The breakthrough on the iPod user interface is what ultimately made the product seem so magical and unique. There were plenty of other important software innovations, like the software that enables easy synchronization of the device with a user's iTunes music collection. But if the team had not cracked the usability problem for navigating a pocket library of hundreds or thousands of tracks, the iPod would never have gotten off the ground. It was a solution that came with ancillary benefits as well. The iPod interface was so well designed that it was able to grow and become even more useful as other technologies in the device improved and became cheaper. And since the thumb-wheel technology was half hardware and half software, it was much easier for Apple to lock in this design advantage with patents and copyrights so tough that no competitor dared try to copy it. Were it primarily a software feature, it would've been far more vulnerable to being aped. Once again, Apple had found a beautifully intuitive way to control a complex, intelligent device hidden underneath a gleaming, minimalist exterior. This is where Ive first showed that he could design far more than the shapes of things. He could help design the user experience, too. There was nothing that mattered more to Steve.

———

BEFITTING THE MEASURED ambitions for the new product, the iPod was introduced at an event held in the tiny Town Hall auditorium at Apple headquarters on October 23, 2001. Reaction from the assembled journalists was anything but measured, however. Following the technology where it led had allowed Steve to create a product with a blend of features that made so much intuitive sense that it would change consumer behavior. The iPod was spectacular and totally unexpected.

To use one was to fall in love with it. Apple gave an iPod to every journalist who attended the October introduction, something it had never done before. These technology writers and reviewers and other cognoscenti wound up raving in print about features Apple hadn't even touted. The showstopper for many was the iPod's random-play capability, something Steve initially considered to be of marginal interest. This so-called "shuffle mode" turned the device into the equivalent of a personal radio station that would play only your own music, in a totally unpredictable sequence. If you had a large library, your iPod operating in shuffle mode was a wonderful way to stumble upon music you had forgotten that you even owned. In that way, the iPod helped people rediscover the pleasures of the music itself.

The iPod gave Apple a new jolt of cool and expanded the appeal of its products to a much broader universe of consumers, especially younger buyers. In time, it would prove to be the Walkman, and then some, of the early twenty-first century. It was also the first new hardware link in a chain of successive innovative and self-reinforcing software and hardware and network products that started pouring forth once Apple got serious about making the Macintosh a genuine digital hub. Slowly, the iPod proved to be the product that would begin to turn Apple back into a growth company. "We followed where our own desires led us," Steve explained, recalling how much his team had hated the existing music players on the market, "and we ended up ahead."

Even the iPod tested Steve's faith in consumers, however. It took them a while to fully warm to the device. It presented an unfamiliar method of interacting with music, and its $399 price was a significant impediment, especially when you could buy a Sony Discman CD player for under $100. Sales started out on the slow side: Apple sold just 150,000 iPods during the first quarter they were available. One year later, Steve cut the price of that first iPod by $100 and introduced a second version with twice as much capacity and a new "touch-wheel" that was a wheel in shape only—it was actually a circular touch-pad that moved users through their music even more smoothly than the mechanical thumb-wheel, and wasn't nearly as prone to break. That second introduction was the first clear outward signal that iPod had transformed more than just the experience of listening to music—it had revitalized Apple's capabilities as a manufacturer as well. The iPod had accelerated Apple's creative metabolism, instilling a new organizational discipline that would make the promise of frequent, market-churning, incremental improvements—the kind that Bill Gates had lectured Steve about in that joint interview in Palo Alto a decade before—into a breathtaking new kind of rapid-fire technological innovation.

The iPod had led Apple to a newfound ability to keep outdoing itself almost like clockwork. Some of this required execution at a very high level. The iPod's low price (at least compared to Apple's computers), forced Apple to learn how to ensure high-quality manufacturing at higher unit volumes than Apple had ever delivered before. These new demands on manufacturing were exacerbated by the competitive dynamics of the consumer electronics market, which expected Apple to refresh the iPod product line far more frequently than its computers. To churn out iPods this way, Apple had to develop disciplines that would fundamentally transform the company into a much more capable enterprise. Tim Cook had to build up an extensive international supply chain, and he and Ruby had to develop relationships with a set of Asian factories capable of delivering lots of high-quality machines in record times. The iPod had quickened the company's metabolism in a way that would pay off for years to come.

But outdoing itself also required Apple's top execs—and Steve himself—to think about the future in a new way, with a willingness to follow the technology wherever it might lead. "Learning about new technologies and markets is what makes this fun for me and for everyone at Apple," Steve once told me, a few years after the iPod's debut. "By definition, it's just what we do, and there are lots of ways to do it. Five or six years ago we didn't know anything about video editing, so we bought a company to learn how to do that. Then we didn't know anything about MP3 players, but our people are smart. They went out and figured it out by looking at what was already out there with a very critical eye, and then they combined that with what we already knew about design, user interface, materials, and digital electronics. The truth is, we'd get bored otherwise." In another interview, Steve said, "Who cares where the good ideas come from? If you're paying attention you'll notice them." When his focus had been directed entirely on fixing Apple's own problems, Steve had almost missed the digital music revolution. Now that Apple was on more solid footing, he was focused outward again, and paying attention very carefully. "When I came back, Apple was like a person who was ill and couldn't go out and do or learn anything," Steve explained. "But we made it healthy again, and have increased its strength. Now, figuring out new things to do is what keeps us going."

Chapter 11
Do Your Level Best

The world was opening up to Apple bit by bit, and vice versa. The iPod was Apple's first mass-market consumer device, but it had come about because Steve and his team had taken one logical step after another: first iMovie, then a correction leading to iTunes, then the iPod. Steve's patience, discipline, and vision had set Apple on a new course, one that was more complicated than its old path, which had simply involved the regular improvement of personal computers. Apple would now follow its explorations to their logical conclusion, even if this led the company into the heart of other industries. If Apple could successfully maneuver in the world of music, it might, under Steve's leadership, be able to do so in other kinds of business as well. The grand scheme—bringing computing tools to people who could employ them creatively to enhance their lives and work—remained the same. But the breadth of Apple's horizon had stretched.

As a mass-market consumer electronics device, the iPod would eventually be sold, of course, all the usual places: Best Buy, Circuit City, big-box department stores, and even the computer retailers like CompUSA. Steve disdained all these outlets. His obsession with his products continued well after they'd been manufactured. The tacky, low-margin hustle of these chains ran completely against the minimalist aesthetic of his products and the clean exuberance of his marketing. There was only one place where he really enjoyed seeing his products sold to the public: his own Apple stores, which had debuted four months ahead of the iPod.

Going back as far as the debut of the Mac, Steve had always groused about the way Apple computers were sold in its resellers' stores. The way his computers were displayed and sold represented the very worst of what could go wrong when things weren't done his way. The salespeople, always interested in quick turnover, seemed to make little effort to understand what was special about a Mac, and had less incentive to do so after IBM and its clones became dominant. Even at NeXT, Steve had talked to Susan Barnes about creating a different kind of computer store, one in which his high-end productions could be shown off to discerning customers.

In early 1998, just a few months after his return to Apple, he asked his chief information officer, Niall O'Connor, to come up with a proposal for an online store where Apple could sell its computers directly to customers, much like Dell Computer was doing then with such great success. O'Connor asked Eddy Cue, who was then an IT technician in the human resources division, to sketch out an initial version of what the store might look like from a programmer's perspective. "I don't think Niall thought I was his best person," says Cue, "but he did think I could deal with Steve, for some reason." Cue, who had never met Steve and knew little about e-commerce or retailing, sought advice from a number of people, including head of sales Mitch Mandich. "Give him your best ideas," Mandich told him, "but it won't matter because we'll never do it. It would piss off the channels [the stores and distributors that had traditionally sold Apple's computers]." One week later, Cue, O'Connor, Mandich, and others attended a meeting to review the initial proposal. Cue handed his presentation to Steve—he'd made it visual, because everyone had told him that Steve preferred visual presentations, and he'd put it on paper, because everyone had told him Steve hated sitting through slides, especially in small meetings. All the research seemed to have gone for naught. Steve looked at his pages, handed them back, and said, "These suck."

Despite his gruff initial reaction, Steve asked the others in the room about Cue's proposal, and about the basic idea of selling direct to customers online. The executives around the table started to talk about all the problems they could foresee with an online store—tying customized purchases into a manufacturing system that had been built to create computers with standardized configurations; not having any research indicating that customers actually wanted to buy computers this way; and, most worrisome, the potential for alienating Apple's existing retail partners, like Best Buy and CompUSA. Mandich, who was senior enough to know that an interesting discussion was developing, kept silent. Finally, one of the senior guys opposing the idea spoke up. "Steve," he asked, "isn't this all pointless? You're not going to do this—the channel will hate it." Cue, who didn't know any better, turned to him immediately. "The channel?" he exclaimed. "We lost two billion dollars last year! Who gives a fuck about the channel?" Steve perked up. "You," he said, pointing at the senior exec, "are wrong. And you," he continued, looking at Cue, "are right." By the end of the meeting, he had asked Cue and O'Connor to create an online store where buyers could customize their purchases—and to have it completed in two months.

The online store went up on April 28, 1998. As Cue prepared to drive home that evening, he walked past Steve's office to tell him they'd sold more than a million dollars' worth of computers in just six hours. "That's great," said Steve. "Imagine what we could do if we had real stores." Nothing would ever be enough, Cue realized. He liked the challenge.

STEVE LOVED GREAT stores. When on vacation in Italy or France, he would insist that Laurene join him in visiting Valentino, Gucci, Yves Saint Laurent, Hermès, Prada, and the like. Wearing the ragged cut-off jeans and Birkenstocks of a bohemian American tourist out for a long day of informal sightseeing, Steve would squire Laurene around exclusive shopping districts. After strolling into one of these bastions of fashion, he and his striking blond wife would head in completely different directions. While Laurene browsed distractedly, Steve would buttonhole the salesclerks and bombard them with questions: Why had they chosen to devote so little space to their merchandise? How did people flow through the store? He'd look at the stores' interior architecture, wondering how the interplay of wood, arches, stairways, and natural and unnatural light helped set a mood that was conducive to spending outrageous sums of money. To Steve, these stores were pulling off something he had never been able to manage: they sold a lifestyle product at an absurdly high margin by presenting it in a beautiful and yet informative way. The presentation itself helped justify the higher prices a customer was asked to pay. The dreary aisles and dull salesmen of Circuit City and CompUSA were making no such argument for Apple.

In 1998, Steve convinced Gap CEO Mickey Drexler to join Apple's board of directors. Then, in 2000, he hired Target's vice president of merchandising, Ron Johnson, and made him part of the executive team, with a bold and simple mandate: Create the ideal store. "The Mac is unique," Steve told me many years later. "The trick was to get it in front of people somewhere where they could see what makes it different and better, and to have salespeople who had something to say about it. We thought if we didn't do that, we'd go broke."

Johnson came from old-school retailing, but he was the right man for the job Steve had in mind. After earning his MBA at Stanford, Johnson chose to start his career unloading trucks for the Mervyn's department store. He then moved up the ranks at Target before making his mark by commissioning the architect Michael Graves to design a teapot exclusively for the department store. Graves had designed a teapot for the Italian appliance icon Alessi in 1984 that was still a global bestseller a decade later, and Johnson wondered, "Why are beautiful objects not available to everyday people, but only to the well-to-do?" It was a question that could have popped full-form out of the brain of Steve Jobs.

When it came time to introduce Graves's teapot, Johnson engineered an event that also could have been dreamed up by Steve: he rented out the Whitney Museum in New York City to "let the press see what design could be for everyday people." The teapot, and a line of other merchandise designed by Graves exclusively for Target, set the department store on the path that eventually led to its becoming the high-end, urbane alternative to Walmart. When Jobs came calling, he wooed Johnson, who was not headed toward a CEO role at Target, with the same kind of promise of unlimited opportunity that had worked with Sculley: "You get to do it all," Steve told him.

"I looked at it as a chance to work with one of the greatest creators ever," Johnson told a group of Stanford MBA candidates during a 2014 interview, "but my friends in the Valley all thought that I was nuts. 'You're leaving Tar-*jzeh* [the Francofied pronunciation that both mocked and trumpeted the chain's high-end position] and going to that loser company?" It was the year 2000, when Apple was still seen as a marginal player in the market for personal computers.

Throughout the interview process, and in Johnson's early days at Apple, Jobs spent more time talking to him about personal matters than retail affairs. "The first time we met," Johnson said, "we talked for two or three hours about all kinds of things. Steve was a very, very private guy. He had grown up fast, and he was only best friends with a handful of people. He told me, 'I want to be good friends, because once you know how I think we only have to talk once or twice a week. Then when you want to do something you can do it and not feel that you have to ask permission.'"

For some time, Johnson was the only retailer employed by Apple. For weeks after his arrival, he sat in on the executive team meetings and mulled over what would make for the ideal store. The key was the customer experience, and as Johnson pondered this, every idea he came up with was counterintuitive. Stores that sell to a customer once every few years generally opt for cheap real estate in remote locations; but the ideal store, for customers and for a brand looking to make its mark, would be right at the center of things. Telephone support should be fine for such occasional customers, but face-to-face interaction is what people really want, especially with computers, which are a lot harder to understand than, say, a raincoat. Salespeople are motivated by commissions, but customers don't want to feel pressured into buying something they don't want. Johnson came up with almost a dozen of these ideas, each of which went against the heart of traditional retailing practice. According to Johnson, Steve supported all of his most far-reaching thoughts. "'If you think something through hard enough,' Steve would say, 'you'll get to the inevitable answer,'" remembers Johnson.

At Mickey Drexler's suggestion, Jobs asked Johnson to develop a prototype for what an Apple retail store might look like. Commandeering a warehouse a couple of miles away from the Apple campus, Johnson built his prototype under the greatest secrecy. Much like an Apple computer under development, the prototype went through several iterations. It was a design project as much as anything, and Steve pushed for a minimalist, clean feel, with easy navigation around tables featuring Apple's laptops and desktop computers.

By late 2000, Jobs and Johnson had a prototype they liked. But on a Tuesday morning in October, Johnson woke up with an epiphany: the layout of the stores, which revolved around areas selling particular product lines, was all wrong. Steve and the executive team had been discussing one subject endlessly in their Monday-morning meetings: the digital hub. Johnson realized that the stores should be laid out to match that concept, with an area built around music, and another built around movies, and so on. It was, once again, a counterintuitive thought—and yet it was also, once again, a thought that would serve customers better than the more common approach that Apple had been on the verge of embracing. That morning, Johnson joined

Steve for a previously scheduled review of the prototype. On the car ride over to the prototype hangar, Johnson told Steve that he thought they'd gotten it all wrong. "Do you know how big a change this is," Steve roared. "I don't have time for this. I don't want you to say a word to anyone about this. I don't know what I think of this." They sat for the rest of the short ride in silence.

When they arrived at the hangar, Steve spoke to the assembled group: "Well," he said, "Ron thinks we've designed our stores all wrong." Johnson waited to hear where this line of thought would go. "And he's right," said Steve, "so I'm going to leave now and you should just do what he's going to tell you to do." And Jobs turned around and left.

Later that day, after he'd returned to the Apple campus, Johnson went to see Steve. "You know," Steve told him, "you reminded me of something I learned at Pixar. On almost every film they make, something turns out to be not quite right. And they have an amazing willingness to turn around and do it again, till they do get it right. They have always had a willingness to not be governed by the release date. It's not about how fast you do something, it's about doing your level best."

The first stores opened in Tysons Corner, Virginia, and Glendale, California, in May 2001. They featured Apple's iMacs, Power Macs, iBooks, and PowerBooks, plus an array of software, a small selection of "how-to" books, some peripheral equipment from other manufacturers like printers and hard disk drives, and an assortment of cables and other accessories. The reaction was fairly uniform: Steve had made a foolish mistake. *BusinessWeek* excoriated the stores as yet another example of Steve's extravagance. One critic after another pointed to the fact that Gateway, perhaps the most marketing-savvy of all the Wintel PC makers, had recently shut down its own chain of more than one hundred retail stores because of poor sales. But just as Jobs had no use for typical market research when formulating product strategy, he dismissed Gateway's misadventure as irrelevant. "When we started opening stores, everyone thought we were crazy," he told me. "But that was because the point of sale had lost its ability to communicate with the customer. Everybody else was selling computers that were the same thing—take off the bezel or company nameplate and it's the same box made in Taiwan. With so little differentiation, there was nothing for the salespeople to explain except the price, so they didn't have to be very sophisticated, and those stores had tremendous turnover in their sales force."

The Apple stores fared fairly well from the beginning, but primarily as havens for those who already loved Apple and its high-priced gear. Early traffic patterns revealed just how deeply the company needed a transformative new product. Basically, Apple had a demographic problem—adolescents and young adults didn't think the company or its products were as cool as their parents did. Part of the reason was that Apple's iMacs and iBooks, as beautiful and compelling as they were, were still too pricey for kids to buy on their own: only their baby boomer parents could afford to write a check or whip out a credit card and bring one home. At the stores, Apple had nothing of its own to sell that appealed directly to the Generation X- and Y-ers.

Enter iTunes and the iPod. With their introduction, the stores quickly became the perfect medium for demonstrating Apple's new digital hub concept. Highly trained salespeople—on salary, not commission—showed customers how to use their iMacs and iTunes to "rip, mix, and burn" their own customized audio CDs. Others taught Mac owners how to use iMovie to edit digital movies. The stores offered group lessons in how to transfer playlists and albums to an iPod, even though it was a very simple process. "The people who work in our stores are the key," Steve said. "And our turnover is very low for retail. So our power is in our people."

As the stores attracted more visitors, Apple expanded its sales of digital cameras, camcorders, speakers, audio amplifiers, headphones, printers, hard drives, CD-ROM burners, and the like made by other manufacturers. Slowly but steadily, over the years, the stores would become the most successful retail outlets in the world, when measured by sales per square foot. Jobs pushed Johnson to be increasingly audacious with the architecture of the stores, which eventually led to iconic features like the cube of glass in front of the GM building in midtown Manhattan. "Steve was the best delegator I ever met," Johnson said at Stanford. "He was so clear about what he wanted that it gave you great freedom."

———

MUSIC REVIVED THE company. Between iTunes, its "Rip Mix Burn" ad campaign, and the iPod itself, Apple was finally generating heat with younger buyers. But the momentum and the insouciant advertising gnawed at some older folks in the music and film business. In 2002, long after the offending ads had ceased running, Disney CEO Michael Eisner complained in a hearing before the U.S. Senate Commerce Committee that Apple was guilty of openly touting illegal behavior. "They are selling the computer with the encouragement of the advertising that they can rip, mix, and burn," he said. "In other words, they can create a theft and distribute it to all of their friends if they buy this particular computer." Steve was livid when he read the transcript, but felt somewhat vindicated after Eisner was widely ridiculed for his somewhat naïve comment. The tone of Apple's ad campaign walked a fine line, but Steve actually sympathized with Eisner and the record labels. He understood the perils of piracy, both as a computer industry executive and as the owner of a movie studio. He had sued Microsoft for what he believed was its theft of the Mac's desktop graphical user interface, and, like everyone in Silicon Valley, he was paranoid about intellectual theft.

In fact, Steve was so attuned to the piracy issue that he knew the issue might help him sell his next big music idea—the iTunes Music Store. Steve believed, with some justification, that iTunes was a more elegant form of digital music management than anything else on the market. And he knew that an iTunes music store, if properly designed, could give the consumers such a fluid and simple way to buy music that they would stop stealing tracks via Napster and the like, which were cumbersome applications that opened up a person's computer to all manner of potential security issues.

The creation of this particular online "store" is a crucial turning point in the evolution of Steve Jobs. It represents the moment when Steve's ambitions for Apple first stretched beyond Cupertino. Up until this point, everything Steve had done had been within the confines of Apple's own operations. He had stabilized the company, focused its mission, rebuilt the staff, shaped a core leadership group of first-rate executives, and produced the striking new iMac and a modern new operating system. Every step he'd taken had naturally proceeded from what came before, ensuring that the company was on a solid foundation in its core business even as it wandered into the uncertain future. Now he was about to make a bet that Apple's bedrock was so strong that it could move beyond its own walls and start looking for opportunities that would reshape the businesses of others.

To accomplish this, Steve would have to work on two fronts, both inside and outside the company. Inside, he would need to have his engineers customize Apple's digital compression and distribution technology in a way that would solve problems the music industry couldn't handle on its own. More expedient options, like buying an existing online retail music distribution website and "Apple-izing" it to get a running start, wouldn't work because such sites didn't yet exist. Nor did it make any sense to simply grant a license to the music labels to promote, sell, and deliver music directly to iTunes users, given how technologically inept the companies had shown themselves to be with their repeated, compromised efforts to sell their wares online. Sony Music, for example, made a hash of its early stab at selling digital music that would play only on players made by its parent, Sony Electronics. Not only did it offer very little music from the other big record companies, but Sony also made the tracks it sold unplayable on personal computers, which was where the lion's share of consumers played digital tracks at that time.

If Apple were to try to sell music itself, Steve would have to convince the heads of all five major record companies that an independent online store operated by Apple was their best, and perhaps their only, choice, given the sophistication of the digital onslaught they faced. Even then, given their temerity, he'd have to bend over backward to give them a comfortable way to try it out.

Selling music online was a complicated challenge. Apple's engineers needed to adapt iTunes so the music could be bought and organized easily, so charges could be recorded and billed appropriately, and so purchased tracks were encrypted to prevent buyers from copying and sharing purchased music indiscriminately. This last bit, a measure that would protect the labels from further piracy, was actually the most straightforward. Software companies had been working to address such security problems for more than a decade, and had developed all manner of digital locks and online verification tricks to protect their own software. Depending on what the label heads would eventually decide they wanted, Steve could easily customize the encryption, or watermarking, of MP3 tracks. It was much easier for Apple to tame that technology into a simple, foolproof lock than it was for the labels.

The more significant challenge facing the store's developers was billing. This seemingly simple problem was profound—existing billing systems might have cost music purveyors more for each transaction than the profit they could earn. This was in large part because of an issue that was becoming as vexing to the industry as piracy—namely, that online buyers were showing a preference for buying individual singles rather than higher-priced albums.

Napster's own traffic had demonstrated this new consumer behavior. When music fans could download whatever music they wanted, they liked to cherry-pick their favorite tunes, rather than get an entire album. This was a complete reversal of what happened to the music business in the late 1960s and early 1970s, when the recording industry all but did away with the single and focused instead on albums that commanded a much higher unit price. Many artists embraced the change and recorded "concept" albums, such as the Beatles' *Sgt. Pepper's Lonely Hearts Club Band,* The Who's *Tommy,* or Pink Floyd's *The Wall.* But labels abused the concept and regularly released albums with just one or two strong tracks, knowing that committed buyers would spend $10 to $15 on the whole album just to get those tracks.

Steve knew that there was no turning back from the "Napster effect." Now that listeners had the option, they would nearly always choose singles over the albums padded with forgettable tracks. Steve thought singles should sell for 99 cents, which more or less represented the imputed value of a track on an album, since the average conventional CD in the 1990s had a dozen or more tracks and sold for about $15. The price also appealed to Steve's nostalgic streak, since it was the same price that he and others our age had paid for the 45 rpm singles we'd purchased in the 1960s.

There was one problem with Steve's idea, however. Historically, Visa and MasterCard charged 15 cents, plus around 1.5 percent of the transaction value for a single purchase; while American Express charged 20 cents plus 3.5 percent of the transaction value. That's not such a big deal when the sale price is in the tens or hundreds of dollars, but when a single song costs just 99 cents, a transaction fee of 17 to 24 cents would be ruinous.

If Apple was going to become a significant music e-tailer, it needed to figure out how to process charges for small purchases without forcing the credit card companies to radically alter their commission structures. (Apple wasn't the first to face this conundrum of finding an affordable way to process and pay for non-cash "microtransactions" of less than a dollar. It had befuddled just about everyone except the phone companies, who solved it by aggregating their own internal accounting and billing for customers' individual phone calls once a month.)

Eddy Cue figured out a couple of ways to get around the problem. First, he suggested that the iTunes music store periodically bundle groups of purchases from an individual customer to send to the credit card clearing companies as a single transaction, rather than post them individually. That wouldn't always be possible, but as the store's traffic increased, the credit card charges could be consolidated into fewer separate transactions. Also, Cue had the store offer a simple way for parents to set up "music allowances" to prepay for their kids' purchases, which would provide up-front payments in large enough increments to cover the cost of reconciling transactions as they trickled in later.

These kinds of intricate answers delighted Steve. When Apple took on a major project, he wasn't just concerned with the design and marketing. He wanted to know *everything* about the project, and he expected his employees to attack *every* conceivable problem—from design and engineering to seemingly mundane tasks such as packaging and billing—with creativity. Steve told me he was just as proud of the microtransaction solution as he was of the redesigned iPod models he would introduce in conjunction with the opening of the online store.

Cue's team made another crucial decision: Apple would build the iTunes digital "storefront" right into the iTunes application, rather than create a public website to serve as its music retail site. If you look for "www.itunes.com" online, you come to an Apple.com marketing page for iTunes, which describes its many wonders but doesn't allow you to buy music. The only way to get to the store is via the iTunes application, which at that time was available only for Macintosh computers. This appealed to Steve for several reasons. It gave Apple control of all the technology behind the store, and it cemented a direct commercial relationship with customers. The simple transaction of buying a song, and of handing over a credit card number to Apple in order to so, became part of what Steve had begun calling "the Apple experience." As a great marketer, Steve understood that every interaction a customer had with Apple could increase or decrease his or her respect for the company. As he put it, a corporation "could accumulate or withdraw credits" from its reputation, which is why he worked so hard to ensure that every single interaction a customer might have with Apple—from using a Mac to calling customer support to buying a single from the iTunes store and then getting billed for it—was excellent. Steve had told me back in 1998 that the only reason for companies to exist was to build products; he was now using his company to build more than just products. Apple was now creating a holistic customer experience. Everything the company did, from technology development to the design of its stores, offline and on, was in service of that customer experience. Apple's broad-based, intense focus on this was far ahead of its time, and would have wide cultural implications. After seeing and experiencing the uniform excellence of Apple's products and service, customers would increasingly demand the same from other companies. Apple redefined the word "quality" and forced other companies to wrestle with the higher expectations of their customers.

There was another key short-term benefit to building the iTunes store into the iTunes application: the limited reach of the iTunes store would be reassuring to the nervous music industry executives Steve had to woo. Half a million iPods had been sold, enough to create a meaningful niche but not nearly enough to affect the broader economics of the entire music industry. After all, Mac users accounted for a measly 4 percent of all personal computer users. For once, that minuscule market share was a competitive advantage. Since online sales of digital music represented a fearsome change to the label chiefs, Steve went to them with a simple, seemingly safe proposition: Why don't you experiment with selling music downloads, to gauge demand and learn the customer and marketing dynamics, in my safe and tiny "walled garden"?

Steve's negotiating challenge was considerable. He needed every leader of the big five labels—Universal, EMI, Sony, BMG, and Warner—to sign on. He was probably right in presuming that any online store that couldn't claim a huge selection across every major label was doomed to fail. And he was charging a stiff price in return for his end-to-end solution: 30 percent of every sale made on the iTunes Music Store.

Fortunately for Steve, he quickly found an ally: Roger Ames, the head of Warner Music, whom he knew through an executive at AOL named Barry Schuler. Ames, an unpretentious realist in a business that was then still floating on the fumes of past profits and successes, saw clearly what Warner could accomplish on its own technologically:

"Absolutely nothing," he says. "We didn't have any real technologists at Warner. It's a record company, not a tech company!" Convinced that Steve had the only reasonable solution to where the industry was headed, Ames introduced Steve to the leaders of the four other major record studios, starting with those he thought would be most receptive. Their progress was steady, if bumpy. The reluctance of the record company executives was palpable and understandable. Some still denied that digital distribution of music was inevitable, while the more pragmatic feared that they would lose pricing power over their own products by ceding distribution to an outside industry that they didn't quite understand or trust. Steve listened to them, and modified the store and the digital protections on singles to their liking. He knew he couldn't just impose a solution on the industry.

Steve also knew how to get what he wanted, and he negotiated with both carrot and stick. While he worked with the studio chiefs and led them to see that he truly did have a safe and complete solution designed for them by the very best technologists, he was also sure to remind them that the digital onslaught they were trying to ignore was inevitable and irrepressible. If they were worried about losing control, well, he invited them to just wait and see what might be wrought by the smarter, sneakier successors to Napster!

Of all the record company heads, Andy Lack at Sony was the most suspicious. Sony had its own consumer electronics division, with its own approach to selling portable digital music players that used a completely different compression and encryption scheme. Furthermore, everything in Lack's decades of experience as a media executive at NBC and other places told him that iPod sales would soar if Apple could offer a full-service music store, and that the company would probably even sell millions more Macs as a result. If that was the case, why weren't the music companies the ones getting a slice of Steve's business, rather than the other way around? Other studio heads sensed this as well, and they—or the CEOs of their parent companies—made equity offers that would have created partnerships that went deeper than mere revenue-sharing on music tracks. But these were halfhearted, and Steve believed that the longer he held out, the more the record companies would see that they needed his solution.

Finally, Lack caved. On April 23, 2003, the iTunes Music Store opened for business with an inventory of 200,000 songs. During the very first week customers downloaded a million tracks, and by the end of the year Apple had sold more than 25 million songs.

———

JUST AS LACK had predicted, iPod sales soared, to the point where several of Steve's lieutenants believed that the market of existing Macintosh users was nearing saturation. They argued that the next logical step in the expansion of the iPod was to create iTunes application software for Windows—which of course meant opening the iTunes Music Store to every computer user in the world, which was exactly what Steve had promised not to do.

Steve initially resisted the idea, for reasons that were both strategic and emotional. Steve had always wanted Macs to have distinctive features that consumers couldn't get from a Windows PC. Also, he still wanted to see if the iPod itself might begin to drive up Mac sales—that part of Lack's prediction had not yet come true. But Ruby, Schiller, and others argued that iTunes for Windows coupled with the iPod would give hundreds of millions of PC users a means to taste for themselves Apple's more inviting approach to personal computing. The idea that the iPod could be a diminutive Trojan Horse to help Apple finally begin to win back some market share for Macintosh personal computers really intrigued Steve. After all, the team reminded him, wasn't he the one who was always saying that if the company could pick up just a few points of PC market share, revenues would soar? Furthermore, even though the expansion would mean that PC users would use iTunes software on Windows, Apple would still control their entire digital music experience, from its iTunes software to its store to its iPod. As it had with iMovie, the team wore Steve down—

quickly, this time—and convinced him to shift direction. Changing his mind now would pay off as much as it had then.

Just a few months earlier Steve had cajoled the music label chiefs into signing off on that "little," Mac-only test of the iTunes Music Store. Now here he came again, wanting to expand the experiment to, oh, every other personal computer user in the entire world. He had to get their permission, because the terms they'd agreed to applied only to the smaller universe of Mac users. But in the few months in between, they had seen that what Steve had forecast was true: consumers really would forgo piracy if given an easy way to acquire digital tracks at a cost that seemed fair. This time they put up minimal resistance; their business was headed in the direction Steve had predicted, whether they liked it or not. The iTunes Music Store gave them a way to like it a little better than the alternatives.

Once again, Sony's Andrew Lack felt he had no choice but to go along with others, even though he felt duped by the speed with which Steve expanded the iTunes Music Store's market. Despite Sony's ample content and history of great consumer electronics devices, its business units were stubbornly independent operating divisions that couldn't possibly collaborate well enough to create any kind of "whole widget" alternative. Years later, Lack still bemoaned the weakness he thought the music studios had displayed in their negotiations with Steve. "The iPod was empty without the music," Lack has said. "I felt strongly that without a dual revenue stream [in which Apple had to give a cut of iPod sales back to the recording companies] the music business was going to struggle. If they'd stuck together, there was a chance they could have gotten somewhere. It's my greatest regret."

On October 16, 2003, Steve announced that Apple was offering free downloads of the iTunes application for Windows PCs. For some of the Mac faithful, this was as shocking as Microsoft's investment back in 1997. Most, however, saw it as a vindication of their faith that Apple software, and its entire approach to personal computing, was far superior to anything offered by the Windows juggernaut. Steve knew it, too; he gleefully made part of his announcement under a slide reading "Hell froze over."

Within three days, a million Windows PC users had downloaded iTunes and purchased a million songs via the iTunes Music Store. By the end of the year, more customers were downloading music from Apple through their Windows computers than through Macs. What the team was beginning to call "the Apple experience" had begun to infect the world of Windows.

It is so hard to remember, given Apple's string of hits, the resulting ubiquity of its later products, and the dominant role it eventually assumed in our culture, that this rise was entirely unexpected, and a surprise even to the people who engineered it. One little thing led to another. One success, one particular challenge, could spur thoughts about another product, or a different iteration of an existing product, or a whole new channel of revenue. As Steve liked to say, "You can only connect the dots of how things really happened in hindsight." Eddy Cue remembers a day in late 2003 when he was waiting for a plane and he looked around the airport lounge at the other passengers waiting with him. Perhaps a dozen folks were listening to music on iPods, earbuds in place; a handful of people were working on PowerBooks with the distinctive white apple silhouette glowing from the back of the lid; and only one guy was tapping away at a laptop PC. "Holy shit, I thought," Cue recalls. "We're really onto something here. We didn't really have time to lift our heads up and look around, you know? But there it was. It was cool."

———

AS STEVE WAS so fond of saying at the end of his meticulously stage-crafted keynote speeches, there was "one more thing" in 2003. In the late summer, he passed a kidney stone and went to the doctor for an ultrasound follow-up, to ensure that there weren't more. In forty-nine years, Steve had never had any serious medical conditions, and when a urologist saw a shadow on the ultrasound and called to urge him to come in for a follow-up visit, he ignored her request. To her credit, she harangued him, and, finally, he returned to see her in October for what he figured would be a routine scan. The results were shocking: he had what appeared to be a cancerous tumor on his pancreas, a scary prognosis that often means the victim has just a few months to live. The next day brought news that what Steve actually had was a slower-growing, more treatable condition—something called a pancreatic neuroendocrine tumor. Both he and Laurene heaved a half-sigh of relieve. But the emotional see-saw of the two days had been exhausting. It was only the beginning of a slow-motion process that would ultimately prove to be beyond Steve's control. And it came at the very moment when his efforts to will his company to success were finally starting to pay off in unimaginable ways.

Chapter 12
Two Decisions

Steve was presiding over a sprawling, growing business that was becoming more demanding by the day. In 2003 and 2004 alone, for example, Apple upgraded its entire product line. The four-quadrant structure still applied to personal computers. Consumers looking for a desktop computer were treated to the transition from the whimsical "sunflower" iMac G4, whose sleek flat-screen monitor swiveled on a post that rose from a bubblelike computer case, to bigger iMac G5s, slablike affairs that packed their entire computing innards behind a flat screen encased by a sleek white plastic frame. The Power Mac G5 was a formidable upgrade of Apple's tower computer for businesses and power users, and received critical hosannas. Laptop buyers were given the choice of white or matte black plastic iBook G4s or the aluminum PowerBook G4s, which came in three different screen sizes. But between the Internet, home networking, music, and the software applications division, Apple was now churning out much more than just personal computers.

New versions of iMovie and FinalCut Pro rolled out, along with a cool new application called GarageBand, which let you record and edit and mix musical compositions on your Mac. Apple also introduced a new version of its OS X operating system called Panther that came loaded with its own browser, Safari. Two new keyboards were introduced, one of them wireless. Apple's beautiful flat-screen Cinema Display monitors grew bigger and sharper. The company that had pushed harder than any other to make Wi-Fi the standard protocol for networking introduced Airport Extreme, a heavy-duty Wi-Fi server for home users, and Airport Express, which could extend a Wi-Fi network throughout an entire McMansion. For users who wanted to make their online chats visual, the company started selling iSight, a Web camera that perched atop their computer monitor. A line of Web servers called Xserve, aimed at businesses, also got an upgrade. And last, but hardly least, iPod users got two special treats in 2004: the sleek and slender iPod Mini, and an iPod Classic with a color screen that could display photos.

Apple was on a roll. The iPod seemed to have years of growth ahead. The product line was focused, beautifully made, and popular. But, of course, Steve didn't see this as cause for celebration or rest. He saw it merely as the foundation for his next "dent in the universe."

Jim Collins, the bestselling author of the management classics *Built to Last: Successful Habits of Visionary Companies* and *Good to Great: Why Some Companies Make the Leap . . . and Others Don't,* has a wonderful phrase to describe an essential characteristic of great leaders: deep restlessness. Collins applies the phrase to Steve, one of the two great leaders who inspire him the most (the other is Winston Churchill, the great English politician who was prime minister during most of World War II, from 1940 to 1945, and again from 1951 to 1955). Collins believes this restlessness is far more important and powerful than simple ambition or raw intelligence. It is the foundation of resilience, and self-motivation. It is fueled by curiosity, the ache to build something meaningful, and a sense of purpose to make the most of one's entire life.

Collins and Steve got to know each other when Collins was a young faculty member at Stanford University's Graduate School of Business from 1988 to 1995. During Collins's first year teaching entrepreneurship, he asked Steve to conduct a session with his students, and they met for the first time. Even though NeXT was not exactly a rousing success, and Pixar was still finding its way, Steve was charismatic, witty, and gracious. Collins, who remained periodically in touch with Jobs throughout his life, believes those years were the best time to meet Steve. "You would have wanted to meet Winston Churchill in 1935, when he was out of favor and no one was paying attention," he says. "Churchill had his detractors, which is not an uncommon experience for great men. But in the end you judge them by the big picture, the arc of how everything unfolded." Churchill, like Jobs, suffered humiliating setbacks early in his career, and persevered through a long, arduous climb back to an even greater prominence.

Steve's restlessness hadn't always been an advantage. When he was younger, his attention could flit from one project to another, as happened when the Apple III development effort suddenly seemed mundane after he'd seen the potential of graphical computing at Xerox's Palo Alto Research Center. Founding NeXT so shortly after leaving Apple under a cloud in 1985 was abrupt, as was his purchase of the computer graphics engineering team that would become Pixar. Back then, his restlessness sometimes seemed like impulsiveness. But he never gave up. He didn't ever quit on Pixar or NeXT. What gave his particular restlessness real depth, then, was its relentlessness. "The things he was trying to do," says Collins, "were always hard. Sometimes those things beat him up. But the response to fighting through that suffering can be tremendous personal growth."

Now, in 2003 and 2004, Steve's restlessness was pushing him forward again, into the uncertain future, and into a test of just how much he had grown. Steve was asking himself the question he always asked himself—"What comes next?"—but this time the answer was particularly complicated. Apple could build something that evolved out of its traditional foundation in personal computing, perhaps something that yet again transformed the user interface. Perhaps it needed to deliver a computer in a new physical form, something like a tablet. Perhaps it could build on the iPod's success with another consumer electronics product, perhaps even a cellphone.

The iPod had changed everything for Apple. The iTunes Music Store, especially now that its customers included millions of PC users, was turning out to be a whole new distribution system, with very little friction and far less overhead cost than the old way of stamping out CDs in a factory and then shipping them to retailers. By the end of fiscal 2004 —just *three* years after the initial introduction of iTunes— revenue from products related to iTunes and the iPod would account for 19 percent of Apple's total sales. Apple sold 4.4 million iPods that year, while Macintosh unit sales slipped by 28 percent, from 4.6 million in 2000 to 3.3 million in 2004. The ultimate proof of the impact of iTunes and the iPod was in the bottom line: In 2004, the company reported net income of $276 million, up from $69 million in 2003.

But the iPod had done more than simply create a huge secondary stream of revenue. It had solidified Apple's foundation and expanded its potential. Tim Cook now managed an intricate supply chain that fed a global manufacturing network capable of churning out tens of millions of iPods a month. Jony Ive had responded to this higher metabolism and greater manufacturing scale by experimenting with new metals, alloys, durable plastics, and super-hard glass that could be sculpted into devices as small as an iPod Mini and as big as a 32-inch computer screen. The executive team was starting to feel that the company would succeed with whatever it took on. "One of the things I've always felt," Steve told me, "is that if you're going to be creative, it's like jumping up in the air; you want to make damn sure the ground is going to be there when you get back." The ground under Steve had never been this solid. The time was right to jump into something radically new that completely changed the game. Steve just didn't know which direction to leap. Resolving the dilemma would turn out to be the biggest decision of his professional life.

APPLE DID NOT have a formal research and development unit per se. Steve didn't like the idea of relegating all forward-looking tinkering to a separate area that somehow wasn't beholden to the people leading his most important product development efforts. Instead, research projects flowered in pockets all around the company, many of them without Steve's blessing or even awareness. They'd come to Steve's attention only if one of his key managers decided that the project or technology showed real potential. In that case, Steve would check it out, and the information he'd glean would go into the learning machine that was his brain. Sometimes that's where it would sit, and nothing would happen. Sometimes, on the other hand, he'd concoct a way to combine it with something else he'd seen, or perhaps to twist it in a way to benefit an entirely different project altogether. This was one of his great talents, the ability to synthesize separate developments and technologies into something previously unimaginable. It's a talent that he would call on to decide what came next.

Two projects had been launched with the intention of exploring the possibilities for creating a new kind of cellphone. Steve himself had asked the folks who developed Apple's Airport Wi-Fi networking product line to do some early research on cellular phone technology. This decision made some on his team just shake their heads—Wi-Fi data-networking technology has very little to do with the cellular radio technology behind wireless phone networks. But there was another, much more immediate project in the works. Beginning in the fall of 2003, several members of Steve's executive team, including Eddy Cue, the mastermind behind the iTunes Music Store, had been engrossed in finding a way to build iTunes-compatible music players and iTunes Music Store accessibility right into cellphone handsets.

"Everybody carried two devices. A cellphone and an iPod," Cue recalls, patting both front pockets of his jeans. "We knew you could add iTunes to a phone and it would be almost like an iPod. It was mostly a software problem. We looked around at the industry, and in early 2004 we settled on working with Motorola, which at the time completely dominated the handset business with its RAZR flip phone.

Everybody had one." Motorola had been a key supplier to Apple for decades. Its microprocessors powered all of Apple's computers up until the mid-1990s, and after that it was part of a consortium with IBM that designed the PowerPC chips that would be CPUs in Macs up until 2006. Motorola promised Apple that it would create a new line of phones, called the ROKR, expressly as a vehicle for iTunes.

The ROKR project was controversial from the start, for one simple reason: most people at Apple didn't like the idea of collaborating with other companies. The iPod hardware team, especially, led by Tony Fadell, couldn't stomach the notion of ceding the development of what they had started to call "musicphones" to the traditional handset industry. And the more Motorola showed them of its plans for the ROKR, the more certain they became that licensing their precious iPod and iTunes software had been a mistake. While Motorola had certainly built sleek and beautiful phones in the past, the company seemed hopeless when it came to designing software that could replicate the simplicity of Apple's iPods. To Apple's whiz kids, Motorola's approach seemed all but inept. The Illinois company assigned separate teams of programmers to build different software components, like a directory of contacts, text messaging, and a crude Internet browser that could only display stripped-down mobile versions of websites. Nothing about these features was as intuitive as the iPod screen interface, and trying to combine the efforts of disparate, disjointed teams led to a hopeless muddle. Steve became so exasperated with Motorola's work that he asked Fadell to develop his own prototypes for an Apple cellphone, the first featuring music and the second focusing on video and photos.

Ironically, two other projects that started out having nothing to do with cellphones would come to have the greatest impact on Steve's decision about what Apple would pursue next. One of these was called Project Purple. It was a skunkworks effort Steve had ordered up to devise a new approach to what was proving to be an elusive "form factor" for personal computing: an ultralight, portable device that resembled a tablet or a clipboard, with an interactive touch screen. The concept had thwarted Microsoft's best researchers and engineers for years, but

Steve believed that *his* guys could make headway where others had failed. There simply had to be a more direct and intuitive way for users to interact with a computer than a keyboard and a mouse. Preferably it would be something he could use anywhere, even when sitting on the toilet.

The other effort was something that developed far from Steve's purview. In 2002, Apple researchers Greg Christie and Bas Ording started looking into a user-interface technology that had been stuck in the mud for years. Christie and Ording decided to reconsider the possibilities of a touch-screen monitor, which allowed people to use a fingertip to activate an icon or button displayed on a video screen. Initially developed by IBM in the 1960s, touch screens had not followed a path anyone would call revolutionary. In 1972, Control Data sold a touch-screen mainframe terminal, called the Plato IV. In 1977, CERN, the European high-energy physics research consortium, built one to control particle accelerators. In the 1980s, Hewlett-Packard became the first big manufacturer to offer a touch-screen monitor as an accessory for some of its early desktop PCs—but most software available at the time couldn't use it. Rudimentary touch screens would become the interface of choice for ATMs, airline check-in kiosks, and cash registers, but they didn't seem to hold out much promise for personal computing.

In the early 1990s, a handful of startup entrepreneurs, along with researchers in the R&D labs of several computer makers, hit upon the idea that they might be able to reconfigure touch-screen technology into something they dubbed "pen computing." Their idea was that users would mimic the actions of a mouse by working directly on the screen of a portable computer with a special stylus. They believed that drawing or writing directly on a screen was so natural and familiar that it would be the best way for people to interact with their computers. This was the nascent technology that John Sculley had counted on to make the Apple Newton MessagePad the next big wave in personal computing when it was introduced in 1993. The Newton failed, of course, partly because its handwriting recognition was embarrassingly inaccurate. Microsoft tried for two decades to make something of pen computing in tablet versions of the PC, but to no avail. The only somewhat successful stab at the genre was Palm's Pilot personal digital assistant (PDA). But the small device was never intended to be a full-featured computer, and its success was fleeting.

Academics and even some forward-looking digital artists took the touch-screen concept in a different direction. In the early 1980s, they started experimenting with technology that allowed for the use of more than just one fingertip to manipulate computer images on a screen. These so-called "multi-touch" interfaces were profoundly different. Performed with combinations of fingers or hands, gestures and coordinated motions could control the screen with far more dexterity than a mouse. You could move icons and files around, or enlarge and shrink images on the screen. You had the tactile illusion of physically interacting with the image on the screen. Seeing the potential, researchers at IBM, Microsoft, Bell Labs, and elsewhere experimented with their own multi-touch projects.

Apple's Greg Christie had been one of the key designers and software engineers of the ill-fated Newton. He had gotten over his romance with pen computing, but he had steadily followed all the multi-touch research efforts in academia and the tech industry. He hoped that partnering with Ording, who had joined Apple in 1998 and who had worked on the iPod's scroll-wheel user interface as well as on OS X, might lead the way to make multi-touch *the* distinguishing technology for a serious new computer. They believed it might serve as the basis for a whole new kind of user interface.

Developing a new interface is one of the most deceptively difficult technological challenges in computer science. It isn't simply a matter of designing some delightful new way to present images of information on a computer. It's just as much a matter of reckoning with—and not simply discarding—past habits. For instance, the QWERTY keyboard has for years been the universally familiar means of typing and entering information into a computer. QWERTY, which refers to the first six keys on the left side of the third row of a keyboard, was a relic, a keyboard arrangement from the era of manual typewriters that was designed to keep the individual letter-embossing hammers from getting tangled up when the user was typing at high speed.

Christie and Ording decided against altering this ubiquitous, albeit hidebound, preference. Instead, they would experiment with having a virtual QWERTY keyboard appear on the screen when you needed to type. As they began to experiment with multi-touch, they found that they could do all kinds of things that were both effective and fun. The new approach was useful for editing and retouching photographic images, for making drawings, and even for annotating spreadsheets and word-processing documents. The more they worked with multi-touch, the more Ording and Christie believed they were onto something big.

Having five different projects sprout up around similar technological possibilities wasn't unusual at Apple. Steve didn't issue a "Let there be the iPad" command one day, and wake up the next to find the whole enterprise devoting itself to his single wish. Instead, the place was always bubbling with possibilities. His most important job was to sort through them and imagine how they could point the way to something entirely new.

———

STEVE HAD ANOTHER critical decision to make during this period: how to treat the cancer that had been discovered in his pancreas. The fact that the islet cell neuroendocrine carcinoma was slow-growing and potentially treatable had given Laurene and him some hope. But the key word was *potentially*. Steve had always taken great care of his body in ways that may have seemed quirky to others but that made sense to him. At one point in his younger days, he had been a fruitarian. He eventually settled into a vegetarian—primarily vegan—diet, as did Laurene, and he had no significant health problems. Now that he had a big one, he wanted to make sure for himself that the tumor was treated in the best way possible. In typical Jobsian fashion, that meant exploring all the alternatives.

He started out talking to close advisers like Larry Brilliant, Andy Grove, Arthur Levinson, the Genentech CEO who was on Apple's board, and the physician/author Dean Ornish. His Stanford doctors recommended immediate surgery to remove the tumor. In fact, the team of doctors included a surgeon who had pioneered a promising new surgical method for just this type of pancreatic cancer. But Steve wasn't immediately convinced that this was the best approach, so he told his doctors he first wanted to try something less invasive, namely treating it through his diet.

There certainly seems to have been a psychological component to his decision to temporarily avoid surgery. Years later, according to his authorized biography, Steve told Walter Isaacson, "I really didn't want them to open up my body, so I tried to see if a few other things would work." It's natural to fear such an invasive operation, but for someone like Steve, who believed so strongly in the value of having control, it must have been especially complicated.

But there were also intellectual reasons to investigate and try to understand his cancer. Steve's particular kind of tumor is a rare one. According to the National Cancer Institute (NCI), only about one thousand cases a year are discovered in the United States. As a result, research on pancreatic islet cell neuroendocrine carcinomas is not buttressed by the kind of massive database available to doctors studying breast or lung cancer, to cite two more common forms, or even other forms of cancer of the pancreas. (His own oncologist/surgeon admitted to me privately that not enough was known at that time to determine statistically what the best treatment should be—surgery, chemotherapy, radiation therapy, something else, or a combination of treatments.) So Steve's indecision about what to do was not completely off-base. "I don't understand," says Brilliant, "how writers can portray him, on the one hand, as this tough-ass businessman, very materialistic, with no mention of the spiritual side. But when it comes to his cancer, they claim that he had this crazy, spiritual belief that he was in a messianic situation to heal it himself."

Steve conducted his research with the same inquisitiveness he applied to understanding what would make a great new product. He scoured the globe for other options, and made surreptitious trips to see doctors in Seattle, Baltimore, and Amsterdam. He was interested primarily in dietary treatments that might work, and alternative cures that meshed more with his inclination toward an organic lifestyle. But he also talked to many expert mainstream doctors. At one point he even convened a conference call where he was able to discuss his cancer with at least a half dozen of the best cancer doctors in the United States.

But he found nothing that was more promising than surgery. The few people who knew intimately of Steve's cancer grew ever more exasperated as his "research" dragged on for months, and his doctors started to feel that the window for a successful operation that would get all the cancer was closing. Finally, in the summer of 2004, Steve acceded and checked into Stanford University Medical Center. On Saturday, July 31, he spent most of the day on an operating table. The surgeons opened him up and removed the tumor.

It was an extremely invasive surgery. Months later, Steve would show me his scar—a squarish semicircle nearly two feet long, starting at the bottom of one side of his rib cage, swooping down to his navel, and curving back up the other side. "The pancreas is back behind your gastrointestinal organs, so the surgeons have to have enough room to pull some of them up and out of the way to get at it," he told me, gesturing with both hands as if he were doing it himself. "They actually took only a small part of my pancreas," Steve continued. "Just getting to it was the hard part."

August 1, the day after his marathon surgery, was a Sunday. Although he was still in the intensive care unit and more than a little logy from anesthesia and painkillers, he asked for his PowerBook so he could put the finishing touches on a letter to Apple employees to inform them of his illness and surgery. In some ways the letter was a marketing challenge: How can you put positive spin on the fact that you have had surgery to treat pancreatic cancer, a disease that in most cases is a death sentence? Here's what he wrote:

Team,

I have some personal news that I need to share with you, and I wanted you to hear it directly from me. This weekend I underwent a successful surgery to remove a cancerous tumor from my pancreas. I had a very rare form of pancreatic cancer called an islet cell neuroendocrine tumor, which represents about 1% of the total cases of pancreatic cancer diagnosed each year, and can be cured by surgical removal if diagnosed in time (mine was). I will not require any chemotherapy or radiation treatments.

The far more common form of pancreatic cancer is called adenocarcinoma, which is currently not curable and usually carries a life expectancy of around one year after diagnosis. I mention this because when one hears "pancreatic cancer" (or Googles it), one immediately encounters this far more common and deadly form, which, thank god, is not what I had.

I will be recuperating during the month of August, and expect to return to work in September. While I'm out, I've asked Tim Cook to be responsible for Apple's day to day operations, so we shouldn't miss a beat. I'm sure I'll be calling some of you way too much in August, and I look forward to seeing you in September.

Steve

PS: I'm sending this from my hospital bed using my 17-inch Power-Book and an Airport Express.

Knowing that the letter would probably wind up being made public, he had even made sure to get a plug in for some Apple products. What he didn't reveal—and it is quite possible that he hadn't been told yet—was that when the surgeons opened him up, they also spotted some incipient cancerous metastases on Steve's liver.

There is, of course, no way of knowing what would have happened to Steve if he hadn't delayed his surgery by ten months. According to the National Cancer Institute, people who have Steve's kind of tumor entirely removed soon after an early diagnosis have a 55 percent chance of still being alive five years later.

Steve would survive for seven years, and those years would prove to be the most astounding and most productive of his life.

————

RECOVERING FROM A radical abdominal surgery is hellish. A massive incision like Steve's generally guarantees a lengthy and difficult convalescence, mainly because so much soft tissue and muscle must heal without too much stress or stretching at a location where your body bends and flexes every time you sit or stand. As Steve tersely told me, "The healing process really sucked." At first, he could hardly move without unleashing a cascade of pain radiating out from his gut all the way to the tips of his fingers and toes. When he finally got home from the two-week hospital stay, it was all he could do to sit upright in a rocking chair. He didn't like his painkillers, because they dulled his brain. Still, he was determined to get back to the office before the end of September.

Many of us would react to a disease like Steve's by taking it slow at the office or by tackling a "bucket list" of things we've always wanted to do. Steve became even more focused on work. "He was doing what he loved," recalls Laurene. "If anything, he doubled down." So he spent much of that seven-week convalescence thinking deeply about Apple, the computer business, and the trajectory of digital technology. He assembled an ambitious to-do list of what he wanted to accomplish once he returned to the office. "When he came back from that surgery he was on a faster clock," remembers Tim Cook. "The company is always running on a fast-moving treadmill that doesn't stop. But when he came back there was an urgency about him. I recognized it immediately."

The first thing Steve did was spend time with each member of the executive team, catching up on what was going on and explaining to each how he intended to approach his work going forward. He told them that he would now focus even more of his attention on things like product development, marketing, and the retail stores, and less attention on manufacturing, operations, finance, and human resources matters. He knew he had less stamina than before, although that wasn't easy to detect. Moreover, his doctors were keeping him on a short leash, he told them, insisting that he come in for regular checkups to make sure he was healing properly and monitoring for any other signs of cancer. He did not tell his senior staff that the cancer had likely spread, nor that he was going to have to endure rounds of chemotherapy. But he had come to accept that his business life would never again be like what it was, and he wanted them to know how that might change things at Apple. When he was done catching up, he turned his attention back to the big decision, which now seemed more urgent than ever. What would come next?

———

OUT OF THE five cellphone- and tablet-related projects that had been percolating, only one was dead by the fall of 2004. Not surprisingly, the Wi-Fi team had failed to come up with anything of note.

Motorola had inched ahead with its iTunes-ready ROKR phone, but the handset was starting to look like what things designed by committee usually resemble—a turkey. For one thing, Motorola opted to build a chunky, so-called candy-bar-style phone, which bore no resemblance whatsoever to its far more stylish forebears, the RAZR flip phone and the iPod. The iTunes MP3s song files would be stored on removable MicroSD flash memory cards—smaller, more fragile versions of the ones that had just begun to show up in most pocket digital cameras. Inexplicably, Motorola decided that those cards would accommodate no more than one hundred songs, even though they could easily hold many times more. And despite the fact that the phone could provide Internet access, you couldn't use it to buy and download music from the iTunes Music Store. Instead, any unlucky ROKR buyer would have to use his computer to buy music via iTunes, and then transfer those tracks to the ROKR via cable. This wasn't any improvement over the existing iPods—which, unlike the ROKR, couldn't boast of having direct Internet access. The more they learned about the ROKR, the more Fadell and Apple's other star engineers dreaded the thing. Motorola would wind up taking eighteen months to deliver it (during that same time, Apple would refresh its entire iPod product line *twice*), so it was no surprise that when Steve finally introduced the ROKR at Apple's September 2005 MacWorld, it was an afterthought. Apple's own sleek new compact iPod, called the Nano, was the star of the show.

Fadell's musicphone prototypes, which he worked on all through 2004, were far more interesting. His first version incorporated the iPod's distinctive thumb-wheel interface as a sort of dialer. Steve liked Fadell's moxie, but there was an obvious problem. The thumb-wheel that worked so elegantly on the iPod turned out to be a serious hindrance on a musicphone. While it was fine for scrolling through a list of music or contacts, "thumb-*dial*" was awkward for actually dialing a new phone number. It was a gimmick. This prototype aimed too low with its technology and user interface design. Fadell's second prototype, which did away with the thumb-wheel and put more emphasis on being a video player, showed great imagination, and was a manifestation of Fadell's irrepressible ambition. It couldn't overcome an external problem—the cellular networks of that time weren't fast or reliable enough to provide consistent video streams. Even though Fadell's videophone could have been produced within a year with the right telecom partner, Steve chose not to go ahead. This prototype had aimed too *high,* since it depended upon cellular infrastructure that was not yet in place.

The Project Purple team was running into a different set of problems. In their desire to repurpose and yet maintain compatibility with traditional Macintosh hardware and software, Project Purple's engineers were running into the bugaboos that Microsoft and the others had encountered with their tablet PCs: bulk, weight, battery life, and cost. Even a relatively small ten-inch screen would guzzle power and quickly exhaust the tablet's rechargeable batteries when operating untethered. Wi-Fi technology, which was the best means for connecting a mobile computer to the Internet or to other computer networks, also sucked power, as did traditional PC microprocessors—even those tailored for laptops. The power demands of a tablet seemed like an intractable problem, given that existing batteries were big and heavy.

So, while the discrete technologies to build an iPad derived from Mac technology were coming together, the actual device you could make would be heavy and impractical, and would carry just about the same price tag as a conventional MacBook. Steve knew that would be a hard sell. Still, he didn't shutter the operation. Until he had a plan B, he wouldn't pull the plug on Purple.

Greg Christie and Bas Ording, meanwhile, had spent several months in 2004 putting together and playing with a rather funky, but working, prototype of a multi-touch screen. The pair projected the live video image of a computer screen on a touch-sensitive surface the size of a conference room table. Using two hands, you could "move" folders around, activate icons, shrink and enlarge documents, and "scroll" around the screen horizontally and vertically with somewhat intuitive dexterity. The multi-touch gestures they had contrived to do all of this were rudimentary at this point, but "Jumbotron," as design chief Jony Ive eventually dubbed their prototype, was intriguing enough to offer a sense of how engaging it would be to control a touch-screen computer with your fingers. Ive, who had become a self-appointed scout for game-changing user interface technologies in Apple's own labs, had been following Christie and Ording's work all along and was mesmerized when he saw the Jumbotron demo in action. He wanted Steve to see this. He believed Apple could make multi-touch the basis of a new kind of device, and he believed it should be a tablet computer.

STEVE, TOO, HAD been thinking that Apple's next step would probably involve some kind of fundamental reconfiguration of the traditional personal computer. He had always been leaning toward making a tablet. That's why he gave the green light to Project Purple in the first place. But shortly after he returned from surgery, during one of their regular brainstorming walks around the Apple campus, Steve told Jony Ive that he was beginning to think differently. "Steve wanted to shelve the project," Ive recalls. "I was so surprised because I was so excited about it. But one of the observations he made—and this is classically brilliant Steve—was that, 'I don't know that I can convince people that a tablet is a product category that has real value. But I know that I *can* convince people they need a better phone.'" This suggestion wasn't made in glorious ignorance of the engineering it would require. He knew absolutely that building a phone was much, much harder than doing a tablet, because it had to be so small, and because it had to be a good phone *and* a good computer *and* a good music player. What he really wanted was to try to sell a whole new category of device. That, to him, was worth the risk.

When Steve finally checked out the Jumbotron multi-touch demonstration prototype by Greg Christie and Bas Ording, "he was completely underwhelmed," says Ive. "He didn't see that there was any value to the idea. And I felt really stupid because I had perceived it to be a very big thing. I said, 'Well, for example, imagine the back of a digital camera. Why would it have a small screen and all of these buttons? Why couldn't it be all display?' That was the first application that I could think of on the spot, which is a great example of just how early this was. Still he was very, very dismissive. It was another example of one of those times when what he says and the way he says it is not personal. You could take it that way, but it wasn't."

After mulling over multi-touch for a few days, however, Steve changed his mind. Perhaps multi-touch really was the user-interface leap he had been looking for. He started to pick the brains of people he respected. He called Jony to talk about it further. He conferred with Steve Sakoman, another former Newton and Palm engineer who now worked for Avie Tevanian as the VP of software technology, and who had been pushing for Apple to make the move into phones. And he wanted to hear what the iPod guys thought about multi-touch, since they'd already built the two musicphone prototypes. He asked Tony Fadell to come check out the Jumbotron, since he had the hardware engineering expertise to judge what it might take to build such a technology into a much smaller device that could be mass-produced. Once he saw it, Fadell agreed that the technology was really interesting, but allowed that it wouldn't be easy to shrink that demo the size of a Ping-Pong table down to something functional that could fit into a pocket-sized device. So Steve gave him exactly that challenge. "You've figured out how to blend music and a phone," he told Fadell. "Now go figure out how to add this multi-touch interface to the screen of a phone. A *really* cool, *really* small, *really* thin phone."

In hindsight, it's clear that seeing Christie and Ording's multi-touch demo was an epiphany for Steve, one that was not all that different from his first visit to Xerox PARC twenty-five years earlier. Helping people interact more directly and intuitively with intelligent devices was the central factor in creating a new genre of smart mobile gadgets. The Mac had been a radical new conception of the user interface for a computer, and the iPod's thumb-wheel had been a user interface breakthrough as well. Multi-touch had the same potential as the Mac's GUI. But he'd have to move quickly.

Thanks to the iPod, Steve knew that his team could strike fast. And also because of the iPod experience, he knew that Apple could make mind-boggling quantities of whatever device it created. So he decided that Apple was going to create a cellphone. The company was going to put in the palm of your hand a gadget as slick and compact as an iPod, that could download or play music and even video streamed directly over a wireless network, that would be a great phone with amazing voice-mail and directory features, and that would be a computer as powerful as the engineering workstations he'd built at NeXT. Most people hated their cellphones, he liked to say. Apple would create one they would love.

All this decision making took place in late January 2005. It was hardly the only big thing going on Apple—after all, at MacWorld Steve had unveiled the Mac Mini computer, the iPod Shuffle, and a new suite of personal productivity applications called iWork, which he hoped would compete directly with Microsoft Office. But the cellphone project quickly became the main topic of discussion when he and Jony met, as they did almost every day now. They would have lunch together three or four times a week, and take long walks afterward kicking around ideas for solving such mundane-sounding problems as how to keep a touch screen from reacting to contact with your ear when you are talking on the phone, or which materials to use so that your screen wouldn't get all scuffed when sitting in your pocket alongside keys and loose change. Steve would sometimes go back to Jony's design lab and sit there for hours, watching designers tinker with prototypes, or else the two of them would stand together at the whiteboard, drawing and modifying each other's design ideas. They were two kindred spirits, and Steve would now collaborate more closely with Jony than he ever had with Woz or Avie or Ruby or even Ed Catmull and John Lasseter.

As he brainstormed with Jony, and as Fadell's team started to get going on a real design, Steve became increasingly confident. Creating a wholly new kind of mobile phone wouldn't be easy. In fact, it would turn out to be even more daunting than the original Macintosh project. But Steve was certain he could negotiate a good deal with a telephone company, now that he'd gained some experience from the ROKR deal. He felt sure that his team could master the software and engineering challenges. He began to have the sense that if it all panned out, this new gadget might be the biggest-selling electronic product of all time. It wasn't just going to be a phone, nor was it going to be a phone that was a media player. It was going to be a full-blown computer, too. That meant it would also be a *smart*phone, one that was perpetually connected to the Internet. The easiest part was coming up with a name for it: *iPhone,* of course.

At Home and Behind the Scenes

After their historic 1991 interview for *Fortune* at Steve's home, Bill Gates and Jobs paused to get their photograph taken with Brent Schlender in the backyard. Bitter competitors at times who publicly sneered at each other repeatedly, Gates and Jobs eventually came around to a mutual respect. © *George Lange*

At NeXT, Jobs hosted annual picnics for the staff. Schlender attended one in 1987 with his daughter, Greta. © *Ed Kashi/VII*

In the late 1990s and early 2000s, Steve relied on software chief Avie Tevanian as much as anyone. While Apple's hardware won most of the kudos, its software—especially Tevanian's masterpiece, OSX—laid the foundation for recovery. *Courtesy of Brent Schlender*

User interface designers watch as Steve reviews the details of OSX in 2001, shortly before its release in beta form. Later during this session, Steve would exclaim, "It looks good enough to lick!" and then lean forward and actually lick the screen. *Courtesy of Brent Schlender*

Pixar employees called their new headquarters in Emeryville "Steve's movie," because he invested so much time in its creation. Here he leads Schlender on a private tour of the grounds in 2000, shortly before it opened. He took pride in the "random" pattern of the bricks on the wall ahead of him, which had been meticulously arranged to appear random. *Courtesy of Brent Schlender*

Rehearsals for product presentations were always intense. Here, the day before a MacWorld Tokyo affair in February 2001, Jobs festers while he and marketing chief Phil Schiller wait for a technical problem to be solved. *Courtesy of Brent Schlender*

Jobs, alone, reviewing his script the day before MacWorld Tokyo in 2001. *Courtesy of Brent Schlender*

At the MacWorld Tokyo keynote on February 22, 2001, he reiterated the "digital hub" strategy that he had laid out a few days earlier back in California. This was the beginning of the broadly defined Apple experience, which would eventually lead to Apple becoming the most valuable company in the world. *Courtesy of Brent Schlender*

The October 23, 2001, introduction of the iPod was a smallish affair, befitting Apple's limited initial expectations for the product. Here Steve shows it off to an audience made up of press and Apple employees, at Apple's Town Hall on its Cupertino campus. *Courtesy of Brent Schlender*

Steve worked hard to repair his relationship with Lisa. She was his daughter from an earlier relationship, and at first he had denied his paternity. Here, in 1994, he plays the harmonica for her while Laurene looks on.

Steve and Laurene attended the wedding of Mike Slade in 2001. Slade, who worked for both Bill Gates and Jobs, believes that he may be the only person to have attended the weddings of both computer industry titans. *Courtesy of Mike Slade*

Steve in his home office in Palo Alto in 2003.

Steve and his family took vacations together at least twice a year, often going to Hawaii or to Europe. In 2005, they went to Mexico, and here they emerge from a sweat lodge together. That's Evie in front, with Erin, Laurene, Reed, and Steve behind her.

What looks like a Steve Jobs "selfie" with Laurene, taken in Paris during a vacation in 2003.

Jobs waves to the crowd assembled for the introduction of the iPad2. It was to be his last Apple product presentation, on March 2, 2011. He died seven months later. © *Paul Chinn/ San Francisco Chronicle/Corbis*

On the morning of June 16, 2005, Steve woke up with butterflies in his stomach. In fact, says Laurene, "I'd almost never seen him more nervous."

Steve was a natural performer who elevated business presentations to something close to high art. But what made him fidgety this day was the prospect of addressing the Stanford University graduating class of 2005. University president John Hennessy had broached the idea several months earlier, and after taking just a little time to think it over, Steve had said yes. He was offered speaking engagements constantly, and he always said no. In fact, he was asked to do so many commencement addresses that it became a running joke with Laurene and other friends who had college or graduate degrees: Steve said he'd accept one just to make an end run around them and get his PhD in a day, versus the years and years it had taken them. But in the end, saying no was simply a question of return on investment—conferences and public speaking seemed to offer a meager payoff compared to other things, like a dazzling MacWorld presentation, working on a great product, or being around his family. "If you look closely at how he spent his time," says Tim Cook, "you'll see that he hardly ever traveled and he did none of the conferences and get-togethers that so many CEOs attend. He wanted to be home for dinner."

Stanford was different, even though speaking there would not turn Steve into Dr. Jobs—the school did not offer honorary degrees. For starters, he wouldn't have to travel or miss dinner, since it was possible for him to drive from his house to the university in just seven minutes. More important, the university was deeply tied into the Silicon Valley tech community in a way he admired. Its education was first-rate and the professors he'd met through the years, like Jim Collins, were top caliber. Despite being a dropout, he always enjoyed spending time around smart college students. "He was only going to do one commencement speech," says Laurene, "and if it was going to be anywhere it was going to be at Stanford."

Getting around to writing the speech proved to be something of a bother. Steve had talked to a few friends about what to say, and he had even asked the screenwriter Aaron Sorkin for some thoughts. But nothing came of all that, so finally he decided to write it himself. He wrote up a draft one night, and then started bouncing ideas off Laurene, Tim Cook, and a couple of others. "He really wanted to get it right," says Laurene. "He wanted it to say something he really cared about." The language changed slightly, but its structure, which summed up his essential values in three vignettes, remained the same. In the days before the event he would recite it while walking around the house, from the bedroom upstairs to the kitchen below, the kids watching their dad spring past them in the same kind of trance he'd sometimes enter in the days before MacWorld or Apple's Worldwide Developers Conference. Several times he read it to the whole family at dinner.

That Sunday morning, as the family got ready to leave for Stanford Stadium, Steve spent some time looking for his keys to the SUV, which he couldn't find anywhere, but then he decided he didn't want to drive anyway—he'd use the short ride to rehearse once more. By the time the family piled into the SUV, they were late. Laurene drove as Steve tweaked the text yet again. Steve was sitting shotgun, with Erin, Eve, and Reed piled into the backseat. As they made their way toward the campus, Steve and Laurene fumbled through their pockets and Laurene's handbag, looking for the VIP parking pass they'd been sent. They couldn't find it anywhere.

As they neared Stanford, it became apparent that they should have built in more time—twenty-three thousand people were descending on the stadium that morning. The stadium is usually easy to get to, since it sits just off El Camino Real, but many roads were blocked off to accommodate the heavy pedestrian traffic of graduates and their families. When they finally got into the eucalyptus grove on the outskirts of the campus that doubled as a parking lot for the stadium, Laurene had to navigate around one roadblock after another. Steve was getting tense—he thought he might miss the only graduation speech he'd ever agreed to give.

Finally the family arrived at what seemed to be the last roadblock before the stadium. A policewoman standing by the sawhorse waved at Laurene to stop. She walked slowly over to the driver's side of the car.

"You can't go this way, ma'am," she said. "There's no parking here. You'll have to go back to Paly [Palo Alto High School], across El Camino. That's where the overflow lot is."

"No, no, no," Laurene said. "We have a parking pass. We just lost it."

The policewoman stared at her.

"You don't understand," Laurene explained. "I have the commencement speaker here. He's right here in the car. Really!"

The officer dipped her head and looked in through Laurene's window. She saw the three kids in the back, the elegant blond driver, and a man in the shotgun seat wearing tattered jeans, Birkenstocks, and an old black T-shirt. He was fiddling with a few pieces of paper in his lap as he looked up at her through his rimless glasses. The officer stepped back and folded her arms.

"Really?" she said, raising her eyebrows. "Which one?"

Everyone in the car broke out laughing. "Really," said Steve, raising his hand. "It's me."

———

WHEN THEY FINALLY reached the stadium, Steve, who had donned a cap and gown, headed for the dais with President Hennessy, while Laurene and the kids accompanied his daughters to a luxury booth above the football field. The scene was the typical Stanford mix of solemnity and frivolity. Some students marched around dressed in wigs and Speedos, participating in what's known as the "wacky walk," while others simply sported the regular graduation gowns. A handful dressed up as iPods. Hennessy spent a few minutes introducing Steve. He spoke of Steve as a college dropout who, ironically, could serve as a model of the kind of broad thinking needed to change the world for the better. The students were thrilled with Hennessy's choice of commencement speaker. Steve seemed so much more accessible than the stuffed shirts who typically address graduating classes. After he tucked away his bottled water in a shelf under the speaker's podium, Steve launched into the fifteen-minute speech that would become the most-quoted commencement address of all time:

> *I am honored* to be with you today at your commencement from one of the finest universities in the world. I never graduated from college. Truth be told, this is the closest I've ever gotten to a college graduation. Today I want to tell you three stories from my life. That's it. No big deal. Just three stories.
>
> The first story is about connecting the dots.
>
> I dropped out of Reed College after the first six months, but then stayed around as a drop-in for another eighteen months or so before I really quit. So why did I drop out?
>
> It started before I was born. My biological mother was a young, unwed college graduate student, and she decided to

put me up for adoption. She felt very strongly that I should be adopted by college graduates, so everything was all set for me to be adopted at birth by a lawyer and his wife. Except that when I popped out they decided at the last minute that they really wanted a girl. So my parents, who were on a waiting list, got a call in the middle of the night asking: "We have an unexpected baby boy; do you want him?" They said: "Of course." My biological mother later found out that my mother had never graduated from college and that my father had never graduated from high school. She refused to sign the final adoption papers. She only relented a few months later when my parents promised that I would someday go to college.

And seventeen years later I did go to college. But I naïvely chose a college that was almost as expensive as Stanford, and all of my working-class parents' savings were being spent on my college tuition. After six months, I couldn't see the value in it. I had no idea what I wanted to do with my life and no idea how college was going to help me figure it out. And here I was spending all of the money my parents had saved their entire life. So I decided to drop out and trust that it would all work out okay. It was pretty scary at the time, but looking back it was one of the best decisions I ever made. The minute I dropped out I could stop taking the required classes that didn't interest me, and begin dropping in on the ones that looked interesting.

It wasn't all romantic. I didn't have a dorm room, so I slept on the floor in friends' rooms, I returned Coke bottles for the five-cent deposits to buy food with, and I would walk the seven miles across town every Sunday night to get one good meal a week at the Hare Krishna temple. I loved it. And much of what I stumbled into by following my curiosity and intuition turned out to be priceless later on. Let me give you one example:

Reed College at that time offered perhaps the best calligraphy instruction in the country. Throughout the campus every poster, every label on every drawer, was beautifully hand calligraphed. Because I had dropped out and didn't have to take the normal classes, I decided to take a calligraphy class to learn how to do this. I learned about serif and sans serif typefaces, about varying the amount of space between different letter combinations, about what makes great typography great. It was beautiful, historical, artistically subtle in a way that science can't capture, and I found it fascinating.

None of this had even a hope of any practical application in my life. But ten years later, when we were designing the first Macintosh computer, it all came back to me. And we designed it all into the Mac. It was the first computer with beautiful typography. If I had never dropped in on that single course in college, the Mac would have never had multiple typefaces or proportionally spaced fonts. And since Windows just copied the Mac, it's likely that no personal computer would have them. If I had never dropped out, I would have never dropped in on this calligraphy class, and personal computers might not have the wonderful typography that they do. Of course it was impossible to connect the dots looking forward when I was in college. But it was very, very clear looking backwards ten years later.

Again, you can't connect the dots looking forward; you can only connect them looking backwards. So you have to trust that the dots will somehow connect in your future. You have to trust in something—your gut, destiny, life, karma, whatever. This approach has never let me down, and it has made all the difference in my life.

My second story is about love and loss.

I was lucky—I found what I loved to do early in life. Woz and I started Apple in my parents' garage when I was twenty. We worked hard, and in ten years Apple had grown from just the two of us in a garage into a two-billion-dollar company with over four thousand employees. We had just released our finest creation—the Macintosh—a year earlier, and I had just turned thirty. And then I got fired. How can you get fired from a company you started? Well, as Apple grew we hired someone who I thought was very talented to run the company with me, and for the first year or so things went well. But then our visions of the future began to diverge and eventually we had a falling out. When we did, our Board of Directors sided with him. So at thirty I was out. And very publicly out. What had been the focus of my entire adult life was gone, and it was devastating.

I really didn't know what to do for a few months. I felt that I had let the previous generation of entrepreneurs down—that I had dropped the baton as it was being passed to me. I met with David Packard and Bob Noyce and tried to apologize for screwing up so badly. I was a very public failure, and I even thought about running away from the Valley. But something slowly began to dawn on me—I still loved what I did. The turn of events at Apple had not changed that one bit. I had been rejected, but I was still in love. And so I decided to start over.

I didn't see it then, but it turned out that getting fired from Apple was the best thing that could have ever happened to me. The heaviness of being successful was replaced by the lightness of being a beginner again, less sure about everything. It freed me to enter one of the most creative periods of my life.

During the next five years, I started a company named NeXT, another company named Pixar, and fell in love with an amazing woman who would become my wife. Pixar went on to create the world's first computer-animated feature film, *Toy Story,* and is now the most successful animation studio in the world. In a remarkable turn of events, Apple bought NeXT, I returned to Apple, and the technology we developed at NeXT is at the heart of Apple's current renaissance. And Laurene and I have a wonderful family together.

I'm pretty sure none of this would have happened if I hadn't been fired from Apple. It was awful-tasting medicine, but I guess the patient needed it. Sometimes life hits you in the head with a brick. Don't lose faith. I'm convinced that the only thing that kept me going was that I loved what I did. You've got to find what you love. And that is as true for your work as it is for your lovers. Your work is going to fill a large part of your life, and the only way to be truly satisfied is to do what you believe is great work. And the only way to do great work is to love what you do. If you haven't found it yet, keep looking. Don't settle. As with all matters of the heart, you'll know when you find it. And, like any great relationship, it just gets better and better as the years roll on. So keep looking until you find it. Don't settle.

My third story is about death.

When I was seventeen, I read a quote that went something like: "If you live each day as if it was your last, someday you'll most certainly be right." It made an impression on me, and since then, for the past thirty-three years, I have looked in the mirror every morning and asked myself: "If today were the last day of my life, would I want to do what I am about to do today?" And whenever the answer has been "No" for too many days in a row, I know I need to change something.

Remembering that I'll be dead soon is the most important tool I've ever encountered to help me make the big choices in life. Because almost everything—all external expectations, all pride, all fear of embarrassment or failure—these things just fall away in the face of death, leaving only what is truly important. Remembering that you are going to die is the best way I know to avoid the trap of thinking you have something to lose. You are already naked. There is no reason not to follow your heart.

About a year ago I was diagnosed with cancer. I had a scan at seven thirty in the morning, and it clearly showed a tumor on my pancreas. I didn't even know what a pancreas was. The doctors told me this was almost certainly a type of cancer that is incurable, and that I should expect to live no longer than three to six months. My doctor advised me to go home and get my affairs in order, which is doctor's code for prepare to die. It means to try to tell your kids everything you thought you'd have the next ten years to tell them in just a few months. It means to make sure everything is buttoned up so that it will be as easy as possible for your family. It means to say your goodbyes.

I lived with that diagnosis all day. Later that evening I had a biopsy, where they stuck an endoscope down my throat, through my stomach, and into my intestines, put a needle into my pancreas, and got a few cells from the tumor. I was sedated, but my wife, who was there, told me that when they viewed the cells under a microscope the doctors started crying because it turned out to be a very rare form of pancreatic cancer that is curable with surgery. I had the surgery and I'm fine now.

This was the closest I've been to facing death, and I hope it's the closest I get for a few more decades. Having lived through it, I can now say this to you with a bit more certainty than when death was a useful but purely intellectual concept:

No one wants to die. Even people who want to go to heaven don't want to die to get there. And yet death is the destination we all share. No one has ever escaped it. And that is as it should be, because Death is very likely the single best invention of Life. It is Life's change agent. It clears out the old to make way for the new. Right now the new is you, but someday not too long from now, you will gradually become the old and be cleared away. Sorry to be so dramatic, but it is quite true.

Your time is limited, so don't waste it living someone else's life. Don't be trapped by dogma—which is living with the results of other people's thinking. Don't let the noise of others' opinions drown out your own inner voice. And most important, have the courage to follow your heart and intuition. They somehow already know what you truly want to become. Everything else is secondary.

When I was young, there was an amazing publication called the *Whole Earth Catalog,* which was one of the bibles of my generation. It was created by a fellow named Stewart Brand not far from here in Menlo Park, and he brought it to life with his poetic touch. This was in the late 1960s, before personal computers and desktop publishing, so it was all made with typewriters, scissors, and Polaroid cameras. It was sort of like Google in paperback form, thirty-five years before Google came along: it was idealistic, and overflowing with neat tools and great notions.

Stewart and his team put out several issues of the *Whole Earth Catalog,* and then when it had run its course, they put out a final issue. It was the mid-1970s, and I was your age. On the back cover of their final issue was a photograph of an early morning country road, the kind you might find yourself hitchhiking on if you were so adventurous. Beneath it were the words: "Stay Hungry. Stay Foolish." It was their farewell message as they signed off. Stay Hungry. Stay Foolish. And I have always wished that for myself. And now, as you graduate to begin anew, I wish that for you.

Stay Hungry. Stay Foolish.

Thank you all very much.

From his earliest days, Steve had always been able to spin a tale. But nothing he ever said before resonated this way. The speech has been viewed at least 35 million times on YouTube. It didn't go viral, in the way of a Web phenomenon of 2015—social networks weren't as developed or extensive a decade ago. But it gradually became recognized as something truly exceptional, of great meaning to a world of people beyond the Stanford Stadium as well. Its popularity surprised him.

"None of us expected it to take off like that," says Katie Cotton, who headed up communications and PR for Apple at the time.

It was not a speech that would have resonated or gotten the same attention a few years earlier. But by the summer of 2005, Apple was back, and Steve's reputation along with it. Revenues and profits were up, and the stock too was beginning to move in the right direction. All thoughts of the dark days, all memories of Spindler and Sculley and Amelio had been banished, at least for the public—Steve himself always kept those times in the back of his mind, as a reminder of what could happen if Apple didn't stay sharp. Much of the public found something deeply admirable about what he had accomplished. Steve was no longer a wunderkind and he had put the has-been label to rest. Now he seemed to be a comeback hero, defying F. Scott Fitzgerald's adage that "there are no second acts in American life." The question was no longer whether Apple would survive; the question was, What would Apple do next? Indeed, the cover story I had written for *Fortune* a few weeks before the speech was titled "How Big Can Apple Get?"

For Jim Collins, Apple's comeback is the starting point for considering the nature Steve's greatness as a businessman. "We all get crushed or decked or knocked down. Everyone does. Sometimes you may not even see that it's happened, but it happens to everyone," says Collins, who besides writing several bestsellers in the last ten years has also turned himself into a world-class rock climber. "Whenever I find myself tired, whenever I'm thinking about whether I want to launch into another creative project, I always think of Steve in that period when he was in trouble. I've always drawn sustenance from that. That's a touchstone for me, that willingness not to capitulate."

Collins has specialized in the study of what makes great companies tick, and what marks the people who lead them. He sees something unique in Steve's unorthodox business education. "I used to call him the Beethoven of business," he says, "but that's more true of when he was young. When Steve was twenty-two, you could consider him a genius with a thousand helpers. But he grew way beyond that. He's not a success story, but a growth story. It's truly remarkable to go from being a great artist to being a great company builder."

After the scattered political and emotional frenzy of his first decade at Apple, and after his failure to deliver what he promised at NeXT, it was hard to imagine that Steve could ever be considered a great business leader. But by the summer of 2005, he had begun to seem just that. Clearly, Apple would have simply disappeared without him. Luck had played a big role in getting Steve back to Apple, but, says Collins, echoing Ed Catmull, "What separates people is the return on luck, what you do with it when you get it. What matters is how you play the hand you're dealt." He continues, "You don't leave the game, until it's not your choice. Steve Jobs had great luck at arriving at the birth of an industry. Then he had bad luck in getting booted out. But Steve played whatever hand he was dealt to the best of his ability. Sometimes you create the hand, by giving yourself challenges that will make you stronger, where you don't even know what's next. That's the beauty of the story. Steve's almost like the Tom Hanks character in *Castaway*—just keep breathing because you don't know what the tide will bring in tomorrow."

"The narrative that was created around Steve 1.0 has dominated," says Collins. "That's partly because the story of a man who matured slowly into a seasoned leader is less interesting. Learning how to have disposable cash flow, and how to pick the right people, and growing, and rounding off the sharp edges, and not merely acting strange— that's not as interesting! But all that personality stuff is just the packaging, the window dressing. What's the truth of your ambition? Do you have the humility to continually grow, to learn from your failures and get back up? Are you utterly relentless for your cause, ferocious for your cause? Can you channel your intensity and intelligence and energy and talents and gifts and ideas outward into something that is bigger and more impactful than you are? That's what great leadership is about."

Part of what makes the Stanford speech so powerful is that it elucidates the very personal, and hard-earned, values Steve brought to his later leadership of Apple. Each of its three stories contains guidance that Steve could only really understand as a mature man. He was always glib, and he perhaps could have said these things as a younger man. But he wouldn't have really known what they meant.

You have to trust that the dots will somehow connect in your future. The young Steve would have had none of this statement from the story about dropping out of Reed College. In the decade after founding Apple, Steve was hell-bent on shaping the future to his vision. He believed he could connect the dots as he moved forward. Time and again, his engineers found themselves hamstrung trying to fit their work into his sometimes brilliant, sometimes misguided, specifications. That first time around at Apple, and again at NeXT, Steve had been convinced he could do just about everything better than the people working around him. But when he returned to Apple, he really did "have to trust that the dots [would] somehow connect." Again and again during his second act, the specifics of Apple's next big things arose from unlikely sources. The iMac was concocted from the design of the eMate, a product that Steve killed. The iPod and iTunes were the direct result of Steve's misguided interest in movie-editing software. Now Apple was developing a phone because five disparate teams knew that they had Steve's backing to explore widely, and their work had led him to decide against pursuing the product he really wanted to build, a tablet. Steve had grown comfortable with only seeing the connections between the dots after the fact. Maturity, and the extraordinary talents of the team he had built, made that possible.

Sometimes life hits you in the head with a brick. Don't lose faith. . . . The only way to do great work is to love what you do. If you haven't found it yet, keep looking. . . . As with all matters of the heart, you'll know when you find it. And, like any great relationship, it just gets better and better as the years roll on. Steve discovered what he loved to do early in his life. But what gave these words—from the second story in the speech, the section about love and loss—such power in 2005 was the fact that the love he had for his work had survived so much, and resulted in so much. It took lots and lots of time—all those years of struggling at NeXT, of reconfiguring Pixar, of stabilizing Apple—for things to get "better and better." Now he could speak with the confidence of someone who had worked on relationships—with Laurene, with the executive team at Apple, and even with his first daughter, Lisa. Steve's struggles, and everything that he had learned as a result, were essential to Apple's ability to again and again create products that people loved. No other huge company, save Disney perhaps, creates products that engender such emotional responses, even from otherwise skeptical journalists. After one product announcement, the *New York Times* ran a wrap-up story with the headline "The magic in Apple's devices? The heart"—and this was three years *after* Steve's death. The company, like its boss, had many faults. But it worked with a sense of mission that was different from other companies in its industry.

Have the courage to follow your heart and intuition. They somehow already know what you truly want to become. Without the proof of Apple's success, these words from the speech's final chapter could be misread as the kind of callow cheerleading intoned by high school valedictorians. But what gives them strength and power is that they come from someone who had proved their value in a corporate setting. Just as Steve thoroughly deviated from the norm, Apple deviated from the norm of its industry, and in many ways from all of corporate America. Steve had learned how to modulate the potential solipsism of "follow your heart." Early in his career, "intuition" had meant a shuttered confidence in the inventions of his own brain. There was a stubborn refusal to consider the thoughts of others. By 2005, intuition had come to mean a sense of what to do that grew out of entertaining a world of possibilities. He was confident enough now to listen to his team as well as his own thoughts, and to acknowledge the nature of the world around him—as he had when learning about the movie industry at Pixar, or in evaluating the openings for Apple upon his return to the company—as he moved toward a course of action. Apple didn't steer toward the iPhone as a result of focus groups or market research. It headed that way because of intuition, but an intuition that was deeper and richer than the selfish preferences of the young man who had founded Apple.

WHEN I FIRST read the speech online, I remembered an interview I'd conducted with Steve in 1998. We had been talking about the trajectory of his career when, in a rambling aside not unlike the road on the back cover of the last issue of the *Whole Earth Catalog,* Steve told me about the impact that the *Catalog* had had upon him. "I think back to it when I am trying to remind myself of what to do, of what's the right thing to do." A few weeks after that interview had been published in *Fortune,* I received an envelope in the mail. It was from Stewart Brand, and it contained a rare copy of that final issue. "Please give this to Steve next time you see him," Stewart asked. When I did, a week or two later, Steve was thrilled. He'd remembered the issue for all those years, but had never had the time to locate a copy for himself.

The end of the Stanford speech focuses on the *Catalog*'s back-cover motto, "Stay Hungry. Stay Foolish," but my favorite line about the catalog in Steve's speech is when he describes it as "idealistic, and overflowing with neat tools and great notions." This is, in fact, a lovely description of Steve's companies at their best. He was an empathetic man who wanted these graduates to head off on foolish, hungry pursuits, and who wanted to give them neat tools and great notions as they began their winding journey. Like Jim Collins, I had gotten close enough to Steve to see beyond his harshness and the occasional outright rudeness to the idealist within. Sometimes it was hard to convey this idealism to others, given Steve's intensity and unpredictably sharp elbows. The Stanford commencement speech gave the world a glimpse of that genuine idealism.

Chapter 14
A Safe Haven for Pixar

On Saturday, March 12, 2005, Bob Iger, then president of the Walt Disney Company, picked up the phone to make a few calls from his home in Bel Air, California. He called his parents, his two grown daughters from his first marriage, and Daniel Burke and Thomas Murphy, his two most important professional mentors. Then he called someone he'd only met a couple of times: Steve Jobs.

Iger had big news to share: The following day, March 13, Disney would announce that he would become the next CEO of Disney, replacing Michael Eisner. Eisner had been CEO since 1984, and had followed a great first decade with a second one that can only be described as mediocre and turbulent. By the end, he had disappointed shareholders and alienated just about every stakeholder who had a vested interest in the company. One of those was Pixar's CEO, who disliked Eisner so much that he had publicly announced that the company would find a new distributor once its existing contract with Disney ended in 2006.

"Steve," said Iger, "before you read it in the paper tomorrow, I'm calling to let you know I'm going to be named the next CEO of the company. I don't fully know what that's going to mean in terms of Disney and Pixar, but I'm calling to tell you I'd like to figure out a way to keep this relationship alive."

There was a long pause on the other end of the line. Iger had pondered this call for several days. He knew that fixing the mess that Eisner was leaving behind at Disney Animation was the most crucial task facing him as CEO, and he had already decided that keeping Pixar was the key to any solution. From what he'd heard, Steve thought of him as a mere extension of Eisner—and frankly, Iger, who had always been a good company man, had given him little reason to think otherwise. He'd been quoted in the press defending Disney's position in the tortuous Pixar negotiations, and he'd never spent any real time with Steve. But now there was this long pause, and Iger was beginning to hope that, just maybe, Steve was conflicted. "Well," he finally heard from the other end, "I think I owe you the right to prove that you're different. If you want to come up and talk about that, then that's what we should do."

————

ONE OF THE most delightful visits of all my years covering Steve occurred early in the summer of 1999, when he invited me to see Pixar's new headquarters and studio in Emeryville, on the Oakland side of the Bay Bridge. The animation company had been growing rapidly in the wake of its first two productions, *Toy Story* and *A Bug's Life,* and had taken over a big lot in the middle of town, which had seen brighter days back when it was home to a slew of different manufacturers. Pixar was erecting its building on the former site of a Dole cannery.

Steve met me in the parking lot. The construction crews had left hours earlier; the only other people on the lot were two security guards. Steve directed me to go in through a side door, rather than the main doors, which were cut into the big glass wall where visitors and employees enter today. "Look up," he said, before I opened the door. "Look up at those bricks. Have you ever seen a brick wall with so many colors? Just look at those bricks!" It was true; the bricks were, and still are, quite lovely. Each is one of twenty-four different earthy shades, from yellowish taupe to rust to maroon to chocolate brown with many more shades in between. The overall effect from a distance is of something like a subtly checkered moiré, with discolorations rippling through the surface in what seems like a totally random fashion. Except that it isn't random at all. The bricks were manufactured by a single beehive kiln in Washington State, one that Steve's supplier had reopened solely for the purpose of manufacturing bricks with the specific shades that Steve demanded. A couple of times, when Steve visited the construction site and saw the wall going up with a randomness that he deemed unpleasing, he had asked workers to tear down the wall. Eventually, the construction team figured out an algorithm of sorts to ensure that the bricks were distributed in a "perfectly" random pattern.

Again and again as we walked around the property, Steve delighted in both showing me a detail and explaining all the work that had gone into getting it just right. Inside the building, enormous steel girders gave off a greenish hue; they were beams from a unique mill in Arkansas, and had been varnished to achieve that extremely natural look. The workers at the mill had been told to handle them with special care; while most of their beams would be hidden within the walls of a shopping mall or skyscraper, these were never going to be covered up. The bolts holding those beams in place were of a slightly different, complementary color; Steve had me climb up a big ladder so I could get close enough to notice. Down in the atrium central lobby, the brick dome atop the cafeteria's wood-fired oven for baking pizza, constructed with the same bricks as the exterior walls, was perfectly round, a mason's masterpiece. Outside, youngish sycamore trees lined the long, broad path to the front door, the same kind of sycamores that line the Champs-Élysées in Paris, a city he and Laurene loved.

He was like a little kid showing me this, albeit a little kid who was hoping to convince a journalist that *Fortune* should devote several pages to a photo portfolio of his creation. My editors chose not to, in part because the building is not so much a jaw-dropping architectural statement. Its greatest beauty is that it is perfectly suited for its function. "It wasn't that he was lovingly crafting a beautiful building," says Ed Catmull. "It's a higher thing. He was lovingly crafting a place to work in. That's an important distinction."

Steve's initial design for the building was minimalist, based mostly on his particular aesthetic taste and his own ideas about how a great building can shape a great office culture. "His theory was very simple," says John Lasseter. "He believed in the unplanned meeting, in people running into people. He knew how everybody works at Pixar, where you're one-on-one with your computer. He had the theory of this big atrium that would be able to house the whole company for a company meeting, and that would have everything that gets you out of your office and into that center spine. It would draw you to the center, or have you crossing it, many times a day." Steve was so set on this idea that he originally proposed that there be no bathrooms in the building's two wings—there would be just one men's restroom and one women's restroom, in the central atrium. Catmull, the most masterful of the many people who had to figure out ways to manage Steve's idiosyncratic excesses, patiently steered Steve clear of this particularly absurd example of his occasional advocacy of unrealistic means designed to achieve laudable ends. (Steve compromised and allowed bathrooms upstairs as well as in the atrium.)

Lasseter and Catmull also resisted the idea of a minimalist, glass-and-steel headquarters. It didn't fit with either their industrial neighborhood or the rich, colorful, fantastical work being done by Pixar employees. "Pixar is warmer than Apple or NeXT," says Lasseter. "We're not about the technology, we're about the stories and the characters and the human warmth." They voiced their concern to Tom Carlisle and Craig Paine, the architects Steve had hired for the job. Carlisle and Paine hired a photographer to shoot the brickwork of the lofts in the surrounding neighborhood, and in San Francisco. Then, at the end of one of the days when Steve was working from Pixar's Point Richmond headquarters, they laid dozens of those photos out on the

table of a conference room. "He walked in and I remember him looking at all these beautiful photographs, all the details, and he walked
around and around," remembers Lasseter. "Then he looked at me and
he goes, 'I get it, I get it, you guys are right. John, you're right.' He got
it, and he became a giant advocate for that look."

The final result is a subtle, intuitive building. The central atrium is
an enormous communal space with a first-rate cafeteria, a post office
where each employee has a wooden slot for flyers, memos, personal
notes, and the like, and plenty of room for informal conversations. It
is bordered on the second floor by eight conferences rooms, labeled
West 1 through 4 and East 1 through 4. "It's like Manhattan," says
Lasseter. "I always hate when conference rooms get those cute names,
because I don't know where any of them are." As movies are developed
at Pixar—and there are usually four or five features and several short
films in the works—the business teams allied with each film move as a
group around the building, nearing the front door as their movie gets
closer to its commercial release. The animators, on the other hand,
don't move. They've each decorated their offices to suit their own eclectic tastes: one looks like the outpost of a desert explorer; another looks
like the room of a poker savant; one woman bought herself a plastic
playground house from Costco and hung plastic plants in her "office,"
while another created a two-story, wooden Japanese-style home with a
tea service on the second floor. If you get on your hands and knees in
one of the offices and press a little red button, you can crawl into the
"Love Lounge," originally a ventilating shaft that's about five feet wide
and that now sports leopard-skin wallpaper, Barry White music, and
a red lava lamp. Steve signed the wallpaper: "This is why we built this
building, Steve Jobs."

"We called it Steve's movie," says Catmull. "This was a labor of
love." Adds Lasseter: "It took the same budget, and the same amount of
time as one of our movies, and he was the director. We love it."

Steve tried to get up to Pixar once a week. While there he met with
Catmull and Lasseter, watched reels of movies in development, and

huddled with folks like Lawrence Levy, the CFO, or Jim Morris, the general manager. Steve, of course, was not a movie director, nor did he try to be one. Catmull had preempted that possibility years earlier, when he wangled from Jobs a promise that he would never try to be a member of the Pixar "brain trust," an advisory council of directors and writers and animators who weigh in on every movie as it develops. But Catmull and Lasseter did use Steve as a critic.

"One of the things we lost when Steve died was an external hammer," says Catmull. "At some point in every film, the director gets lost in the forest. So once or twice a film, I might call Steve up and say, 'Steve, I think we've got a problem.' That's all I would say. You never try to tell Steve what to think. I wouldn't prep him." Steve would drive up to Emeryville, settle into one of the small screening rooms, and watch whatever had been assembled of the movie up to that point. Then he'd offer his own critique, usually talking to the director and the whole brain trust. "Steve never said anything that hadn't already been said by one of the other brain trust members, because they're all really good at the storytelling," Catmull continues. "But there is something about his presence, and he was so articulate, that he could take the same thing said by somebody else and just cut right through it. He was very careful about how he went about this. Steve would preface it by saying, 'I'm not a filmmaker, you can ignore everything I say.' He literally said that every time. He would then just say what he thought the problem was. Right? Only the fact that it was articulate was the gut punch. He didn't tell them to do anything, he just told them what he thought.

"Sometimes," Catmull says, "if it were a big enough of a gut punch he'd go for a walk with the director. Steve was this incredibly intelligent, strong-willed person who made things happen, but at the same time he enabled people. He was always big on going for walks with people. So he would take the director out on a walk, where you talked more slowly, you think through things . . . just talking, just a friendly back-and-forth talking. His goal was just to help them make a better movie. It always made it easier for the director to move forward. It wasn't ever like 'Oh, you screwed up.' It was 'What are we gonna do to move forward?' The past can be a lesson, but the past is gone. He believed that."

This kind of one-on-one mentoring was something Steve learned over time. "Early on, if somebody didn't measure up Steve wouldn't hide it," says Catmull. "That kind of behavior wasn't something I ever saw during his last ten years. Instead, he would take you off in private, and turn what could have been an embarrassing thing into something that actually became very productive and bonding. He learned; he had taken the mistakes that he made, internalized and processed them, and made some changes."

Steve was more relaxed at Pixar than he was at Apple. "He never tried to make us like Apple," says Catmull, "or to run us the same way." Andy Dreyfus, a designer at Pixar who had previously worked at Apple and CKS Group, says that whenever he and his boss Tom Suiter wanted to present something to Steve, they tried to meet him at Pixar. "We were always happy when we had a Friday meeting with Steve," Dreyfus recalls, "because Friday was the day he was at Pixar, and he was always in a good mood there."

Week after week, year after year, Pixar provided Steve with a series of uncomplicated highs. He attended the Oscars regularly, as Pixar accumulated more and more honors. He loved showing friends preview reels from unfinished movies. "Steve was our biggest fan. Every time we did an internal reel, he would want a copy," remembers Lasseter. "And I'd find out from people I knew, he's showing it to every neighbor at his house. Hey, everybody—come see this! He loved it. He was like a kid."

———

THERE WAS ONLY one problem with Pixar, as far as Steve was concerned, and his name was Michael Eisner.

The relationship between the two high-powered men had deterio-

rated since they had signed the 1997 contract in which they agreed that
the companies would share billing and profits equally. There had been
issues between the two companies: Steve was never satisfied with the
kind of attention Pixar films got from Disney's marketing folks, and
he wasn't impressed with the plans once they finally got developed. But
things had gone well. *A Bug's Life, Toy Story II,* and *Monsters Inc.,* the
first three movies on the contract, had all gotten raves from critics. And
it was hard to argue with their box-office results; each had debuted at
number one, and each had made well over $500 million.

After delivering *Monsters Inc.* in 2002, Pixar was free to start negotiations with any studio for a new distribution pact. Catmull and
Lasseter wanted to continue with Disney, since the company owned
the rights to all the Pixar characters they'd created, and since Pixar's
films had done so well with Disney as distributor. Steve hoped Eisner
would call to open negotiations, but Eisner chose to wait him out. He
believed he would be able to negotiate a better deal after the release of
Finding Nemo. He'd seen two previews at Pixar, and, as he wrote Disney's board of directors, in a memo that was leaked to the *Los Angeles
Times,* "It's okay, but nowhere near as good as their previous films."
Eisner, of course, was dead wrong. *Finding Nemo* became one of Pixar's
most beloved films and grossed $868 million around the world.

Now Steve laid out a set of aggressive terms: in return for distributing Pixar movies, Disney would get 7.5 percent of the box-office
gross—and nothing else. It would have no ownership of the new characters. No ownership of the films. No DVD rights. At the same time,
Steve went public with his dissatisfaction with Disney, harping on the
creative excellence of Pixar versus the forgettable disasters that were
being released by Disney Animation: *Treasure Planet, Brother Bear,*
and *Home on the Range.*

The negotiations caused Catmull and Lasseter no end of distress.
"He had stayed at the negotiating table with Disney largely for me,"
says Lasseter, "because of how much I cared about the characters we
had created." As the months dragged on, things just seemed to get
worse and worse. Steve believed that Eisner leaked his demands to the

press in an effort to make him seem greedy. In early January 2004, things seemed to reach an endpoint: Jobs told Lasseter and Catmull that Pixar would no longer negotiate with Disney. He would not work with Eisner. Not now. Not ever. "It was the worst day of my life," says Lasseter, who, besides facing the loss of all his old characters, was now facing the prospect that *Cars,* which he was just finishing up, would also belong to Disney, and to a CEO who had visited Pixar just twice since the original deal was signed. Lasseter cried as he, Catmull, and Jobs announced the impasse to the Pixar staff, and he swore that the company would never again make a movie without owning the characters.

As soon as the news went public, other studios began calling. Steve played it cool. Disney would distribute *Cars* regardless of a new deal, and Pixar had so much cash after all its successes that it was in no rush. While Steve dickered with other studios, Eisner began to lose the support of his own company. In the fall of 2003, Walt's nephew Roy Disney had resigned after Eisner tried to force him off the board of directors, but only after writing a sharp and public critique of the CEO. Investors who had watched Disney's stock lag for years were tiring of Eisner's imperiousness. When 43 percent of shareholders voted against Eisner's reelection to the board of directors at the company's 2004 shareholder's meeting, the board stripped him of his chairmanship. Eisner said he would serve out the rest of his contract, which ran through 2006, but the odds against that suddenly seemed quite high.

Steve watched all this unfold with glee, especially since his threat to take Pixar elsewhere had helped undermine Eisner. He had never had anything against Disney, after all; it was just Eisner he couldn't stand.

When Steve returned from his postoperative convalescence in the fall of 2004, he told Catmull and Lasseter that he wanted to find a way to ensure that Pixar would be in good shape even if he wasn't around. It wasn't that he feared an imminent death. But as he pondered a future in which he might have to further pare down his responsibilities, he knew that Pixar would survive without him more easily than Apple. It wouldn't be easy. Steve always believed that he, Catmull, and Lasseter worked like a three-man version of the Beatles, complementing one another's strengths while making up for individual weaknesses. The prospect of operating without Steve made Catmull nervous. "He wasn't a [film] director, or anything like that. It wasn't so much the creative side that would be hurt," says Catmull. "But I'm not really a public CEO kind of person. It's just not who I am. So if he goes, then we are actually missing a key component."

Pixar seemed to have three options: find a new distributor and enter into an unproven relationship; build its own distribution arm, which would have entailed a massive investment of money and people to create a service that neither Catmull nor Lasseter really wanted to manage; or stay with Disney—which in fact was not an option so long as Eisner was CEO. The choices seemed even more dire given that the first two scenarios would mean that Disney, not Pixar, would own the characters from all the movies that Lasseter and his team had created under the old contract.

Disney had the theme parks, where Pixar characters lived on in new ways. It had the proven distribution network that had successfully launched every Pixar movie. And its name was still magical for Catmull and Lasseter, who grew up dreaming of joining the great animators from Disney's fabled past. "I knew right from the very beginning that Steve's long-term game plan was to sell to Disney," says Catmull, even though Steve never overtly acknowledged this to him. "I never had any question about it. He was doing all this stuff, and playing these games, but I knew that was the long-term game plan."

For three years, Steve displayed remarkable patience as he waited out Eisner. His public attitude put pressure on the Disney CEO, since his directors couldn't see any way to secure Pixar with him still at the helm. But behind the scenes, Steve made sure that his public ire did nothing to harm the working relationship between the companies. "We were working hard to maintain a good relationship with Disney," Catmull remembers. "When Eisner was going through his war with Roy Disney, a book was being written, [*Disney War*, by James B. Stewart, which was eventually published in January 2006]. Steve said, 'Whatever we do, we don't talk. We don't know what's going to happen, so they get nothing from us for the book.' So there is nothing that came from us, because Steve didn't want any ill will towards us at Disney.

"With things like this," Catmull adds, "you connect a few dots and you figure, okay, I know what this means. And then the war finally comes to an end, and they bring in Bob Iger."

IGER'S ASCENSION WAS announced in March, but he didn't move into the CEO job until September 1. After informing Eisner that he was going to try to repair relations with Steve, he set about doing so. One month after their first phone call, he called Steve with an idea: What if there were a way for consumers to have access to view all kinds of TV episodes, both current and past, on Macs or PCs or other kinds of devices? Couldn't Apple do for the television industry what it had done for the music industry, and become, in essence, the retail outlet for TV? Iger said he knew the idea was fraught with complexity, but that he would love the opportunity to discuss it with Steve.

"You're kidding," Steve replied. Iger insisted he wasn't. "Can you keep a confidence?" Steve asked, clearly still wary of any Disney executive. When Iger said he could, Steve told him that he was very intrigued, and that he would have something to show him in a month or two.

Iger's call had been strategic—he thought it would help his chances if Steve knew that he, unlike his predecessor, was determined to make Disney technology-friendly. Steve was in fact impressed, and, while Iger waited to find out what Steve's big surprise could be, the two men began to discuss a possible framework for a new film distribution deal. They couldn't make the numbers work. At one point they considered having Disney sell back to Pixar the right to make sequels, in return for a 10 percent equity stake in Pixar. But Iger called it off. "It was a one-sided deal," he remembers. "I'd get an announcement that the relationship is continuing, but the actual relationship wouldn't have been good for Disney's bottom line. We wouldn't own the intellectual property, we'd have basically a silent ownership in Pixar, and we'd have done nothing to fix Disney Animation."

A few weeks later, Steve visited Iger at Disney's headquarters in Burbank. "I've got something to show you," he told Iger, and pulled one of the first video iPods out of his pocket. "Would you really consider putting your TV shows on this?" he asked. "I'm up for that," Iger replied without missing a beat. He secured the deal even faster than Steve had won Bill Gates's investment in Apple back in 1997. Iger became CEO on September 1, and by September 5 Apple had a deal to sell downloads of *Desperate Housewives, Lost,* and *Grey's Anatomy* episodes from the iTunes store for viewing on iPods. The two made the announcement on the stage of MacWorld on October 5. "He was blown away that, one, I would even do this," says Iger. "Two, that we could make a deal in five days without Disney lawyering it to death. Three, that I would have, I don't know, the presence to go on *his* stage with Steve Jobs, even though Disney had been the mortal enemy in some ways."

In early September, Iger had asked his board of directors to allow him to explore the outright purchase of Pixar. As he recalls it, "This was my first meeting as CEO, and I hadn't been the absolute choice of everyone in the room. I looked around and they were all a little taken aback. A third didn't know what to say, a third were really intrigued, and a third thought this was ridiculous, but since it's never going to happen anyway, let him go ahead." A couple of days after the MacWorld event, Iger called Steve. "I said, 'I've got a crazy idea. Maybe Disney should just buy Pixar outright.' Steve paused, and then he said, 'That might not be the craziest idea in the world. And anyway, I like crazy ideas. Let me think about it!' He called me back a couple of days later."

Iger and Steve were now speaking just about every day, and their relationship was building into one of mutual respect. Iger was pleasantly surprised by Steve's honesty—his primary source on the Apple CEO had been Michael Eisner, who had painted a somewhat less than flattering picture. Steve, meanwhile, began to realize that Iger was smart, as well as straightforward, a combination that Steve appreciated, according to Catmull. Iger was a welcome change from Eisner, who Steve had found plenty smart but deeply political and evasive. At the very beginning of the negotiation, Iger simply laid his cards on the table. "My wife told me that the average tenure of a CEO is three and a half years," he told Steve. "Mine will be less unless I fix Animation, and getting there goes through you. I've got a problem; you've got a solution. Let's get this done."

Steve asked Lasseter and Catmull to come visit him at his home in Palo Alto. When they showed up, he wasted no time dropping his bomb. "I'm thinking about selling Pixar to Disney," he explained, before laying out the reasons he was now considering such a move. He revealed that, as part of the deal, the two of them would have to run Disney Animation as well as Pixar. "If you guys say no, we're not going to do it. But the only thing I ask of you is that you get to know Bob Iger."

Catmull flew down to Burbank for a one-on-one dinner with Iger. But Lasseter, who was particularly wary, asked Iger to fly up and have dinner with him at his home. So Iger flew to Charles M. Schulz–Sonoma County Airport in Santa Rosa, where Lasseter picked him up and drove him to his home near the wine country town of Glen Ellen. "We sat and talked until the wee hours," Lasseter remembers. "We talked about the importance of Disney Animation, the importance of bringing it back. I told him all I could see was the risk of dividing my time, and he said, 'Well, I look at it the other way. I see it as giving you a bigger canvas because I think you can handle it.'

"Then he said, 'The number one thing is, I don't want to change Pixar,'" Lasseter recalls. "He said, 'I was at ABC for two acquisitions. The first one, with Capital Cities, was great. I learned a lot from Tom Murphy, the Cap Cities CEO. And then Disney bought Cap Cities/

ABC, and everything about it was bad. Disney came in and took ABC from the number one network to the number four network. The first time one of the top three networks fell below Fox. They came in and thought they knew more than we did, but they didn't.' "

Just as Steve had, Lasseter and Catmull grew comfortable with Iger, and as they talked over the deal with Steve they came to see other benefits. Being part of Disney would mean that Pixar would be protected in ways it couldn't as a stand-alone public company. "Our board," says Lasseter, "did amazing due diligence. They told us that having one hit per year for a decade going forward was *already* built in to our valuation. And since the shareholders, whom the board represented, would always want growth, eventually that one-movie-per-year model was not going to cut it. We would have to start making television shows, or many more movies a year." It did seem, he decided, that the best way for Pixar to cement into place the way of life it loved was to sell itself to the company it had battled for so long.

Iger did his own personal due diligence, of course. One day he flew up to Pixar, for a series of one-on-one meetings with the directors of Pixar's next few movies. "We had only had one movie, *Cars,* left to distribute," he recalls, "and people within Disney had spent months pooh-poohing the idea for the next movie, about a rat in a restaurant in Paris. So I go up to Emeryville, and for six or seven hours the directors pitch me every single upcoming movie. I see a couple of movies that they didn't wind up making [one called *Newt,* and the other an unnamed Lee Unkrich project about dogs in a New York City apartment building]. I also see work in progress from *Ratatouille, Up, Wall-E.* Disney hadn't seen any of this, and I went back to my guys—including Alan Braverman, the general counsel—and told them that it wasn't even close. The richness of the creativity, the quality of the people, was so obvious. We *had* to do this deal."

With Lasseter and Catmull feeling more comfortable, Steve homed in on the final details of a deal. He didn't overreach by demanding an exorbitant premium over Pixar's market value. Believing that Pixar might someday be purchased, investors had already overvalued Pixar with a very high market capitalization of around $5.9 billion. Steve and Iger settled on a price of $7.4 billion. They agreed that Pixar and Disney would get equal billing on every film. They even agreed to a side deal that Catmull and Lasseter had proposed: To ensure that Disney wouldn't change the culture of Pixar, Iger agreed that his company would never change or cancel any of seventy-five items on a list of Pixar cultural touchstones that Lasseter drew up. The list protected the cereal bar in the dining room, the annual paper airplane contest, the employee car show, the right of animators to do whatever they like to their office spaces, and so on.

Iger knew that the price he had paid could not be justified by any conventional reasoning. "There wasn't an analysis in the world that would make the deal pencil out," he says. But he argued to the Disney board of directors that the deal had more potential than could be captured by the numbers: if Catmull and Lasseter could revive Disney Animation, and if *both* studios, rather than Pixar alone, were creating memorable characters, the ancillary revenue from theme parks, merchandise, and other divisions could soar. "All the way back to Walt's time," says Iger, "Disney has been most successful in terms of its bottom line and its reputation when animation has been strong."

Iger also knew that many so-called experts thought he was nuts for inviting Steve Jobs to join the board of directors as Disney's biggest shareholder. "Many people who were deeply involved in the process told me that bringing Steve in as the biggest shareholder was the dumbest thing I could do," Iger remembers. "I won't name names, but one of the investment bankers we used told me that. He said, 'You're a brand-new CEO who's going to try to run Disney. Jobs is going to be in your life at a level that will drive you crazy. You don't have the clout to fight that. If you want to run this company in an unfettered way, don't do this.'" Iger trusted his gut. "Steve and I had talked about the fact that he was going to take all stock, and hold it. I knew there was some risk in letting him into the tent. On the other hand, I had a good relationship with him, and I felt I could benefit from having Steve Jobs around. And if for some reason it didn't work out for me, Disney would still have Steve Jobs and that would be a great thing."

Like many others, Bill Gates was astounded by what Steve had been able to negotiate. "When he has the upper hand, he's good at using time," says Gates. "You know, he would wait people out. Just look at how much of the resulting company ends up being owned by this fairly small—and yes, very high tech, very brilliant—animation studio. They end up owning a very substantial percentage of the entire Disney-ABC-ESPN entity. It's owned by a little animation studio! That took three rounds of negotiations, and by the time the acquisition is being done, Disney is just flat on its back saying, 'Take me.' Because of the political dynamics of Disney at the time, they needed that win, and Steve knew they needed it."

Selling Pixar to Disney was a singular triumph. Steve had gotten Lasseter and Catmull the corporate parent they needed for their unique institution to thrive for decades. He'd even put the two of them in a position to revive the greatest animation studio of all time, Disney. And he'd done all this by developing, in the space of less than a year, a trusting relationship, in fact a friendship, with the man who'd been the go-to executive for one of the two people he most detested. Compare this with the wary antipathy Steve displayed during the NeXT/IBM negotiations, and you realize just how much Steve had changed over the intervening years.

It was a deeply personal negotiation, one that tested both Iger and Jobs right up until the end. After both boards had signed off, the announcement was set for Tuesday, January 24, 2006. Iger flew up from Los Angeles to be with Lasseter, Catmull, and Steve in Emeryville when they announced the deal to the Pixar staff. But with about an hour to go before the announcement, Steve surprised Iger by suggesting that the two of them go for a walk around the campus. Steve had something important to tell him.

Iger excused himself for a minute to chat with Braverman, his general counsel. "I'm not sure what he wants," Iger confessed. "Maybe he wants to get out of the deal. Maybe he wants more money." Then Iger and Steve left the building. Steve led him to a bench in an isolated nook on the campus. They sat down, and there, he put his arm around Iger's shoulders. Here is how Iger recalls what happened next:

> *He says, "Bob,* there's something really important I've got to tell you. I've got to get this off my chest with you, and it's really important as it relates to this."
>
> I ask him, "What is it?"
>
> He says, "My cancer is back." This is January of 2006. Since the operation there's been no hint to the outside world that he has cancer again. So, of course, I ask him to tell me more. He talks about spots on his liver, chemotherapy. . . .
> I pressed him for more details. He said, "I've made myself a promise that I'm going to be alive for Reed's graduation from high school."
>
> So I say, of course, "How old is Reed?"
>
> He tells me that Reed is fourteen, and will be graduating in four years. He says, "Frankly, they tell me I've got a fifty-fifty chance of living five years."
>
> "Are you telling me this for any other reason than wanting to get it off your chest?" I asked.
>
> He says, "I'm telling you because I'm giving you a chance to back out of the deal."
>
> So I look at my watch, and we've got thirty minutes. In thirty minutes we're going to make this announcement. We've got television crews, we've got the board votes, we've got investment bankers. The wheels are turning. And I'm thinking, We're in this post Sarbanes-Oxley world, and Enron, and fiduciary responsibility, and he is going to be our largest shareholder, and I'm now being asked to bury a secret. He told me only two people know this. Laurene and his doctor. He told me, "My kids don't know. Not even the Apple board knows. Nobody knows, and you can't tell anybody."
>
> Basically, thanks.

I have to make a decision sitting on this bench with him whether I can even go through with this deal. I don't even know. So I took a chance, and I said, "You're our largest shareholder, but I don't think that makes this matter. You're not material to this deal. We're buying Pixar, we're not buying you. We're going to hype the fact that you become the largest shareholder, but that's not how you value the deal. You value the deal on the assets of Pixar."

So we announce the deal.

The two men walked back into the building, the one that Catmull and Lasseter would name the Steve Jobs Building after his death. Iger had just sworn himself to secrecy, but he felt he had to tell Braverman. He felt he needed a second opinion. Braverman quickly agreed that Disney could go ahead with the deal. Steve went off to find Lasseter and Catmull and brought them into his office. He put his arms around the two of them. As Catmull explains, "He looked at us and said, 'Are you guys good with this? If you say no, I'll send them away right now.' And we both said we were okay, and Steve just started weeping. We just held each other for the longest time. He loved this company."

After Steve and Iger signed all the papers, the four men walked out into the atrium to tell the staff. Rumor of a deal had leaked out the day before, but the employees were nonetheless shocked when Steve confirmed that Pixar was in fact being sold to Disney. "The problem was that Ed and I had gone through this three-month journey of getting to know Bob Iger, doing our due diligence, and eventually realizing this was the right decision to do," Lasseter recalls. "But everybody else in the company was in the same place we had been when Steve first mentioned the idea to us, of 'How can you do this?' Standing up in front of them in that moment was very hard. This gasp went through the crowd, like, 'Oh my God.' I'll never forget [*A Bug's Life* producer] Katherine Sarafian sitting down right in the front, just weeping when Steve said it."

IGER TOLD TWO other people about Steve's cancer. That night he told his wife, the television journalist Willow Bay. A day later he let Zenia Mucha, Disney's communications chief, in on the secret. Steve's cancer recurrence wasn't publicly revealed until 2009, when he finally had to take another medical leave from Apple to get a liver transplant. "In that three-year period," says Iger, "I always knew exactly what was going on with Steve medically. He and I would talk all the time, and since I kept things secret he confided in me. I knew about the trips to Rotterdam, or Amsterdam, and heard about the radioactive receptors that would attach themselves to cancerous cells."

Before the deal had been announced, Steve had talked to Laurene about revealing his secret to Iger. They both felt that it was the right thing to do, given the magnitude of the sale. Their discussions had revolved around a single question: Could Steve really trust Iger to keep the secret? Steve told her they could. "I love that guy," he told Laurene.

Taking care of Catmull, Lasseter, and their staff was a deeply satisfying resolution to what had turned into one of the great joys of his life—the Pixar adventure that had started as such a curious whim. But it was also just one small element of the most productive period of Steve's life, which happened to be the four years immediately following his return from abdominal surgery in the fall of 2004.

During these years, Steve's cancer didn't overshadow Apple's daily operations. The board of directors discussed succession plans, but most members did not know that the cancer had spread past his pancreas. Steve's occasional tiredness seemed reasonable, both for a man who had turned fifty in 2005 and for someone who had had cancer. He would take a few days off here and there to see his doctors and get treatments, but he worked from home a fair amount anyway, so that wasn't alarming. Of course, Steve's colleagues continued to worry that the cancer would recur, and looked for signs that it had come back.

But there was nothing unusual to see until the summer of 2008, when Steve abruptly seemed to be losing weight in alarming fashion.

What the world did see was an effective and visionary leader at the height of his powers. These were complicated years for Apple, but Steve handled almost every challenge in exactly the manner he wanted. He had fallen into leadership at such a young age, but he was comfortable in that role now, and justifiably sure of his capacity to guide Apple's tens of thousands of employees to the goals he set for them. During these years, he would ensure the company's continued success in personal computers by engineering a deft switch to a new kind of microprocessor; ruthlessly and successfully managing some major transitions in his executive team; and optimizing and building upon the efficiency and ambition of the company's product development "treadmill," as Tim Cook describes it. This is also when he delivered what is likely to be remembered as the most notable product of his life, the iPhone, and then improved even that by pivoting once again into a strategy he personally had not wanted to pursue, thereby transforming the application software business in an almost Gatesian fashion.

These are the years when he got almost everything right. They are also the years that show most completely how he had changed, and that manifest the prolifically creative person and the genuine *business* genius he had become. "I am who I am," Steve liked to say. This was most true during the last seven years of his life.

———

AFTER HIS FORAY into music, Steve knew that even he had underestimated the potential of a digital hub of Apple products linked to a computer. As the world of computers subsumed the world of consumer electronics, Apple steadily improved the experience of enjoying and managing music, photos, and videos on personal electronic devices, making the various technologies coherent in a way that no other company came close to matching. Apple promised to provide a simple and yet magical (to use one of Steve's favorite adjectives) encounter with technology at every stage, as opposed to the disjointed and geeky mess that served mainly to confuse consumers when they tried to coordinate products from different companies. Purchasing music or computers from Apple online was almost too easy, while shopping in the company's gleaming glass emporiums, staffed with all those smart young men and women and the whiz kids at the Genius Bar, could be a form of entertainment in itself. Apple was even starting to do a pretty good job of tying it all together via Wi-Fi, although this was the trickiest link in the continuum. Steve embraced the marketing adage that every single moment a consumer encounters a brand—whether as a buyer, a user, a store visitor, a passerby seeing a billboard, or someone simply watching an ad on TV—is an experience that adds either credits or debits to the brand's "account" in his imagination. The "Apple experience" was an unprecedented merger of marketing and technology excellence that made customers want to come back for more.

This was a new kind of quality, something consumers had never expected from technology or electronics, which had always reflected their origin in the gnarly world of engineering. Buyers of products from Olympus, Panasonic, IBM, Motorola, Canon, or even Sony waded through instruction manuals that were confounding at best, and often nothing more than a step up from the technical Heathkit directions Steve had encountered as a kid. More often than not, buyers of Apple products had little more to do than open a sleek and solid package, connect their stylish device to an outlet or a Mac, and turn it on.

Buyers of PCs had heard about the quality of Apple computers for years. But now that millions of consumers had played with their iPods and used iTunes software on their PCs, Apple's reputation for building products that made even Sony's look stodgy was more universal. It had taken just a couple of years, in fact, for Apple to develop a phenomenal reputation among that younger generation that had ignored its products when the first retail stores opened. By 2006, the Apple emporiums from Tokyo to Johannesburg to the new gleaming cube that opened on Fifth Avenue in the heart of Manhattan were flooded primarily by young buyers. For these new customers, and of course for the Apple faithful of old, the company had an open invitation to enter any new field it liked. They were primed for any new addition to the Apple experience.

Just as significantly, Steve's skill at figuring out an industry's soft spot, and maneuvering Apple into a position to solve that problem, finally matched his confidence that he could do so. Steve had always been able to suss out the weak spots in other adjacent industries (just as he had always been able to quickly pinpoint the personal foibles of other people). But now that Apple had pulled off its iTunes coup, Steve knew that the company could successfully enter another industry and alter its business model in a way that would benefit both Apple and the industry's consumers. Releasing a new phone, he knew, might take that strategy to a whole new level of complexity, affecting the lives of not merely tens or hundreds of millions of individual human beings, but *billions* of potential buyers. All he had to do was figure out how to work with the telephone carriers.

THE FIRST TIME Steve ever railed on to me about "the stupid carriers" was back in 1997. That's how long he had been thinking about a phone, even though he swore again and again that he'd never do business with "those bozos." I once said to him, "Steve, methinks you doth protest too much! You sure seem to be thinking about this a *lot*." He didn't laugh. He just got angrier. "Yeah, I *do* think a lot about what a crock of shit it is," he ranted, "that our only choice if we want to get into the phone handset business is to work with one of the goddamn telecom carriers." When Steve agreed to launch the ROKR, Motorola was the one that dealt primarily with the carriers. The disappointing experience reinforced Steve's belief that the carriers always stiffed handset makers. Nevertheless, the carriers held the keys to a market he couldn't ignore. By 2004, worldwide unit sales of cellphone handsets already had topped 500 million units a year, dwarfing unit sales of PCs and iPods and PDAs combined. And they were growing.

There was one way that Apple could have avoided the carriers: by operating a network itself. A new strain of carrier had emerged in the United States called a "mobile virtual network operator" (MVNO). The MVNO model made it possible for an independent company with its own strong brand to have its own eponymous network by leasing wireless capacity wholesale from one of the telecom giants. Sprint once approached Steve about starting an Apple-branded MVNO. But as much as he wanted to avoid the carriers, Steve knew that operating a network was a complex, transaction-intensive business and way outside Apple's area of expertise. So he swallowed hard, and asked Eddy Cue to start knocking on doors.

Cue and Jobs knew there was one big obstacle to negotiating a successful deal: Steve wanted Apple to have complete control over the handset. Since the phone was also going to be a top-notch iPod, *and* an Internet client, *and* a serious computing device, the user experience would be critical to its success. The multi-touch interface on the iPhone would be utterly different from anything consumers had experienced before. Furthermore, if websites were going to display at a big enough size for consumers young and old, the screen would have to take up virtually the entire front surface of the phone. All of this was doable, Steve thought—but only if the carriers kept their hands off his design. Finally, Steve knew the team would go through a few designs before getting it perfect; Apple needed the freedom to experiment without anyone second-guessing its engineers. So any carrier that committed to a deal would have to do so without knowing all of the specifics of what kind of phone Apple would finally deliver.

"We actually knew Verizon better than we knew AT&T," recalls Cue. (At the time, Cue was dealing with Cingular, a joint venture of Bell South and SBC that bought AT&T Wireless in 2004. In 2006, after SBC acquired AT&T Corp. and Bell South, it changed its name to AT&T.) "We knew Verizon because we had consulted them when we did the deal with Motorola for the ROKR, even though they didn't end up selling the phone. When we went back to them to talk about our own phone, they were pretty tough. They thought cellular was their playground. Sort of like, 'You're gonna play our game by our rules.' And they were pretty powerful. So when you looked at what we wanted to do, it didn't match well, because they said, 'Whaddya mean, you're gonna control the phone's UI?' "

AT&T's wireless executives weren't nearly as tough. They had more customers than Verizon, but their network was derided for its spotty coverage. So when Cue and Jobs came for a visit, the results were different. "When we went to see [AT&T]," says Cue, "we spent four hours with Ralph de la Vega and Glenn Lurie in a room in the Four Seasons. And right off we really liked them. You could tell they were hungrier and wanted to show what they were capable of. So we started a relationship that same day."

Steve regaled the AT&T folks with the myriad ways the iPhone would send consumption of wireless data bandwidth soaring, painting a vision that made them salivate. For the first time, he explained, consumers would have a device in their hand that could do much of what they could do on their desktop computer. The iPhone's big touch screen would make unmodified, full-featured Internet websites usable just about anywhere. Consumers would download and share photographs, which are rich with data. They would spend lots of time doing email. They could edit documents or manage information about their sales contacts remotely, right on the phone, by interacting with either built-in applications or over the Internet, with specialized websites that worked regardless of whether the user's main computer was a PC or a Mac. They would purchase and download music from the iTunes store. They could text easily. And that was all without even mentioning video! Once people started looking at videos and movies online, data usage would skyrocket. Maybe someday they'd make video phone calls. He told them about a site that had just started up in February, something called YouTube, where people uploaded and shared video clips with anyone else online around the world. Maybe that too would turn into something big! This is what AT&T had to look forward to, he explained—being *the* carrier for all these kinds of new activities.

And Steve had learned something else along the way, he told them. He knew that once you made this kind of powerful technology available to the world, it would take off in ways you couldn't predict, in ways that *even he* couldn't predict. Surely those developments, too, would drive usage of the AT&T wireless network.

This was why Steve had one other demand above and beyond having total control of the design and manufacture and sales price of the phone. If Apple's phone was going to be an instrument that drove consumption of wireless data, Steve felt that his company also should be compensated for bringing the carrier the extra business. So if AT&T wanted the right to be the initial, exclusive carrier for the iPhone, it would have to pay Apple a sales commission for the added data traffic the iPhone would inevitably foster. In other words, Steve wanted a piece of the carrier's action. After all, Apple kept 30 percent of the take on anything sold in the iTunes Music Store. So why not do the same thing with phone data carriage fees?

All in all, his demands were every bit as bold as the vision he painted. But AT&T could see that the iPhone might give its network a highly needed boost, and something else none of its competitors could claim—a phone from what had become the hottest gadget manufacturer in the world. So it was willing to strike what, in hindsight, seems like an extraordinary deal for Apple. Steve got all that he wanted, and perhaps a little bit more than he should have. AT&T gave Apple unprecedented freedom to produce, almost sight unseen, whatever phone Steve and his wizards wanted to make. It allowed Apple to set the price for the new phones, which AT&T could not change or discount. And, last but not least, the Cupertino company would receive up to about 10 percent of the data carriage revenues a user generated each month, for the duration of that customer's iPhone service contract. These were terms no handset maker had ever received. Never had a carrier shared its fees with a telephone manufacturer.

As it would turn out, sharing fees was something neither side liked. One year later, they changed the deal so that AT&T paid Apple the full price for each phone, instead of getting the distributor's price, which was about $200 below retail. Since accounting rules allowed Apple to spread the price AT&T paid per phone across two years, Apple was able to smooth out revenue stream and buffer the ups and downs of usage. And AT&T was happy to get Apple's fingers out of its own revenue stream. It was a cleaner arrangement for both sides—and many telecommunications analysts believe it has been an even better deal for Apple than the old model.

After the development of iTunes, Steve had come to fully appreciate the power Apple now commanded. He used it aggressively but intelligently. He didn't overreach with AT&T. He knew they needed something like the iPhone, he knew nobody else could provide it, and so he made a deal that gave them what they wanted, but on terms that would make Apple very, very rich. He had Cue to handle the day-to-day business of the relationship, and Cue was on the phone with AT&T's Glenn Lurie constantly—no one wanted a repeat of Apple's Motorola partnership. It all worked out brilliantly for Apple. By some analysts' estimates, the Cupertino company now pockets as much as 80 percent of the profits of the *entire* cellphone handset business.

———

STEVE WAS DEEPLY focused during these years. He had pared his life down so that he could be as expansive as possible in very specific aspects of his work. The dividing lines were clear. Family mattered. A small group of friends mattered. Work mattered, and the people who mattered most at work were the ones who could abet, rather than stifle, his single-minded pursuit of what he defined as the company's mission. Nothing else mattered.

This is why, during the last decade of his life, Steve built so much of his work life around his collaboration and deep friendship with Jony Ive. Their relationship was unlike any creative partnership either had experienced previously. Not only were they both extremely productive, but they seemed to get along even when they disagreed. "People have talked about that roller coaster of falling in and out of favor with Steve," Jony mused during one of two lengthy interviews we had in 2014. "I was fortunate in that we didn't have that experience. We had a very consistent relationship that weathered his illnesses and the huge transitions the company went through."

They had come a long way since that day in 1997 when Steve first walked over to the Design Lab, where Jony was anxiously assuming that his new boss intended to fire him on the spot. But Steve told me that he immediately recognized Jony as a "real keeper." He could tell instantly that he liked his taste, judgment, and ambition. Nevertheless, Jony had remained intimidated during that first year, fearful that if he did a single thing wrong, he'd have to pack his bags. Such was Steve's reputation. While Jony thoroughly enjoyed the process of working with the boss on that very first iMac, he always felt self-conscious when trying to describe some of his design decisions to Steve. But a visit to Pixar helped him realize that he and his boss were on the same wavelength. "When we visited Pixar with the first model of the iMac, it was a revelation, because I didn't know Steve very well, even then," says Jony. "But to hear his introduction of me to the whole of Pixar, I realized that he really understood what I was trying to achieve at an emotional level. At some level, he knew what I was trying to articulate."

As Steve spoke, it became clear to Jony that he had an even more sophisticated and intuitive sense than Jony did of why the unusual new design made sense. This was before the product had been announced or shown to anyone else outside Apple. "He could do that," Ive continues. "He could refine and describe ideas so much better than anyone else could. I think very quickly he understood that I had a specific proficiency in terms of having good taste and understanding of aesthetics and form. But one of my problems is that I'm not always as articulate as I would like to be. I can feel things intuitively, and Steve could sense the full meaning of what I was getting at. So I didn't have to justify it explicitly. And then what would happen was I would then see him articulate those ideas but in a way that I was completely incapable of doing. And that's what was so amazing. I learned, I got better at it, but obviously I was never ever in his league."

Their relationship deepened as Apple's metabolism accelerated. Personal computers have always been works in progress, thanks in large part to the escalator effect of Moore's law, which forces you to redesign constantly in an effort to do more with components that keep becoming more capable. The iPod only accelerated that cycle. Jony and Steve could never pause for long to bask in the afterglow of shipping a new device. But integrating these faster cycles into the company's routine was a deeply satisfying challenge, Jony contends. "I've always thought there are a number of things that you have achieved at the end of a project," he says. "There's the object, the actual product itself, and then there's all that you learned. What you learned is as tangible as the product itself, but much more valuable because that's your future. You can see where that goes and demand more of yourself, being so unreasonable in what you expect of yourself and what we expect of each other, that it yields these even more amazing results, not just in the product but in what you've learned."

Ive believes that the lessons gained from each successive product development cycle fueled Steve's unquenchable restlessness. Each product somehow fell short, which meant that the next version not only *could* be better but *had* to be better. Looking at their work this way, Steve turned the incremental development of products into an ongoing and impossible quest for perfection. What got left out of each product merely served as the basis for the next, improved edition. Steve always wanted to look forward, and the completion of a device was just one more call to the future.

Ive, like Cook and Laurene, believes Steve came back from his 2004 cancer operation more focused than ever. "I remember walking and us both being in tears very, very early on, wondering whether he would see Reed graduate," he says. "At one level there was a daily 'What did they say? What did the tests show?' conversation." But Ive doesn't think cancer is what motivated Steve during the incredibly productive end of his life. "I think it's hard to maintain a singular focus in reaction to an illness that lasts many, many years," he continues. "There were other things beside his illness that motivated him to focus more intensely on his work. Things like selling product in very high volume for the first time in the company's history. I'm talking about selling tens or hundreds of millions of units of a single product. That was a huge change for Apple.

"I remember a conversation in which we talked about how do we define our metrics for feeling like we have really succeeded? We both agreed clearly it's not about share price. Is it about number of computers we sell? No, because that would still suggest that Windows was more successful. Once again, it all came back to whether we felt really proud of what we collectively had designed and built. Were we proud of that?

"There was definitely pride, in that the numbers reflected that we were doing good work. But also I think Steve felt a vindication. This is important. It *wasn't* a vindication of 'I'm right' or 'I told you so.' It was a vindication that restored his sense of faith in humanity. Given the choice, people *do* discern and value quality more than we give them credit for. That was a really big deal for all of us because it actually made you feel very connected to the whole world and all of humanity, and not like you're marginalized and just making a niche product.

"There were many things that overlapped or aligned to make Steve much more sharply focused than before," he concludes. "One was his illness, but one was an unprecedented momentum as a business that none of us had ever felt before. Feeling that momentum was as important as his illness to his creativity and success, because the excitement was still fresh."

By the time the two got around to focusing on the iPhone, Steve had become closer to Jony than anyone he had ever worked with. "The bond became so strong between us," says Ive. "We could just be honest and straightforward and not have to articulate precisely why this is a good idea or why this is a valuable idea. And we also were honest enough to be able to say 'Nah, that's a terrible idea,' without worrying about each other's feelings so much."

Not surprisingly, some on the executive team thought Ive held un-warranted sway over Steve. In the years after Steve's death, more and more unaccredited stories came forth alleging that Jony was the one who really decided who got fired and who got promoted, as if he were Steve's Svengali. The truth was simpler than that. Steve prioritized ruthlessly, in just about every aspect of his life. To maintain his focus, Steve made clear decisions about what mattered and what didn't. His time and friendship and discussions with Jony mattered, even at the expense of other relationships. It proved to be a relationship that was as expansive as Steve's ambition.

"The main reason we were close and worked in the way we did was that it was a collaboration that was based on more than just the tradi-tional view of design," Ive says. "We both perceived objects in our en-vironment, and people, and organizational structures intuitively in the same way. Beauty can be conceptual, it can be symbolic, it can stand as testament to progress and what humankind has managed to achieve in the last fifteen years. In that sense, it could represent progress, or it could be something as trivial as the machined face on a screw. That's why we got on well, 'cause we both thought that way. If my contribu-tion was simply to the shapes of things, we wouldn't have spent so much time together. It makes no sense that the CEO of a company this size would spend nearly every lunchtime and big chunks of the afternoon with somebody who just was preoccupied with form.

"Honestly, some of the loveliest, strongest, most precious memories are those of talking at a level that was very abstract. He and I could talk philosophically about aspects of design in ways we wouldn't with other people. I would get self-conscious if I had to talk in such philosophi-cal terms before a group of engineers, who are brilliantly creative, but when you go on and on about the integrity and meaning of what they are building, well, that's just not their focus. There were times when

Steve and I would talk about these things and I could see in people's eyes that they're thinking, Oh, there they go again.

"But then we also talked about the very particular. I would say to him 'Look. This is how we're designing this bracket.' Then I'd watch him take his glasses off, because he couldn't see for shit, and I'd watch him just enjoy the beauty of all that's inside. Even things like those special screws."

The screws were the flattened ones used on the inside of an iPhone. When it finally debuted in 2007, the iPhone was a thing of beauty, its look almost more that of a piece of jewelry than a gadget. Even now, it still stands as perhaps the greatest physical manifestation of Steve and Jony's remarkable creative friendship.

The iPhone was the product of the efforts of thousands of people, from Tony Fadell and Greg Christie to the workers in the Foxconn factories in China. The inventions and engineering breakthroughs necessary to make it work are too numerous to count. But it could never have been even imagined, much less made, without these two kindred spirits—Steve and Jony—working so closely together.

———

THE IPHONE WAS introduced on January 9, 2007, at the annual Mac-World conference at San Francisco's Moscone Center. It was a high-wire act. The handset was nowhere near ready to ship. There were serious software shortcomings and hardware glitches. Its individual components had been put through the wringer, but the device had hardly been tested "in the wild," when Apple treats its prototypes the way it expects consumers to use them, shifting back and forth from phone to music player to computer quickly and indiscriminately.

Steve had never liked to "pre-introduce" a product in this way (with the exception of major operating system upgrades). There was always the possibility that the software or the screen or something else might wig out during the demo, and he also worried about tipping his hand too early in a highly competitive business. But Steve had three good reasons for pre-announcing the iPhone. The first was that he had to finally show AT&T *something*. The company had seen nothing for years—no mock-ups, no prototypes—and it had a clause in its deal that allowed it to pull out if Apple failed to meet certain development milestones. That was unlikely to happen, but he couldn't take any chances. Second, as Lee Clow observed, Steve was P. T. Barnum incarnate. He loved the element of surprise when he debuted a product. While Apple had remained poker-faced on the subject of a phone for nearly three years, he wasn't sure he could preserve a cone of silence for another few months. The iPhone would need to be tested by employees out in the real world, and sooner or later one would be spotted. He preferred to control the message. Finally, the January MacWorld confab was by far the best showcase for Steve; not only did he own the forum, but his announcement would upstage anything coming out of the Consumer Electronics Show in Las Vegas, where other handset makers would be showing off their wares. He wanted to steal their headlines.

There was one other reason to make the announcement early, on the very best stage available: Steve and his team knew, in their bones, that the iPhone was something truly special. They were eager to show the world. Eddy Cue recalls: "iPhone was the culmination of everything for Steve, and of everything I had learned. It was the only event I took my wife and kids to because, as I told them, 'In your lifetime, this might be the biggest thing ever.' Because you could feel it. You just knew that this was huge."

Despite all the worries, the demo went off without a hitch. The multi-touch user interface seemed almost magical as Steve showed off the little nips and tucks that made it truly engaging. Scrolling through lists had an almost liquid smoothness. A double tap on a website column would make it fill the screen. The Google Maps application that came built in was already far more useful and versatile than most dedicated GPS devices, which had only recently shrunk down to pocket size. It was a delightful presentation of a delightful device. There was just one problem, and it was obvious to everyone except Steve.

PETER LEWIS, *FORTUNE* magazine's technology critic, had arranged for one of the handful of short, private interviews that Steve granted after the keynote that day, so I tagged along. It was the first time I'd seen him in the flesh since shortly after I had started a sabbatical from the magazine to start work on a book project eighteen months earlier. This was the longest stretch of time that we hadn't spoken in the entire time I knew him, so I was looking forward to the visit. Steve was visibly relieved that the demo had gone so well, but he bristled a little when Pete and I kept trying to steer him back to one particular subject: Why wasn't Apple allowing software developers to build applications for the iPhone? After all, it was as powerful a computing device as an early Mac or PC, wasn't it? I mentioned that Google Maps and the YouTube video-viewing app both demonstrated that it was perfectly possible to "open up" the iPhone to third-party software developers. "We had to help them build those apps, you know," Steve said. "So we know what went into them." Then he said he was concerned about how third-party apps could be vetted and policed, to make sure there would be no chance of software viruses infecting the phones. "We want to understand better how apps affect the network, too, before we throw things wide open," he added. "We don't want to create a monster." He also suggested that if developers really wanted to create custom applications for the device, they could always design special websites that would perform the computing tasks on Web servers, with the phone acting simply as a terminal.

Steve had already heard from a slew of people, inside and outside the company, that he had whiffed by not opening up the iPhone to outsiders' applications from the get-go. John Doerr, the managing partner of the most prominent venture capital firm of them all—Kleiner Perkins Caufield & Byers—had become neighborhood friends with Steve after their daughters had met at Palo Alto's Castilleja School and started having sleepovers. Doerr had never had direct business dealings with Apple, but he knew all the main players there and was tapped into everything in Silicon Valley. Steve had first showed him an iPhone several months before they shipped. Doerr immediately asked Steve the very same question: Why wasn't he allowing third-party applications? "At the end of that conversation, I said, 'Look, I disagree with you,'" Doerr recalls. "'And if you ever do decide you want to put applications on it, I'd like to form a fund to encourage people to build them. I think there's a big opportunity there.' He said, 'Okay, I'll call you back if we change our mind.'"

When the iPhone finally shipped on June 29, 2007, the biggest problem customers encountered wasn't the lack of applications—it was the fact that AT&T's network coverage was so spotty. To cite just one high-profile case, Mike Slade couldn't get any reception at his house in Seattle on either of the two phones Steve had sent him. When Slade teased Steve about this in an email, Steve called the CEO of AT&T. The next day, a service rep visited Slade's home. But there was no solution, and Slade wasn't able to try out the phones until he traveled out of Seattle.

Worse yet, AT&T's network was weaker than Verizon's in the San Francisco Bay Area, so the early-adopter techies who'd bought their units on day one found their calls being dropped regularly as they commuted up and down I-280, which connects San Francisco and San Jose. In those areas where AT&T had sporadic voice coverage, Internet connectivity was even more of a hassle.

Apple and AT&T sold about 1.5 million units in the first quarter the iPhone was on sale, but they probably could have sold many more. Between its cellular woes and the absence of more applications like the ones supplied by Apple and Google, the iPhone proved to be a tougher sell than many would have imagined. People had expected something that would support video games and reference books and fancy calculators and word processors and financial spreadsheets right out of the box. The phone they got couldn't yet do that. Jean-Louis Gassée, Steve's former Apple nemesis who had segued into venture capital, puts it bluntly: "The iPhone was crippled when it first came out."

This time Steve turned around even faster than he had when his team had convinced him to go for iTunes rather than pursue iMovie any further. He didn't do so gracefully—"Oh, hell, just go for it and leave me alone," is how Eddy Cue recalls his edict—but he did so quickly. In the fall of 2007, Doerr got a phone call. "From out of the blue, Steve said, 'I think we should talk. Come on down to Cupertino and tell me about this fund idea that you have.' So I went to work, and we hastily pulled some materials together and proposed something we called the iFund. I told him we'd commit fifty million dollars to it. Scott Forstall, the Apple guy then in charge of the iPhone operating system, was in the meeting. He said, 'Come on, John, *fifty* million dollars? Surely, you could do a hundred.' So we bumped it up to one hundred million."

In November, just over four months after shipping its first iPhone, Apple revealed that it would make available a software development kit for anyone who wanted to develop apps. "That's when we knew Steve had finally come to see the light," Gassée says. "Suddenly, that was all anyone was talking about in the Valley and in the VC community. Hundreds of little guys signed up, and the race was on. Then they announced the App Store. And then they released the iPhone 3G [the second version, which shipped in July 2008, and had better wireless and a faster microprocessor]. It was only then that the iPhone was truly finished, that it had all its basics, all its organs. It needed to grow, to muscle up, but it was complete as a child is complete."

——

IN THE EIGHT years since that January 2007 MacWorld, Apple has sold more than a half billion iPhones. It is the most successful, most profitable consumer electronics product ever, by just about any measure—units sold, dollars of profit generated, number of global carriers that sell it, the number of apps written for it. When you think of it, who sells a half billion of *anything* costing hundreds of dollars? Sure, Procter & Gamble sells billions of tubes of toothpaste and Gillette sells billions of razor blades. But those don't come with two-year service contracts that can effectively drive the price of ownership to nearly $1,000 over the life of the product.

When it first appeared in the summer of 2007, there were other devices on the market that described themselves as smartphones. Palm had been selling its Treo for several years, and a Canadian company, Research In Motion, had done well with its BlackBerry. All of these models had pint-sized keyboards and squarish screens. They were all adequate for checking email, looking at your calendar, or finding contacts in your address book. And their businesses were basically doomed, although BlackBerry would hang on for years. The iPhone changed the category forever. Google understood this, and within eighteen months developed Android, a free knockoff of the iPhone's operating system software that powered phones made by the likes of Samsung, LG, HTC, and later an upstart Chinese handset maker named Xiaomi. A new race was on, and Apple had the lead. Android handsets would eventually outsell iPhones, but this has not been a redux of the Macintosh experience. At least not yet.

Marc Andreessen, the cofounder of Netscape who has become a highly successful Silicon Valley venture capitalist, calls the introduction of the iPhone a seminal event that "flipped the polarity" of what makes Silicon Valley go. Once upon a time, wealthy entities like the military and big corporations drove technological change. They were the only ones who could afford machines with leading-edge components. No more. Now it's consumers like you and me who lead the way. "The scale economics are gigantic, since these are being sold in such volume," says Andreessen, whose shaved head looks like an artillery shell, and who talks like a machine gun spraying clipped, staccato bursts of forward-thinking analysis. "We're talking eventually billions of these things. As a result of that, the smartphone supply chain is becoming the supply chain for the entire computing industry. So the components going into the iPhone [like Corning's Gorilla Glass, and especially the cellular microprocessors based on a design by ARM Holdings, a British firm] are going to take over computing. By end of decade, even servers will be ARM-based, because the scale economics will be so great that anything else will not be able to compete."

In other words, Steve had just turned the computer industry on its head. The iPhone marked the emergence of a new form of computing that was more intimate than what had been called personal computing. "My theory about the turnaround of Apple is that what they have accomplished is relatively *under*appreciated," says Andreessen. "Mac, iPhone, and iPad are all Unix supercomputers packaged into a consumer form factor. That's basically what they did. That's the part that nobody talks about, because everybody's so design-obsessed." He leans forward to drive home his point. "That iPhone sitting in your pocket is the exact equivalent of a Cray XMP supercomputer from twenty years ago that used to cost ten million dollars. It's got the same operating system software, the same processing speed, the same data storage, compressed down to a six-hundred-dollar device. That is the breakthrough Steve achieved. That's what these phones really are!"

Chapter 16

Blind Spots, Grudges, and Sharp Elbows

A few weeks after the debut of the second iPhone, I got a call from John Nowland, the head engineer at Neil Young's recording studio at his ranch near La Honda, California. John and Neil's publicist and I had spoken for a year or so about possibly working on a *Fortune* profile about the rock star's serious technological forays into audiophile-quality digital recording and biofuels for cars. Like me, Neil has a hearing disability, so during our initial meeting he and I spent some time comparing notes about what it's like for a musical person to live with damaged ears.

Nowland told me that Neil wanted to send Steve a set of new, remastered vinyl editions of every album he had ever recorded. It was intended as a peace offering of sorts, and as a reminder of the peerless sound quality of old-style analog recorded music. Neil contends, with some justification, that the demonstrably inferior recorded sound quality of digital music, which was introduced with CDs, only got worse with the shift to compressed digital audio files. Half a decade earlier, shortly after the iPod hit the market, Neil had complained publicly about the fact that the digital format Apple used for the music sold on the iTunes Music Store compressed sound files so much as to render the music unbearably "compromised," in his words.

Steve could be pretty thin-skinned when someone prominent criticized the aesthetics of his products. He took great umbrage that Neil would, as Steve put it, "pop off in public like that without coming to talk to us about his technical concerns first." From that point on he had rebuffed all of Neil's attempts to smoke the peace pipe.

Still, I knew that Steve enjoyed listening to records on vinyl from time to time, so I agreed to call him to see if he'd like to get the LPs. Steve answered the phone on the second ring, and I explained what I was calling about. We had talked about Neil's criticisms a year or so before, and I thought this might soften his grudge.

Fat chance. "Fuck Neil Young," he snapped, "and fuck his records. You keep them." End of conversation.

Yes, Steve Jobs had grown and changed enormously over the course of his lifetime. If personal evolution is the long process of making more of our strengths and learning to moderate our weaknesses, Steve can be said to have succeeded brilliantly at the first, but not always so well at the latter. He had blind spots, grating behavioral habits, and a tendency to give in to emotional impulse that persisted his entire life. These characteristics are often used to make the case that Steve was an "asshole" or a "jerk," or perhaps simply "binary"—that odd adjective often used to convey the sense that he was half asshole/half genius from birth to death. These aren't useful, interesting, or enlightening descriptions. What's more illuminating is to take a look at the specific ways in which Steve failed to do an effective job of tempering some of his weaknesses and antisocial traits, and to consider how, when, and why some of them continued to flare up even during the years of his greatest effectiveness as a leader.

DURING THE LAST decade of his life, the issue of Steve's character would come up periodically. With all his heady success at Apple since the turn of the century, there seemed something incongruous about the occasional, stubborn persistence of certain problematic behaviors. They didn't resonate with the image of Apple as a company all about creativity, potential, and the good that came to humanity when imaginative people used ingenious technological tools to amplify their own potential.

Apple's cool, creative reputation wasn't just a veneer, even though the company did work hard and masterfully to propagate that image with Lee Clow's brilliant ad campaigns, Jony Ive's minimalist designs, and Steve's exacting product introductions, where music players and cellphones were associated with words like *magical* and *phenomenal*. It was also deserved and hard-earned, especially after the iPhone became the most popular consumer electronics device ever. Apple now was bigger and more influential than Sony had ever been. But Steve's own actions could sometimes undermine the vision. How did that sleek, clean, and austere façade square with, for example, the moment in 2008 when Steve called Joe Nocera, the *New York Times* columnist who had once profiled him for *Esquire,* "a slime bucket who gets most of his facts wrong"? How could a company with Apple's cherubic marketing glow make its devices in Foxconn factories where the drudgery and difficult working conditions resulted in more than a dozen assembly-line workers committing suicide? What about those deals encouraging book publishers to switch en masse to the agency model Apple preferred, where publishers set (and raised) ebook prices in a concerted effort to pressure Amazon to raise the prices it charged? What was the justification for the mutual under-the-table agreement with other Silicon Valley powerhouses not to hire one another's engineering talent? And how "nice and cuddly" could a company or CEO be that let former top executives take the fall when the Securities and Exchange Commission took exception to the way the company doled out stock options worth hundreds of millions of dollars?

In some of these cases, the perceived moral transgressions were likely overstated, or failed to take into account all the circumstances. But Steve exacerbated many contentious situations with behavior that ranged from rude to insouciant to arrogant. Even for those of us who knew Steve well enough to have seen the significant mellowing in his personality over the years, his continued penchant for antisocial behavior was obvious, and a subject for debate. No one I have spoken to has a unified theory for the staying power of Steve's childish behavior, not even Laurene. But it's possible to understand the separate parts of Steve's personality well enough to go deeper than simply characterizing him as wholly good, bad, or binary.

So when Steve spat his expletives about Neil Young, I just laughed. I wasn't surprised. He could hold on to grudges for decades. Even after Steve had gotten what he wanted from Disney, Eisner remained a curse word to him. Gassée's "sin" of telling Sculley that Jobs intended to oust him as CEO occurred way back in 1985; a quarter century later, Steve still snarled whenever the Frenchman's name came up.

His grudges could even extend to companies that Steve believed had wronged Apple. His passionate antipathy for Adobe, for instance, was based in part on the fact that founder John Warnock had decided to also support Windows with his company's software at a time when Apple was foundering. It was a perfectly rational decision at the time, when Macs held less than 5 percent of the personal computer market. But Steve saw it as a betrayal.

So when Steve himself was back on top of the world, he stuck it to Adobe by refusing to have the iPhone support a program called Flash. Flash was the leading software for viewing video and other interactive or animated content online. Adobe had done a good job with Flash, which was easy for developers to work with. But it had security holes, and could crash unexpectedly. Adobe had not been as diligent about correcting those problems as Steve would have liked. The iPhone was a brand-new networked-computing platform, and the last thing he wanted was to leave it vulnerable to hacking or security problems, especially in its infancy. So he left the program off the iPhone, and eventually off the iPad as well. Flash had been such a popular piece of software that Apple was deluged with complaints. But Steve was adamant, and in 2010 he issued a lengthy statement with six reasons he had not supported Flash. His reasoning was sound, but his words nonetheless smacked of revenge. Apple's power was such that Adobe paid a price for its supposed betrayal. Flash survives, but Adobe has begun to focus more energy and investment on other streaming media technologies.

Steve's biggest grudge of his later years was directed toward Google. There were many reasons for Steve to feel personally betrayed when Google introduced Android, the mobile operating system that mimicked many of the features of Apple's own iOS, in 2008. What really galled him was that Eric Schmidt, Google's CEO and chairman, had been a board member and a friend for years. Now his company was releasing an able, direct competitor to the product Apple had been working on intensely during Schmidt's years on the board.

Even harder for Steve to accept was the fact that Google decided to make Android available to handset manufacturers for free, thus guaranteeing that phones made by Samsung, HTC, LG, and others could undercut Apple in the new marketplace it had created with their cheaper devices. Steve was downright livid. Google was pulling a page from the first chapter of Microsoft's handbook for dominating the world. Clearly, Steve believed, Google's intent in offering a free operating system was to propagate a standard across all cellphones and mobile devices, leading to nothing less than a replay of what Gates had done to Apple's Macintosh with the release of Windows two decades before.

Determined not to let that happen again, Steve was not content to rely only on great products. In 2011, just months before he died, Apple unleashed a torrent of litigation seeking damages from Samsung, the leading maker of Android-based phones and tablets, and even asking for an injunction to prevent the Korean manufacturer from selling its phones in the United States. Steve didn't sue Google directly, since the company was getting little direct financial benefit from Android, which was free. But he could go after the device manufacturers. (Apple also sued HTC and Motorola Mobility, a handset maker that Google bought in 2012.) He accused the companies of copying outright many of the key user-interface features of Apple's iOS, launching a panoply of suits that were not settled until 2014. Apple won a major victory in U.S. courts, but the company still has not actually collected any money from Samsung. Meanwhile, both sides agreed to drop all Android-related lawsuits outside the United States in 2014. It seemed an acknowledgment that the litigation had become an albatross for all involved. Venting Steve's anger against Google had cost the company at least $60 million in lawyers' fees. Steve, whose intense focus was a huge competitive advantage, had created a massive legal effort that will likely prove, in the long run, to have been nothing but a distraction.

EVERYTHING ABOUT WORK was personal for Steve. Over the years, he had learned to trust this passion, and that trust had led him to intuitive leaps that had moved the whole industry forward. But the passion had a flip side, too.

For one thing, deriving so much of his own sense of personal identity from work meant that Steve, a man who could really dish it out, was surprisingly sensitive to criticism. Like most great public figures, Steve had fundamentally inured himself to the envious admonishments of others. But he did feel he deserved the occasional pat on the back for his contributions to modern life. More than once, after some of the tougher stories I wrote in *Fortune* criticized him personally, he emailed or called to say, "You hurt my feelings." I had half expected him to be nonplussed, after some of those stories. But personally wounded? He didn't always take the criticism so personally, however. When I wrote a column snarkily suggesting that the first version of Apple TV would make a great doorstop, and wondering if it might be of some actual use as a modernistic sushi tray, Steve emailed me as soon as he'd read it to say, "I can't disagree with anything in this one." He was the only CEO—with the possible exception of Gil Amelio—who ever reacted so personally to my coverage.

Steve brought an unguarded and painfully blunt version of his personality to his relationships at work. That helped him inspire a unique kind of loyalty that was the glue that held together the great teams that ran Apple with him. But his persona also presented a challenge when he had to make changes in the team, as he did a few times during his last decade. Steve would not indulge any laziness, entitlement, or overreaching ambition from members of his core team. He regularly pitted one against another in order to see whose ideas or intelligence would prevail. Everyone had to be in top form, solidly contributing and fully engaged, or they would find themselves subtly marginalized by Steve. His relationships with Avie Tevanian, Jon Rubinstein, Fred Anderson, and Tony Fadell, among others, demonstrated how quickly Steve could revoke the special insider status that was his to grant.

Anderson was the first to leave the executive team. He was ten years Steve's senior and old enough to be the father of some of the newcomers. He'd had a great run as CFO and was widely recognized in the company as the man who had kept Apple alive long enough to bring Steve back. He had operated as one of the most autonomous members of the executive team, since Steve wasn't expert in his field. There was symbolic significance in the fact that his office was just a couple of doors down from Steve's. If the CEO wanted to make a big change to the budget, he'd just walk over and ask Fred to help him find the money. "Steve and I had a mutual, genuine respect for each other as business partners. It was genuine," remembers Anderson. "So if he wants five million or ten million dollars more for this great idea or marketing program, he wouldn't just haul off and do it. He'd walk down the hall and see me, and use his persuasive powers. 'Fred, come on, can't you find room for this?' You know? That's the way we worked."

Fred had stayed on longer than he had intended, despite feeling a little weary. In fact, he'd thought he was ready to move on or retire as early as 2001. That year, Dell Computer had recruited him. Steve responded by convincing the board to make a onetime special award to Fred of options for one million shares, just to let him know how much he was appreciated. Steve also requested options grants of the same size for Avie, Ruby, and Tim Cook, and smaller amounts for other members of the executive team. It was a gesture that would come back to haunt Steve—and Anderson—but at the time it was welcome and enriching. Anderson stayed on three more years, despite the fact that Steve wouldn't let him join the board of directors of any other companies. "Steve liked to control you. He liked to have you under his sphere of influence," says Anderson. Eventually, Steve did let Fred join the boards of 3Com and eBay, and when Fred finally did retire, Steve asked him to join Apple's own board.

When Fred's retirement was announced in June 2004, Ed Woolard, the former Apple chairman, sent him a note thanking him for, among many other things, serving as "Chief Tantrum Controller of Steve." At the last Top 100 meeting of Apple management that Fred attended as an employee, Steve broke down and cried during a video he showed in Fred's honor. In his remarks at a going-away party at Cafe Macs, the company commissary, Steve reflected on the warmth everyone felt for Fred. Anderson still keeps two mementos from his retirement in his office at venture capital firm Elevation Partners: a plaque from Steve calling him "The World's Greatest CFO" and a commissioned caricature portrait signed by all his closest coworkers, including Steve.

Jon Rubinstein and Avie Tevanian were the next members of the "Save Apple" team to depart. Ruby and Avie had been a buddy act of sorts, managing the hardware and software sides of Apple's whole widget. Says Ruby, "There's as much of the turnaround team's DNA in Apple as there is of Steve's, and you can still see it today." They had been involved in every key decision at Apple since 1997. And before they left they helped pull off a move that they'd been talking about with Steve and with Tim Cook for years—switching the microprocessors that powered every Apple personal computer from the PowerPC chip to one made by Intel.

The primary buyers of the PowerPC chip were IBM and Apple.

This was a customer base that paled next to Intel's enormous market for Windows PCs and servers—millions of units a year for the PowerPC versus *hundreds and hundreds* of millions for Intel. Motorola could not match Intel's manufacturing prowess. Intel reinvested much of the profit from selling all those processors into building more state-of-the-art manufacturing facilities (called "fabs"), which had come to cost in excess of $1 billion each. The bottom line was that switching to Intel held irresistible price and performance advantages, especially after Steve negotiated yet another sweetheart deal, this time with Intel CEO Paul Otellini.

The whole executive team at Apple anticipated that the switch would be difficult. For starters, the change would infuriate some customers, because users who wanted the latest and greatest software would eventually be forced to replace their older iMacs, PowerMacs, MacBooks, and PowerBooks. Second, Avie and his team had to make sure there would be no software glitches, so that buyers of the new Intel-powered Macs would be able to use the OS X–ready software they'd purchased for their older machines. Despite all that, the move was far smoother than anyone had anticipated. Since Avie's team had ported the NeXT operating system to run on Intel-based systems years and years earlier, they were very familiar with the strengths and idiosyncrasies of the Intel's microprocessors. The first Apple machines switched over in February 2006. The rest made the transition by that summer. The operation came off without any noticeable glitches.

This was the kind of technological excellence Avie and Ruby had helped ensure throughout their time at Apple. Nevertheless, neither one could see an interesting career path forward there, especially now that the iPod and other mobile devices had become Apple's growth engines. Steve saw Avie and Ruby as, first and foremost, "old-time" computer guys. Tony Fadell and Scott Forstall were early members of the post-PC generation, and seemed destined to be the key leaders of the iPhone hardware and software efforts. The wheel was turning for Avie and Ruby, just as it had for Fred.

"Steve kept people in a box," says Avie. Tevanian had talked to his boss several times about his itch to do something new, and in 2003, Steve had moved him into a role as the company's "chief software technology officer." It was unquestionably a promotion, but it turned out to be a job without much of a portfolio. Tevanian found himself with little concrete responsibility. He felt out of the loop, and realized that his new role would not work. "Being a pseudo individual staff person working for Steve doesn't work, because he already has all the answers. He didn't like it when I would be in a meeting where he was reviewing a product, and I would have an opinion. He just didn't like it. And he grew to not like that I could be a senior person like that without having day-to-day responsibilities to deliver something," he says.

Tim Cook, now Apple's CEO, says that he worried about Tevanian leaving, and urged Steve in 2004 to figure out another challenge to keep the brilliant software engineer at Apple. "Steve looked at me," Cook remembers, "and goes, 'I agree he's really smart. But he's decided he doesn't want to work. I've never found in my whole life that you could convince someone who doesn't want to work hard to work hard.'" Another time, shortly after Steve had learned that Tevanian had taken up golf, Steve carped to Cook that something was really amiss. "Golf?!" he thundered incredulously. "Who has time for golf?"

Rubinstein, meanwhile, noticed that he too was getting less and less attention after Steve returned from his cancer operation in 2004. "In the beginning at Apple, it was a pleasure because we were all really in it together. I mean, it was really a team, we were partners," he says. "But once Apple started getting really successful, Steve moved himself to the next level and started separating himself from all of us. It started to become all about him versus about the team. Over time it changed, where you were much less working *with* Steve and much more working *for* Steve."

Ruby saw himself as CEO material, and envied Cook's growing role. He also had started clashing with Ive, who had once reported to him but now reported directly to Steve. And he couldn't stand Tony Fadell, the lead engineer for the iPod. Ruby and Fadell would resent one another for years, long after they'd each left Apple, each claiming responsibility for the iPod's success, and each demeaning the other's contribution. (Some wags took to calling Fadell "Tony Baloney.")

Finally, it all got to be too much. Ruby says he went in to Steve's office one day and told him he was tired, that he was ready to quit and go build his dream house in Mexico. He left on March 14, 2006—just a few weeks before Avie's own departure. "It was a great experience," Ruby says. "I wouldn't have traded it for anything. It was wonderful in so many dimensions. I mean, it changed my life in so many different ways and I learned a lot from Steve. Steve could be a real jerk, no question about it, but I feel very warmly about him. I really do."

Steve had considered himself friends with both men. But that personal level of involvement made their departures personally fraught. Every personable executive must confront this problem, but it was especially tough for Steve. While he had changed over the years, he still didn't have a natural soft touch when it came to discussing career options with his closest colleagues. So things ended badly with both Avie and Ruby. Steve's relationship with Avie, who had organized his bachelor party back in 1991, just petered out. His relationship with Ruby, on the other hand, ended with a bang.

Ruby built his dream house after leaving, but he was still ambitious. In late 2007 he was hired by Palm Computing, which remained a significant player in the handheld market. Ruby sent Steve an email to give him a heads-up that he was heading to Palm. Steve called him back about four seconds later, according to Ruby, and started saying things that left him flabbergasted. "He couldn't understand," Rubinstein remembers. "He said, 'You've got plenty of money, why are you going to Palm?' I'm like, 'Steve, what are you talking about? I mean, you've got orders of magnitude more money than I have and you're asking me? Are you joking?'"

To Steve, Ruby's move was akin to treason. By taking another job, at an ostensible competitor to Apple, Ruby had, "failed the loyalty test," to cite the words of Susan Barnes.

Ruby tried to reason with Steve, even suggesting that Apple and Palm "didn't necessarily have to compete." That wasn't realistic, of course, given the clear faceoff between Palm's handheld devices and the iPhone. In fact, it may have been just wishful thinking. In the end, it didn't really matter. Palm fizzled out, unable to compete with the iPhone either on its own or as a division within Hewlett-Packard, which bought the company but closed it shortly thereafter. Ruby and Steve only spoke to each other a few times again.

Steve *had* made an effort to keep Ruby and Avie on board. But the fact that the new jobs he promoted them into turned out to be hollow is an indication of the ambivalence he felt about keeping them. In one critical way, Steve hadn't changed much. He put the needs of the company ahead of any work relationship. He became even more pragmatic about this kind of thing during his later years. In important ways, his assessment of the team—measured by the same high standards he applied to himself—was clear-headed and brilliant. Losing employees, colleagues, and personal friends was hard on a personal level, for Steve and for everyone else involved in the transitions. But Steve had always believed that when the time came for a change in personnel, a company should move on as quickly as possible. It will soon find that circumstances change, and that it can do just fine without The departure of the old heroes.

Where Steve failed in these transitions is in the aftermath. The departure of Ruby, with whom he'd worked for sixteen years, was characteristic, even though the hardware chief delayed his official resignation in order to better prepare Tony Fadell to succeed him as head of the newly formed iPod group Ruby had put together. When others could no longer match his level of effort and intensity, when they became less important to his plans for Apple, or when they left the company, Steve would lose interest. Steve cared more about the potential buying power of his customers than he cared about propping up departing veterans whose contributions he deemed waning. Avie or Ruby should never have expected anything different. Steve had treated his Apple co-founder, Woz, this way, and others along the way had been dismissed in similar fashion. He prioritized ruthlessly, and when Avie and Ruby tumbled down in the ranks of people who could deliver what he believed Apple needed, he moved on.

TWO MONTHS AFTER Avie and Ruby retired, Apple made a seemingly innocuous announcement, in which it tersely acknowledged that Nancy Heinen, the company's general counsel—and one of just two women on Steve's executive team—had quietly resigned. She was only forty-eight years old at the time of her "retirement," yet the news made barely a ripple. One month later, however, the plot thickened when another Apple press release noted that the company had embarked on an "internal investigation," at the behest of the Securities and Exchange Commission, into apparent "irregularities" in stock option grants made to senior management between 1997 and 2001. Nearly a year later, on April 24, 2007, Heinen would be formally charged by the SEC of being complicit in improperly managing the "backdating" of two 2001 stock grants: one of 7.5 million options to Jobs, and another—the one Jobs himself had initiated after Fred Anderson was recruited by Dell—of 4.8 million options to other members of the executive team. By backdating the options, Heinen had given Steve and his team better strike prices. That in and of itself wasn't illegal—what crossed the line, however, was how the records accounting for the options were doctored, by someone, in a way that made Apple's earnings report look slightly better than it was at the time. Eventually, Heinen settled with the SEC without admitting any wrongdoing, after paying a $200,000 fine and returning $1.575 million of proceeds from options she received from the grants in question.

Anderson had been chief financial officer at the time of the alleged backdating, and the SEC produced an email in which he cursorily approved Heinen's suggestion of a specific strike date for backdating the options. He too was implicated by the SEC, for supposedly not paying proper attention to the grants, and settled the charges after paying $3.65 million of proceeds derived in the same way as Heinen's.

All kinds of mitigating factors complicate the backdating story. Apple's outside counsel, Palo Alto–based Wilson Sonsini Goodrich, had advised Heinen that backdating was probably legal; much the same advice it gave to several other tech companies who were eventually pursued by the SEC, including Pixar. Steve had authorized the backdating, albeit with the assumption that it was legal. And he did himself no favors with his testimony to the SEC. Explaining his own 7.5 million options grant, Steve sounded self-pitying. "It wasn't so much about the money," he said. "Everybody likes to be recognized by his peers." He had hoped, he explained, that the board would come forward on its own with an offer of new options, given his success and the fact that a previous grant was underwater. "It would have made me feel better," he told investigators.

Talk about tone-deaf. Even allowing for the fact that Steve was not feeling well on the day of his testimony, and that he never imagined his testimony would become public, his words accurately, if unintentionally, reflected a certain callousness that he applied to Anderson and Heinen's plight. Anderson had resigned from Apple's board about six months before the SEC came to its decision, when it became clear that the company's internal investigation would lay the blame for the trouble at his feet, and at Heinen's. Meanwhile, Steve himself was left untouched by the SEC. "I was hurt," says Anderson, "because I have tried to live my life as a Boy Scout. The most important things to me are my set of values and how I conduct myself, you know? And everybody that knows me, whether at Apple or anywhere else, will tell you that I have incredibly high ethical standards and that I would never, ever knowingly do anything wrong. I mean, even with people. I *always* treated people with respect and protected a lot of people from Steve's idiosyncrasies."

Anderson deserved better treatment than he got from Steve and from Apple. (Heinen has not spoken publicly about her departure.) But by the time the backdating scandal became a public matter, he was no longer CFO, making him less important to Steve than he had been. Steve could be tremendously helpful to friends and colleagues in times of need, especially when they or their families needed medical treatment. He could also be cold and insensitive to coworkers when their personal issues obstructed what he saw as the company's mission, or distracted them from giving Apple their full attention. With a little more empathy, and a little more caring for those who weren't critical to his cause, Steve could have saved himself, and Apple, from a handful of unnecessary headaches.

———

FOR THE REST of his time at Apple, Steve would manage the company with a mix of old-timers and newcomers. Cook and Ive had been with him for years by now, as had communications chief Katie Cotton, and Phil Schiller, the good-natured head of marketing. Sina Tamaddon and Eddy Cue had gradually become part of the core, and Steve promoted Fadell to head up the hardware side of the iPhone project, and Forstall, another former NeXT whiz, to handle the software. Forstall and Fadell could have become the next "Avie and Ruby," had they not viewed each other as rivals from the very start. They would clash and undercut each other even more than Fadell had banged heads with Ive and Ruby. Steve found himself refereeing disputes that were beginning to threaten the vaunted synergy that had always been Apple's "secret sauce"—the blending of clever hardware and ingenious software into a single, magical digital widget. In fact, Fadell was such an explosive force that he would leave the company in 2009, and head off to form a new company, called Nest Labs, which makes a thermostat and a smoke detector that work with your home Wi-Fi network. Fadell is not remembered fondly in the Apple executive boardroom. When certain Apple higher-ups speak of him now, they sneer at the designer of "that little thermostat." The definition of *little* is relative, of course. In 2014, Google paid $3.2 billion to acquire Fadell's Nest Labs.

In the last years of his life, two avoidable controversies distracted Jobs from what he really wanted to be doing: working with this group on great new products. The two events played out, even after his death, in ways that made Apple, and Steve, seem arrogant, willful, and above the law. Starting in the mid-2000s, Steve was the informal leader of a group of Silicon Valley CEOs who agreed not to poach senior employees from one another. In 2010, the Justice Department filed a complaint in 2010 against Apple, along with Adobe, Google, Intel, Intuit, and Pixar, alleging that the companies had entered a series of agreements, recorded formally and informally, to not hire from one another. A class-action lawsuit followed in 2011, filed by an engineer at Lucasfilm on behalf of 64,000 employees of these companies, and others in Silicon Valley. (This lawsuit added Lucasfilm, which like Pixar is now owned by Disney, to the list of companies.) The plaintiffs alleged that the anticompetitive scheme cost workers billions of dollars in unrealized wage gains they might have enjoyed with unrestricted job mobility.

Emails subpoenaed during the investigation show that Steve was clearly involved. They also show him taking mordant pleasure at the fact that a Google recruiter was fired for poaching an Apple employee, after Steve had complained to Eric Schmidt, who was then CEO of the giant search engine company. When Jobs heard the news, his email reply was a smiley-face icon. Steve was hardly the only CEO to be caught with incriminating emails, but he was the only one shown making light of the personal impact of the collusion. Other chief executives seemed motivated primarily by a desire to not piss off Steve, who had become the most powerful employer in the technology business.

Tim Cook doesn't see anything egregious in Steve's thinking—even though he has since tried to settle the lawsuit by offering to pay hundreds of million of dollars to participants in the class-action suit. "I know where Steve's head was," he says. "He wasn't doing anything to hold down salaries. It never came up. He had a simple objective. If we were working together on something—like with Intel, where we threw everything in the middle of the table and said let's convert the Mac to the Intel processor—well, when we did that we didn't want them poaching our employees that they were meeting, and they didn't want us poaching theirs. Doesn't it make sense that you wouldn't, that it's an okay thing? I don't think for a minute he thought he was doing anything bad, and I don't think he was thinking about saving any money. He was just very protective of his employees." It's a rational argument, insofar as it goes. All CEOs want to keep their best employees at their company. But it ignores the simple fact that making such an agreement with other companies, explicitly or otherwise, is illegal, according to the U.S. government and most antitrust lawyers. Steve, apparently, couldn't be bothered even with acknowledging those rules.

That same attitude hurt Apple in another case it had to settle, in which the government alleged that Apple conspired with book publishers to raise the price of ebooks. As Steve prepared to launch the iPad, he was sure that reading books on the device would be seen as an attractive feature, one that he hoped would create profits for Apple while stealing customers from Amazon. He and Eddy Cue strongly encouraged book publishers to adopt the agency model Apple used on its app and iTunes stores—publishers could set the price of their ebooks, as long as Apple got 30 percent of the sale. Furthermore, they wouldn't allow their titles to be sold at lower prices elsewhere. In this scenario, prices of ebooks would have risen uniformly from the low, $9.99 price Amazon often charged for new releases. The publishers would have enjoyed smaller profits but would have been able to set higher prices and avoid permitting Amazon to drive book prices down. Here, too, Steve's emails did nothing to help Apple. His aggressive negotiating notes show that he was fully aware of the impact of getting all the publishers on the same page. Writing to James Murdoch, the son of News Corp CEO Rupert Murdoch, Jobs said that News Corp's best option, he believed, was to "Throw in with Apple, and see if we can all make a go of this to create a real mainstream ebooks market at $12.99 and $14.99."

It's possible that Steve really didn't see anything wrong with trying to build solidarity among publishers, because he had done the same thing with record company executives when setting up the iTunes Music Store. Nobody accused him of collusion then, even though he had insisted on setting a price of 99 cents a track. It's also possible that a variety of assorted corporate safeguards—better legal counsel, better compliance efforts, and so on—could have kept Apple on the right side of the law in both the ebooks case and the labor collusion. But Steve had molded Apple into a tool for turning what unfolded in his imagination into real products, not an organization that conservatively guarded against the downside of his impulses. So the safeguards that did exist weren't powerful enough to prevent the troubles that arose.

"Steve created a management approach that worked for the type of product that he had been thinking about," Bill Gates told me after Steve's death. "You know, if you were going to do hardware and software together, and you're going to do a few super, super nice designs, and you're going to do it end-to-end where partnerships aren't the key thing, where you control that experience totally. He managed a great organization that was purpose-fit to that." We had been chatting about why so many books had been written promising to reveal how to do business "the Apple way," or "the Steve Jobs way." Bill was describing why Steve is a unique managerial case, someone whose model has limited applications. "Maybe you should call your book *Don't Try This at Home*," he said, only half joking. "So many of the people who want to be like Steve have the asshole side down. What they're missing is the genius part." One downside to the Steve Jobs way of running a company, he opined, is that "This is not an organization with checks and controls."

———

ALL HIS LIFE, Steve had tried to control the narrative about Apple by being the sole employee to tell its story to the public. There was a cost to this choice that didn't really become apparent until the last years of Steve's life, when his notoriety and Apple's success drew attention to Cupertino as never before. Apple became the lightning rod for everything from criticism of the tech industry's sustainability problems to corporate governance controversies that affected many other companies as well. And its spokesman was a mortally unhealthy man with a desperate impatience to deal with things that really mattered to him, not this broad array of nagging distractions.

Ever since getting sick in 2004, Steve had kept goals in his head of things he wanted to be alive for. Some were personal, like the school graduations of his kids. Some were corporate, like his desire to live long enough to introduce the iPad tablet computer. Dealing with the media circus that erupted in 2010 when a technology blog came into possession of an iPhone 4 prototype that a young Apple engineer left in a bar was nowhere on Steve's list. Nor was flying back from a Hawaii vacation to manage an uproar that became known as "Antennagate," the result of the discovery that the iPhone 4, if held at certain angles, would drop calls more frequently than past iPhones. And he had only passing sensitivity to corporate governance issues. Yet all these incidents, and more, added to the already immense task he faced of managing a sprawling international company with nearly fifty thousand employees during these years when he was quite truly dying.

It is part of the CEO's job description to manage such distractions, and Steve was not particularly good at this even when he was healthy. He had always been impatient. But the cancer was exhausting him and bringing the kind of wearing pain he had never before experienced. Not surprisingly, Steve bollixed up things that he might have handled with ease under different, healthier circumstances.

For instance, reasonable people can disagree on the subject of whether Steve had a fiduciary responsibility to disclose his cancer earlier than he did, and to then keep the public informed of its progress. Steve felt, and perhaps naively wished, that this was a private matter, and so he skirted the truth about his disease again and again. But calling Nocera a "slime bucket" when the *Times* columnist called to address the issue did little for the reputation of Apple or its CEO. Similarly, Steve's public comments about Apple's response to the controversy that was set off when a spate of suicides occurred at the Chinese campuses of Foxconn, its leading assembler of iPhones, did more to hurt Apple than help it, in a situation where its record was actually fairly good for a big global corporation.

As Apple built up a supply chain that delivered more and more iPhones, iPods, iTouches, Nanos, and the like, it annually audited working conditions at the factories of its suppliers, and even of its suppliers' subcontractors. But problems slipped past these audits. That's not unusual; not surprisingly, the conditions of Asian manufacturing plants have been worrisome for decades. That's unlikely to change. In a system set up purely to secure the lowest costs for U.S. and European manufacturers, workers are unlikely to be paid or treated particularly well. When Apple learned of the suicides, it actually responded quickly, pulling together a noteworthy task force to investigate Foxconn's factories, and taking other actions that some observers have deemed forward-looking. Again, reasonable people can disagree about the quality of Apple's response. But what everyone can agree on is that Steve didn't help matters with some of his public responses to the crisis, including the moment at a tech conference when he said, "Oh, we're all over this one." He sounded glib, in the way of any corporate CEO trying to smooth over an inconvenient truth.

Steve had come a long way in moderating some of the behaviors that had made the young man at the Garden of Allah such a volatile, difficult presence. Some of his old foibles hung on with persistence. Others had been tamed. And at the moment when the pressures of his job would have benefited most from his evolution, his illness added to the complexity of his task.

Heroic narratives aren't supposed to have chapters like this. In the typical Pixar movie, or in the Disney animations that started getting better and better toward the end of Steve's life, true emotions are unfrozen, reconciliations are wholly achieved. But Steve's life wasn't a movie. It was inspiring, confounding, and unabashedly human, to the very end.

Chapter 17
"Just Tell Them I'm Being an Asshole"

In early December 2008, Steve called me at my home office in Foster City, California. He said he had something important to tell me.

For several months, I had been working to set up a joint interview of Steve, Andy Grove, Bill Gates, and Michael Dell. The confab was supposed to kick off the reporting for a book I had in mind. I had what I thought was a snappy title—*Founders Keepers*—and a plan to describe how a handful of geeky entrepreneurs had evolved into captains of industry; how self-absorbed inventors morphed into self-taught empire builders; how shaggy-haired idealists managed to stay in the saddle even as the companies they created grew rapidly by orders of magnitude, and as their own wealth and influence over the world itself became far more than the stuff of dreams.

I had intended to get started on the book in 2005. But while traveling on a road trip to Nicaragua for what was supposed to be a long vacation, I became very sick. Endocarditis lodged on the artificial heart valve that had been implanted in my aorta eight years before, and it had spread from there throughout my body. In my spinal column the infection gestated into meningitis, and from there entered the lining of my brain. Other infections landed in a lung, in my intestines, and elsewhere throughout my body. Doctors in a Managua hospital saved my life, but only by inducing a coma and blasting me with antibiotics that, while quelling the infection, caused me to lose 65 percent of my hearing, including going completely deaf in one ear. My employer, Time Inc., had me medevacced by jet back to Stanford Hospital in Palo Alto, where I endured three weeks in the intensive care unit. The doctors there were puzzled by what exactly was keeping me so sick.

During this time, Steve came to visit me in the hospital a couple of times. I was so addled with sedatives and painkillers and my own delirious hallucinations that during one visit I expressed my sincerest regrets at not being able to play saxophone in a Beatles retrospective show he was planning to put on in Las Vegas with Ringo Starr and Paul McCartney. Somehow I had thought he had taken up guitar in order to play the part of John Lennon himself, and he had asked me to be part of the backup band. Unfortunately, I explained to Steve, with my new hearing-loss problem, I'd never be able to pull it off. Apparently, Steve and my wife, Lorna, had a good laugh. At least that's what she told me later when I had regained my senses. She also said that before leaving, he said, "I've told them to give you the VIP treatment here. Call me if you need anything."

We stayed in touch off and on by email over the coming few years, as I slowly recovered in Santa Fe, New Mexico. I managed to write one last cover story for *Fortune* by turning a series of four interviews with Pixar's John Lasseter into his own first-person narrative. Steve didn't make time for photographs or even a short interview for the story, despite his closeness to Lasseter. It turns out that he had decided not to work with me on magazine stories anymore. Perhaps my zany behavior during the hospital visits had convinced him that I would never be able to tell Apple's (or Pixar's) stories with the same level of sophistication I had applied in the past, or perhaps it was something else. I never did learn his reason.

Despite having no interest in working with me on magazine articles, Steve seemed genuinely curious about the book idea. He and I had discussed the project a few times, and in the spring of 2008 I told him I wanted to set up a roundtable discussion of around eight founders, as the centerpiece of my reporting. "That's way too many people," he snorted. "Everybody will want their camera time, and nobody will say much of anything honest or real." Instead, he suggested, "Focus your book on the emergence of the PC. There are four of us, really. Me, Bill, Andy [Grove], and Michael [Dell]. Get us together and we'll have a good discussion. It will be more focused. We know each other's weaknesses and strengths. It will make a much better story for you to tell, and we'll all have to be more honest."

He even offered to help me wrangle the other three, although I told him I didn't think that was necessary. Just being able to tell them that Steve wanted to do it was enough to get them to readily buy in to the idea. Announcing Steve's involvement was like waving a magic wand. I got immediate responses from the other three, despite their very tight schedules. After some back and forth, we set a date for converging at the offices of Andy Grove's family foundation in downtown Los Altos, California, on Thursday, December 18. All four committed to spend lunch and the entire afternoon together. Andy's longtime admin, Terri Murphy, arranged for the food after I had consulted with Lanita Burkhead, Steve's administrative assistant, about what would work for her notoriously finicky boss—sushi, perhaps a salad, and herbal tea.

But here Steve was, in the early afternoon of December 11, calling me at home on the phone. "Hi, Brent, this is Steve." Before waiting for me to respond, he immediately announced, "I really hate to have to say this but I just can't make it next Thursday."

I couldn't believe what I was hearing. "Steve, we have been planning on this for six months. Everybody else cleared out a whole day on their schedules so they could be here for this. Lanita said everything was all set last week. We can't do it if you aren't there."

"Sure you can," he said.

I didn't say anything. I just sat there and waited for him to explain.

"I have to tell you, Brent, my health has really gone downhill. I can't put on any weight. You know me, I'm a vegan, and I've even started getting chocolate milk shakes now, eating cheese, anything. But I keep wasting away. You wouldn't want to see me like this. The others wouldn't, either. Laurene says I can't wait any longer. I have to deal with this. And she's right."

I asked him about the earlier surgery, and why he had insisted so strongly that he had been cured. Was it his pancreas still? Or was it something else? He told me it was some sort of endocrine disorder that seemed to have made it difficult for his body to digest food. "I eat something, and it goes right through me," he said.

"Whatever it is, I have to drop everything else and figure it out now. It has to be my only priority. I owe it to my family. I haven't even told the board or Tim and the others this yet, but I am going to have to take another medical leave. MacWorld is coming up, so I have to announce it before then, because I don't think I can do that, either."

Then his tone changed. "I've always told you what was happening with my health, because you can relate. So I'm sure you know you can't tell anyone else about this. It's just between you and me. That's why I called. Because I wanted to tell you myself. I wanted you to know that I really wanted to do this with you, too. But I just can't."

Sitting there on the edge of the daybed in my home office, I tried to imagine what Steve must look like. I hadn't seen him in the flesh since the Worldwide Developers Conference at Moscone Center in San Francisco the previous June. He had looked thin then, but he had also had a spring in his step. iPhones were flying out of the stores and the App Store was selling apps by the millions. iMacs, now pristine white rectangular slabs that floated in front of you, were selling better than ever. And the new MacBook Air—the laptop equivalent of a sleek supermodel—was the latest "it" device.

"So, what am I supposed to say to Bill and Andy and Michael?" I asked. "They're going to want to know why you are pulling out at the very last minute. Should I tell them you aren't feeling up to it? I won't say anything more than that."

At first Steve didn't answer. Then, after a few beats, with a mordant giggle, he said, "Just tell them I'm being an asshole. That's what they'll probably be thinking, anyway, so why not just say it?"

I was dumbfounded. "Do you really want me to say that?" I replied, thinking that none of them would buy it for a minute. They knew that Steve wouldn't have put me up to the whole roundtable thing, only to back out. He could be a jerk, but he wasn't an asshole. "All I ask is that you just don't tell them the real reason. Not yet."

I didn't tell Michael or Andy or Bill anything other than that Steve had to cancel because of a personal conflict that had come up. A month or so later, after Apple had announced Steve's medical leave for "complex" health-related issues, I saw Bill at his office in Kirkland, Washington. He told me he wanted to get in touch with Steve and wasn't sure of the best means. It had been a long time since they had spoken. I gave him Steve's home phone number and his cellphone number, and also the email address and phone number of his assistant Lanita, but not before relating the story of the "asshole" excuse Steve had suggested. Bill loves a smart riposte as much as anyone, so we had a good laugh.

ACCORDING TO TIM COOK, he and Katie Cotton, Apple's communications chief, first learned about Steve's need for a liver transplant in January 2009, a few weeks after Steve and I spoke. But he had watched Steve wither away during 2008. By early 2009 Steve wasn't coming into the office at all, and Cook would visit him at home just about every day. He started to worry that things might finally be headed in a fatal direction. "It was terrible going over there day after day and talking with him, because you could see him slipping day after day," says Cook. Steve was starting to look alarmingly frail. He developed ascites—an accumulation of fluid in the peritoneal cavity that caused his belly to protrude in ghastly fashion—and he just lay in bed all day, gaunt and tired and irritable.

He was on the list of people in California who were awaiting a liver transplant. This isn't a list that can be gamed. At one of their many bedside meetings, Steve told Cook that he thought he might have a better chance at a liver transplant than others because he had a rare blood type. It wasn't a statement that made any sense to Cook, because while there were fewer applicants on the list with Steve's blood type, there were also fewer people of that blood type whose livers could be transplanted to him. In fact, Steve's chances of getting a donor were not good at all.

One afternoon, Cook left the house feeling so upset that he had his own blood tested. He found out that he too had a rare blood type, and made the assumption that it might be the same as Steve's. He started doing research, and learned that it is possible to transfer a portion of a living person's liver to someone in need of a transplant. About six thousand living-donor transplants are performed every year in the United States, and the rate of success for both donor and recipient is high. The liver is a regenerative organ. The portion transplanted into the recipient will grow to a functional size, and the portion of the liver that the donor gives up will also grow back.

Cook decided to undergo a battery of tests that determine if someone is healthy enough to be a living donor. "I thought he was going to die," Cook explains. He went to a hospital far from the Bay Area, since he didn't want to be recognized. The day after he returned from the trip, he went to visit Steve. And there, sitting alone with him in the bedroom of the Palo Alto house, Tim began to offer his liver to Steve. "I really wanted him to do it," he remembers. "He cut me off at the legs, almost before the words were out of my mouth. 'No,' he said. 'I'll never let you do that. I'll never do that!'"

"Somebody that's selfish," Cook continues, "doesn't reply like that. I mean, here's a guy, he's dying, he's very close to death because of his liver issue, and here's someone healthy offering a way out. I said, 'Steve, I'm perfectly healthy, I've been checked out. Here's the medical report. I can do this and I'm not putting myself at risk, I'll be fine.' And he doesn't even think about it. It was not, 'Are you sure you want to do this?' It was not, 'I'll think about it.' It was not, 'Oh, the condition I'm in . . .' It was, 'No, I'm not doing that!' He kind of popped up in bed and said that. And this was during a time when things were just terrible. Steve only yelled at me four or five times during the thirteen years I knew him, and this was one of them."

"This picture of him isn't understood," says Cook. "I thought the [Walter] Isaacson book did him a tremendous disservice. It was just a rehash of a bunch of stuff that had already been written, and focused on small parts of his personality. You get the feeling that [Steve's] a greedy, selfish egomaniac. It didn't capture the person. The person I read about there is somebody I would never have wanted to work with over all this time. Life is too short." In saying this, Cook echoed the feeling of many of Steve's close friends—in interview after interview, they complained that very little of what has been published offers any sense of why they would have worked so long and so hard for Steve. Those former employees share another common thread, too: the idea that they did the very best work of their lives for Steve.

"Steve cared," Cook continues. "He cared deeply about things. Yes, he was very passionate about things, and he wanted things to be perfect. And that was what was great about him. He wanted everyone to do their best work. He believed that small teams were better than large teams, because you could get a lot more done. And he believed that picking the right person was a hundred times better than picking somebody who was a little short of being right. All of those things are really true. A lot of people mistook that passion for arrogance. He wasn't a saint. I'm not saying that. None of us are. But it's emphatically untrue that he wasn't a great human being, and that is totally not understood.

"The Steve that I met in early '98 was brash and confident and passionate and all of those things. But there was a soft side of him as well, and that soft side became a larger portion of him over the next thirteen years. You'd see that show up in different ways. There were different employees and spouses here that had health issues, and he would go out of his way to turn heaven and earth to make sure they had proper medical attention. He did that in a major way, not in a minor, 'Call me and get back to me if you need my help' kind of way.

"He had the courage to admit he was wrong, and to change, a quality which many people at that level, who have accomplished that much, lack. You don't see many people at that level who will change directions even though they should. He wasn't beholden to anything except a set of core values. Anything else he could walk away from. He could do it faster than anyone I'd ever seen before. It was an absolute gift. He always changed. Steve had this ability to go through a learning curve quickly, more quickly than anybody I've known, about such a wide variety of things.

"The Steve I knew was the guy pestering me to have a social life, not because he was being a pest, but because he knew how important family was in his life, and he wanted it for me, too," continues Cook, who came out publicly as a gay man in 2014. (Steve and others at the company had known this for years, of course.) "One day he calls my mom—he doesn't even know my mom, she lives in Alabama. He said he was looking for me, but he knows how to find me! And he talked to her about me. There are lots of these things where you saw the very soft or caring or feeling or whatever you want to call it side of him. He had that gene. Someone who's viewing life only as a transactional relationship with people . . . doesn't do that."

———

EVENTUALLY STEVE DID get a liver transplant. He had also registered on another list in Memphis, Tennessee, which was perfectly legal; the only requirements to get on an out-of-state list were that he could make his way to the hospital within eight hours of being told that a liver was available—since Steve had a private jet, he could do so—and that he be judged healthy enough to recover from the surgery by a team of doctors from the admitting hospital. He and Laurene flew to Memphis for the surgery on March 21, 2009. Because of complications, he required a second surgery a couple of days later. He and Laurene remained in

Memphis for two excruciating months, during which things were so touch-and-go that relatives and close friends such as Jony Ive, Mona Simpson, Steve's lawyer George Riley, and others came to visit and perhaps say goodbye to him. Ive even brought a special present from the Apple design team—a meticulous miniature aluminum replica of the Macbook Pro that would ship in June. The designers had made these nano-models for Steve after every product release. Given the circumstances, this one was special.

Steve survived, of course. He later told Bob Iger that he had considered leaving Apple after the operation, to spend more time with his children at home. But, as Eddy Cue says, "Steve really just had two things he cared about in his life, Apple—and to some extent, Pixar—and his family." He needed both. He returned to work, and just as he had after his 2004 operation, he did so with vigor. He had a new milestone he wanted to achieve before he died: the introduction of the iPad.

———

DEVELOPING THE IPAD was easier, technologically, than creating the iPod or the iPhone. In the first instance, the team had had to learn an utterly new way to operate. In the case of the iPhone, Apple pushed the personal computer revolution to its pinnacle, by melding three devices into one handheld supercomputer. Now, armed with the experience of those two battles, Steve and his team were able to create something whose attributes were ethereal and unexpected. Back in 2004, Steve had shifted Project Purple away from the tablet and toward the phone. By doing so, he ensured that Apple's tablet device would be a line extension of the iPhone; when his team turned to building the iPad, they *maximized* an iPhone, rather than opt to minimize an iMac. That meant using ARM-based microprocessors, which are common in smartphones, rather than the more power-hungry Intel chips that drive many computers. That meant adopting the iPhone's multi-touch screen and virtual keyboard. Perhaps most important of all—and most ironic, given Steve's initial resistance—the iPad would benefit enormously from the iTunes App Store. The iPad gave software developers a much more powerful target to shoot for than the iPhone, mainly because the larger screen made it possible and practical to do some really cool things that you could not do on a pocket-sized device. Often sold at the same low price points as iPhone apps, these cool new iPad apps seemed like an even better deal as they exploded on those bigger screens. The iPad multiplied the importance of the App Store, and the influence of the new market and business model for software that it had created.

With the one-two punch of the iPhone and the iPad, Apple had completely reshaped the business of making and selling consumer software. Where once upon a time developers had to price their software applications so that they might make a profit from the sale of a few thousand copies, they now could sell into a market of hundreds of millions of people. This tremendous opportunity has led to all kinds of developments that never would have even had a glimmer of a chance in a smaller market. Name what you want to do now, and there is probably an app (or two or three or ten) for that. That wasn't true in the PC world, because the price points necessary to achieve profitability on a much smaller volume of sales were simply too high.

Looked at in the context of Steve's career as a technologist, the iPad is not as significant a product as the iPhone. But in some ways, it is the most elegant evocation of some of his enduring goals: to create technology that is a window into the limitless world of information, and to create technology that is so simple and so powerful that it basically disappears. His sense of those essential goals is what distinguished him from the more tech-savvy hobbyists back at the start of his career. His restless desire to reach that goal had betrayed him more than once, causing him to try to leap before the technology was ready even to walk. But by the time he and his team got around to creating the iPad, he had learned enough, finally, to make the technology essentially invisible. A true artist, he'd finally hidden all evidence of his labor.

Steve's sense of pleasure and satisfaction with this outcome was evident on January 27, 2010, when he introduced the iPad at San

Francisco's Yerba Buena Center for the Arts. This time the stage was set with a small couch and a table, props that weren't the standard for his product demos. When Steve walked onto the stage, looking gaunt, he received, as always, a standing ovation. He paced confidently and energetically as he proudly recounted some of the company's achievements. A slide of him with Woz from the early days was projected above him as the statistics rolled out: 250 million iPods sold; 3 billion downloads from the App Store in a year and a half; revenues exceeding $50 billion annually. Apple, he explained, is now a mobile device company; in fact, by revenues it is the largest mobile device company in the world.

There was something elegiac about all this, even though Steve often used the first moments of a presentation to update the crowd on Apple. This, after all, was a recitation of the story of his professional life. And the sentimental nature of the event grew when, after a dozen or so minutes, Steve sat down in the leather love seat to demonstrate how easy it was to use an iPad. This was, of course, a concession to his weakened state of health. But it served the product, too. He leaned back, and navigated through a series of things you could do with your fingers on the iPad: send email, surf the Web, open up apps that let you listen to music, watch videos on YouTube, or even make "digital" finger paintings. "It's so much more intimate than a laptop," he stated, with great satisfaction. His every move was projected on the big screen. Like every other presentation he had ever given, this one was staged with a clear intention: to show that this device was actually an invitation to a new kind of computing, something so natural and relaxed that it would slip right into your daily life with unimaginable ease.

While the iPad drew its fair share of initial criticism, the public instantly understood its appeal. The first-generation iPad was the fastest-selling debut product Apple had ever unleashed, racking up numbers that made the launches of the iPod and the iPhone pale by comparison: by the end of 2010, the company had sold nearly 15 million iPads.

IN 2009, STEVE had returned with vigor, just as he had after the initial operation back in 2004. But this time it was different. This time, everyone understood that his return would end, and they understood how it would end, even if they didn't know when. There was no talk of being cured; instead, Steve was going to "live with it" as long as possible. Steve didn't talk to many people about his medical woes, and he didn't even spend much time discussing it overtly with his inner circle. But the real prospect of his death was there, and it was noticeable.

Bob Iger was aware of it. As Iger had expected, Steve had been a meaningful and yet unthreatening member of the Disney board ever since the Pixar sale in 2006. His relationship with Iger had become so strong that Steve had wanted Iger to join the Apple board, which Iger couldn't do for fiduciary reasons. In fact, because of their friendship, Iger also turned down an invitation from Sergey Brin, Larry Page, and Eric Schmidt to be on Google's board. "He told me he'd be jealous," says Iger, with a wistful grin, although given how Apple's relationship with Google eventually disintegrated, there was likely more to Steve's reluctance than mere envy.

Before the liver transplant, Iger and Steve talked three or four times a week. They even saw each other over winter vacations in Hawaii. "I was at the Four Seasons, and he was at Kona Village. We'd walk together a lot. He had a daily walk that ended at the Four Seasons. We would walk and he'd try to convince me of stuff like, say, that white pineapple is better than yellow pineapple. And we'd sit on benches, and talk about music and the world. That's where I told him the exciting news that we were looking to build a resort in Hawaii, a nine-hundred-million-dollar resort. I could tell he didn't like the idea. I said, 'Why not?' He said it wasn't a big enough idea. I said, 'Nine hundred million dollars, Disney comes to Hawaii, that's not a big idea? What's a big idea in your mind?' He said, 'Buy Lanai' [a small island in the state that was eventually purchased by Larry Ellison]. He thought we should build a theme park on the island, have all the visitors brought there by a special Disney transportation service. It was totally impractical."

Most often, the two would meet in Burbank, when Steve came

down to Disney headquarters for board meetings. Even though Iger was not on the Apple board (he would join it after Steve's death), Steve would seek his advice about things going on at the company, and walk him through Jony Ive's design lab whenever he came up to Cupertino. "We would stand at a whiteboard brainstorming," remembers Iger. "We talked about buying companies. We talked about buying Yahoo! together." By the time the Disney board meetings came around, Steve had usually been fully briefed by Iger. "We saw eye to eye on most things," says Iger. "It wasn't anything preplanned, but when Steve opined, the board generally listened."

That wasn't true on everything, but Steve voiced his disagreements in a forceful but civil fashion. Steve hated stock buybacks, when companies purchase their own shares on the public market—a move that is supposed to be both a good investment for the company and a signal of its confidence to big investors. He made a strong case against it at one board meeting, but the company proceeded nonetheless. On the other hand, when Disney was about to enter a joint venture with Carnival Cruise Lines because Iger didn't think he could get the board's support to build two new, billion-dollar cruise ships, Steve passionately urged him, and eventually the board, to have Disney build the ships itself. "If this is a good business," he said, "why are you going to put your brand in someone else's hands?" Disney built the two new ships on its own.

Steve also helped with Disney's retail business. In 2008, the company had bought back its stores, after having licensed them to outside operators for years. When the new head of retail first pitched the board on his plans, Steve, who always sat next to Iger, grew restless and started rolling his eyes. At one point during the presentation he just burst out, muttering "Bullshit!" in a way that everyone could hear. Iger kicked him in the shins to try to get him to muzzle himself. Once the presentation had ended, Steve asked the executive two simple questions: "What message are you sending to your customer when they walk through the door? What statement are you making?"

"The guy couldn't answer the questions," remembers Iger. "There was silence in the room." Afterward, Steve told Iger he should fire the executive immediately. But Iger didn't. "Steve was quick to judge people. That was a fault," says Iger. "If he got better on that, it wasn't something I saw. I always found that a shortcoming. I'd say to him, 'First of all, I haven't decided about the person, so you've got to give me a chance to form my own opinion.' Or I'd tell him, 'You're just flat-out wrong about this person.' In some cases he was proved right, and in others I was. Either way, I never got an 'I told you so' from him."

A few weeks later, Iger brought the retail chief and a couple of others up to Cupertino for a daylong brainstorming session with Steve and Apple retail chief Ron Johnson. "He didn't redesign our stores," says Iger. "He didn't even set foot in them, as far as I know. But he did give us a full day of his time, and they helped us come up with a guiding statement about the stores: This is going to be the best twenty or thirty minutes of your kid's day."

In the last couple of years it grew harder for Steve to travel, and he had to call in to some board meetings. But when he could make it down to Burbank for a meeting, he and Iger always tried to spend time together. Iger remembers the night when it really hit him that Steve was going to pass away, during a 2010 dinner at his home with his wife, Steve, and Laurene. "We all kind of knew there was an inevitability to him dying, not that any of us was willing to truly accept it, believe it, or articulate it," Iger recalls. "But it was pretty evident. Steve made a toast that night. He said, 'The two of us did an unbelievable thing, didn't we? We saved Disney and we saved Pixar.' He thought that being part of Disney had breathed a whole new life into Pixar. And clearly, Disney has never been the same since. Tears came to his eyes. Our wives had a hard time maintaining dry eyes. It was one of those moments: 'Hey, look at what we did, my goodness! Wasn't that cool, wasn't that really special?'"

At Apple, Steve still did everything he could to have people treat him as if he were not sick. "He was working his ass off till the end, in pain," remembers Eddy Cue. "You could see it in the meetings, he was taking morphine and you could see he was in pain, but he was still interested."

He did make some adjustments upon his return, most of which were simply extensions of the shifts in priority he'd made after his 2004 operation. He focused on the parts of the ongoing business he cared about most—marketing, design, and the product introductions—and he started to take active steps to ensure that he would leave Apple in good shape after his death. This was a process that had started earlier—Tim Cook says that Steve started thinking of succession and the post-Steve era of the company back in 2004—but everything accelerated now.

He spent some of his time working with Joel Podolny, a professor he had hired away from the Yale School of Management, to develop the curriculum for an executive education program he wanted to create called Apple University. Unlike Pixar University, where all employees can choose from a range of eclectic courses that instruct them in creative arts and skills employed by others at the studio, Apple U. is designed as a place where future leaders of the company can review and dissect momentous decisions in the company's history. It's an attempt to reverse-engineer, and then bottle, Steve's decision-making process, and to pass on his aesthetics and marketing methodologies to Apple's next generation. "Steve cared deeply about the why," says Cook. "The why of the decision. In the younger days I would see him just *do* something. But as the days went on he would spend more time with me and with other people explaining *why* he thought or did something, or why he looked at something in a certain way. This was why he came up with Apple U., so we could train and educate the next generation of leaders by teaching them all we had been through, and how we had made the terrible decisions we made and also how we made the really good ones."

Steve also focused on Apple's new headquarters, which are now being built on the grounds of the old Hewlett-Packard campus in another neighborhood of Cupertino. He was very actively involved in the design, working with Norman Foster Architects. The building will reflect many of the same thoughts that went into the creation of Pixar's headquarters, albeit with an Apple spin. It will be one huge circular structure, four stories tall and housing up to thirteen thousand employees. Some people compare it to a space station. Its design is intended to promote interaction among employees. A common hallway stretches around the entire circle of each floor. A single café area will seat three thousand people. Some 80 percent of the grounds will be covered in shrubs, bushes, and trees, including a huge area in the middle of the circular structure. And the building will be its own technological marvel; its exterior won't have a single pane of flat or rectilinear glass. Instead, the "walls" of the building will consist of enormous panels of perfectly curved glass. The cafeteria will have sliding, curved-glass doors four stories tall to open up when the weather is nice. "I think we have a shot," Steve told the Cupertino City Council, "at building the best office building in the world."

Steve's approach to the creation of the campus was driven by the same principles as always. What kind of design would make the new headquarters complex the ideal place for Apple to create its own future? The closer you could get to that ideal, the better for Apple. He wanted to do everything he could to ensure that Apple would remain what he believed it had become—the most important, most vital, and most creative industrial company in the world. "Steve wanted people to love Apple," says Cook, "not just *work* for Apple, but really *love* Apple, and really understand at a very deep level what Apple was about, about the values of the company. He didn't write them on the walls and make posters out of them anymore, but he wanted people to understand them. He wanted people to work for a greater cause."

This belief in Apple as a special place—as a company as magical, perhaps, as an iPad—was something Steve shared with Cook, and was certainly part of the reason he urged the board of directors to sign off on Cook as his successor. "This was a significant common thread we had," says Cook. "I really love Apple, and I do think Apple is here for a bigger reason. There are very few companies like that on the face of the earth anymore."

THE PAIN FROM the cancer was relentless, and Steve spent more and more time at home. Lee Clow visited him there, to work on the ad campaign for the iPad 2, which would be launched in the spring of 2011. "We had to go to his house when he was sick, because he wasn't coming in," says Clow. "But he had the same kind of laser-intense focus. He wanted to talk about the ad or the product or whatever we were doing." With Clow, Steve didn't spend much time looking back, or looking into dark corners of the future. "To the end, he tried to will that it [his death] wasn't going to happen, that he was going to somehow keep going. He really didn't want to dwell on that."

They worked hard on that introductory iPad 2 ad. Its stentorian tone and poetic language would bear a striking resemblance to the "Think Different" campaign that signaled the beginning of Apple's miraculous turnaround after Steve had returned to Cupertino. "This is what we believe, that technology alone is not enough," were the words they settled on. "Faster, thinner, lighter, those are all good things. But when technology gets out of the way everything becomes more delightful, even magical. That's when you leap forward, that's when you end up with something like this." The words accompanied a video showing a single finger manipulating iPad apps with casual ease. "It was the last thing that he blessed as the message that should go out for that particular product," remembers Clow, "and it came off of Steve's vision very clearly. It summed up his vision from day one that somehow technology should change people's lives and make them better. It should be something that everyone uses."

There was considerable doubt as to whether he'd be well enough to introduce the product himself, but when he did make it onto the stage to introduce the iPad 2 on March 2, 2011, his words echoed the themes of the ad: "It's in Apple's DNA that technology alone is not enough," he told the crowd. "We believe that it is technology married with the humanities that yields us the results that make our hearts sing." The iPad 2 was a significant improvement over the first version. It was lighter, it had two digital cameras—one on the screen side to facilitate videoconferencing and taking selfies, and another with a higher-resolution camera and flash, on the back side, courtesy of that crew of camera engineers that had been brought on board after the first iPhone.

Still, the obvious improvements in quality of the product came second, at least for that day, to the bigger news that Steve Jobs was, clearly, dying. His appearance was such that the stock dropped immediately after he stiffly walked onto the stage. This time, he relied even more on other Apple executives to fill out the program and demonstrate key features.

Steve had been living with illness for so long, with the bad times coming in unpredictable waves, that neither he nor his colleagues nor his doctors had any sense of when the end would come. When Steve presented his plans for the ambitious new Apple corporate campus to the Cupertino City Council on June 7, he was visibly hurting, and his voice was weak. Steve seemed to know that it was his last big contribution to the company, and to the community it had always called home. So he steeled himself to spend fifteen minutes walking the council members through the proposal for the building, and about five minutes answering questions. When one councilwoman tried to joke with him that perhaps the city should get free Wi-Fi in return for approving the move, Steve said, "Well, you know, I'm kind of old-fashioned. I believe that we pay taxes, and that the city then gives *us* services."

Over the last few months, a steady flow of visitors came by the house in Palo Alto. Bill Clinton came to visit, as did President Obama, for dinner with a select group of Silicon Valley leaders. John Markoff, of the *New York Times,* and Steven Levy, who had written several books about Silicon Valley, including ones about the development of the Macintosh and the iPod, dropped by together to pay their respects. Bill Gates wound up spending four hours with Steve one afternoon. "Steve and I will always get more credit than we deserve, because otherwise the story's too complicated," Gates says. "I mean, yes, Steve did brilliant work, and if you had to say—you know, leave me out of it— one person who had the most impact on the personal computer industry, particularly from where we sit now, you'd pick Steve Jobs. That's fair. But the difference between him and the next thousand isn't like, you know, God was born and he came down from the hill with the tablet." The two had developed a friendship and a sense of mutual respect despite their differences. "There was none of that need to put the other person down that afternoon," says Gates. "We just talked about the things we'd done, and where we thought things were headed." Gates wrote him a final, personal letter just weeks before his death.

The members of his executive team came by regularly. His worsening health made an already tight group of executives even closer. They talked with him about work, and sometimes they'd just hang around to watch a movie or have dinner. Their work together on what Cook calls the "treadmill" of Apple's perpetual innovation machine had only intensified as the company gained momentum. "Steve had been close to the first group," says Laurene, referring to the team with Fred Anderson, Avie Tevanian, and Jon Rubinstein that had saved Apple with Steve, "but he loved the last group. I think it was because of the amazing, amazing work they did together."

On August 11, a Sunday, Steve called Tim Cook and asked him to come over to the house. "He said, 'I want to talk to you about something,'" remembers Cook. "This was when he was home all the time, and I asked when, and he said, 'Now.' So I came right over. He told me he had decided that I should be CEO. I thought then that he thought he was going to live a lot longer when he said this, because we got into a whole level of discussion about what would it mean for me to be CEO with him as a chairman. I asked him, 'What do you really not want to do that you're doing?'

"It was an interesting conversation," Cook says, with a wistful laugh. "He says, 'You make all the decisions.' I go, 'Wait. Let me ask you a question.' I tried to pick something that would incite him. So I said, 'You mean that if I review an ad and I like it, it should just run without your okay?' And he laughed, and said, 'Well, I hope you'd at least ask me!' I asked him two or three times, 'Are you sure you want to do this?' because I saw him getting better at that point in time. I went over there often during the week, and sometimes on the weekends.

Every time I saw him he seemed to be getting better. He felt that way as well. Unfortunately, it didn't work out that way."

Cook had been the obvious candidate for years. He had already run the company twice, during Steve's medical leaves in 2004 and 2009. And Steve preferred an internal replacement. "If you believe that it's important to understand Apple's culture deeply, you wind up clicking to an internal candidate," explains Cook. "If I were leaving this afternoon I'd recommend an inside candidate, because I don't think there's any way somebody could come in and understand the complexity of what we do *and* really get the culture in that deep way. And I think Steve knew that it also needed to be somebody that believed in the Beatles concept. Apple would not be served well to have a CEO that wanted to, or felt like they needed to, replace him precisely. I don't think there is such a person, but you could envision people trying. He knew that I would never be so dumb as to do that, or even feel that I needed to do that."

Steve had discussed the subject with Cook for years, so none of this came as a surprise. And they had talked often about the fate of Apple after Steve's death. As Cook puts it, "He didn't want us asking, 'What would Steve do?' He abhorred the way the Disney culture stagnated after Walt Disney's death, and he was determined for that not to happen at Apple."

Eight weeks after Steve told Cook he was making him CEO, things took a sudden turn for the worse. "I watched a movie with him the Friday before he passed away," Cook remembers. "We watched *Remember the Titans* [a sentimental football story about an underdog]. I was so surprised he wanted to watch that movie. I was like, Are you sure? Steve was not interested in sports at all. And we watched and we talked about a number of things and I left thinking that he was pretty happy. And then all of a sudden things went to hell that weekend."

John Lasseter got a call from Laurene, who told him he should come quickly for one last visit. "We just hung out in that study they had turned into a bedroom for him. We talked all about Pixar, all the things at Disney, and stuff like that. And then I kinda looked at him and he said, 'Yeah I need to get a nap now.' I got up to go, and then I stopped, and I looked at him and came back. I gave him a big hug, and a kiss, and I said, 'Thank you. Thank you for everything you've done for me.'

"He's special," says Lasseter. "It's funny, there's a little group of people who were very close to Steve up until the very end. And we all miss him very much. I was at Laurene's birthday party [in November 2013], her fiftieth birthday, in San Francisco. I got there a bit early, and Tim came in. He came over and we started talking, and of course we started talking about Steve. I said, 'Do you miss him? I really miss Steve.' And I showed him this," says Lasseter, pointing to the favorites list on his iPhone. "I still have Steve's number on my phone. I said, 'I'll never be able to take that out.' And Tim took out his iPhone and showed me— he still had Steve's number in his phone, too."

———

"LIFE SHOULD BE about renewal and growth," says Jim Collins. "Most great leaders don't start out that way, they grow into it. And that's what Steve did. I don't see it as a success story, but a growth story. I wish I could have seen Steve Jobs 3.0. Seeing him from age fifty-five to seventy-five would have been fascinating. If you're in good health at that age, 3.0 should be the best. But we don't get to see that."

"There are three things you need to be considered a truly great company," Collins continues, switching gears to Apple. "Number one, you have to deliver superior financial results. Number two, you have to make a distinctive impact, to the point where if you didn't exist you couldn't be easily replaced. Number three, the company must have lasting endurance, beyond multiple generations of technology, markets, and cycles, and it must demonstrate the ability to do this beyond a single leader. Apple has numbers one and two. Steve was racing the clock [to help it get number three]. Whether it has lasting endurance is the final check, something we won't know for some time. There are lots of good people there, and maybe they'll get it."

By the time of his death, Apple was truly extraordinary in just about every way that mattered to Steve. By 2011, it could safely be said that no other American corporation had a comparable record of innovation and success. Its internal goal, of continually developing great products in an efficient, unbureaucratic method built around the productivity of and collaboration between small teams, had been successful in ways that defy the fact that the company had grown to 60,000 employees at the time of his death. Its revenue stream was so much more profitable and diversified than it had been when he returned in 1997. Its management team was a veteran group that had been remarkably stable over the years. Avie Tevanian, Jon Rubinstein, Fred Anderson, and Tony Fadell were notable departures, but others remained with institutional memory and remarkable chops. Most important of all, the company had shown an astounding capacity to conceive, develop, manufacture, and market products that really and truly were insanely great. It was doing everything Steve had ever hoped a company could do.

STEVE DIED ON Tuesday, October 5, 2011. There were three services after his death. He was buried on October 8, with some three dozen people attending, including four Apple employees—Tim Cook, Katie Cotton, Eddy Cue, and Jony Ive—along with board members Bill Campbell and Al Gore, Bob Iger, John Doerr, Ed Catmull, Mike Slade, Lee Clow, the four children and Laurene and some members of her extended family, his sisters Patty and Mona Simpson. They gathered at Alta Mesa Memorial Park in Palo Alto, and walked on tatami mats to, and then around, Steve's coffin. Several of the mourners spoke, and some read poetry. After the ceremony the group repaired to John Doerr's house to reminisce.

On October 17, several hundred people attended a memorial service at the Memorial Church on Stanford University's campus. The iPhone 4S had been introduced two days earlier, in the company's first public event after Steve's death, with presale orders that exceeded those of any previous model. The memorial service was an invitation-only event, and the guests ranged from his closest friends and family to the Clintons, Bono, Rahm Emanuel, Stephen Fry, Larry Page, Rupert Murdoch, and John Warnock, the Adobe cofounder. Bono and the Edge from U2 performed Steve's favorite Dylan song, "Every Grain of Sand"; Joan Baez sang "Swing Low, Sweet Chariot"; and Mona Simpson read a moving tribute about Steve on his deathbed. Larry Ellison and Jony Ive also made remarks. Steve's daughter Erin lit the candles at the beginning of the service, while the other children all spoke: Reed read his own thoughts, Lisa read a poem, and Eve read the text of "Think Different." It was, despite the number of people there, a deeply intimate and emotional event, which opened with Yo-Yo Ma playing the prelude from Bach's Cello Suite No. 1. Laurene's own remarks about Steve were especially poignant:

> *Steve and I met* here, at Stanford, the second week I lived in California. He came here to give a talk, and afterwards we found each other in the parking lot. We talked until four in the morning. He proposed with a fistful of freshly picked wildflowers on a rainy New Year's Day. I said yes. Of course I said yes. We built our lives together.
>
> He shaped how I came to view the world. We were both strong-minded, but he had a fully formed aesthetic and I did not. It is hard enough to see what is already there, to remove the many impediments to a clear view of reality, but Steve's gift was even greater: he saw clearly what was not there, what could be there, what had to be there. His mind was never a captive of reality. Quite the contrary. He imagined what reality lacked, and he set out to remedy it. His ideas were not arguments but intuitions, born of a true inner freedom. For this reason, he possessed an uncannily large sense of possibility—an epic sense of possibility.
>
> Steve's love of beauty—and his impatience with ugliness— pervaded our lives. Early on in our marriage we had long

dinners with Mona and Richie. I remember a particularly wide-ranging discussion that lasted late into the night. As we were driving home, Steve launched into a devastating critique of the restaurant's sconces. Mona agreed with his assessment. Richie and I looked at each other, whispering, "Is a sconce a light fixture?" No object was too small or insignificant to be exempt from Steve's examination of the meaning, and the quality, of its form. He looked at things, and then he created things, from the standpoint of perfection.

That could be an unforgiving standpoint, but over time I came to see its reasons, to understand Steve's unbelievable rigor, which he imposed first and most strenuously on himself.

He felt deeply that California was the only place he could live. It's the slanting evening light on the hills, the palette, the fundamental beauty. In his very soul, Steve was a Californian. He required the liberty it afforded, the clean slate. He worked under the influence, and the inspiration, of the sublimity of the place. He needed to be refreshed by the primal rhythms of the natural world—the land, the hills, the oaks, the orchards. California's spirit of newness invigorated him, and ratified his own spirit. Its scale is contagious: such natural grandeur is the perfect setting for thinking big. And he did think big. He was the most unfettered thinker I have ever known. It was a deep pleasure, and a lot of fun, to think alongside him.

Like my children, I lost my father when I was young. It was not what I wanted for myself; it is not what I wanted for them. But the sun will set and the sun will rise, and it will shine upon us tomorrow in our grief and our gratitude, and we will continue to live with purpose, memory, passion, and love.

I left shortly after the ceremony closed. I was overcome with emotion, and with regret over my last conversation with Steve, which had occurred earlier that summer. He called to ask if I wanted to go for a walk with him and chat. In retrospect, I understand that it was an invitation to have one of those farewell talks that he had with quite a few people that summer. But I was in a dark mood then for a variety of reasons, and I didn't realize how very, very sick he was. So instead of responding to his invitation I lit into him, telling him my grievances about our relationship, especially my anger at the fact that he had refused to work with me on *Fortune* stories after my battle with meningitis. He seemed stunned. After a few minutes, once I'd had my say, there was a silence on the line. And then he said he was really sorry. He sincerely meant it, I'm sure. He also told me that he would still like me to come see him, and maybe go for a walk around the neighborhood. I made a halfhearted attempt to schedule a visit with his assistant, but when there was a slight complication I quickly gave up, to my everlasting regret.

Had I gone to the reception after the memorial service in the Rodin Sculpture Garden of the Cantor Arts Center, a short stroll from the Stanford Chapel, I would have received a copy of Paramahansa Yogananda's book *The Autobiography of a Yogi,* which was handed to each guest, in brown paper wrapping. I also would have walked into a who's who of Silicon-Valley, a gathering of the men, and a smattering of women, who had started the PC and Internet revolutions. John Doerr, Eric Schmidt, and Michael Dell were there, and the younger generation was represented by Sergey Brin and Jerry Yang and Marc Andreessen. But the core members from Apple's birth were there, too; Woz, Regis McKenna, Bud Tribble, Andy Hertzfeld, Bill Atkinson, and others. Lee Clow and James Vincent were there, as were NeXT veterans such as Susan Barnes and Mike Slade. The latter came with Bill Gates in tow.

"When Bill had gone to visit Steve at his house in May," says Slade, "he got to know Steve's youngest daughter, Evie, because both she and Bill's daughter, Jennifer, do horse showing. After we got to this reception I kind of ditched Bill because I knew more people there than he does. I kind of felt bad, but I was like, oh, whatever, he's a big boy. Half an hour goes by and I've lost track of him. So I went to find him. In the middle of the sculpture garden they had set up these really long couches in a rectangle where the family was. Laurene was there, and the kids were there. And that's where Bill was, over on a couch, talking to Evie about horses. He just sat there and had been talking to her for a half an hour. He didn't talk to anybody else."

————

THE LAST MEMORIAL service occurred at the Apple campus in Cupertino, on October 20. Nearly ten thousand people gathered on the lawn within the ellipse formed by the campus's main buildings. Every Apple retail outlet around the globe had been closed for the occasion, with the store employees gathered to watch video of the event streamed live to them over Apple's virtual network. Tim Cook was the first speaker. Coldplay and Norah Jones, whose music had been featured in Apple television advertisements, played short sets for the crowd. But two speakers provided the highlights: Jony Ive and Bill Campbell, the Apple board member who had been a close adviser of Steve for many, many years.

"Steve changed," said Campbell. "Yes, he had been charismatic and passionate and brilliant. But I watched him become a great manager. He saw things others couldn't see. He dismissed as arrogant the tech leaders in the world who thought we were all stupid because we couldn't use these devices. He said, '*We're* stupid if they can't use these devices.'" And then Campbell went on to address the Steve he had known personally. "In the last seven and a half years, as he became more vulnerable, he made sure that those he loved, those who were closest to him, knew it. To those people he exuded the phenomenal warmth and humor he shared. He was a true friend."

Speaking later, Ive too talked about friendship. "He was my closest and most loyal friend. We worked together for fifteen years," said the Brit, "and he still laughed at the way I said 'alu*mi*nium.'" But mostly Ive talked about work, the pleasures of work, and the pleasures of working specifically with Steve. "Steve loved ideas and loved making stuff, and he treated the process of creativity with a rare and wonderful reverence.

He, better than anyone, understood that while ideas ultimately can be so powerful, they begin as fragile, barely formed thoughts, so easily missed, so easily compromised, so easily just squished. His was a victory for beauty, for purity, and, as he would say, for giving a damn."

The ceremony, which anyone can watch these days on their iMac or iPhone or iPad, or on their Samsung Galaxy or Microsoft Surface if they prefer, was both sober and rousing. "Look right, look left, look ahead of you and behind you," said Campbell. "You're it. Results counted. You're the people who made this happen." It was an event that celebrated the past, and that also made clear, as Steve would have, that there was much still to be done. "We won't keep you too long," said Chris Martin, the lead singer of Coldplay, as they launched into a song to close the ceremony. "We know Steve would want you to get back to work."

Source Notes

Having reported and written about Steve Jobs from 1986 through 2011, Rick and I have literally thousands of pages of our own notes and transcripts, hundreds of hours of recorded interviews, scores of published stories, and who knows how many unrecorded experiences to draw from. We suppose it would have been easier in some ways to simply recycle parts of what I wrote at the time because that was when it was freshest in my mind and when the impressions were most vivid.

But those stories were written with a different and more immediate objective than what we are trying to achieve with this book, which is this: providing a deeper understanding of Steve Jobs's ever-evolving arsenal of entrepreneurial skills and capabilities, and the deepening of his almost messianic drive to have an impact on his world. We want to show how it was fueled to an unusual degree by his unique gift for being an autodidact, and by genuine idealism as well as his occasionally scary obsessions, his rigid and austere yet consistently well-thought-out aesthetic standards, his often pompous sense of mission. All along, he held a genuine compassion for the anxieties and needs of ordinary people who want to find new tools to empower and improve themselves in a world that grows more complex, cacophonous, and confounding every day.

So for us, this is an entirely new story. One that is in part recycled from the old, but also augmented with fresh observations and reflections from those who were closest to our subject; people who shared particular memories that have had a chance to settle and steep into a deeper understanding of who their friend or colleague or rival Steve Jobs really was. With these source notes, we attempt to provide more specific information about the breadth of sourcing of information and analysis that helped to inform various passages throughout the book.

Prologue

Most of the prologue is based upon my own recollections and notes from my first interview with Steve Jobs, which took place in Palo Alto on April 17, 1986. Other observations were drawn from the cumulative experience of my more than one hundred fifty meetings, interviews, phone calls, emails, and informal conversations with him between that date and his death on October 5, 2011. All the quotations from him throughout this book are from those meetings, phone calls, or email exchanges, unless otherwise noted. Some of the quotations have appeared previously, in whole or in part, in feature articles that I wrote that were published by *Fortune* or the *Wall Street Journal*. None of those articles is reprinted or excerpted in any form in this prologue, however, or elsewhere in the book, unless specifically noted.

Steve Jobs's birthdate is February 24, 1955; mine is April 9, 1954. Both of us graduated from high school in the spring of 1972. Aside from snippets from my own encounters with Jobs, this chapter also drew from an interview with Regis McKenna on July 31, 2012, and another with Ed Catmull on January 16, 2014.

Chapter 1: Steve Jobs in the Garden of Allah

This chapter establishes a baseline from which Steve Jobs would evolve over the rest of his life. The central anecdote of this chapter was provided by Dr. Larry Brilliant, then CEO of the Skoll Global Threats Fund and a close friend of Jobs since the mid-1970s. We interviewed him on two occasions— August 23, 2013, and again on January 17, 2014. We also visited the Garden of Allah in Mill Valley, California, with Brilliant and his wife, Girija, who was a cofounder of the Seva Foundation. Other key interviews included one with Laurene Powell Jobs on October 14, 2013, one with Lee Clow on October 14, 2013, and one with Regis McKenna on July 31, 2012.

Biographical dates and details for the chapter were culled from many published sources, including *Steve Jobs,* Walter Isaacson's authorized biography, and *The Little Kingdom,* Michael Moritz's history of early Apple. Details about Stephen Wozniak's life and contributions to Apple came primarily from his memoir *iWoz: Computer Geek to Cult Icon: How I Invented the Personal Computer, Co-founded Apple, and Had Fun Doing It,* which he wrote with the help of Gina Smith. This is also a source for many of the details about the collaboration between Wozniak and Jobs on the Blue Box digital telephone dialers.

For background information on the Homebrew Computer Club we relied primarily upon *iWoz,* by Wozniak with Smith, although we also drew from Moritz's *The Little Kingdom* and other sources. I also discussed the club with Bill Gates and Steve Jobs on several occasions during meetings during the past twenty years.

The filing of the prospectus with the Securities and Exchange Commission for Apple Computer Inc.'s initial public offering on December 12, 1980, provided the statistics about Apple's early growth—"Apple sold approximately 570, 7,600, 35,100, and 78,100 Apple II computer mainframes during the six-month period ending September 30, 1977, and during the fiscal years ending September 30, 1978, September 30, 1979, and September 26, 1980, respectively."

We also relied upon the following online sources: The Seva Foundation website at www.seva.org; the Ralston White Retreat (the current official name of the Garden of Allah) website at www.ralstonwhiteretreat.org/history.asp; *Fortune*'s "Most Admired Company in the World" 2008–2014 compendium, published online at www/time.com/10351/fortune-worlds-most-admired -company-2014; and the Smithsonian Institution's Oral and Video Histories interview of Steve Jobs on April 20, 1995, posted at http://americanhistory. si.edu/comphist/sj1.html. Another useful resource for this chapter was a website called foundersatwork.com, www.foundersatwork.com/steve-wozniak. html, an online adjunct to Klaus Livingston's book *Founders at Work: Stories of Startups' Early Days.*

Chapter 2: "I Didn't Want to Be a Businessman"
This chapter explains Jobs's idiosyncratic early attitudes toward being a business executive and drew many of its details from books and magazine articles about the early days of Apple Computer Inc., informal reminiscences of Jobs himself during one of our many meetings, and the recollections of other people who worked with him at that time. Of particular value were the reminiscences and personal archives of Regis McKenna, who generously shared his collection of notes, drawings, advertising copy, annual reports, and correspondence from this period. We also relied upon our interviews with him in the summer of 2012, and upon his book *Real Time: Preparing for the Age of the Never Satisfied Customer.* In all, we interviewed him at length on three occasions in 2012 and 2013.

Other books we consulted were Wozniak and Smith's *iWoz;* Moritz's *The Little Kingdom; Swimming Across: A Memoir,* by Andrew S. Grove; *Andy Grove: The Life and Times of an American,* by Richard S. Tedlow; *The Chip: How Two Americans Invented the Microchip and Launched a Revolution,* by T. R. Reid; and *The Man Behind the Microchip: Robert Noyce and the Invention of Silicon Valley,* by Leslie Berlin. We also quoted at length from "Digitization," an article in the Talk of the Town department of *The New Yorker* magazine that was published on November 14, 1977. And we also culled information from the 1980 SEC prospectus for Apple Computer's initial public offering.

Chapter 3: Breakthrough and Breakdown
This chapter describes the circumstances that led to Steve Jobs being stripped of executive authority and eventually quitting under pressure from the board of directors. Once again we synthesized information from many different sources, from books to our own interviews and government filings, such as annual reports, and Jobs's own episodic reminiscences during our many

meetings over the years after we first met in 1986. The narrative of the sequence of events leading to Jobs's demotion in April 1985 and the ultimate conflict with Apple's board that led to his resignation also benefitted from many recent interviews of people who were there at the time, as well as published reports from the time of the event.

Aside from snippets from my own encounters with Jobs, most of the direct quotations in this chapter were drawn from interviews with Susan Barnes on July 24, 2012; Lee Clow on October 14, 2013; Regis McKenna on July 31, 2012; Bill Gates on June 15, 2012; Mike Slade on July 23, 2012; and Jean-Louis Gassée on October 17, 2012.

We also relied on passages from the following books: *Gates,* by Stephen Manes and Paul Andrews; *Odyssey: Pepsi to Apple, A Journey of Adventure, Ideas, and the Future,* by John Sculley; *The Bite in the Apple: A Memoir of My Life with Steve Jobs,* by Chrisann Brennan; *Apple Confidential 2.0: The Definitive History of the World's Most Colorful Company,* by Owen W. Linzmayer; *Dealers of Lightning: Xerox PARC and the Dawn of the Computer Age,* by Michael A. Hiltzik; and *Insanely Great: The Life and Times of Macintosh, the Computer That Changed Everything,* by Steven Levy; as well as Moritz's *The Little Kingdom,* and Wozniak and Smith's *iWoz.*

Other journalistic sources included "The Fall of Steve" by Bro Uttal, published in *Fortune* on August 5, 1985; and the PBS television documentary *The Entrepreneurs,* broadcast in 1986. The Golden Gate Weather website, http://ggweather.com/sjc/daily_records.html#September, provided the precise weather data for the day of Jobs's visit to the Garden of Allah. And statistical data on unit sales were drawn from Apple Computer's annual reports from 1980 to 1984.

Chapter 4: What's Next?

This chapter marks the beginning of my frequent meetings with Jobs, first as a reporter for the *Wall Street Journal,* and later as *Fortune*'s Silicon Valley writer. Ironically, I didn't write all that many stories about Steve or his two pet entrepreneurial projects, NeXT and Pixar, for the first three years because neither company was publicly held and hence neither was a high priority for the *Journal.* After moving to *Fortune* in 1989, however, I made it a point to write about Steve with much greater frequency, and tried to cultivate what was becoming a closer personal relationship. Much of what is described in this chapter is drawn from my own notes and interview transcripts and recollections of events. Lengthy recent interviews with Jobs's colleagues at that time provided valuable background for the chapter.

Aside from snippets from my own encounters with Jobs, most of the direct quotations in this chapter were drawn from interviews with Dan'l Lewin on July 26, 2012; Susan Barnes on July 24, 2012; Avie Tevanian on November 12, 2012; and Jon Rubinstein on July 25, 2012. We also benefitted from lengthy email correspondence with Allison Thomas on January 20, 2014.

We relied for some additional general background about NeXT on two books: Randall Stross's *Steve Jobs and the NeXT Big Thing*; and Owen W. Linzmayer's *Apple Confidential 2.0*.

The descriptions of the rapid growth of Sun Microsystems and the competitive landscape for computer workstations were drawn from reporting for my own stories in *Fortune* from 1998 to 2004 (see bibliography). The narrative details of the introduction of the NeXTcube is drawn primarily from my own experience at the event and my reporting for a *Wall Street Journal* front-page story that followed it on October 13, 1988, titled "Next Project: Apple Era Behind Him, Steve Jobs Tries Again, Using a New System."

Statistics about the relative capacities of hard drives and the transistor counts of semiconductors were drawn from two primary sources: For our descriptions of semiconductor transistor densities we relied upon Pat Gelsinger's article "Moore's Law—The Genius Lives On," which appeared in the *Solid State Circuits* newsletter, July 13, 2007; and our data on trends in hard drive densities came from Chip Walter's "Kryder's Law," which appeared in *Scientific American*'s July 25, 2005, issue.

Other magazine articles we found helpful were a *Newsweek* story from October 24, 1988, by John Schwartz, titled "Steve Jobs Comes Back," and we refer at length to a magazine article by Joe Nocera from the December 1986 issue of *Esquire* titled "The Second Coming of Steven Jobs." We also refer again to the PBS television documentary *The Entrepreneurs* broadcast in 1986.

Online resources for this chapter include the digital archive of the National Mining Hall of Fame, Leadville, Colorado, http://www.mininghallof fame.org/inductee/jackling; Philip Elmer-DeWitt, "Inside Steve's Teardown Mansion," April 27, 2009, Fortune.com, http://fortune.com/2009/04/27/ inside-steve-jobs-tear-down-mansion/; and http://www.sec.gov/cgi-bin/ browse-edgar?company=sun+microsystems&owner=exclude&action=get company for financial information about Sun Microsystems gleaned from the company's SEC filings.

Chapter 5: A Side Bet

This chapter describes the origin of Jobs's purchase of what eventually came to be called Pixar. Once again, this chapter draws primarily from my own extensive previous reporting for stories that appeared in *Fortune* from 1989 to 2006 (see bibliography). We also benefitted from recent interviews with Ed Catmull and from Catmull's recently published book about his experiences at Pixar, *Creativity Inc.: Overcoming the Unseen Forces That Stand in the Way of True Inspiration*. For verification of some of the historical facts we also relied upon Karen Paik's book *To Infinity and Beyond: The Story of Pixar Animation Studios*.

Aside from snippets from my own encounters with Jobs, most of the direct quotations in this chapter were drawn from interviews with Susan

Barnes on July 24, 2012; Ed Catmull on January 16, 2014; John Lasseter on May 8, 2014; Bob Iger on May 14, 2014; and Laurene Powell Jobs on October 25, 2013.

Chapter 6: Bill Gates Pays a Visit

This unusual chapter is based upon a single historic meeting, one of only two "on the record" lengthy encounters between Bill Gates and Steve Jobs. As such, there aren't many outside sources beyond my interview transcripts, my notes, and my own recollections and analysis of the industry at that time.

We retrieved statistical information from the U.S. Bureau of Economic Affairs, Annual Industry Accounts—1976–2012, which can be found at https://www.bea.gov/scb/pdf/2005/01January/0105_Industry_Acct.pdf.

For background information on Gates we consulted an article by Bro Uttal, published in *Fortune* on July 21, 1986, called "The Deal That Made Bill Gates, Age 30, $350 Million"; an interview with Mike Slade on July 23, 2012; and an exclusive, more recent interview with Gates himself on June 15, 2012.

Chapter 7: Luck

This chapter describes how Pixar evolved into a maker of computer animated feature films. It is based in large part on our own recent interviews with Pixar's principals, and is supplemented by the many feature stories I had written over the years about Pixar's remarkable run as a maker of animated feature films (see bibliography). Ed Catmull and John Lasseter were both very generous with their time for profile stories I had written about each, and made themselves available again during our research for this book. We also drew from my previous interviews with Jeffrey Katzenberg of Dreamworks and Michael Eisner of Disney in the late 1990s. Ed Catmull's book *Creativity Inc.* also provided lots of useful background information.

Other published sources included two books: Karen Paik's official corporate history, *To Infinity and Beyond: The Story of Pixar Animation Studios;* and *The Pixar Touch: The Making of a Company,* by David A. Price. And for information on how it was his investment in Pixar that eventually made Steve Jobs a genuine billionaire, we consulted the website for *Forbes;* specifically an interactive article called "Two Decades of Wealth," located at www.forbes.com/static_html/rich400/2002/timemapFLA400.html.

We also relied upon the website of the Securities and Exchange Commission, to confirm details of Netscape Communications Inc.'s initial public offering on August 9, 1995. The company offered 3.5 million shares at a price of $28 a share, generating proceeds of $98 million.

Above all, however, we benefitted from our lengthy interviews with Ed Catmull on January 16, 2014; John Lasseter on May 8, 2014; and my many encounters over the years with Jobs.

Chapter 8: Bozos, Bastards, and Keepers

This chapter reflects an unusual period in my relationship with Jobs because it coincides with a time that Jobs, who was CEO of both NeXT and Pixar, was calling me seemingly out of the blue to talk about what was going on at Apple Computer. Previously, we hadn't talked much about his original entrepreneurial fling, mainly because he wasn't one to look in the rearview mirror. But he seemed genuinely alarmed at what appeared to be the beginnings of a death spiral for Apple. I spent the better part of a year reporting off and on to prepare what was supposed to be a cover story about the breadth and depth of Apple's troubles, informed not only by what Steve whispered in my ear, but also by grumblings from other people inside and outside the company. The story, called "Something's Rotten in Cupertino," wasn't published until the March 3, 1997, issue of *Fortune*, more than two months after Apple's hasty decision to acquire NeXT Computer. The reporting that went into that particular story, plus other stories I reported and wrote about Microsoft, NeXT, and Pixar during 1995 through 1997, informed much of this chapter. Numerical data about Apple came from Apple's annual reports during this period. Two lengthy interviews with Fred Anderson in August 2012 were particularly helpful in explaining how he was able to mastermind Apple's escape from a dire fiscal situation when he arrived there in the spring of 1996.

Aside from snippets from my own encounters with Jobs, most of the direct quotations in this chapter were drawn from those interviews with Anderson; and others with Mike Slade on July 23, 2012; Ed Catmull on January 16, 2014; Jean-Louis Gassée on October 17, 2012; Avie Tevanian on November 12, 2012; Andy Grove on June 20, 2012; and Bill Gates on June 15, 2012.

Other sources of information include archival video of Jobs addressing MacWorld Boston, August 6, 1997, http://www.youtube.com/watch?v=PEHNrqPkefI; and an article in the *New York Times* of March 19, 1992, titled "Business People: NeXT Finds a President in Telephone Industry," by Lawrence Fisher, which provided background information about Peter van Cuylenberg.

Chapter 9: Maybe They Had to Be Crazy

This chapter covers the first four years after Steve Jobs had returned to the helm of Apple, and relies primarily upon my own reporting and writing about Apple during the time period that it covers, 1997 through 2001. Despite Apple's precarious situation and widespread skepticism, there was tremendous interest among techies and businesspeople of all stripes in what Jobs might have up his sleeve that could turn things around at the iconic company. Jobs knew it was in his interest to be fairly open with me about his initial strategies to stabilize things, and by this time we had developed solid trust. Consequently, he was not nearly as secretive during these first few years back at Apple than he would be after the turn of the century.

Aside from snippets from my own encounters with Jobs, most of the quotations in this chapter were drawn from interviews with Lee Clow on October

14, 2013; Jon Rubinstein on July 25, 2012; Avie Tevanian on November 12, 2012; Rubinstein and Tevanian together on October 12, 2012; Jony Ive on June 10, 2014; Bill Gates on June 16, 2012; and Mike Slade on July 23, 2012.

The financial numbers and headcount statistics and other numerical information in this chapter came primarily from Apple's SEC filings reporting its financial results for 1996 through 2000, so we are not citing them here individually. The notorious quote from Michael Dell suggesting that Jobs should simply liquidate Apple came during a Q and A session at the Gartner Symposium and ITxpo97 in Orlando, Florida, on October 6, 1997, http://news.cnet.com/Dell-Apple-should-close-shop/2100-1001_3-203937.html. Background information about Dieter Rams, the design genius who was the primary inspiration of Jony Ive, Apple's head of design, came from the website of the German furniture design company Vitsœ, https://www.vitsoe.com/us/about/dieter-rams and https://www.vitsoe.com/us/about/good-design. The technical details we cite about the iMac and other computer models came from www.everymac.com/systems/apple/imac/specs/imac_ab.html.

Chapter 10: Following Your Nose

This chapter describes how Apple finally invented its way back to growing again namely by entering and shaking up an entirely different business, in this case personal audio electronics with the introduction of the iTunes music management application and the iPod portable digital music player. It also demonstrates in great detail the new methodology Jobs had come to embrace, which he called "following your nose," rather than plotting out some sort of predetermined strategic "road map." The significance of iTunes, the iPod, and later the iTunes Music Store is in how one led to the next and then to the next. I described this process in piecemeal fashion at *Fortune* as these products rolled out. Only in hindsight can you see how each was a case of Steve and his team following their noses, seeing what might be possible after each successive step. Again, the stories we reported, wrote, and edited for *Fortune* provide most of the factual basis of this chapter.

Aside from snippets from my own encounters with Jobs, most of the direct quotations in this chapter were drawn from interviews with Tony Fadell on May 1, 2014; Eddy Cue on April 29, 2014; Jony Ive on June 10, 2014; Tim Cook on April 30, 2014; and Jon Rubinstein and Avie Tevanian on October 12, 2012.

The information and background about Gates's keynote presentation at CES was drawn from Microsoft's online press release archive. Financial statistics came from online SEC filings. Apple Computer Inc. online business document archive was the source of a press release dated January 16, 2001, "iTunes Downloads top 275,000 in First Week" and Apple Computer Inc.'s Annual Report for the fiscal year ending September 30, 2001. Other online resources for this chapter include Gartner Group website for various market statistics, http://www.gartner.com/newsroom/id/2301715; and Quora.com,

http://www.quora.com/Steve-Jobs/What-are-the-best-stories-about-people
-randomly-meeting-Steve-Jobs/answer/Tim-Smith-18.

Chapter 11: Do Your Level Best

This chapter essentially tells the story of Steve Jobs, the merchandiser. Two stories by other *Fortune* writers provided some of the background: a 2003 cover story by Devin Leonard about the evolution of iTunes into a music retailing juggernaut, and another story by Jerry Useem, published in 2007, that describes how Apple's retail stores became some of the highest-grossing stores of any kind in the world. Rick's experiences as editor of *Entertainment Weekly* also contributed to our explanations of the dynamics of the music industry as they made a leap of faith into the digital future, by signing onto Apple's iTunes Music store.

Aside from snippets from my own encounters with Jobs, most of the direct quotations in this chapter were drawn from interviews with Eddy Cue on April 29, 2014; Tim Cook on April 30, 2014; and Laurene Powell Jobs on October 14, 2013.

Magazine articles we cited include "Apple: America's Best Retailer," by Jerry Useem, which appeared in the March 8, 2007, issue of *Fortune;* "Songs in the Key of Steve Jobs," by Devin Leonard, which appeared in the May 12, 2003, issue of *Fortune*; and "Commentary: Sorry Steve: Here's Why Apple Stores Won't Work," by Cliff Edwards, which appeared in the May 20, 2001, issue of *BusinessWeek*.

Chapter 12: Two Decisions

This chapter primarily chronicles the circuitous process of Jobs and his team arriving at the decision to make a mobile "smartphone." We relied upon several new interviews to tell this story, as well as on Fred Vogelstein's *Dogfight: How Apple and Google Went to War and Started a Revolution* for some of the background details, and Walter Isaacson's *Steve Jobs*.

We also consulted various books and online articles, including Myron W. Krueger's *Artificial Reality II,* to provide background on the evolution of the multi-touch user interface.

Aside from snippets from my own encounters with Jobs, most of the direct quotations in this chapter were drawn from interviews with Jim Collins on April 15, 2014; Jony Ive on May 6, 2014, and on June 10, 2014; Tony Fadell on May 1, 2014; Laurene Powell Jobs on October 14, 2013; Tim Cook on April 30, 2014; and Eddy Cue on April 29, 2014.

Online resources we consulted include the Mitsubishi Research Laboratories website for an article titled "DiamondTouch: A Multi-User Touch Technology," by Paul Dietz and Darren Leigh, published in October 2003, and reproduced online at http://www.merl.com/publications/docs/TR2003 -125.pdf; the National Cancer Institute website, for background information on pancreatic cancer, http://www.cancer.gov/cancertopics/pdq/treatment/

isletcell/HealthProfessional; and Apple's online press release archive for
Apple Computer Inc. financial results, August 2, 2004, and other corporate
data.

Chapter 13: Stanford

This chapter describes Steve Jobs's commencement address to the Stanford
University graduating class of 2005. It was an unusual event because Jobs so
rarely spoke publicly at anything other than Apple or Pixar events, and even
then, only when he had a new product or technology to tout. Much of the
chapter is derived from one of our interviews with Laurene Powell Jobs, who
shared her recollections of her husband's obsessive preparation for the speech,
and also of the family's misadventures on Commencement Day. Apple and
Laurene Powell Jobs also granted permission to reproduce the memorable
address in its entirety.

Aside from Jobs's speech, most of the direct quotations in this chapter
were drawn from interviews with Tim Cook on April 30, 2014; Katie Cotton
on April 30, 2014; Jim Collins on April 15, 2014; and Laurene Powell Jobs on
October 25, 2013, December 6, 2013, and April 30, 2014.

Chapter 14: A Safe Haven for Pixar

This chapter is the largely untold, inside story of how Steve Jobs came to sell
Pixar Animation Studios to the Walt Disney Company in early 2006, at a
time when the relations between the two companies was particularly fraught.
We relied upon the recollections of Disney CEO Robert Iger, Pixar founder
Ed Catmull, and Pixar's driving creative spirit John Lasseter to tell this tale,
not unlike the plot of a Pixar movie, which almost always chronicles the personal growth of characters who sometimes stumble over their own feet. We
benefitted from lengthy, enlightening interviews with all three in early 2014.

For background we also relied on two books: James B. Stewart's *Disney
War* and Walter Isaacson's *Steve Jobs*.

Aside from snippets from my own encounters with Jobs, most of the direct quotations in this chapter were drawn from interviews with John Lasseter on May 8, 2014; Tim Cook on April 30, 2014; Ed Catmull on January
16, 2014; and Robert Iger on May 14, 2014.

Chapter 15: The Whole Widget

This chapter has several threads that reflect the new complexity in managing
the company, soon to be called simply Apple Inc., as its business and product line broadened. Between late 2004 and 2008, Apple gave birth to the
iPhone, endured a changing of the guard in the executive ranks, and entered
into a new kind of business partnership with AT&T even as the company's
sales and ranks of employees nearly tripled. Meanwhile controversy returned
to Cupertino, in the form of an SEC investigation into its procedures for
awarding executive stock options, public criticism of working conditions at
its contract manufacturer in China, and accusations of antitrust violations

in its collusion with book publishers over electronic book prices and with other Silicon Valley employers to reduce "poaching" of key employees. Apple kept on growing, and with the iPhone's surging success, Jobs had completed his trifecta of landmark computers. All this despite the fact that his health continued to decline visibly. We benefitted from lengthy interviews with key current and former executives at Apple, including CEO Tim Cook, senior vice president of design Jony Ive, senior vice president of Internet software and services Eddy Cue, vice president of corporate communications Katie Cotton, and Tony Fadell, the founder of Nest Labs, which is now a subsidiary of Google. We also relied upon Apple press releases and SEC filings and court records about the stock option controversy.

Aside from snippets from my own encounters with Jobs, most of the direct quotations in this chapter were drawn from interviews with Eddy Cue on April 29, 2014; Fred Anderson on August 8, 2012; Avie Tevanian on October 11, 2012; Tim Cook on April 30, 2014; Jon Rubinstein on July 25, 2012; Jony Ive on May 6, 2014, and June 10, 2014; John Doerr on May 7, 2014; Jean-Louis Gassée on October 17, 2012; and Marc Andreessen on May 7, 2014.

Online resources we consulted include Fastcodesign.com, the *Fast Company* magazine website that focuses on design, May 22, 2014, http://www .fastcodesign.com/3030923/4-myths-about-apple-design-from-an-ex-apple-designer; and the blog by former Apple engineer Don Melton, donmelton .com/2014/04/10/memories-of-steve/. Also, Apple SEC filings provided unit sales data each quarter from Fiscal Year 2000 through Fiscal Year 2013.

Chapter 16: Blind Spots, Grudges, and Sharp Elbows
This is an unusual chapter because rather than explain a sequence of events, we try to put into perspective certain of Steve Jobs's more controversial characteristics and patterns of behavior, especially in the context of both Apple's meteoric growth and success, and the pressures brought on by living with a terminal illness. Some of Jobs's decisions and actions led to legal challenges in court and reprimands from federal regulators. Others resulted in nagging public relations problems. Still others were merely examples of a man who refused to sugar coat his opinions. We relied mainly upon court records and newspaper and magazine stories for the background of several of these debacles, and also asked Jobs's closest work colleagues to reflect upon them. We don't try to pass definitive judgment, especially on those legal cases that are ongoing. But we felt it was important to try to describe how these issues reflected aspects of Jobs's personality and temperament at the peak of his success. We also describe some of the interpersonal dynamics of the executive team Jobs had assembled, and the period of transition in the mid-2000s when several key members left.

Aside from snippets from my own encounters with Jobs over the years, most of the direct quotations in this chapter were drawn from interviews with Tim Cook on April 30, 2014; Eddy Cue on April 29, 2014; Katie Cotton on

April 30, 2014; Fred Anderson on August 8, 2012; Jon Rubinstein on July 25, 2012; Avie Tevanian on October 11, 2012; and Bill Gates on June 15, 2012.

Online sources quoted or consulted include a *New York Times* op-ed column "Talking Business: Apple's Culture of Secrecy" by Joe Nocera, published on July 26, 2008, http://www.nytimes.com/2008/07/26/business/26nocera.html?pagewanted=all; the online press release archive of the Securities and Exchange Commission litigation archive for Release No. 20086 regarding the settlement of stock option dating issues, http://www.sec.gov/litigation/litreleases/2007/lr20086.htm; the online archive of the U.S. Department of Justice regarding the antitrust complaint against Apple, Adobe, Google, Intel, Intuit, and Pixar for conspiring to prevent competition for the hiring of technical employees, http://www.justice.gov/atr/cases/f262600/262654.pdf, and the complaint against Apple and several book publishers for conspiring to fix prices of ebooks, http://www.justice.gov/atr/cases/f299200/299275.pdf; "Thoughts on Flash," an open letter from Steve Jobs explaining his reasoning for not allowing Adobe Corp.'s Flash media player software on the Apple iPhone, https://www.apple.com/hotnews/thoughts-on-flash/; Apple Inc.'s archive of news releases for information about the company's litigation against Samsung, which for many years was the leading maker of smartphones that used Google's Android operating system; "How the U.S. Lost Out on iPhone Work," by Charles Duhigg and Keith Bradsher, published in the *New York Times* on January 21, 2012, http://www.nytimes.com/2012/01/22/business/apple-america-and-a-squeezed-middle-class.html; "In China, Human Costs Are Built into an iPad," by Charles Duhigg and David Barboza, published in the *New York Times* on January 25, 2012, http://www.nytimes.com/2012/01/26/business/ieconomy-apples-ipad-and-the-human-costs-for-workers-in-china.html; "How Apple Sidesteps Billions in Taxes," by Charles Duhigg and David Kocieniewski, published in the *New York Times* on April 28, 2012, http://www.nytimes.com/2012/04/29/business/apples-tax-strategy-aims-at-low-tax-states-and-nations.html; "Apple's Retail Army, Long on Loyalty but Short on Pay," by David Segal, published in the *New York Times* on June 23, 2012, http://www.nytimes.com/2012/06/24/business/apple-store-workers-loyal-but-short-on-pay.html.

We also consulted Vogelstein's *Dogfight: How Apple and Google Went to War and Started a Revolution* for background information.

Chapter 17: "Just Tell Them I'm Being an Asshole"

This final chapter also covers a lot of ground, from my own interactions with Jobs over the last few years of his life, to the unusual circumstances surrounding his liver transplant in 2009, to the public criticism of working conditions at Apple's contract manufacturer in China, to accusations of antitrust violations in its collusion with book publishers over electronic book prices and with other Silicon Valley employers to reduce "poaching" of key employees. We also describe how the iPad came to be Apple's fastest-selling new product ever. The chapter's primary intent, however, is to put in perspective the evolution of Steve Jobs from a reckless young entrepreneur into a seasoned builder of new consumer technologies and the businesses infrastructures required to deliver and support them. For this we draw largely upon the comments and experiences of many who knew him best.

Descriptions of the private burial service were provided to us by several individuals who were present but did not want their recollections attributed to them. The transcript of Laurene Powell Jobs's tribute given at the public memorial for Steve Jobs on October 17, 2011, is used with her permission.

Aside from snippets from my own encounters with Jobs, most of the direct quotations in this chapter were drawn from interviews with Tim Cook on April 30, 2014; Bob Iger on May 14, 2014; Eddy Cue on April 29, 2014; Lee Clow on January 20, 2014; Bill Gates on June 15, 2012; Laurene Powell Jobs on April 30, 2014; John Lasseter on May 8, 2014; Jim Collins on April 15, 2014; and Mike Slade on July 23, 2012.

We relied on the Cupertino City Council video archive to obtain exact quotes from Jobs's presentation of plans for a new Apple headquarters, June 7, 2011, http://www.cupertino.org/index.aspx?recordid=463&page=26; and upon Apple's online video archives to obtain the comments by Bill Campbell and Jony Ive speaking at the memorial for Jobs at Apple Inc. headquarters, October 20, 2011, http://events.apple.com.edgesuite.net/10oiuhfvojb23/event/index.html.

Bibliography

Books

Amelio, Gil. *On the Firing Line: My 500 Days at Apple*. New York: HarperBusiness, 1998.

Berlin, Leslie. *The Man Behind the Microchip: Robert Noyce and the Invention of Silicon Valley*. New York: Oxford University Press, 2005.

Brennan, Chrisann. *The Bite in the Apple: A Memoir of My Life with Steve Jobs*. New York: St. Martin's Press, 2013.

Catmull, Ed. *Creativity Inc.: Overcoming the Unseen Forces That Stand in the Way of True Inspiration*. New York: Random House, 2014.

Collins, Jim. *Good to Great: Why Some Companies Make the Leap . . . and Others Don't*. New York: HarperBusiness, 2001.

Collins, Jim, and Jerry I. Porras. *Built to Last: Successful Habits of Visionary Companies*. New York: HarperBusiness, 2004.

Deutschmann, Alan. *The Second Coming of Steve Jobs*. New York: Crown Business, 2001.

Esslinger, Hartmut. *Keep It Simple: The Early Design Years at Apple*. Stuttgart: Arnoldsche Verlaganstalt, 2014.

Grove, Andrew S. *Swimming Across: A Memoir*. New York: Grand Central Publishing, 2001.

Hertzfeld, Andy. *Revolution in the Valley: The Insanely Great Story of How the Mac Was Made*. Sebastopol, CA: O'Reilly Media, 2004.

Hiltzik, Michael A. *Dealers of Lightning: Xerox PARC and the Dawn of the Computer Age*. New York: HarperBusiness, 1999.

Isaacson, Walter. *Steve Jobs*. New York: Simon & Schuster, 2011.

Kahney, Leander. *Jony Ive: The Man Behind Apple's Greatest Products*. New York: Portfolio Hardcover, 2013.

Krueger, Myron W. *Artificial Reality II*. Boston: Addison-Wessley Professional, 1991.

Lashinsky, Adam. *Inside Apple: How America's Most Admired—and Secretive—Company Really Works*. New York: Business Plus, 2012.

Levy, Steven. *Insanely Great: The Life and Times of Macintosh, the Computer That Changed Everything*. New York: Penguin, 2000.

————. *The Perfect Thing: How the iPod Shuffles Commerce, Culture, and Coolness*. New York: Simon & Schuster, 2006.

Linzmayer, Owen W. *Apple Confidential 2.0: The Definitive History of the World's Most Colorful Company*. San Francisco: No Starch Press, 2004.

Livingston, Jessica. *Founders at Work: Stories of Startups' Early Days*. New York: Apress, 2009.

Lovell, Sophie. *Dieter Rams: As Little Design as Possible*. London: Phaidon Press, 2011.

Manes, Stephen, and Paul Andrews. *Gates*. New York: Touchstone, 1994.

Markoff, John. *What the Dormouse Said: How the Sixties Counterculture Shaped the Personal Computer*. New York: Penguin, 2006.

McKenna, Regis. *Real Time: Preparing for the Age of the Never Satisfied Customer*. Boston: Harvard Business Review Press, 1999.

Melby, Caleb. *The Zen of Steve Jobs*. New York: Wiley, 2012.

Moritz, Michael. *The Little Kingdom: The Private Story of Apple Computer*. New York: William Morrow & Co., 1984.

Paik, Karen. *To Infinity and Beyond: The Story of Pixar Animation Studios*. San Francisco: Chronicle Books, 2007.

Paramahansa Yogananda. *Autobiography of a Yogi*. Oakland, CA: Self-Realization Fellowship, 1998.

Price, David A. *The Pixar Touch: The Making of a Company*. New York: Vintage, 2009.

Reid, T. R. *The Chip: How Two Americans Invented the Microchip and Launched a Revolution*. New York: Simon & Schuster, 1985.

Sculley, John. *Odyssey: Pepsi to Apple, A Journey of Adventure, Ideas, and the Future*. New York: HarperCollins, 1987.

Segall, Ken. *Insanely Simple: The Obsession That Drives Apple's Success*. New York: Portfolio Hardcover, 2012.

Simpson, Mona. *A Regular Guy*. New York: Vintage, 1997.

Stewart, James B. *DisneyWar*. New York: Simon & Schuster, 2006.

Stross, Randall. *Steve Jobs and the NeXT Big Thing*. New York: Scribner, 1993.

Suzuki, Shunryu. *Zen Mind, Beginner's Mind: Informal Talks on Zen Meditation and Practice*. Boston: Shambhala, 2006.

Tedlow, Richard S. *Andy Grove: The Life and Times of an American*. New York: Penguin, 2006.

Vogelstein, Fred. *Dogfight: How Apple and Google Went to War and Started a Revolution*. New York: Sarah Crichton Books, 2013.

Wozniak, Stephen, and Gina Smith. *iWoz: Computer Geek to Cult Icon: How I*

Invented the Personal Computer, Co-founded Apple, and Had Fun Doing It. New York: W. W. Norton & Company, 2007.

Young, Jeffrey S. *Steve Jobs: The Journey Is the Reward.* New York: Scott Foresman Trade, 1987.

Articles by the Author

Schlender, Brenton R. "Jobs, Perot Become Unlikely Partners in Apple Founder's New Concern." *Wall Street Journal,* February 2, 1987.

———. "Next Project: Apple Era Behind Him, Steve Jobs Tries Again, Using a New System." *Wall Street Journal,* October 13, 1988.

———. "How Steve Jobs Linked Up with IBM." *Fortune,* October 9, 1989.

———. "The Future of the PC: Steve Jobs and Bill Gates Talk About Tomorrow." *Fortune,* August 26, 1991.

———. "What Bill Gates Really Wants." *Fortune,* January 16, 1995.

———. "Steve Jobs' Amazing Movie Adventure." *Fortune,* September 18, 1995.

———. "Something's Rotten in Cupertino." *Fortune,* March 3, 1997.

———. "The Three Faces of Steve." *Fortune,* November 9, 1998.

———. "Apple's One-Dollar-a-Year Man." *Fortune,* January 24, 2000.

———. "Steve Jobs' Apple Gets Way Cooler." *Fortune,* January 24, 2000.

———. "Steve Jobs: Graying Prince of a Shrinking Kingdom." *Fortune,* May 14, 2001.

———. "Pixar's Fun House." *Fortune,* July 23, 2001.

———. "Apple's 21st Century Walkman." *Fortune,* November 12, 2001.

———. "Apple's Bumper Crop." *Fortune,* February 3, 2003.

———. "What Does Steve Jobs Want?" *Fortune,* February 23, 2004.

———. "Incredible: The Man Who Built Pixar's Innovation Machine." *Fortune,* November 15, 2004.

———. "How Big Can Apple Get?" *Fortune,* February 21, 2005.

———. "Pixar's Magic Man." *Fortune,* May 17, 2006.

———. "Steve and Me: A Journalist Reminisces." *Fortune,* October 25, 2011.

———. "The Lost Steve Jobs Tapes." *Fast Company,* May 2012.

Other Newspapers and Magazines

BusinessWeek/BloombergBusinessweek
Esquire
Fast Company
Fortune
New York Times
The New Yorker
Newsweek
San Francisco Chronicle
San Jose Mercury News
Time
Wall Street Journal
Wired

Websites

allaboutstevejobs.com

apple.com

apple-history.com

Computer History Museum: www.computerhistory.org/atchm/steve-jobs/

cultofmac.com

donmelton.com/2014/04/10/memories-of-steve/

everystevejobsvideo.com

Fastcodesign.com, a Fast Company website that a focuses on design news, May 22, 2014, http://www.fastcodesign.com/3030923/4-myths-about-apple-design-from-an-ex-apple-designer

Forbes billionaires list: "Two Decades of Wealth," www.forbes.com/static_html/rich400/2002/timemapFLA400.html

foundersatwork.com; interview with Stephen Wozniak, www.foundersatwork.com/steve-wozniak.html

Gartner Group: http://www.gartner.com/newsroom/id/2301715

Golden Gate Weather: http://ggweather.com/sjc/daily_records.html#September

National Cancer Institute: http://www.cancer.gov/cancertopics/pdq/treatment/isletcell/HealthProfessional

National Historic Trust for Historic Preservation: preservationnation.org (Jackling Mansion details)

National Mining Hall of Fame, Leadville, Co.: http://www.mininghalloffame.org/inductee/jackling

news.cnet.com

paloalto.patch.com/groups/opinion/p/my-neighbor-steve-jobs

quora.com; http://www.quora.com/Steve-Jobs/What-are-the-best-stories-about-people-randomly-meeting-Steve-Jobs/answer/Tim-Smith-18.

The Ralston White Retreat: www.ralstonwhiteretreat.org/history.asp

The Seva Foundation: www.seva.org

Smithsonian Institution's "Oral and Video Histories" Steve Jobs interview on April 20, 1995: http://americanhistory.si.edu/comphist/sj1.html

Steve Jobs addressing MacWorld Boston, August 6, 1997: http://www.youtube.com/watch?v=PEHNrqPkefI

Steve Jobs open letter "Thoughts on Flash," explaining his reasoning for not allowing Adobe Corp.'s Flash media player software on the Apple iPhone: https://www.apple.com/hotnews/thoughts-on-flash/

stevejobsarchive.net

U.S. Bureau of Economic Affairs, Annual Industry Accounts 1976–2012, https://www.bea.gov/scb/pdf/2005/01January/0105_Industry_Acct.pdf

Vitsœ: https://www.vitsoe.com/us/about/dieter-rams; https://www.vitsoe.com/us/about/good-design

Other

Cupertino City Council video archive of Steve Jobs's presentation of plans for a new Apple headquarters, June 7, 2011, http://www.cupertino.org/index.aspx?recordid=463&page=26.

Dietz, Paul, and Darren Leigh. "DiamondTouch: A Multi-User Touch Technology." Mitsubishi Electric Research Laboratories white paper, October 2003, http://www.merl.com/publications/docs/TR2003-125.pdf.

The Entrepreneurs. PBS, 1986.

Leonard, Devin. "Songs in the Key of Steve Jobs." *Fortune,* May 12, 2003.

Securities and Exchange Commission S-1 filing of the prospectus for Netscape Communications Inc.'s initial public offering on August 9, 1995.

Securities and Exchange Commission S-1 filing of the prospectus for Pixar's initial public offering on November 29, 1995. (Filing date October 11, 1995.)

Securities and Exchange Commission S-1 filing of the prospectus for Apple Computer Inc.'s initial public offering on December 22, 1980. (Filing date December 12, 1980.)

Securities and Exchange Commission litigation press release No. 20086, *Securities and Exchange Commission v. Nancy R. Heinen and Fred D. Anderson, Case No. 07-2214-HRL,* April 24, 2007, http://www.sec.gov/litigation/litreleases/2007/lr20086.htm.

Useem, Jerry. "Apple: America's Best Retailer." *Fortune,* March 8, 2007.

Uttal, Bro. "The Fall of Steve." *Fortune,* August 5, 1985.

———. "The Deal That Made Bill Gates, Age 30, $350 Million." *Fortune,* July 21, 1986.

Acknowledgments

Thank you to Kris Dahl, our agent, who has been steady, wise, and inspiring as our early idea blossomed into this book. Our editor at Crown, Roger Scholl, championed this project from the get-go, offering unflagging support at every turn. We couldn't have asked for a better guide through the editorial process. John Huey initiated our working relationship, which led to deep friendship and this collaboration. Cathy Cook has been our sage, skeptical counselor and friend in Silicon Valley for years. Jenny Lyss delivered the title over a dinner that reflected the warmth and generosity she brings to everything. There's a long list of folks who have helped us along the way, but we especially want to thank Larry Brilliant, Annie Chia, Larry Cohen, Katie Cotton, Mia Diehl, Steve Dowling, Caroline Eisenmann, Heather Feng, Sadie Ferguson, Sarah Filippi, Veronica Garcia, Celine Grouard, Bill Joy, Ted Keller, George Lange, Kristen McCoy, Regis McKenna, Gretchen Menn, Doug Menuez, Michelle Moretta, Zenia Mucha, Terri Murphy, Karen Paik, Emily Philpott, Derek Reed, Abby Royle, Wendy Tanzillo, Allison Thomas, Fred Vogelstein, and Tom Waldrop.

Without naming them individually, we also would like to thank the many people close to Steve Jobs—family members, longtime friends, work colleagues, mentors, rivals, and competitors—who chose to trust us with their personal memories, impressions, and insights. The source notes give a complete listing of those who provided on-the-record interviews. We are grateful for the generosity of spirit they showed by sharing their reminiscences and feelings despite their understandable reluctance.

—BS and RT

I'd like to thank my family. Lorna, my wife of three decades, who has patiently tolerated the unpredictable hours and mood swings and sudden transoceanic moves that sometimes go with being married to a journalist; and my two daughters, Greta and Fernanda, who both have cameo roles in our story and who, like their mother, encouraged me to put my own traumatic illness behind me, and just do it. I also must thank my late mother, Charlotte, an eighth-grade English teacher who taught me the importance of learning the Greek and Latin roots of most words, and to realize, too, that there is almost always a better word—unless there isn't. And I want to especially thank my father, Harold, a lifelong homebuilder and craftsman who turned ninety the month this book was published. He taught me very early that your mistakes always cost you in three ways: you waste effort and materials; you then have to dismantle what you messed up; and after that you have to do it all over again to get it right. That's a good rule of thumb to keep in mind for just about any endeavor. By example, my father also showed me that it is never too late in life to take on your biggest challenge. His was the restoration of a magnificent, historic opera house in my hometown of McPherson, Kansas, that reopened, thanks in large part to his own sweat and muscle when he was eighty-five. And finally, I'd like to give a special shout-out to one of my oldest and dearest friends, Rodney Pearlman, a genuine polymath whose valuable and cogent suggestions for the manuscript were of immense help late in the writing process.

—BS

Bob Safian, editor of *Fast Company,* encouraged the project and gave me room to complete something that took far more time than either of us anticipated. The world needs more leaders like Bob—that'll embarrass him, but it's true. David Lidsky was an invaluable reader of our first draft. I am truly grateful to David, Lori Hoffman, and Jill Bernstein for leading the print team at *Fast Company* while I was on book leave. Frank Davis and Nancy Blecher Davis helped at critical moments along the way; they are the greatest in-laws around. Christine Pierre has been a model for the entire family for years now, and has helped in more ways than she would ever acknowledge. My brothers, Bill and Chris, have been steady confidants, as have Adam Bluestein, Nicole Gueron, Carter Strickland, and Steve Tager. My children, Jonah, Tal, and Anya, have been occasionally exasperated but always curious and loving participants in the process of "*that* book." They add meaning to everything and are a welcome reminder of both the value and the limits of this project. Finally, Mari, my wife of seventeen years, has been our most rigorous and tireless reader; her heavily marked-up manuscript pages informed every draft. She has pushed us to be as clear, ambitious, and thorough as possible. More important, she is my best friend and everything anyone could ever hope for in a partner. Who knew, Mari, that walking you home sixty-five blocks that first night would transform my life? My gratitude for any good things that have come my way in life begins with meeting and marrying you.

—*RT*

Index

Join a literary community of
like-minded readers who seek out
the best in contemporary writing.

From the thousands of submissions Sceptre
receives each year, our editors select the books
we consider to be outstanding.

We look for distinctive voices, thought-provoking
themes, original ideas, absorbing narratives and
writing of prize-winning quality.

If you want to be the first to hear about our
new discoveries, and would like the chance to
receive advance reading copies of our books
before they are published, visit

www.sceptrebooks.co.uk

Follow @sceptrebooks

'Like' SceptreBooks

Watch SceptreBooks